Discovering Indian Philosophy

Discovering Indian Philosophy

*An Introduction to Hindu, Jain
and Buddhist Thought*

Jeffery D. Long

BLOOMSBURY ACADEMIC
LONDON · NEW YORK · OXFORD · NEW DELHI · SYDNEY

BLOOMSBURY ACADEMIC
Bloomsbury Publishing Plc
50 Bedford Square, London, WC1B 3DP, UK
1385 Broadway, New York, NY 10018, USA
29 Earlsfort Terrace, Dublin 2, Ireland

BLOOMSBURY, BLOOMSBURY ACADEMIC and the Diana logo are trademarks of
Bloomsbury Publishing Plc

First published in Great Britain 2024

Cover design by Charlotte James
Cover image: Sunrise at Gadisar Lake in Jaisalmer, Rajasthan © Nora Carol Photography /
Getty Images

A catalogue record for this book is available from the British Library.

Library of Congress Cataloging-in-Publication Data

ISBN: HB: 978-1-7845-3645-9
PB: 978-1-7845-3646-6
ePDF: 978-1-3503-2481-7
eBook: 978-1-3503-2482-4

Typeset by Deanta Global Publishing Services, Chennai, India
Printed and bound in Great Britain

To find out more about our authors and books visit www.bloomsbury.com and
sign up for our newsletters.

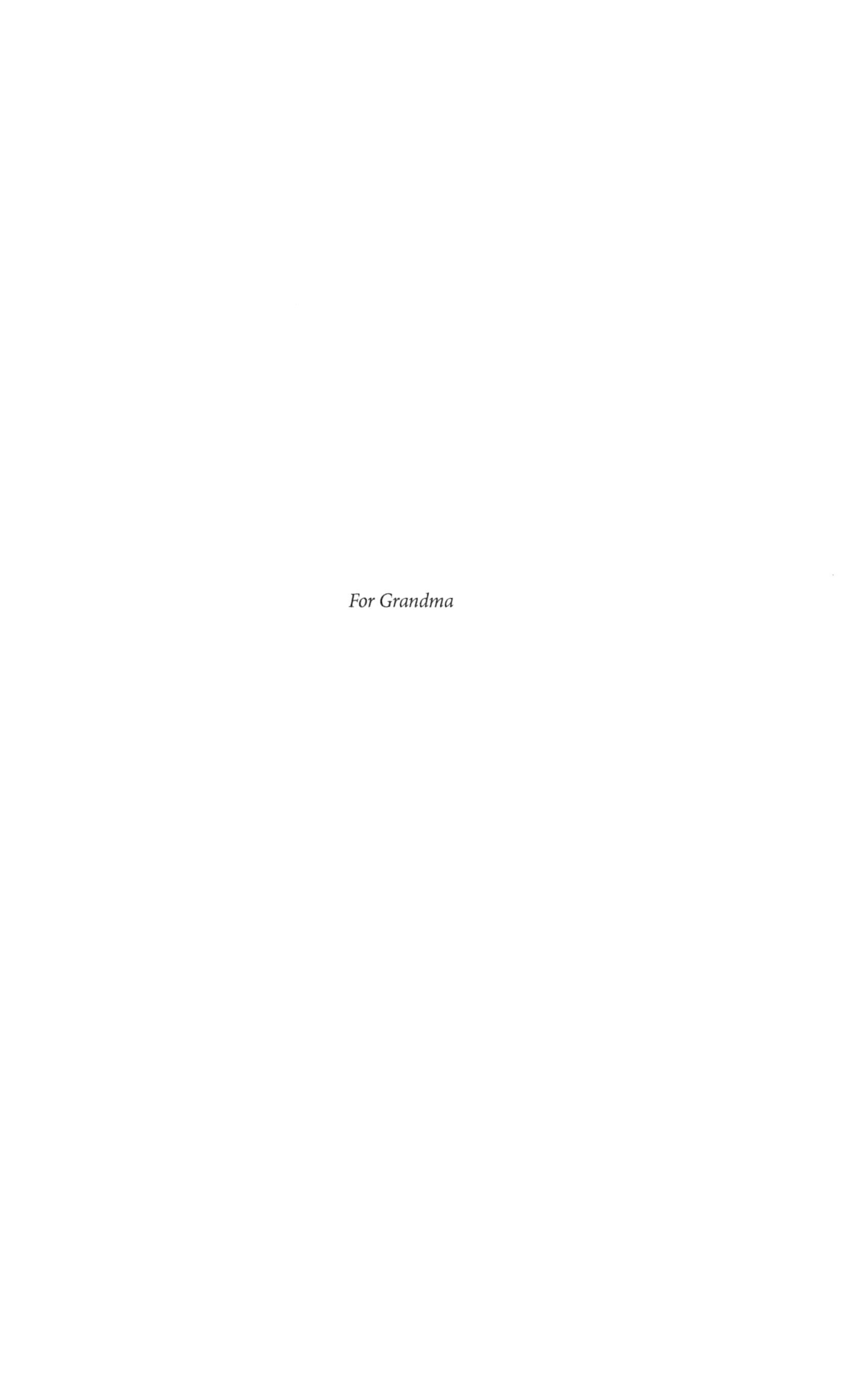

For Grandma

Contents

Acknowledgements

This book has been ten years in the making. The reasons for the delays in its writing and publication have been many, mostly involving other writing projects or my work at a small college with a strong emphasis on teaching. There have also been some family health crises during this time, the worst being my grandmother's struggle with cancer, culminating with her departure from us in the spring of 2015. Grandma was dearer to me than words could ever express, and this book is dedicated to her.

I wish to thank all those who have made this book possible. The bodhisattva-like patience of Alex Wright, who first suggested this book to me as a project for I. B. Tauris, was a tremendous gift. I am certain he, too, would like to have seen this book published in 2013, which is what we had both originally envisioned. The fact that he stuck with me and tolerated my delays is something I do not take for granted. In the same vein, I would like to thank Olivia Dellow and David Avital, who inherited the management of this project when it migrated from I. B. Tauris to Bloomsbury, and who have been similarly kind and patient with me.

I wish to give special thanks to the anonymous peer reviewers who meticulously examined the early drafts of this book and who generously offered many constructive criticisms which I have incorporated and which I find to have strongly improved the final product. This is how peer review, at its best, is supposed to work. Of course, any errors that remain are entirely my own.

I also wish to thank my colleagues and the administration of Elizabethtown College for the semester-long sabbatical that enabled me to write the first draft of this book in the spring of 2017. I am also grateful to the many students who have allowed me to 'test drive' earlier drafts of this book in my courses on Indian philosophy, taught both in person and online. This includes both my students at Elizabethtown College and at Embodied Philosophy. I owe a special debt of gratitude to Jacob Kyle, at Embodied Philosophy, for first connecting me with that organization, which does such great work to spread knowledge of Indian culture and wisdom globally. I have now had the opportunity to teach several courses for them, and each experience has been excellent.

I would also like express to my gratitude for the grant from the Consortium of Independent Colleges which enabled me to develop the initial online version of my Indian philosophy course at Elizabethtown College, future offerings of which will incorporate this book.

The development of the online courses, as well as my in-person teaching of this material, has been helpful to my writing on many levels. Getting a sense of which concepts students found the most difficult to grasp, which concepts they grasped readily and the areas that could benefit the most from further explanation has shaped the contours of this book, which is mainly for college students, as well as interested laypersons who are new to the subject and want a simple overview. It is likely to be of less interest to advanced scholars and graduate students, except – I hope! – as a teaching tool.

Andrew Nicholson's kind recommendation enabled me to become an Affiliated Scholar at the South Asia Center of the University of Pennsylvania, and avail myself of its many resources, especially the Van Pelt library. For this, as well as for his generally collegial and helpful nature, I am grateful to Andrew, as well as to the University of Pennsylvania, and to its South Asia Center in particular.

I also want to thank Loretto Taylor, Sven Wilson and Darren Hackler, for patiently reading drafts of chapters to ensure that I remained clear and comprehensible. With that being said, if there are parts of this book that remain neither clear nor comprehensible, the fault is mine, not theirs!

Finally, to my mother, Diana Long, who made the author of this book possible, to my wife, best friend and companion for life, Mahua Bhattacharya, and to my wise and kind Gurudeva, no thanks I can offer can ever be enough.

Pronunciation guide

Many terms in this book are from either Sanskrit or other Indic languages. The scripts ('alphabets') of these languages are phonetic – that is, each character stands for exactly one sound, and there is a character for each sound. As a result, the Indic scripts have far more characters than the twenty-six of the Roman alphabet used in English and other western European languages. To render words from Indic languages into the Roman script in an exact way, scholars have developed a system of diacritical marks to distinguish between, for example, the short *a* of Sanskrit (which is pronounced like the 'u' in 'bud') and the Sanskrit long '*ā*' (which is pronounced like the 'a' in 'father'). Writing both sounds as 'a' would lose this important distinction, leading to incorrect pronunciation and, in some cases, to incorrect meanings as well. (*Mayā*, for example, a first-person pronoun that means 'by or with me', is different from *māyā*, the power by which the world becomes manifested to us.)

The correct pronunciation of Indic sounds, as depicted using this system, is as follows:

a: 'uh', as in 'bud'
ā: 'ah', as in 'father'
i: like the 'i' in 'bit'
ī: like 'ee' in 'beet'
u: like the 'oo' in 'book'
ū: like the 'oo' in 'boot'
ṛ: like the 'ri' in 'rig', with a slight roll of the tongue, though not as hard a roll as in Spanish
e: like 'ay' in 'say'.
ai: like 'aye' or 'eye'.
o: 'oh', as in 'Ohio'.
au: like 'ow' in 'cow'.

Consonants are mostly pronounced as in English, but consonants with a dot under them (like 'ṭ') are pronounced with the tongue touching the roof of the mouth. Consonants immediately followed by an 'h' (like 'dh') include an exhalation. The 'h' is thus pronounced, producing somewhat of a softening of the consonant. The 'h' is *not* a separate syllable, so 'dha', for example, is pronounced as 'dha', and not 'daha'. Also, the letter 'c' is not pronounced like a 'k', as it typically is in English, but is pronounced as 'ch'. So *Yogācāra* is *not* pronounced *Yogākāra*, but *Yogāchāra*.

The 'ś' and 'ṣ' sounds are almost indistinguishable from one another and are sometimes confused even by native speakers. The 'ṣ' sound is pronounced with the tongue at the roof of the mouth, but 'ś' is not. Both sound somewhat like the 'sh' in 'she'. So *Śiva* is *not* pronounced *Siva*, but *Shiva*.

The sound 'ḥ', is always preceded by a vowel and produces a slight echoing of that vowel. So 'aḥ' is pronounced 'aha'. The sound 'ṃ' is slightly nasalized, sounding almost like an 'n'.

Finally, the consonant conjunct 'jña' is the one non-phonetic sound in Sanskrit. It is typically pronounced 'gya,' though sometimes as 'ña,' with the 'j' kept silent.

I have used this system for most terms, except modern proper names that have a popular spelling (so Ramakrishna, not Rāmakṛṣṇa). For the sake of consistency, I have used Sanskrit terminology, even when the corresponding Hindi term is better known (so *avatāra* instead of *avatār*, or *avatar*, which has essentially become an English word).

I would finally add, to anyone who has read up to this point and is now thoroughly intimidated at the prospect of pronouncing Indic words correctly, please do not panic! Correct pronunciation will come with practice. The most important thing is to understand the meanings of the terms that will be introduced, and how these terms work in Indian philosophical contexts.

Introduction

Approaching Indian philosophy

A universal quest

We are all potentially philosophers. It is true that few of us pursue the technical training to become philosophers in a formal, professional sense. Many of us, though, especially if we face a major life crisis, find ourselves at some point asking the 'big questions' of life, death and meaning. We seek answers that will satisfy us at least enough to help us get up and face each day with a sense that there is some purpose to all of this, the life we are experiencing. *Does* this life have a purpose? Does our existence come to an end when we die, or is there something beyond death? What is the good life? Why do we exist at all? Why are we here? Who are we? What is real? Why is there anything? How would one go about finding answers to questions like these? Can they be answered at all? How would we know if our answers were true? In fact, how do we know anything? How do we know *that* we know? Do we truly know anything, or are we deceiving ourselves? The philosophies explored in this book address questions such as these, and many more.

Questions like these became quite urgent to me in my childhood. My father was injured in a terrible accident when I was ten years old, leading eventually to his death when I was twelve. Why, I asked myself in the aftermath of these events, did all of this happen? Why did my family have to suffer so much? What is the point of a world where so much suffering happens, suffering often even worse than what my family experienced? Are the events of this life, both the happy ones and the sad ones, taking us in a particular direction – to a place where we might like to go – or are all our struggles pointless? As I wrestled with these questions, I began to study as many of the world's philosophies and religions as I could, casting as wide a net as possible in my search for answers. I also had a strong interest in science, and my search included it as well.

As I explored the world's religions and philosophies, I found something good, true and beautiful in all of them. I also found that each had its limitations and needed to be supplemented by the others. I came to believe that no philosophy is, by itself, a complete picture of truth, but that one must study many viewpoints to have as full an understanding of reality as possible.

My view is not that we are incapable of knowing the truth. I am not a complete sceptic. But if we try to formulate truth in language, in a philosophical system, this expression always falls short of the full truth, because languages and concepts are necessarily finite. Also, our knowledge base is always changing and our ability to visualize past it – to see beyond our horizon – is limited by our location in a particular place, time and culture, with its own strengths and blind spots. In the words of Alfred North Whitehead, 'There is no first principle which is in itself unknowable, not to be captured by a flash of insight. But, putting aside the difficulties of language, deficiency in imaginative penetration forbids progress in any form other than an asymptotic approach to a scheme of principles, only definable in terms of the ideal which they should satisfy.'[1] Again, it is not that we are incapable of knowing the truth, whatever it may be; but all our attempts to express it remain incomplete, never quite capturing the full picture. I believe this is even true of the great Masters of the world's wisdom traditions, because they have taught so many different things, often differing radically from one another, and have yet managed to convey some important insight to those with the capacity to receive it. In other words, if a radical awakening of consciousness of the kind posited in many of the Indian traditions does indeed occur, even those who attain it and seek to communicate their wisdom in words end up producing statements which require interpretation.

If words always fall short of offering us a complete picture of truth, it follows that the best policy is to maintain an open mind, learning from what others have to say and adding their insights to our own, ever mindful that even if truths are eternal, knowledge is a process. It is in this spirit that I offer this book on Indian philosophy to those wishing to supplement their current views of life, whatever they may be, with the insights of varied traditions and ways of thinking. And even for those who do not see themselves on a personal quest for truth, understanding the ideas of great minds from a variety of cultural backgrounds is itself a worthwhile exercise, particularly in a world like ours, which is wrought by frequent misunderstandings and clashes across worldviews that all too often end in tragedy.

As my personal quest has unfolded, I have found answers in the philosophies of the Hindu, Jain and Buddhist traditions that have shed much light upon the questions that have preoccupied me for much of my life. Far more than exotic historical curiosities, I have found Indian traditions to be sources of deep insight and wisdom. Much like Indian classical music and Indian cuisine, the philosophies of India are subtle and complex. They have changed my life in ways that I cannot even begin to describe. To be sure, each system has its limits, as all philosophies do. But each adds its unique contribution to the sum total of human wisdom. I would, in fact, argue that some important insight can be gained from each of the systems of thought outlined in this book, as well as in those philosophies which I have not included, due to the limits of space and my own expertise.

Defining the field

When scholars speak and write about 'Indian philosophy', we are referring not only to the philosophies of the modern Indian nation-state, the Republic of India, which became independent from the British Empire on 15 August 1947, but to a broader and more ancient family of traditions. The word *Indian* in *Indian philosophy* is used as this word has been used since ancient times: to refer to the peoples and cultures of the entire Indian subcontinent. This region is known by many scholars today as *South Asia* because it encompasses not only the country named India, but also such nation-states as Pakistan, Nepal, Bangladesh, Bhutan, Sri Lanka, the Maldives, and Afghanistan (although Afghanistan is sometimes categorized as part of Central Asia). It is a long-held convention to use the terms *India* and *Indian* in this more extensive way (and to refer to the study of India and Indian culture as *Indology*). These usages are employed in this book as well: *India* and *Indian* in the broader cultural sense, not in the narrower sense defined by current political borders (which did not even exist during most of the period covered in this book).

It is also important to point out that the *Indianness* of Indian philosophy does not imply that philosophies derived from India are relevant only to India or Indians. Systems of thought and practice and ideals derived from Indian philosophy, in fact, claim adherents from around the world, and from a wide array of nationalities and ethnic origins. The most obvious example is Buddhism, which has long had an international following, extending in the premodern era from Sri Lanka to Japan, and in the modern era reaching even into the West.[2] Hindu systems of thought and practice have also come to have global followings in the modern era, beginning with the Vedānta tradition first brought to the West by Swami Vivekananda in the late nineteenth century.[3] Even Jain thought, which has long been the preserve of a relatively small minority of Indian adherents (roughly five million today),[4] has a global following, and not only among Jains in the Indian diaspora.[5]

To be sure, there are Indian philosophical traditions, including currently living traditions, that emphasize the concept of *adhikāra*, or 'eligibility' to have access to philosophical knowledge.[6] The criteria for such eligibility have included birth into the right community (or 'caste'), as well as more individualized criteria related to intellectual aptitude, moral development, one's age, and one's having performed certain rituals. There are ideas presented in this book which would at one time have been the preserve of only a few scholars deemed eligible by such traditional norms, but which have long since been globally circulated, both through books and, more recently, through the internet.

Although there are Indian philosophies which have traditionally been deemed the special property of an elite few, my point here is that Indian philosophy is, first and foremost, philosophy. It should not be seen as something merely provincial in its scope or relevance, but as containing plenty to be of interest to Western philosophers and students of philosophy. In the words of scholar Roy W. Perrett, 'There is enough in common between Indian and Western philosophy to suggest that the philosophers in both traditions are often engaged with similar problems and hence should be able to communicate with each other. However, there are also sufficient differences between the traditions to suggest that they may have some novel perspectives to offer each other.'[7]

An influential definition of philosophy in the Western world is that of Aristotle (384–22 BCE), who defines philosophy as, 'the science of the universal essence of that which is actual'.[8] Another way to put this is that philosophy is the search for the general principles held to underlie particular instances of fact. One example of this is modern science, which searches for the general principles – the 'laws of nature' –

underlying the experience of the natural world. Indeed, science is, in its origins, a type of philosophy, formerly known as *natural philosophy*. It is the application of the principles of philosophy, as defined by Aristotle, to the examination of nature.

Indian philosophy overlaps with Aristotle's understanding of the philosophical enterprise, both in content and method. Both Indian and Western traditions are on a search for universal truths underlying the experiences which make up our lives.

There are important differences, though, as Perrett notes, between these traditions as well. It has become common to stereotype Indian philosophy as focused purely on spiritual and mystical realms, as full of exotic, paradoxical ways of thinking, and as akin to religion. At the same time, it has become equally common to see Western philosophy as dryly logical and as akin to science. Many Western philosophers, however, such as Plato, have been every bit as intent upon achieving mystical insight as have many Indian philosophers. By the same token, entire systems of Indian philosophy have been sharply focused upon the correct use of logic to argue for a view, and upon accurate observation and description of the physical world. To again cite Roy W. Perrett, 'Contrary to popular Western belief, classical Indian philosophy was not indistinguishable from Indian religion . . . But religious concerns did motivate the work of many Indian philosophers (as they did too the work of many of the great Western philosophers).'[9]

Indian philosophy: World views and ways of life

Understanding Indian philosophy requires us to understand the ways in which it is both similar to and different from philosophy as known in the West, including the ways that both Indian and Western philosophy are related to the complex phenomenon known as *religion*. In using the term 'Indian philosophy', we are using a term for an intellectual discipline which developed in the Western world and extending it to refer to an analogous discipline which developed in the cultural environment of India. The ideal to which I aspire in this book is for the reader to understand Indian philosophy, as much as possible, on its own terms. This requires us to stretch our sense of what philosophy is to enable us to enter imaginatively into Indian thought worlds (and most of the time, Indian thought worlds from much earlier periods of history than the present) with, we can hope, minimal distortion or misunderstanding.

The word *philosophy*, derived from the Greek *philosophia*, or 'love of wisdom', carries the implication of knowledge pursued for its own sake. What is the Indian equivalent of this term? And what is the activity this term describes?

First, it is important to know that there is no such language as *Indian*, any more than there is a language called *European*. India has always, so far as anyone can tell, been a multilingual and multicultural environment. The language of formal learning in India for most of history has been Sanskrit. The role of Sanskrit in Indian intellectual history is akin to that of Latin in Europe. Indian intellectual traditions have thus typically operated in the medium of Sanskrit, or languages closely related to it, like the Pāli language often used in Theravāda Buddhist thought.

Several Sanskrit terms have been used as Indian equivalents to *philosophy*. One such term is *jijñāsa*, or 'enquiry'. Literally meaning 'the desire for knowledge', *jijñāsa* is an exceptionally good equivalent to the term *philosophy*, particularly bearing in mind that both, in their roots, refer to a desire to know. Another is *anvīkṣikī*, which refers to the application of logic to a topic, which might be seen as equivalent to William James' definition of philosophy as 'the unusually stubborn attempt to think clearly'.[10] It also brings to mind the Analytic tradition of philosophy in the West.

The most common Indic term for philosophy, though – the one whose equivalent in modern Indian languages, like Hindi, is most frequently used to translate this word – is *darśana*. *Darśana* (or *darśan*, in Hindi), literally means *view*. It is derived from the Sanskrit verbal root *dṛś*, or 'see'. *Darśanam* literally means *seeing*. One who sees is a 'seer' or *ṛṣi*. Building upon this linguistic foundation, the word *darśana* has come to hold two specific meanings in Indian traditions.

One well-known meaning of *darśana* is a religious one. *Darśana* in this sense refers to the act of seeing (and being seen by) a deity in the context of worship, usually in a temple setting. The deity is present in a *mūrti*, or an image, which a devotee beholds. A spiritual communion thereby occurs between the devotee and deity through the medium of sight. It is not uncommon in Hindu contexts to hear a person refer to making a brief visit to a temple 'to take".darśan'._

The other meaning of *darśana*, more relevant to our discussion here, is a system of ideas used to perceive reality: that is, a *perspective* or *world view*.

In relation to philosophy, then, *darśana* can be identified as a system or school of thought. Throughout this book, whenever I refer to a *tradition*, system or school, I am translating the term *darśana*. *Darśana* refers not so much to philosophy in general (although it can mean this) as to *a* philosophy: a particular philosophical outlook, with certain ideas and methodologies. It is philosophy in the sense that one uses when one speaks of a particular system of thought, such as Aristotelian philosophy, Heideggerian philosophy, Continental philosophy, Analytic philosophy and so on. In the Indian traditions, one similarly speaks of the Yoga darśana, the Vedānta darśana, the Nyāya darśana and so on.

Though it has become a common practice, even in India, to translate *darśana* as *philosophy* (and *philosophy* as *darśana* or *darśan*), no translation is perfect. In the minds of many, philosophy is an academic activity of a highly technical nature pursued by university professors, with little or no reference to lived human experience outside of the academic conversation. If this denaturalized activity is what one has in mind when one encounters the word *philosophy*, then it serves as a poor translation of *darśana*.

This is because darśana is understood to occur in the context of a way of life. Usually, this way of life is aimed at realising some ideal of the highest good, and is thus, in important respects, akin to the concept of *religion*. In most of the darśanas, the highest good is identified as *mokṣa* – or freedom from the cycle of death and rebirth and the suffering this cycle involves. This freedom is seen in many darśanas as the highest aim of human existence, although we shall see that there are important exceptions to this tendency, such as the adherents of the Cārvāka, or Lokāyata darśana, who reject the entire concept of rebirth, and so the idea of liberation from it as well.[11]

Certainly, darśana can be every bit as technical and intricate in practice as philosophy has become in modern university settings. *Philosophy* is a better word for translating *darśana* than *religion*, even though many darśanas are connected to a way of life aimed at realising a highest good and can thus certainly be said to have religious dimensions. To practise a religion, however, does not typically require a specialized educational process. It is usually a matter of acculturation – something that one absorbs from one's family and wider community. Darśana is like philosophy in being a specialized, technical discipline. This discipline, though, is not pursued disinterestedly or for its own sake, but in the context and in the service of a way of life aimed, for most Indian traditions, at a spiritual end. Again, this does not mean we should think of Indian philosophy in a stereotyped way as 'spiritual', and thus as unconcerned with real-world issues or with the right and rigorous application of logic to truth claims. Indeed, recent scholars of Indian philosophy have taken great pains to move away from a widespread tendency to simply identify Indian philosophy with religion. To again cite Roy W. Perrett, 'Indian philosophy [is] not indistinguishable from Indian religion.'[12]

It is also not the case, even when darśanas *are* focused on what might be called religious or spiritual ends, that this means they abandon rationality and rigorous standards of logic. On the contrary, its situation in a way of life aimed at an ultimate end makes logical rigour and clarity all the more urgent in Indian philosophy, given the stakes involved; for it is not merely an intellectual exercise. Rather than taking its concern with spiritual ends as indicative of a lack of intellectual seriousness, it is better to see Indian philosophy as deeply concerned with *pragmatic outcomes*. It would seem to be a peculiarly modern bias to see intellectual rigour and spirituality as mutually antagonistic concerns.

Indeed, Sikh philosopher and scholar, Arvind-Pal Singh Mandair argues – persuasively, in my opinion – that the imposition in the early modern period of Western concepts of 'religion' and 'philosophy', and the resulting notion of an antagonism between these two, on Indian traditions is a violent colonizing act which has the precise effect of delegitimizing and marginalizing Indian traditions, just as it has marginalized much religious discourse in the West:

> The purpose of creating the modern category of 'religion' was to help authorize and naturalize secular rationality as the dominant form of modern consciousness, and as the essential language of conventional thinking, or 'common sense'. It is precisely this common sense which persuades us of the apparent naturalness of oppositions such as religion versus politics or materiality versus ideality, to give two well-known examples.[13]

The Sanskrit term which is most often used to translate *religion* is *dharma* (or its equivalent in modern Indic languages, such as the Hindi *dharm*). Here, too, though, the correlation is far from perfect. Indeed, translating *religion* as *dharma* is arguably even more problematic than rendering *darśana* as *philosophy*. In the words of scholar Pankaj Jain:

> [T]he general understanding of the term 'religion' is largely based on . . . Western theological connotations with [a] definite scripture, founder, historic events, and

specific theologies and practices . . . Transcending the boundaries of 'religion', some Indian thinkers . . . have included Jesus Christ and Muhammad as the eleventh and twelfth incarnations of Viṣṇu, thus incorporating Christianity and Islam into Indic traditions . . . '[D]harma' is a better representation of Indic spiritual phenomena than 'religion.'[14]

In addition to the fact which Jain points out that the content and structure of dharma are in many ways quite distinct from those of religion, at least as popularly conceived, dharma is often seen by its adherents as being a far more encompassing activity than religion, including both sacred and mundane aspects of life, and to some extent erasing or subverting the distinction between the two.

Dharma, however, like religion, is something in which a large number of people participate, whereas darśana, like philosophy, is a far more specialized, elite activity. The distinction between dharma and darśana, then, at least in this sense, maps reasonably well onto the Western distinction between religion and philosophy. Again, philosophy and darśana are universal activities, to the extent that they are concerned with problems which are of interest to thinkers from many cultural backgrounds. But relatively few people pursue the educational process that is needed to make these activities a full-time occupation, in either India or the West.[15] This is what is meant by philosophy (or darśana) being a specialized activity and religion (or dharma) being a more generalized one.

To the degree that darśana is, on the one hand, religion-like, in its being rooted in a way of life aimed at realizing an ideal of the highest good, but is also a specialized activity requiring a technical, intellectually rigorous training, it is tempting to translate *darśana* as *theology*. Theology has come, in the Western academy, to refer to reflection on the big questions of life which occurs self-consciously within a lived tradition of practice: a religion. This is a pretty good description of *darśana* as well. Due to the long association of theology with Christianity, though, as well as the original Greek meaning of *theologia* – reflection on the nature of divinity – many in both India and the West have a deep aversion to applying this term to activity rooted in non-Christian traditions.

For one thing, we shall see that many of the darśanas are non-theistic. They either deny or are simply uninterested in the question of a supreme being who creates and upholds the cosmos. Alternatively, we shall see that there are also darśanas where some notion of what might be called divinity is affirmed, but that this has nothing to do with the creation or maintenance of the world.

At the same time, there is also much Indian philosophical activity that overlaps a great deal in both method and content with Christian theology. The debates among the schools of Vedānta, for example, are deeply theological, being about the nature of God and the best way to realize the highest good. Some Naiyāyika arguments for the existence of a supreme God – called *Īśvara*, 'the Lord' – are quite similar to classical Christian arguments for the existence of God. But there are also darśanas that engage vigorously in refuting these very same arguments.[16] To again cite Perrett:

One fundamental difference [between Indian and Western philosophy of religion] is that theism is not central to all the Indian religions in the way it is to the Western religions. While there certainly were classical Indian philosophers who were staunch monotheists (e.g., the Viśiṣṭādvaitins, the Dvaitins, the Śaiva Siddhāntins), overall this was not the dominant trend. In the first place, Buddhism and Jainism are both non-theistic religions. Then within Hinduism, orthodoxy is traditionally determined by an acknowledgement of the authority of the Vedas [a set of sacred texts], not a belief in God. Hence among the orthodox Hindu philosophical schools Sāṃkhya and Mīmāṃsā are both atheistic, Advaita is ultimately non-theistic, and Yoga and Nyāya-Vaiśeṣika are minimally theistic in that they allow only significantly attenuated powers to God.[17]

Beyond the fact that theism is not the central theme of Indian philosophy that it has been in Western theology and philosophy of religion, there is also much in Indian philosophy with no equivalent in any Western theological tradition. Though not absent in Western thought, the concept of rebirth (also known in the West as *reincarnation*, transmigration, or metempsychosis) tends to be rejected by most thinkers in the West, certainly within the ambit of Christian orthodoxy. There is also no Western equivalent to the extensive and highly technical literature on karma, which can be found in, for example, the Jain tradition.

If, again, one is attentive to the original Greek meaning of theology (i.e. discourse about God, or the Gods) then *theology* becomes a highly inappropriate term for referring to the numerous darśanas that are non-theistic, or that are theistic in ways which differ considerably from classical Western theism, such as the Yoga tradition's affirmation of an Īśvara who exists primarily as an object for meditation, or the Jain view of all liberated souls as divine.[18] Theism is, of course, belief in a supreme being, and this is an idea that some systems of Indian philosophy explicitly reject, and that some do not engage at all, while others are deeply theistic and theological. In this book, therefore, I utilize the common practice of translating *darśana* as *philosophy*, and usually as a specific system, school or tradition of philosophy, and not as *theology* or *religion*, even when its content comes quite close to that of theology and religion as these are widely known in the West.

One needs to bear in mind, though, that Indian philosophies, even when they are at their most abstract, remain rooted in ways of life aimed at realizing the highest good. In thinking of Indian philosophy, one should not think of a contemporary university faculty debating an abstract topic, even when much of the content and method of Indian philosophy becomes as abstract and technical as contemporary philosophical debates, and instead bear in mind *philosophia* as conceived by the ancient Greeks. *Philosophia*, in its origins, was not an abstract set of claims, but rather reflection occurring in the context of a way of life often involving some kind of spiritual practice, as famously affirmed by Pierre Hadot.[19] Hadot defines 'spiritual exercises' as activities 'intended to effect a modification and a transformation in the subjects who practice them'.[20] This definition certainly applies to the various ethical, ritual and contemplative practices that are understood to accompany most of the darśanas of Indian philosophy. Indeed, it can sometimes be very difficult to grasp what Indian philosophers are saying if one is not attentive to the context of practice in which they are operating, particularly when they refer to meditative states, ritual injunctions and so on.

Religion and philosophy: Differences in Indian and Western sensibilities

Does affirming the rootedness of Indian philosophy in a way of life not imply that we are dealing here with something which is fundamentally of a spiritual, or even a religious, nature? Is not Indian philosophy therefore radically different from Western philosophy, which typically takes a sceptical stance and questions everything? Or do these questions simply arise from stereotyped ways of thinking about India and the West, which are really oversimplifications?

It is here that one becomes keenly aware of cultural difference. First, the split which many in the Western world take for granted between philosophy as a sceptical enquiry that is objective and disinterested, like modern science, and religion, which is seen as a matter of faith that cannot be subjected to logical proof or demands for evidence, is a split which is foreign to the traditional Indian sensibility (though not necessarily to a *contemporary* Indian sensibility, due to the colonial experience).

The sundering of philosophy and religion, the division of the old *philosophia* into a rational science called *philosophy* and a faith-based way of life called *religion*, has a very specific history. This history is closely connected with the crisis in European Christianity, in which the division of the tradition into numerous sects or denominations following the Protestant Reformation created the need for an objective foundation for knowledge: a foundation that would be separate from the hotly contested realm of faith. Religion thus became, particularly with the rise of secular nation-states, part of the private realm. One was free to believe whatever one wanted. Philosophy and science, however, were part of the realm of public knowledge. They thus required agreed-upon standards of argumentation and evidence.[21] This division is now taken for granted by many in the West as something natural and given, as well as by many in contemporary India, to the extent that India, like much of the world, has been deeply influenced, in the wake of European colonization, by Western thought. In its origins, though, this is actually a quite localized and Western way of thinking. Indeed, it is rejected by many thinkers even in the West, such as Christian philosophers and theologians who do not see reason and faith as necessarily being in conflict with one another.

Second, to say that this split is foreign to the traditional Indian sensibility is *not* to say that classical Indian philosophies are lacking in rationality or rigorous standards of evidence and logical argumentation. Again, it betrays a peculiarly Western bias, rooted in a specific Western history, to assume that adhering to a spiritual path or way of life is incompatible with scepticism and logic. It is also not to say that religious concerns necessarily suffuse every single Indian system of thought, or that they dominate every Indian philosophical conversation. They do not.

For the adherents of systems of Indian philosophy who do take their activity as being in the service of the realization of the highest good, precisely because so much is at stake, it becomes essential to examine all truth claims with maximum rigour. This conviction is the basis for one of the most pervasive features of Indian philosophical texts: the use of the *pūrva-pakṣa* or 'other side' as a foil for one's own perspective.[22]

For every claim one makes, one must consider the objections of those who hold other views.

Two ways of introducing Indian philosophy: By tradition and by topic

There are many ways to organize an introduction to Indian philosophy. The one that was long standard in the field was to introduce students to traditions or schools of thought. Typically, the emphasis would be on what are regarded as the classical systems of Indian philosophy. Critics of the traditional format for introducing Indian philosophy argue that it can be confusing to those who are at an early stage in their acquaintance with Indian thought. Many books which follow this format end with the classical period.

Some do go beyond the classical period, exploring the development of the classical systems in the medieval era: the proliferation of the Vaiṣṇava schools of Vedānta and the Navya Nyāya, or 'new logic', school. There might also be some discussion of modern Indian philosophy, though there has also been a disturbing trend among some authors to dismiss modern Indian thought as 'neo' Indian philosophy, and as somehow inauthentic, rather than as simply a new development.[23]

The relative rarity of the inclusion of recent Indian thought in introductory texts creates the unfortunate impression that Indian philosophy is a 'dead' tradition, when in reality, nothing could be further from the truth. The tendency not to include this material is, in some cases, due to an assumption of a major break separating modern and premodern Indian thought: that a massive gulf of differences in world views and methodologies divides recent and earlier Indian philosophies.

While there is some validity in this view, it can be overstated. There is continuity as well as divergence between premodern and modern Indian philosophy, just as there is both continuity and divergence across earlier eras of this tradition as well. It is an ancient intellectual heritage that has passed through many transitions, and a living heritage which continues to change through time.

An alternative model, which has become popular recently, is to organize an introductory text topically. In this kind of textbook, one might find a chapter on the nature of reality, which would include the views of various schools of Indian philosophy on this topic. Such a text would also have similarly organized chapters on other topics (like the nature of knowledge and so on).

Both approaches, by tradition or by topic, have virtues and drawbacks. Students who want to know, quickly and at a glance, the views of various schools of thought on a particular topic are not well served by the first approach, having to dig through chapters on many schools of thought to locate the information which they are trying to find. On the other hand, a student who wants to know the views of a particular system of thought on a range of topics – Patañjali's Yoga school, for example – is served equally poorly by the second approach, having to dig through chapters on varied topics to find their references to the views of the Yoga school.

One also loses, in the second approach, a sense of the flow of the conversation across the various Indian systems of thought. A good image for Indian philosophy as a whole is, indeed, that of a conversation that has been going on for over three thousand years. To understand why a school of thought holds the view it does on a given topic, it may be important, and perhaps even essential, to understand that this view is seen by its adherents as a corrective to the view of another system. What was this other system? What were its views? And why were they found to be problematic by the school of thought one is studying?

Entire systems of Vedānta, for example, have emerged historically as critical reactions to the Advaita Vedānta promulgated by the renowned thinker, Śaṅkara. Understanding these systems therefore involves understanding Advaita Vedānta, the system which they are critiquing. Similarly, understanding Advaita Vedānta involves understanding Buddhism, to which Advaita Vedānta can be seen as a reaction. Understanding Buddhism, in turn, involves understanding both Jain and early Vedic thought.

These examples illustrate the fact that Indian philosophy is neither a set of discrete systems of thought with no bearing on one another (as the first approach might suggest), nor a set of topics explored in the abstract (as suggested by the second approach). It is also not a series of lists of terms and claims, though it is sometimes presented in this way, even in India. It is a discourse that is highly contextual and intra-relational.

This book's approach: Telling a story

I have constructed this book based on my twenty-five years of teaching Indian philosophy using textbooks of both of the kinds I have just described. Both approaches have their virtues and their shortcomings. I have learnt much from every book on Indian philosophy I have used. My intention in writing this book is not to criticize previous authors on Indian philosophy. I am grateful to them all.

I have found, though, that the most natural and effective way for me to approach Indian philosophy is as a story: to see this tradition as the millennia-old conversation that it is, with each system and tradition flowing into and affecting the others, each giving its particular insight into questions like the nature of being, knowledge and morality. Rather than presenting a list of either traditions or topics, I have endeavoured to summarize this conversation, as I understand it. I hope I have done so clearly and in a way which gives insight, with a minimum of confusion, while also conveying a sense of the complexity of the material involved. At times, for the sake of simplicity, I have not gone into the depths of some aspects of the Indian philosophical conversation and have simply moved chronologically from one tradition to the next.

The danger of this approach is that it might inadvertently suggest that, as the conversation has moved on through history, earlier systems of thought have thereby been superseded or rendered obsolete. As most of these are living traditions today, that clearly is clearly not the case.

I have therefore sought, as much as humanly possible, to represent each tradition in a way with which its adherents would, I hope, agree.

Another question with which authors of introductory texts wrestle is terminology. How much Sanskrit terminology should be included and how much should be translated into handy English terms? Should diacritical marks be used?

I have opted to trust the intelligence of my readers and have used the terms used by these traditions, both to give a flavour of their original sensibility, but also to acknowledge the fact that, for many of these terms (like *Brahman* and *karma*), there simply is no single English equivalent. It is not that these terms are, as it is sometimes claimed, untranslatable: that is, incapable of being explained in English. But they do not have any easy or obvious one-to-one correspondences with English terms which could be used without massively distorting their meaning. I have given an English explanation of each new term as it appears (and will sometimes repeat this explanation, in the case of less-used terms).

Regarding the book's title, I am aware that *Discovering Indian Philosophy* might have the effect of conveying a colonialist mindset. One immediately thinks of the widespread claim that Columbus 'discovered America' when in fact many people had already been living in America for thousands of years before Columbus 'discovered' it. The intent of this title is not to imply that Indian philosophy is some kind of wild territory which needs to be 'tamed' through being written about and described by scholars like myself. The hope, rather, is that this title will convey some of the excitement which comes whenever any of us encounters something that is new *to us*. Given the profound sense of indebtedness that I personally feel towards the traditions of India, my aim is not to shape these traditions in my own image, but rather, I hope, to communicate as authentically as I am able, given my own limitations and context, ideas that I have found transformative, as well as, in some cases, puzzling and challenging, because I believe that encountering ideas from diverse cultural sources is important to human growth, and even to our future survival as co-inhabitants of the planet we call home. I have assumed a readership that is largely unfamiliar with this material, but that does not limit its relevance only to, say, an audience of college students in North America and Europe. Even though it is an introductory text, it is my hope that even people who have grown up with one or more of the traditions discussed in this book will learn something worthwhile from reading it.

Finally, as an introductory text, there is much material that this book does *not* cover. I have touched on major themes and explored topics with which I am most familiar. This is not the kind of topic on which anyone can really have the last word. I would like for readers to know that there are many layers of complexity in Indian philosophy that are beyond the scope of an introductory text like this one. Especially in regard to the teachings of various schools of thought, it is important to bear in mind that important thinkers within each school of thought have often diverged from a 'textbook' version of the teachings of their darśanas. There is variety internal to each school that is inevitably glossed over when one is trying to summarize things in a comprehensible way. John Cort, a renowned scholar of Jainism, has observed that, 'Anyone who has ever taught about India knows that for every true statement about India there is an opposite, yet equally true statement'".[24] This is as true of Indian philosophy as it is for other aspects of life in India. Sāṃkhya philosophers, for example, are non-theistic, except when they are not. Many other examples could be cited.

In short, Indian philosophy is a vast field, impossible to encompass in one book; but, as the saying goes in India, I have tried my level best!

Notes

1 Alfred North Whitehead, *Process and Reality (Corrected Edition)* (New York: The Free Press, 1978), p. 4.

2 And Buddhism was not unknown in the West in ancient times. See Christopher I. Beckwith, *Greek Buddha: Pyrrho's Encounter with Early Buddhism in Central Asia* (Princeton: Princeton University Press, 2015).

3 See Jeffery D. Long, *Hinduism in America: A Convergence of Worlds* (London: Bloomsbury, 2020), pp. 92–101.

4 Jeffery D. Long, *Jainism: An Introduction* (London: Bloomsbury, 2009), p. 13. The number of Jains globally was roughly 4.2 million in 2009, but it has since increased.

5 For an example of a Western expression of Jain philosophy, see Herbert Warren, *Jainism in Western Garb as a Solution to Life's Problems* (New Delhi: Crest Publishing House, 1993). Warren became a Jain practitioner after his encounters with Virchand Gandhi (1864-1901), who represented the Jain tradition at the Chicago World Parliament of Religions in 1893.

6 Torkel Brekke, *Makers of Modern Indian Religion in the Nineteenth Century* (Oxford: Oxford University Press, 2002), p. 8.

7 Roy W. Perrett, ed., *Indian Philosophy: A Collection of Readings, Volume Four, Philosophy of Religion* (New York: Routledge, 2001), p. ix.

8 Charles G. Herberman, Edward A. Pace, Condé B. Pallen, Thomas J. Shahan, and John J. Wynne, eds, *The Catholic Encyclopedia*, vol. I (New York: Robert Appleton Co., 1907), p. 714.

9 Perrett, *Indian Philosophy*, p. xiii.

10 Cited in David L. Hall and Roger T. Ames, *Thinking Through Confucius* (Albany: State University of New York Press, 1987), p. 29.

11 'It is more or less an accepted fact that philosophy . . . is not independent of the religious background on which it grows. It is markedly so in the Indian tradition where all systems – except the little known *lokāyata* materialism – are aiming at salvation or release, *mokṣa, niḥśreyasa,* apavarga, kaivalya, or nirv. The terminology may be different, but the fundamental idea, leaving the karmic cycle of transmigration forever, is the same.' Ferenc Ruzsa, 'The Fertile Clash: The Rise of Philosophy in India', in *Indian Languages and Texts Through the Ages: Essays of Hungarian Indologists in Honour of Prof. Csaba Töttössy*, ed. Csaba Dezso (Delhi: Manohar, 2007), p. 63.

12 Perrett, *Indian Philosophy*, p. xiii

13 Arvind-Pal Singh Mandair, *Sikh Philosophy: Exploring Gurmat Concepts in a Decolonizing World* (London: Bloomsbury, 2022), p. 11.

14 Pankaj Jain, *Dharma and Ecology of Hindu Communities: Sustenance and Sustainability* (New York: Routledge, 2016), p. 25.

15 Either as a matter of choice or because this education is unavailable due to issues of class, race, caste, gender and so on.

16 See Parimal Patil, *Against a Hindu God: Buddhist Philosophy of Religion in India* (New York: Columbia University Press, 2009).

17 Perrett, *Indian Philosophy*, p. xiii. We shall see that there are some exceptions to the characterizations that Perrett has given to various systems of thought as either theistic or non-theistic. It is not always the case that the adherents of a particular darśanas hold a uniform view on a given topic, including the topic of theism. His broader point, however, that theism is not the dominant theme of Indian philosophy of religion that it is in its Western equivalent is nevertheless correct.

18 See Richa Pauranik Clements, 'Being a Witness: Cross-Examining the Role of Notion of Self in Śaṅkara's *Upadeśasāhasrī*, Īśvarakṛṣṇa's *Sāṃkhyakārikā*, and Patañjali's *Yogasūtra*', in *Theory and Practice of Yoga: Essays in Honour of Gerald James Larson*, ed. Knut A. Jacobsen (Leiden: Brill, 2005), pp. 75–97; and Jeffery D. Long, 'From a Certain Point of View: Jain Theism and Atheism', *Sophia* 60, no. (2021): pp. 623–38.

19 See Pierre, Hadot *Philosophy as a Way of Life* (Oxford: Blackwell Publishing, 1995).

20 Ibid., p. 6.

21 Richard Tarnas, *The Passion of the Western Mind: Understanding the Ideas That Have Shaped Our World View* (New York: Ballantine, 1991), p. 286.

22 See Michael Allen, 'Inquiry as Spiritual Practice: The Role of Philosophy in Late Advaita Vedānta', in *Proceedings of the XXIII World Congress of Philosophy*, vol. 16 (2018), pp. 15–19.

23 A particular instance of this tendency has been well critiqued by James Madaio in his article, 'Rethinking Neo-Vedānta: Swami Vivekananda and the Selective Historiography of Advaita Vedānta', *Religions* 8, no. 1 (2017): 3.

24 John Cort, *Jains in the World: Religious Values and Ideology in India* (Oxford: Oxford University Press, 2001), p. 15.

1

Vedic thought

Philosophies of action and knowledge

Introduction

This chapter explores the roots of Indian philosophy: the concepts found in the body of literature known as the Vedas. The Vedas are an extensive collection, beginning with the hymns and ritual-based reflections of the *Ṛg Veda* and concluding with the more abstract and what some might call the more 'philosophical' (in a conventional sense) teachings of the *Upaniṣads*.

In the Vedas, including the *Upaniṣads*, one does not find *systematic* philosophy of the kind one finds in later periods of Indian intellectual history. Such systematic thought begins to emerge in the later commentarial literature written to explicate more poetic and evocative texts such as the Vedas. The Vedas contain numerous expressions of wonder at the mysterious depth and beauty of the cosmos: the external cosmos of the physical world as well as the internal cosmos of the mind and consciousness. These two levels of reality, outer and inner, are linked, in early Vedic thought, through ritual, which is believed to sustain and bind the cosmos together.[1] By the time of the later Vedic texts, the *Upaniṣads*, the underlying, binding reality of the universe, and of the outer and inner worlds, comes to be understood more abstractly as *Brahman*, the Infinite.

Further developments of the Vedic period that become foundational for Indian philosophy and culture, and which are touched upon in this chapter, include the idea of a single reality beyond the diverse realm of deities and natural phenomena, the interlinked concepts of karma and rebirth, and the practice of *renunciation*, in which a person gives up life in society and pursues ascetic practice. This is seen in these texts as a kind of sacrifice: as a substitute, in a sense, for the earlier Vedic sacrificial ritual. One engages in such renunciation to pursue a higher spiritual realization: specifically, to reach the state of mokṣa, or liberation from the cycle of karma and rebirth.[2]

It has become conventional among scholars to see the transformations of thought which can be discerned in the Vedic literature as historical developments. This is the way this material will also be presented here. It is important to note, however, that from a traditional point of view, what is observed both in the Vedic literature and in subsequent periods of the history of Indian philosophy is not so much a *development* as an *unfolding* of potentials and implications already present from beginning: the eternal truths perceived by the seers of the past.[3]

Prehistoric roots? The Indus civilization

The Indian philosophical conversation most likely began in the first civilization to emerge in the subcontinent, if not earlier. This civilization, now widely known as the Indus or Harappan civilization, was one of the major river-based civilizations of the ancient world, alongside Egypt, Mesopotamia, China and the Oxus civilization. It is likely that its inhabitants called it *Meluhha*.[4]

We do not know precisely what the people of this civilization believed, or how, or even if, they argued for their worldview or worldviews. The very small samples of writing found amidst the archaeological remains of this civilization have yet to be deciphered.[5]

It is worth mentioning, however, that a technologically advanced, culturally sophisticated civilization existed in the Indian subcontinent as early as the third millennium before the Common Era (the urban phase of the Indus civilization having lasted from roughly 2600 to 1900 BCE). This civilization was also widespread, occupying not only the valley of the Indus River, in what is today Pakistan, but extending into Afghanistan and a considerable portion of north-western India as well. With a population and a territorial extent larger than the Egyptian and Mesopotamian civilizations, certainly this civilization had an impact on later thought and practice, both in India and beyond.[6] However what, precisely, this impact might have been remains something of a mystery.

The Vedas: Fountainhead of the Sanskrit tradition

To the best of our knowledge, the first recorded Indian philosophy is found in the Vedas. The Vedas are a vast collection of texts whose composition spanned a period of over a thousand years. Scholars typically date the compilation of the oldest of these texts, the *Ṛg Veda*, to the period between 1500 and 1000 BCE. Many Hindu scholars argue that they are even older than this.[7]

The *Ṛg Veda* is made up of 1028 hymns, or *mantras*, all of which are in an archaic version of Sanskrit, a language spoken in north-western India in ancient times. The reverence in which the Vedas have been held in many Indian traditions eventually led to Sanskrit becoming the standard language of literature and philosophy – of 'high' culture – among Indian elites. Sanskrit held this prestigious status until being supplanted by English in the modern period. Knowledge of Sanskrit is still regarded in India today as an achievement, and a sign of a deep, sincere devotion to Indian cultural ideals. In fact, the word *Sanskrit* literally means 'cultured' or 'refined', and its mastery is still seen as a mark of cultural literacy and intellectual acuity.

The nature of Vedic revelation: Eternal truth, spiritual science or word of God?

Hindu tradition attributes the compiling of the Vedas to a figure named Veda Vyāsa, whose name literally means 'the compiler of the Vedas'. The texts themselves, however, are attributed to figures called *ṛṣis* or seers.[8]

According to a tradition of Vedic interpretation called Mīmāṃsā, the seers did not compose the Vedas from their own imaginations, as with conventional poetry. Rather, they perceived eternal truths directly and expressed them in the medium of Sanskrit. Although *apparently* composed by human authors, the Vedas absolutely transcend human subjectivity. For this reason, the Mīmāṃsā tradition teaches that the Vedas are *apauruṣeya*: 'authorless', or 'not-man-made'. The Vedic texts are thus described not as having been 'crafted' or 'authored', but as *śruti*, or 'heard'. The idea is that the seers did not author the Vedas, which are eternal, but enunciated what they had perceived.[9]

There is another system of Vedic interpretation, that upheld by the Nyāya school of Indian philosophy, which teaches that the Vedas are the word of God in much the same way as this is understood in Western, Abrahamic, religions. According to this line of thought, the Vedas are a special revelation from Īśvara, 'the Lord', having been 'heard' by the ancient seers to whom the Lord spoke.

Nyāya is a system of logic which is aimed at establishing knowledge on a firm foundation. According to Nyāya, there are several means by which valid knowledge is acquired. Such means to valid knowledge are called *pramāṇas*. They include relatively uncontroversial foundations for knowledge, like sensory perception and inferential reasoning (i.e. logic applied to observation). Thus, I can know something because I have seen it for myself, or I can know something because I have seen something else and can infer from what I have seen. I can see, for example, smoke that is coming from a mountain and conclude there is a fire there, even if I have not seen the fire myself. Another source of valid knowledge is the word of a trustworthy person. Unlike Mīmāṃsā, which does not teach that a personal divinity presides over the cosmos, Nyāya teaches that a supreme being, the Lord, does necessarily exist. The Lord is, of course, the most trustworthy person that one can imagine. Because the Vedas, according to Nyāya, are the Lord's word (as transmitted through the also reliable Vedic seers), they constitute a sound basis for knowledge about those truths which are unavailable to sensory perception or logic.[10]

Acceptance or rejection of Vedic authority: A major dividing line of Indian philosophy

The question of the authority of the Vedas is a major dividing line in Indian philosophy. A number of Indian philosophical systems accept the premise that the Vedas are authoritative texts, either in the impersonal sense of Mīmāṃsā or the theistic sense of Nyāya. Others, though, reject the idea of Vedic authority entirely and are critical of many Vedic teachings and perspectives, even to the point of ridiculing the notion of an authorless text as an oxymoron.

In the modern period, those systems which accept Vedic authority have come to be called *Hindu* and make up the philosophies of the religious tradition known today as *Hinduism*. Although the Vedas and the systems of thought and practice based on them are ancient, the terms *Hindu* and *Hinduism* are of relatively recent origin and are not utilized by Indian philosophers until quite late in the medieval period.[11] Referring to these systems as *Hindu* prior to this period is anachronistic, but one nevertheless sees this usage in many texts, especially older works on Indian philosophy.

Among ancient Indian traditions which reject Vedic authority, the two that continue to have a major following today are the Buddhist and Jain traditions. Buddhists live primarily in East and Southeast Asia, although there are Buddhist communities in Nepal, India and Bangladesh, and Buddhism is the predominant tradition of Sri Lanka and Bhutan. Jains live mainly in India, though there is today a global Jain community, just as there are Buddhists and Hindus living around the world as well. In addition to Buddhism and Jainism, other ancient Indian schools of thought which reject the authority of the Vedas include the now-extinct Ājīvika tradition and a variety of sceptical traditions, most prominently the Cārvāka or Lokāyata system of materialist philosophy.

Two streams of Vedic thought: Philosophies of action and of knowledge

The term *Veda* means *wisdom*. The Vedas are regarded by those who revere them as the repositories of the highest wisdom, as well as the means by which human beings can achieve true happiness. Indeed, human happiness is a central concern of the Vedas. How can human flourishing be ensured? Of what does it consist? What is a good life, and how can it be achieved?

Two answers to these questions can be found in Vedic literature. The first focuses upon *action*, particularly ritual action, as essential to human flourishing. The second focuses on a special *knowledge* believed to create a radical transformation in those who attain it, a transformation which leads to a state of perfect freedom and bliss.

These two responses to the question of happiness represent yet another dividing line within Indian philosophy, and one not limited to the Vedic traditions. The Vedic philosophy that affirms the centrality of action represents a stream of thought called *pravṛtti*: a philosophy of engagement with the world, affirming life in human society and one's role within it. The Vedic philosophy that emphasizes transformative knowledge represents, on the contrary, a stream of thought known as *nivṛtti*: a philosophy of world renunciation, in which worldly life is seen not as the way *to*, but as an impediment in the way *of*, true happiness.

The latter philosophy has come to be stereotypically associated with most Indian thought, as focused on otherworldly or spiritual aims at the expense of worldly life, though in fact it is the philosophy of action which has more often tended to define the way of life of the average person in India throughout history. There have also been significant attempts to integrate the two, to infuse a spiritual sensibility into worldly life and transform it into a spiritual practice. The philosophy of the *Bhagavad Gītā*, as we shall see later, is an important example of this approach.

We shall first examine the Vedic philosophy of action, which is the main focus of the oldest portion of the Vedic literature – a set of texts called, in the tradition, the *Karma Kāṇḍa*, or the 'action portion' of the *Vedas*. The *Karma Kāṇḍa* begins with the *Ṛg Veda*.

The *Ṛg Veda* in a global historical and cultural context

The 1028 hymns of the *Ṛg Veda*, compiled into ten books, or *maṇḍalas*, consist primarily of songs of praise to powerful divine beings known as the *devas*, or 'shining ones'. The devas, for the most part, appear to be personifications of natural forces. Indra, lord of the devas, who leads them in battle and also ensures human success in warfare, is associated with thunder. His weapon is the thunderbolt.[12] He bears many resemblances to deities in other cultural traditions, such as the Greek Zeus and the Norse Thor, who also wield thunderbolts. All these deities are part of what is called the *Indo-European* cultural sphere, united by similarities in language, culture and religion.

The philosophy of the *Ṛg Veda*: Devas, the Oneness of Being, cosmic order and sacrifice

In addition to the thunderbolt-wielding Indra, other important devas include Sūrya, lord of the sun, Varuṇa, lord of the waters, Vāyu, lord of the wind, Soma, identified in later literature as lord of the moon and the realm of sleep and dreams, Yama, lord of death, Mitra, lord of friendship, Uṣas, goddess of the dawn, and Sarasvatī, goddess of a river of the same name, later revealed to be the goddess of wisdom. Each deva is associated with narratives to which the hymns of the *Ṛg Veda* allude. These stories are typically not found within the *Ṛg Veda* itself, but in a later set of texts called the *Purāṇas*. Indra, for example, is known to have used his vajra to slay the serpentine monster, Vṛtra. Yama is said to be the first human being to die, and so the first to enter the realm of the dead, thus becoming Lord of Death. *Soma*, lord of the moon and of dreams in the *Purāṇas*, is, in the Vedas, the name for a sacred drink which appears to have had hallucinogenic effects.

There are many other devas as well, including two who would later become major deities of the Hindu tradition, but who receive relatively little attention in the *Ṛg Veda*: the omnipresent Viṣṇu, whose footsteps span the entire universe, and Rudra, 'the roarer', a storm deity who is later and more widely known as Śiva, the benevolent one. Both are later seen as the Supreme Being.[13]

The devas do not fit easily within Western conceptions of either monotheism (belief in one deity) or polytheism (belief in many deities). While the multiplicity of the devas is affirmed, one also finds Vedic verses suggesting that these beings are forms or manifestations of a single higher reality. The *Ṛg Veda* famously proclaims: 'They say it is Indra, Mitra, Varuṇa, and Agni, and. . . the winged, well-feathered bird of heaven [the sun]. Though it is One, inspired poets speak of it in many ways'[14] The idea of a singular, unmanifest (or 'Unborn') ultimate reality is also suggested in the following verse: 'I ask the wise who know, myself not knowing: who may he be, the One [*tad ekam*] in the form of the Unborn, who props in their place the six universal regions'?[15]

The idea of a singular supreme reality manifesting through the forms of many deities would become a prominent feature of later Indian philosophies, and Hindu thought in particular. In later Vedic thought, this reality comes to be known as *Brahman*, the basis not only of all deities, but of all existence. In modern Hinduism, this idea becomes the basis for a pluralistic approach to the world's religions generally, seeing all concepts of divinity as pointing to the same reality.

To be sure, it is not clear that the intention of the composers of the Vedic verses was to affirm the philosophy of religious pluralism found in modern Hindu thought; but it can certainly be seen as an implication of the Vedic idea that behind the diversity of the phenomena of the world there exists a deeper unity. Beyond the devas is *tad ekam*: 'the One'. This is interpreted in various ways by subsequent Hindu traditions. Some, like the Vaiṣṇava traditions, see it as an affirmation of something akin to monotheism in a Western, Abrahamic sense, in which the multiplicity of phenomena is dependent upon a singular supreme being. Others, like the Advaita Vedānta darśana, see it as teaching *monism*, a philosophy of the oneness, or non-duality, of all being.[16]

One of the most important devas is Agni, lord of fire. Fire is essential to civilization. It brings light in the darkness and protection from wild animals. It makes cooking possible. It is also dangerous, if uncontrolled. All these features of fire give rise to philosophical reflection. Light in the darkness can represent the power of knowledge to dispel ignorance. The protective power of fire can represent protection from all the malevolent forces, internal and external, that can threaten us. Cooking – the transformation of inedible matter into edible, life-giving food – represents personal transformation. The danger of uncontrolled fire – its ability not only to give life and light and cook food but also to burn and destroy life and property – represents the enormity of divine power. The very first mantra of the *Ṛg Veda* is, in fact, a prayer to Agni: 'I magnify the Lord, the divine, the Priest, minister of the sacrifice, the offerer, supreme giver of treasure . . . To you, dispeller of the night, we come with daily prayer offering to you our reverence. For you are Lord of sacrifice, enlightener, shepherd of the world, who wax mighty in your own abode.'[17]

Throughout Vedic literature, one can trace the process by which people in ancient India developed their philosophies, much as the ancient Greeks would do a few centuries later, through observing and reflecting on the forces of nature and the interplay between the outer world of nature and the inner world of human life and consciousness. Vedic hymns appearing, at first glance, to be about nature, are also revealed, upon closer analysis, to be deeply psychological.[18] One example of such a hymn, which explicitly connects the external world of nature with the inner realm of the mind is the *Gāyatrī Mantra*: 'May the beautiful light of the sun be ours; that our thoughts may be inspired.'[19] The poet clearly perceives the light of the sun not only as a physical light, illuminating the earth, but also as a spiritual light which can arouse thoughts in the mind. An emphasis on such metaphorical correspondences between the outer world of the universe – the macrocosm – and the inner world of the mind of the individual – the microcosm – are a central feature of Vedic thought. The history of Vedic thought can be seen as a movement from the poetic to the philosophical, from the metaphorical to the metaphysical, from the concrete (fire, the sun) to the abstract (Brahman). It is from reflections on the utterances of texts such as the *Ṛg Veda* that Indian philosophy, at least that branch of it which is identified with Hinduism, begins its long history of development.

In Vedic thought, the intermediary process which connects the outer world of nature and the inner world of the mind, the macrocosm and the microcosm, is ritual.[20] Agni, the sacred fire, is central to Vedic religious practice, as the focus of rituals that are aimed at maintaining the cosmic order. According to Vedic thought, human flourishing is made possible by the order of nature: called *ṛta* in the Vedic literature and, in later Hindu literature, *dharma*. If nature did not follow an orderly flow, all would be chaos. If all were chaos, life would be unpredictable, and in fact, impossible. How could one guarantee the changes of the seasons on which agriculture depends, or that the sun would rise the next day, or that cows would give milk if all were chaos? Importantly, human activity, and ritual activity in particular, is also seen as integral to this process.

This assumption of a basic order of the cosmos is fundamental to all forms of philosophical thought, and even to the practice of modern science. A basic axiom of the scientific method is that repeated observations of the same phenomena will yield the same results, such that an experiment performed on one day in a certain manner will not yield a radically different result if performed in the same manner at a later time. If this could not be presumed, no predictions could be made and knowledge would be impossible. As Whitehead observes, 'Apart from a certain smoothness in the nature of things, there can be no knowledge.'[21] Order is essential to knowledge and to life itself. The ancient Vedic thinkers understood this principle. It was the basis for their ritual practice. The Vedic term for the fundamental order of existence is, again, *ṛta*, which later comes to be known as *dharma*. The root meaning of *dharma* is 'that which provides support'. The cosmic order supports the world and makes life and human flourishing possible.

While some sense of a basic order of things is a universal necessity of philosophy, one of the distinctive views about this cosmic order in Vedic literature is that this order is not simply a given. It cannot be taken for granted and must be maintained by human activity. Human beings are not detached, passive observers of the cosmos. We participate in it. Certain duties are required of us in order to ensure the smooth continuity of existence. Just as the cosmic order itself comes to be called *dharma*, the particular duties of human beings in that order also come to be denoted by this same term. In fact, if one asks an Indian friend the meaning of *dharma*, the answer one is most likely to hear is 'duty'.[22] 'In short, *dharma* is a harmonizing principle of the cosmos. Humans, through virtuous and religious disciplines and ritualistic actions, sustain this order'.[23]

This ancient Vedic concept of duty and its fulfilment as essential to maintaining the world later becomes central to Indian thinking on ethics, society and politics, and remains so even today. The cosmos is not only an object for abstract contemplation.

We are part of the cosmos. Its nature therefore places a demand upon us, a set of obligations. Our failure to fulfil these duties leads to chaos and a breakdown in the order of things. The Vedas, as the self-revelation of the cosmos (or, in the Nyāya view, the supreme being's revelation of the nature of the cosmos), are the ultimate guide to the fulfilment of these obligations.

From a contemporary perspective, this idea of our embeddedness in the cosmos, and our presence within it as imposing certain obligations upon us, could be seen as profoundly ecological. For everything we take from the world, we should return something. At the same time, such an organic view of the cosmos, if applied to human society, can also lead to the deeply conservative view that we are each born to specific duties and social roles that we cannot escape in this lifetime. Both implications were drawn in ancient India from the core philosophy of the Vedas. If, for everything we take from the world, we should give something back, this implies a concept of reciprocity, which develops into the idea of karma. The specific duties and social roles applying to each person are developed into the social system called, in the modern period, 'caste'.

The primary duty of human beings in the Vedas is to give something back to the devas for the blessings they bestow on us: all the things that make life possible, like rain in sufficient measure to grow food (but not so much as to cause destructive flooding), fire, cattle, sunlight and so on. This giving back takes the form of *yajña* or sacrifice. Sacrifice is the central Vedic ritual.

It is important to note that while it may appear that the Vedic sacrifice consists of human beings giving gifts to the devas in the hope that the devas will thus look kindly upon human beings and give us something in return, the concept is really closer to that of a symbiosis. It is not the case, in other words, that sacrifice consists of 'bribing' the devas, on whose whims human beings depend. Just as humans need food to survive and do our work, including our duty of performing sacrifice, the devas also need the sacrifice in order to sustain themselves and carry out their work of maintaining the world. The obligations between human beings and the devas are mutual.

Over time, the Vedic sacrifice comes to be seen as a source of great power in its own right: a technology not only for the maintenance, but also for the transformation of the world in accord with the desires of the sacrificer. One who comprehends the mystery of the sacrifice can command the devas. One who understands how ritual action, well and rightly performed, leads to specific, concrete results, can achieve anything. This is one reason the study of the Vedas is, from an early period, restricted to a relatively small group in the larger Indian society: the Vedic ritual experts, or priests, known as *Brahmins*.[24]

The Vedic sacrifice, from the beginning, is seen as a kind of model of the universe. Indeed, scholar Paul Mus coined a new term –*mesocosm*, or 'middle cosmos' – to refer to the mediating realm of the Vedic ritual in its role of connecting the macrocosm – the universe – and the microcosm consisting of the individual person.[25] It is a useful term for helping grasp these concepts; for the Vedic universe has many layers, all linked to one another by correspondences. An element of the external, physical cosmos is linked to an element of the sacrificial ritual, which is also linked to an element of the consciousness of the individual. The light of the sun, for example, is also the light of the sacred fire, which is also the light of knowledge which drives away ignorance. The efficacy of Vedic ritual, its ability to have transformative effects upon the world and the individual person, rests on this set of correspondences. They are what make a Vedic ritual 'work'. The manipulation of elements of the ritual corresponding to a desire in the mind of the sacrificer also influences the corresponding facets of the wider world that need to be transformed in order for the desire to be fulfilled. The ritual realm mediates between cosmos and sacrificer through the correspondences described in the Vedas. One could speculate that Vedic ritual serves as a means for visualizing the desires in the mind of the sacrificer which the sacrificer wishes to manifest into the external world, thus helping make those desires a reality.

What is the origin of Vedic correspondences? Some may seem quite obvious or natural, like the correspondence invoked in the *Gāyatrī Mantra* between the light of the sun and the light of awareness. Others are more obscure, at least from a contemporary perspective, and require texts like the later Vedic commentaries to elaborate upon them.

The *Hymn of the Cosmic Man* (or *Puruṣa Sūkta*), a famous hymn of the *Ṛg Veda*, describes how the devas fashioned the universe from the body of a being called the *Puruṣa*, or cosmic person, who sacrifices himself to give life to all beings. Correspondences are an essential element in this creative process; for each part of the body of the creator corresponds to (i.e. it *becomes*) a portion of the cosmos: 'The moon was born from his mind. From his eye the sun was born. From his mouth Indra and Agni, from his breath Vāyu was born".[26] The body of the creator becomes not only the physical cosmos, the natural world, but also the social world of human beings, with all its various categories and classes: 'The Brahmin was his mouth. The ruler was made [from] his two arms. As to his thighs – that is what the freeman was. From his two feet, the servant was born.'[27]

All that exists proceeds from this original sacrifice and is tied to it through correspondence: the moon to the mind of the creator, the sun to the creator's eye and so on. Every Vedic sacrifice gains its power, in part, due its being a repetition or a re-enactment of this original sacrifice. The sacrifice, correctly performed, participates in the original sacrifice which creates the universe, and taps into the original creative power, Brahman, which then manifests through the correspondences across the levels of reality: microcosm, mesocosm and macrocosm.

Vedic sacrifice is therefore a model of the universe: a miniature re-enactment of the cosmic process of creation. Similarly, on the microcosmic level, each living being is a recreation of the primordial cosmic man, the creator, the divine being whose life, on the universal level, gives life to all.[28] Only one who fully grasps these connections can perform the sacrifice effectively, tapping into and utilising its power.

Finally, it is important to note that in the worldview of the Vedas, creation is an ongoing process. This is why sacrifice must be repeated. Despite the fact that the *Hymn of the Cosmic Man* reads as though it describes a singular event occurring in the past (how the world was created) it actually describes an ongoing, ever-unfolding process of creation, in which all beings participate. In fact, this hymn is only one of several accounts of creation in the *Ṛg Veda*. The various Vedic creation stories are not seen in the tradition as contradictory or in conflict, but as revealing various facets of the complex, ongoing process of the emergence of the cosmos.

The other three *Vedas*: *Yajur, Sāma* and *Atharva*

While the *Ṛg Veda* consists largely of hymns to the devas, the Vedic rituals are described in another collection of texts called the *Yajur Veda*.

Vedic sacrifice, in concrete terms, involves the creation of a fire altar made of bricks where the sacred fire can be safely kindled and, throughout the course of the ritual, 'fed' with offerings. Agni, the sacred fire, is the 'mouth' of the devas into which their offerings are 'fed'. The first offering always goes to Agni himself; for if Agni is not fed, he will consume the offerings to the other devas. Usually, these offerings consist of aromatic wood and a clarified butter called *ghee*. A source of controversy, in ancient times as well as today, when many Hindus have embraced an ethic of non-violence and vegetarianism, is the fact that some sacrifices described in the *Yajur Veda* appear to involve the slaughter of animals. As we shall see, this practice constitutes a major objection to the Vedic tradition from philosophies that reject Vedic authority, like Jainism and Buddhism. It has also been critiqued within the Vedic tradition itself. Vedic animal sacrifices have generally been replaced, where they are still performed, with <u>non-violent, vegetarian</u> substitutes.

Offerings to the fire are accompanied by the singing or chanting of select verses from the *Ṛg Veda*. The *Yajur Veda* indicates which verses should be chanted when in specific rituals.

The major life rituals of the Hindu tradition, such as a young person becoming an adult and receiving a sacred thread as a mark of this transition, a couple getting married, the funerary ritual and many other rituals as well, involve the sacred fire and follow principles set forth in the *Yajur Veda*.

Numerous rituals are described in this text. Some are performed to achieve specific goods: timely rain, abundant cattle, protection from enemies and wild animals, healthy children, and, for warriors, success in battle. These rituals are optional and recommended for those who wish to achieve the goods at which they are aimed.

Other rituals are obligatory and must be performed regularly to maintain the cosmic order. These include daily rituals and occasional rituals performed on special holy days. Vedic tradition observes a lunar calendar, and the correct times for rituals are based on close observation of the stars and planets to determine when they should be performed. One also wishes to determine the most auspicious time for optional rituals. The performance of Vedic ritual becomes the basis for a number of sciences in ancient India, called *Vedāṅgas*, or 'limbs of the Vedas': astronomy, for finding auspicious times for rituals, geometry, for constructing fire altars, poetics, for correct recitation and so on.

In addition to the *Ṛg Veda* and the *Yajur Veda*, the *Sāma Veda* is a guide to chanting Vedic verses correctly. The musical principles of the *Sāma Veda* later have considerable influence on Indian classical music, particularly in the areas of singing and intonation.

Together, these three texts constitute a guide to Vedic ritual, with the *Ṛg Veda* providing the hymns sung during sacrifice, the *Yajur Veda* being the guide to performing the sacrifice itself, and the *Sāma Veda* being the guide to the chanting of the *Ṛg Vedic* hymns during the sacrifice.

A fourth Veda, the *Atharva Veda*, was added later to the Vedic canon.[29] What differentiates it from the other three Vedas? The rituals described in the *Yajur Veda* are sufficiently elaborate to require a class of specialists to perform them. The *Atharva Veda*, though, describes simpler rituals performable by any person to ward off evil and protect from illnesses and other misfortunes. This text also includes material on healing, such as lists and descriptions of medicinal herbs, that would later become part of the Indian science of medicine: *Āyurveda*, the 'science of longevity'.[30]

Further reflections on the sacrifice: Priestly texts, forest texts and secret teaching

The oldest portions of the four Vedas are called *Saṃhitās*, or 'collections'. They had been compiled and were in use by roughly 1000 BCE. They do not, though, constitute the entirety of the Vedic canon. In fact, the process of composing and compiling the Vedas had, at this point, just begun. If one is looking at the Vedas in their entirety, one must be attentive not only to the original four collections, but also to three additional collections appended to these texts. Reflecting on the meaning of sacrifice, these appendices to the Vedas are commentaries upon the original Vedic collections, delving into and elaborating upon the contents of the Vedic hymns. As such, they establish a pattern that becomes central to Indian philosophy. Most Indian philosophers, at least until the modern period, present their ideas not as new innovations, but as elaborations on ideas already revealed by their ancient predecessors. Their preferred genre of writing is the *bhāṣya*, or commentary, in which insights are drawn forth from earlier sources.

The first commentarial appendix to the Vedas is a group of writings called *Brāhmaṇas*, or 'priestly texts'. The *Brāhmaṇas*, in combination with the *Saṃhitās*, form the *Karma Kāṇḍa*: the action portion of the Vedas.

A Vedic priest, responsible for performing ritual and memorizing portions of the Vedas relevant to his duties, is called a *Brahmin*. The Brahmins were organized in ancient times based on their roles in Vedic rituals. Some Brahmins, for example, were responsible for kindling and tending the sacred fire. Others built the fire altar. Others sang verses. One was tasked with observing the work of the other Brahmins and mentally correcting their mistakes. Brahmins were also dispersed geographically. They were divided into branches, or *śākhās*, based on their location and the portion of the Vedas forming their specialization. Each of these branches had its own *Brāhmaṇa* text, its own commentary on the *Veda* that was its domain.

Some *Brāhmaṇas* may have been lost to history. Nineteen remain: two that comment on the *Ṛg Veda*, eight on the *Yajur Veda*, eleven on the *Sāma Veda* and one on the *Atharva Veda*.[31]

How and why does sacrifice work? What is its inner meaning? These are the questions the *Brāhmaṇas* address and that continue to be addressed in subsequent genres of Vedic literature that comment and build on the *Brāhmaṇas*. The focus of the *Brāhmaṇas* is the correspondence between the elements of the sacrifice and various aspects of the natural world and human psyche, often presented through stories and riddles.

Although the *Brāhmaṇas* were not the last portion of the Vedas to be composed, and though they form the basis for reflections that eventually lead to an entirely different way of understanding the Vedic world view, it should not be thought that the older, ritualistic philosophy that these texts express ever became obsolete. The Vedic philosophy of ritual action continues to be present in India today. In the twenty-first century, there are Brahmin priests who continue to faithfully fulfil their obligations to perform daily rituals to maintain the cosmic order, as well as performing rituals aimed at specific this-worldly goods, such as bringing much needed rainfall to farmlands parched by drought. This ancient way of thinking also exerts influence on the Indian philosophical tradition at a number of points in the unfolding of its long history, shaping concepts of social order and of personal responsibility through the ideal of dharma.

Philosophical speculation continued as the Vedic tradition was passed from one generation to the next. Scholars typically place the date of the *Brāhmaṇas* between 900 and 600 BCE. Before the middle of the first millennium BCE, between 700 and 500 BCE, another set of commentaries begins to emerge: commentaries on the *Brāhmaṇas* called the *Āraṇyakas*, or 'forest texts'. These texts take their name from the fact that by this period, the Brahmins had begun teaching their knowledge to students in forest retreats called *āśramas*.[32] The belief that knowledge of Vedic ritual is a source of great power was taken seriously by the ancient Brahmins. They therefore chose to pass their knowledge to their students in secluded places, where they could not easily be overheard. Forest retreats were also seen as places free from distraction, where students could pursue a way of life focused fully on learning and absorbing the knowledge and values of the tradition.

This ideal of withdrawing from society to pursue higher knowledge would prove to have profound implications for the Indian philosophical tradition the more radical practice of *sannyāsa*, or renunciation, developed, in which one would not temporarily, but permanently withdraw from the social world to pursue spiritual aims: the path of *nivṛtii*.

Bands of wandering hermits engaged in ascetic practice had already existed as early as the time of the *Ṛg Veda*, where they are known as *Vrātyas*: 'those who observe vows'. In the *Ṛg Veda*, Vrātyas are outsiders to mainstream society, viewed with suspicion and believed to wield magical powers. It is possible they represent an independent tradition from that of the Vedas which could perhaps be a predecessor of Jain or Śaiva traditions, or both. Indus Valley depictions of long-haired figures may represent these ascetics (though this is a highly speculative suggestion). It has also been suggested that they were warrior monks.

In the second millennium before the Common Era, withdrawal from social life for spiritual purposes came to be seen increasingly as a legitimate option in Vedic society, although it continued to be viewed with ambivalence. This is the case even today, as such renunciation often involves the giving up of traditional family ties, including the severing of contact with loved ones.

The *Āraṇyakas*, which reflect the beginning of the acceptance of this ascetic way of life, make up the *Upāsana Kāṇḍa*, or 'contemplation portion' of the *Vedas*. They mark the transition between the pure action focus of the first portion of the *Vedas* and the final, knowledge portion, in which renunciation is not only accepted, but elevated as the path to the highest good.

Around the middle of the first millennium BCE, the final set of Vedic appendices began to be composed. This set of texts, called the *Upaniṣads*, or 'secret teaching', would later become the foundation for a system of philosophy which is today the dominant mode of Hindu thought. This philosophy, called *Vedānta*, or 'end of the *Veda*', takes its name from the fact that its foundational texts are the final portion of the Vedas to be studied in a traditional Vedic curriculum, and from the fact that this philosophy is seen as expressing the deepest secret, the ultimate goal and aim, to which all previous Vedic literature and practice are directed. The *Upaniṣads* make up the *Jñāna Kāṇḍa*, or 'knowledge portion', of the *Vedas*.

From *Veda* to *Vedānta*: From ritual action to transformative knowledge

If one follows the development of Vedic thought from the earliest collections of the *Ṛg, Yajur, Sāma* and *Atharva Vedas*, through the *Brāhmaṇas*, and then the *Āraṇyakas*, and finally, the *Upaniṣads*, one finds a shift in focus from ritual acts to the attainment of transforming knowledge. In relation to this knowledge, ritual is, at best, a preparation, and at worst, a distraction. How does this shift occur?

In the philosophy of ritual action found in the *Saṃhitās* and *Brāhmaṇas*, human beings are integral to maintaining the cosmos. It is the duty, or *dharma*, of human beings to maintain this order – also called *dharma* – by performing sacrifice. The Vedas are the guide to how this action is to be performed, through repetition of the original sacrifice that continually re-creates the world. This could be called the external focus of Vedic ritual.

From the beginning, however, Vedic ritual had an internal focus as well. The sacrifice was an occasion for observing the natural world and reflecting on its relationship to the human world – the social world of humans in interaction with one another and the wider world of plants, animals and other phenomena, but also the inner world in the mind of the sacrificer. In such Vedic hymns as the *Gāyatrī Mantra* and the *Hymn of the Cosmic Man*, correspondences are revealed between these inner and outer worlds and the sacrifice established as the essential link between them. As Vedic thought develops further, or unfolds, in the *Brāhmaṇas* and *Āraṇyakas*, the inner dimension becomes the primary focus. The ritual sacrifice is gradually seen less as a duty to be performed and more as an image or metaphor for an inner process of personal transformation, and a realization of one's ultimate unity with the process of creation.

In the *Upaniṣads*, this inner process is the primary concern. While sacrifice is still present, it slips increasingly into the background. Scholars call this the 'internalisation' of the sacrifice. Simple acts like eating and breathing, performed with right knowledge, become sacrificial acts. In some *Upaniṣads*, the outer sacrifice even comes to be seen as problematic – a line of thought carried further by the Jains and Buddhists, who see the Vedic sacrificial ritual as an actual impediment to the process of inner transformation.

The evolution of the idea of karma

Accompanying this shift from outer to inner, and from ritual action to knowledge, is a shift in world view. An important dimension of this shift involves the concept of karma.

A Vedic ritual act is called a *karma*. A karma well performed–a 'good karma' – leads to the desired result being produced by the ritual. The devas will be sustained and the cosmos upheld. A karma performed poorly – a 'bad karma' – will not be effective or may even yield the opposite of the desired result. By the time of the *Upaniṣads*, though, *karma* has come to refer to *all* deliberate action and its results. How does this occur?

If the Vedic sacrifice is made up of actions – karmas – which can be performed either well or badly, leading to correspondingly good or bad results – and if this reflects the nature of the universe and the individual within it, then one can also conclude that one's own life is similarly made up of actions, good and bad, and that one's current circumstances are the results of these actions. This follows from the correspondences across the various levels of reality: the macrocosm, mesocosm and microcosm. The Vedic sacrifice is a model of the universe. By the time of the *Upaniṣads*, all of life has come to be seen as one great Vedic ritual, with the focus shifting from actual, concrete ritualistic performance to the character of all actions at all times, and the effects of these actions in the wider universe and upon oneself. In the words of scholar Herman Tull:

> While the *Brāhmaṇas* exhibit an overwhelming concern with the ritual world, the *Upaniṣads* look outward to the larger cosmos. The Upaniṣadic thinkers did not, however, abandon the principles that are the hallmarks of Brāhmaṇic thought: to look outward from the carefully delimited boundaries of the ritual world, they simply extended the principles that governed the ritual.[33]

This is essentially the origin of the doctrine of karma affirmed in all the systems of Indian philosophy but one: that every right action produces good results for the doer of the action and that every wrong action similarly produces bad results. The only system of Indian philosophy that does not affirm this concept is the sceptical Lokāyata or Cārvāka school of materialist thought. To be sure, interpretations of the mechanics of karma differ across systems; but the concept is accepted.

Karma and rebirth

In its fully developed form, the idea of karma is closely linked with the concept of rebirth, or 'reincarnation', as this idea is known in the West. According to this conception, karma is a law governing action, much as the laws of physics govern physical motion. Analogously to Newton's third law of motion, according to which, 'For every action, there is an equal and opposite reaction', the law of karma states that for every good or bad thought, word or action, one will experience a correspondingly good or bad result. These results may occur immediately or after a long span of time. We are ultimately responsible for the good or bad experiences we have.

The fact that we observe many unfair instances of suffering in the world, and experience them ourselves, necessitates the concept of rebirth to account for events which would otherwise appear to violate the principle of karma. Essentially, in a world of unfair events, one must either give up the concept of karma, understood as a kind of universal justice, or extend the scope of our understanding of what constitutes our field of experience. Indian philosophies, on the whole, opt for the second choice, maintaining that karma does exist, but that its effects are not all felt within a single lifetime. The sufferings of those who do not deserve to suffer are due to choices made in a previous life. Similarly, the occasions when those who do evil do not appear to suffer negative consequences suggest that there must be a future in which those consequences will be felt.

This does not mean we should hold ourselves blameworthy every time we suffer. In times of misfortune, one might recall the phrase, 'I must have done something bad in a past life.' This could be the case, according to the doctrine of karma. But when one is victimized by the evil deeds of another whom one has not knowingly harmed, one may well be justified in seeing this as a case of undeserved suffering. What the idea of karma suggests, at least on some interpretations, is that life is akin to a vast school in which one learns the deep truths of existence through the joys and sufferings, the trials and errors, that one experiences. We do not typically remember the events of our past lives, but they do serve to shape our character. Our character is made up of our collective habits or *saṃskāras*. These are transformed by the ways in which we respond to the experiences of our lives. We thus learn and grow, or regress, in response to events.

Even when the idea of karma was limited to the context of Vedic ritual, it was tied, albeit indirectly, to the idea of the afterlife. A karma is, of course, any ritual action, and one wishes for one's karmas to be performed well to achieve the desired result of the ritual. Vedic ritual, though, is performed not only to ensure the maintenance of the cosmic order and human flourishing in the here and now. There are also Vedic rituals aimed at ensuring the continuity of one's existence in a positive, happy state after death: *amṛta* or immortality. In the early Vedic context, immortality does not refer to a state of literal deathlessness, but to a long, healthy life and the continuation of this state beyond the death of the body, consisting of another long, healthy life, in another form.

The early Vedic conception of the afterlife, much like that of other Indo-European cultures, such as that of the Celts, is of birth in another realm, usually conceived as divided into the world of the devas and the world of the ancestors. Passage to one of these realms is not guaranteed. It requires the right performance of the correct Vedic ritual: in this case, a ritual known as the *Soma* ritual.

Vedic rituals are of course not performed once and for all. They need to be repeated so the cosmic order can be maintained, or to achieve specific, finite goals. Their efficacy is limited. One, therefore, does not remain forever after death in the other world one has entered with the help of the Soma ritual. One eventually dies there as well, once the efficacy of the ritual actions, the karmas that have led to that realm, has been exhausted.

What happens then? One possibility is that one returns to a new life in this world.[34] This seems to be the origin of the concept of rebirth: a view which, like the idea of karma which accompanies it, is held in all but one system of Indian philosophy (the materialist school). Good karma does not lead to an eternal afterlife in the heavens, nor does bad karma lead to eternal punishment in a hellish abode. Rather, both good and bad karma, having limited efficacy, lead to finite realms. These realms can be predominantly good, predominantly bad or mixed, depending upon one's actions. One eventually dies and returns, and the process begins again.

When, in the *Upaniṣads*, belief in the efficacy of ritual acts becomes expanded to include all volitional acts, this has implications for the afterlife. If all one's actions, good and bad, and not only ritual actions, lead to corresponding results, then the idea of rebirth follows logically; for the fact of one's physical death does not necessarily mean one has experienced all the results of one's past actions. Again, it can be observed that those who have done great good often suffer terrible misfortunes, and those who have done evil often prosper. If good necessarily follows from good and evil from evil, by the logic of Vedic ritual, one lifetime is insufficient to balance one's karmic debt, or we would see this occurring with greater frequency, with the good being rewarded and the evil suffering. The suffering of good people and the prosperity of evil people must be explained by the bad or good actions they have committed in the past (or through some sense of the cosmos as a learning process for the development of character). The alternative to karma and rebirth is a random, often cruel universe in which, ultimately, there is no justice: an option from which most schools of Indian philosophy recoil.

What, however, makes an action good or bad? What determines whether an action leads to a good or bad result, either in one's current lifetime or a future rebirth? In a Vedic ritual context, a good action is one conforming to the principles of Vedic practice and a bad action violates these principles, either wilfully or out of carelessness. Building on Vedic ritual thinking, later texts, like the *Dharma Śāstras* and epics, further develop the idea that dharma is both the cosmic order and the actions, the obligatory duties, required to maintain it. If all of life is a Vedic ritual, one way of discerning what constitutes a good or bad action is to apply the principles of Vedic ritual to it.

One of these principles is *reciprocity*. If one wants to receive the blessings of the devas, one must offer them sacrifice. If one wishes to receive good from the universe, one must do good. If one wishes to avoid harm, one needs to avoid doing harm. 'This is the sum of dharma: Do not do to others that which would cause you pain if done to you'.[35] In a cosmos where all is ultimately one, to harm another is to harm oneself. The idea of karma is a logical extension of this principle.

Liberation from desire and rebirth

If one is from a cultural background in which the idea of reincarnation is unfamiliar, it is often the case that one finds great comfort in this idea. Our loved ones who have died have not ceased to exist. They have merely changed form. Perhaps we will meet again. And perhaps those to whom we feel instinctively drawn in this life are our long-lost friends and loved ones from other lifetimes with whom we have resumed our association. It can be seen as a kind of immortality.

In the *Upaniṣads*, though – and, as we shall see, in most systems of Indian philosophy – the cycle of death and rebirth is something to escape, a bondage from which one seeks freedom. For all the joys one experiences in life, there are also sorrows. Even if one believes in rebirth, death is an indefinite separation that brings great sorrow. The goods of the world are also impermanent. The shadow of death hangs over everything. As long as one is bound to the cycle of karma and rebirth, one is bound to experience, at best, temporary moments of happiness, interspersed with the suffering that inevitably comes with embodied life: illness, old age, death and all our various other limitations as inhabitants of a material world.

How might one escape from this process? Is this not simply the way the universe works, according to Vedic thought? Part of the 'secret teaching' contained within the *Upaniṣads* is the answer to the question of how to become free from the cycle of karma and rebirth. If one wants to become free from this cycle, one must first understand how it works.

How does it work? What makes a good action lead to a good result and a bad action to a bad result? According to the *Upaniṣads*, one must first look beyond action itself. It is not that all actions automatically attract corresponding effects to their doer. What decides the good or bad quality of an action is the *desire* which motivates it. Desire, finally, is the cause of all action. We do things because we want things. It is one's desires that eventually determine the nature of one's rebirth. The power of action to lead to a result is due, ultimately, not to the action itself, *but to the fact that one desires the results of those actions, and so clings to them*. It is this clinging, or *rāga*, also translated as *attachment*, that attracts the results of our actions to us. We ultimately get what we desire, as well as the implications that come with it (some of which may be quite undesirable).

The Vedic cosmos is driven by desire. It is from the desire to create that the creator deity engages in the act of creation. In the words of the *Nāsadīya Sūkta* of the *Ṛg Veda*: 'Then, in the beginning, from thought there evolved desire, which existed as the primal seed[36] It is out of our desire to live well and achieve various goals that we engage in action and thus contribute to the creative process of the cosmos. In the Vedic cosmos, we ultimately do achieve what we desire. This is, however, often accompanied by a number of unintended or unforeseen consequences, a result of our ignorance of the deeper interconnectedness of events. The infusion of desire into an action leads that action to produce results, either in this life or in a future rebirth. This is what determines the kind of rebirth one experiences. According to the *Bṛhadāraṇyaka Upaniṣad*,

> One who is attached goes with his action to that very place to which his mind and character cling. Reaching the end of his action [the exhaustion of the results of his karma], of whatever he has done in this world, from that world he returns, back to this world, back to action. That is the course of one who desires[37]

We are driven to rebirth by our desires: because we *want* to experience things.

In the *Upaniṣads*, though, one also finds the insight that a life driven by desire is not a truly happy life. If one is constantly pursuing happiness in the form of external objects, outside oneself, and if this is a process that must constantly be repeated, given that the effects of action are never final or permanent, when does one experience lasting contentment? In earlier Vedic literature, one finds the assumption that happiness comes from fulfilling desires, and that desires are fulfilled through (ritual) action. But when are desires fulfilled once and for all? One may fulfil a desire, but that is then followed by another desire, and one must continue to engage in action to pursue the fulfilment of that desire, and then the next, and then the next, from one lifetime to another.

If desire fuels the process of rebirth, then this also suggests the means by which the process might be ended, and ultimate fulfilment achieved: through the extinction of all desire directed at external objects and conditions.

It is important to emphasize the qualifier, 'directed at external objects and conditions'; for what is under discussion is not the extinction of *all* desire. The desire to be free from desire, for example, is not an impediment to freedom from the rebirth cycle, but a necessary condition for it. Freedom from desire is not an external object or condition, but an inward state. It is the desire for external objects and conditions which leads to karmic effects, including rebirth. One may object that we pursue external objects out of desire not for the objects themselves, but for the inward states we believe they can create within us. This, however, is precisely the point: that *we confuse the things we believe will give us happiness with happiness itself.*

Happiness can only come when we are free from desire because happiness *is* freedom from desire. It is contentment. It is satisfaction. External objects make us happy temporarily because, in those moments during which they satisfy our desires, we are briefly free from desire. We are fulfilled. But this is temporary. To experience it again requires further action, leading to further results, and the cycle continues. The ultimate aim of the *Upaniṣads* is an enduring, permanent fulfilment that does not require further actions, external objects or conditions for its continuation.

If this happiness does not come from external objects or conditions, from where does it come?

It comes from within: from oneself; for one's true nature is infinite joy. It is the experience of ultimate inwardness. If one were able to strip away all one's desires, all one's limitations, paring away all that is inessential, what would be left? What would be left would be one's essential self: the core of one's being. This essential self is called, in the *Upaniṣads*, the *ātman*. It is the ātman that undergoes the cycle of rebirth and experiences desire and limitation, falsely believing external objects and conditions can lead to happiness when happiness is already, in fact, its own true inner nature.

If we put this question in Vedic terms, if one pares away all the elements of the Vedic ritual of sacrifice, including the desires which motivate it, with what would one be left? All that would be left, if the mechanics of the sacrificial ritual were to be removed, would be the power of creation into which the ritual taps, the power underlying the creative process of existence itself: Brahman.

According to the *Bṛhadāraṇyaka Upaniṣad*, 'Now, a man who does not desire–who is without desires, who is freed from desires, whose desires are fulfilled, whose only desire is his self [*ātman*] .... *Brahman* he is, and to *Brahman* he goes. . . When they are all banished, those desires lurking in one's heart; then a mortal becomes immortal and attains *Brahman* in this world.'[38] The ātman is Brahman, viewed from the perspective of the microcosm. Brahman is the macrocosmic ātman, the Self of all beings.

Brahman: The infinite

The concept of Brahman is elaborated in the *Upaniṣads*. The nature of Brahman and how to attain it is the 'secret teaching' from which the *Upaniṣads* take their name. The word *upaniṣad* can literally refer to sitting close to one's teacher. The image is of a teacher delivering knowledge to students in a forest retreat. The knowledge not being delivered in a town or village because it is secret knowledge. Now, though, the teacher has come to the deepest and most secret knowledge of all and asks the students to lean in close so he can whisper it to them. That secret is Brahman.[39]

The main element which distinguishes the *Upaniṣads* from the earlier collections of Vedic literature is their emphasis on the concept of Brahman. Brahman is mentioned numerous times in earlier Vedic texts, but it is in the *Upaniṣads* that it becomes the central topic of discussion.

In earlier references, *Brahman* refers to creative power which energizes the Vedic sacrifice, thus enabling chants, gestures and other actions that make up the rituals to have an effect in the world. As has already been discussed, Vedic ritual functions through correspondences between the elements in the various levels of reality–macrocosm, mesocosm and microcosm. But what is it that links these varying elements? What is the name for the underlying unity which makes the cosmos a *universe*, a unified, interconnected reality, and not a mere chaos of disparate elements? This is the question which Vedic thinkers reflected on for generations in their pursuit of the deep truth behind the sacrifice.

In the *Upaniṣads*, the secret is revealed: Brahman is the unifying reality which underlies this universe of actions and changes and diverse elements, of people and things, of desires and sacrifices. Brahman is 'the Whole', the sum total of existence, and the infinite, the source of all that is. In realizing Brahman, one becomes the Whole, all of one's desires are fulfilled, and one is freed from all bondage, including bondage to the desire-fuelled process of rebirth.

What does it mean to 'realise Brahman'? The *Bṛhadāraṇyaka Upaniṣad* poses the question in the following way, in a dialogue between student and teacher:

[Student:] 'Since people think they will become the Whole by knowing *Brahman*, what did *Brahman* know that enabled it to become the Whole?'

[Teacher:] 'In the beginning this world was only *Brahman*, and it knew only itself, thinking, "I am *Brahman*." As a result, it became the Whole. Among the gods, likewise, whoever realised this, only they became the Whole . . . If one knows "I am *Brahman*" in this way, he becomes this whole world. Not even the gods are able to prevent it, for he becomes their very self (*ātman*). So, when one venerates another deity, thinking, "He is one, and I am another," he does not understand.'[40]

Brahman becomes Brahman by knowing itself. We, too, become Brahman by knowing ourselves, by realising that our true self–the ātman – is not different from the Brahman underlying the cosmos. Indeed, because Brahman is the reality underlying everything, and has literally become everything – including ourselves – because we are, in fact, Brahman, we can say that when we know ourselves as Brahman, Brahman is 'becoming' Brahman by knowing itself. The very existence of conscious beings in the cosmos is a function or manifestation of the self-knowledge of Brahman. Although not an adherent of the philosophy of the *Upaniṣads*, the astronomer Carl Sagan makes a somewhat similar observation when he says, 'We are a way for the Cosmos to know itself.'[41]

One can see here several themes of the *Ṛg Veda* brought to their logical conclusion. If the sacrifice is a model of the cosmos (the macrocosm) and the person (the microcosm), and if what underlies the sacrifice, its inner essence and source of creative power, is Brahman, then it follows that Brahman is also the inner essence and source both of the cosmos and the person. In the case of the person, we call this essence *self* – ātman. In the case of the cosmos, it is Brahman.

The non-duality of Brahman and ātman is illustrated most famously in a series of dialogues in the *Chāndogya Upaniṣad* between the Brahmin Uddālaka Āruṇi and his son, Śvetaketu:

Good lad, just as bees secrete honey by collecting the nectars from different kinds of trees, and combine the nectar into oneness, and just as there they do not keep any distinction, so as to be able to say, 'I am the nectar of that tree,' 'I am the nectar of *that* tree,' so, good lad, all creatures, once they have entered into being, do not know that they have entered into being. Whatever they are here – a tiger, a lion, a wolf, a boar, a worm, a flying thing, a gnat, or a mosquito – they become *that*. This subtle part is what all this has as self. It is truth: it is the self. *You* are that, Śvetaketu.

'Bring a banyan-fruit from this tree.'
'Here it is, sir.'
'Break it.'
'I have broken it, sir.'
'What do you see there?'
'Tiny seeds, sir.'
'Now break one of them.'
'I have broken it, sir.'
'What do you see there?'
'Nothing, sir.'
He said to him, 'Good lad, on this subtle part – the subtle part which you do not see – rests the great banyan tree. Good lad, have faith. This subtle part is what all this has as a self. It is truth: it is the self. *You* are that, Śvetaketu.'

'Put this salt in water, and come to me in the morning.'
He did so. His father said to him, 'Now, bring me the salt that you put in water last night.'

He felt for it, but did not find it.

'Quite,' said his father, 'for it has dissolved. But sip from the side of it. What is it
    like?'

'Salt.'

'Sip from the middle of it. What is it like?'

'Salt.'

'Sip from the other side of it. What is it like?'

'Salt.'

'Throw it away, then come to me.'

. . . His father said to him, 'You do not see *being* here, but it *is* here. This
    subtle part is what all this has as a self. It is truth: it is the self. *You* are that,
    Śvetaketu.'[42]

Brahman is the subtle essence of all that exists. It is being itself. It is not different in a substantive sense from ātman, because ātman is the essence of an individual being, of the person.

It is important to note here that an alternative reading of the refrain of this passage, *tat tvam asi*, which I have rendered here as '*You* are that', is possible, in which 'you' are not simply being identified with 'that' (the essence of being), but rather being likened to it.

As pointed out by Indologist Joel Brereton, grammatically speaking, if one wanted to write in Sanskrit, 'You are that', one would not use the neuter pronoun *tat*, or 'that', but a pronoun that would match the gender of the person being addressed: in Śvetaketu's case, 'he', or, in Sanskrit, *saḥ*.[43] The use of *tat*, as Brereton explains, could suggest not that one is being identified with 'that', but again, compared or likened to it. On the basis of this understanding, Patrick Olivelle translates this passage as 'That's how you are'[44] or 'You are like that.'[45]

The Advaita Vedānta tradition interprets '*tat tvam asi*' to mean, 'You *are* that.'[46] *That*, again, refers to Brahman, the essence of all that exists. According to Advaita Vedānta, it is the core of one's being, the ātman.

The importance of interpreting '*tat tvam asi*' as either 'You *are* that' or 'You are *like* that' will become clearly as we delve into the later development of Vedānta philosophy. Briefly, though, the difference between the two interpretations is the difference between a philosophy like Advaita Vedānta, which teaches that Brahman, ultimately, is all that exists, and other systems of Vedānta which affirm Brahman as either the foundation or substratum of all existence, in which other beings participate but from which they are numerically distinct, or as a personal deity, in a monotheistic sense, whose nature beings share but who are, again, distinct from Brahman itself.

Brahman is also called 'the Real' (*sat*) and is seen in Advaita Vedānta as coextensive with reality as such. It is that which is real pre-eminently, from which the existence of all other entities is derivative. It is that, by knowing which, all things are known.[47] It is also the object of religious aspiration, of the famous *Upaniṣadic* prayer, 'Lead me from the unreal to the Real, from darkness to light, from death to immortality'". It is eternal. 'It is immortal; it is Brahman; it is the Whole.'[48] It is unique, 'One alone, without a second.' It can, again, be seen as 'it' or 'that', as an impersonal foundation of being, or as a personal deity who can hear and answer prayers and so on.

How else is Brahman characterized? The root meaning of the Sanskrit term *Brahman* can be translated as 'the expansive' or 'that which makes things great'. It is described in the *Upaniṣads* as the sweet essence of all that is, the 'honey of all beings'.[49] Brahman has, according to many forms of Indian philosophy, become all things. It is that in which they live, move and have their being. It is from Brahman that all have emerged and to which all inevitably return. It is Brahman that all things *are*, in their essence, throughout the course of their existence. Brahman is our very self. Nothing exists that is not, at the core of its being, Brahman. 'All this is indeed Brahman.'[50] Being infinite, Brahman is ultimately beyond verbal description: the one 'before whom words recoil'.[51] Brahman is *neti, neti*, 'not this, not that'.[52] As the essence of all things, it cannot be identified exhaustively with anything. It is, literally, 'no-thing'. 'It does not exist. It is existence itself.'[53] Perhaps the truest statement one could make about Brahman would be to remain silent.

It should be underscored that when the non-duality of Brahman and ātman are emphasised, the 'self' to which the word *ātman* refers is not the ego or personality: the *self* as this term is used in conventional speech. The self, in the conventional sense, refers to those 'layers' of our being that must be stripped away to reach our 'true self', the ātman. This stripping away is done through the practice of renunciation, the complete sacrifice of one's socially constructed identity. In modern Vedānta, the distinction between ātman and ego is indicated by referring to the ātman as the Self with a capital 'S', in contrast with the lower-case 's' self: the selfish, clinging ego.

It is to the ātman that the Upaniṣadic sage, Yajñavālkya, refers in a famous dialogue with his wife, Maitreyī. Yajñavālkya is about to undertake renunciation and wants to reassure his wife that all shall be well. He has ensured that she and Kātyāyanī, his other wife, will be provided for economically in his absence.[54] Maitreyī, though, is wise, and asks him, 'If I had this whole earth, filled with riches, would I become immortal by it?'

> 'Oh, no, no,' said Yājñavālkya. 'Your life would be as life of the wealthy, but there is no hope of immortality through riches.'

> Maitreyī said, 'What use to me is something by which I cannot become immortal? Blessed one, teach me what you know.'

> He said, 'It is not for the love of a husband that a husband is dear: it is for the love of the Self [ātman] that a husband is dear. It is not for the love of a wife that a wife is dear: it is for the love of the Self that a wife is dear. It is not for the love of children that children are dear: it is for the love of the Self that children are dear . . .'

Yajñavālkya continues in the same vein, explaining to Maitreyī that riches, cattle, the Brahmin priesthood, the royal class, the worlds, the gods, the *Vedas*, all beings – in short, everything – is dear not for its own sake but because of the Self of which all these are manifestations. Brahman is the source of all joy and love. The love of people and the enjoyment of the good things in life is an experience of Brahman, mediated through these varied forms. The ultimate joy is the experience of Brahman itself, to experience which all else must be set aside. The immortality which Maitreyī mentions, and that appears in the prayer, 'lead me from death to immortality', refers not to the earlier Vedic idea of long life, but to liberation from the process of death and rebirth.

Is Brahman God?

One might recall from earlier in this chapter a reference to two distinct traditions of Vedic interpretation, Mīmāṃsā and Nyāya, one of which is non-theistic, seeing the revelation of eternal truth to the ancient seers in impersonal terms as the self-revelation of the cosmos, and the other of which is theistic, affirming the necessity of a divine being to oversee the order of the cosmos. In the service of this task, this divine being reveals the Vedas to the seers, much as God is believed to have revealed the sacred scriptures of the Abrahamic religions. One may also recall the singular higher reality of whom the various Vedic devas are forms or manifestations. 'They say it is Indra, Mitra, Varuṇa, and Agni, and . . . the winged, well-feathered bird of heaven [the sun]. Though it is One, inspired poets speak of it in many ways.'[55] Finally, one might recall the foregoing discussion about the interpretation of *tat tvam asi*. Are we identical with Brahman, or akin to Brahman?

Is the Brahman of the *Upaniṣads* the Supreme Being of theistic Hindu philosophies like Nyāya, and Hindu movements like the Vaiṣṇava and Śaiva traditions (focused, respectively, on the deities Viṣṇu and Śiva)?

The answer to this question is not clearly stated in the *Upaniṣads*. In fact, this question becomes a major topic of debate in later Indian philosophy, particularly among Vedānta schools.

The *Upaniṣads*, like the rest of the Vedic literature, do not present a systematic philosophy, beginning with premises and developing a world view based on them. They are more like inspired poetic utterances: accounts of revelatory conversations between teachers and students, whether it be Yajñavālkya speaking to his wife, Maitreyī, or Uddālaka speaking to his son, Śvetaketu, just to cite a couple of examples.

In some parts of the *Upaniṣads*, Brahman appears to be not a personal deity, but the ground of all being, with which we ourselves are identical in our deepest essence. In other parts of these texts, Brahman is represented as a personal being, engaged in speech, thought and other activities. We shall see that, as Vedānta develops, each of these views has its adherents, who see the parts of the text that contradict their particular worldview as speaking not literally, but metaphorically.

The layers of the mind: Upaniṣadic psychology

Another observation that can be made about the *Upaniṣads* is that more than two thousand years before Freud, ancient Indian thinkers were advancing the idea that the mind is made up not only of that level of which we are conscious in our waking life, but that it has many dimensions, many 'layers'. According to the *Upaniṣads*, these layers do not consist merely of two levels: the conscious and the unconscious. We are, in fact, multi-layered beings.

One Upaniṣadic model of the multi-layered self is presented in the second chapter of the *Taittirīya Upaniṣad*. This model utilizes the idea of *kośas*, or 'sheaths', each of which encloses a more essential layer or level of self. The outermost layer is the 'layer made of food': the physical body. Co-extensive with and residing 'within' the physical body is the 'layer made of breath': the life force of any living being. When this layer leaves the physical body, death occurs, and the life force moves to another physical form in the process of rebirth.

Within the life force is the 'layer made of mind': the intellect. This layer, in turn, contains the 'layer made of awareness', which, in turn, contains the 'layer made of joy'. Within this layer resides the ātman: the true self, which is the essential core of all living beings, the Self of all.

Another, similar model is presented in the *Māṇḍūkya Upaniṣad*. This text speaks not of 'layers', but levels of consciousness. These levels are the waking state of ordinary life, the dream state, dreamless sleep and a mysterious 'fourth state' (*turīya*), which is the state in which one experiences enlightenment: the direct awareness of the non-duality of ātman and Brahman, leading to liberation. It is 'unseen, inviolable, unseizable, signless, unthinkable, unnameable, its essence resting in the one Self, the stilling of proliferation, peaceful, gracious, without duality. That is the Self: so it should be understood'.[56]

In later Indian philosophy, these two models were integrated with one another and further developed into a system of 'subtle bodies', each co-existing with the others and corresponding to a different level of consciousness.

The *Upaniṣads* as internal Vedic critique: Going beyond ritual

The totality of the Vedic corpus of literature, from the *Ṛg Veda* to the *Upaniṣads*, is seen in the Hindu tradition as sacred *śruti*, the revelation of the true nature of existence 'heard' by the ancient seers. Again, the 'hearing' of the Vedas by the seers can be seen either as an impersonal process or a special divine revelation. A great variety of world views and philosophical approaches co-exist within Hindu thought; and, as many scholars would point out, it was not always the case that these approaches were even seen as part of the same tradition, but were instead independent, and often debating, systems, with the term *Hindu* being added later to give a sense of unity.

The Vedas themselves are a vast literature. This chapter has hopefully given some sense of the range of thought it encompasses. The task of subsequent commentators, operating from out of various world views, agendas and assumptions, was to interpret this literature in ways they found coherent and relevant to their concerns, and true to what they took to be the intent of these texts.

There are various ways in which one might interpret the totality of the Vedic corpus as a unity, and as expressing a coherent, self-consistent worldview. This task is not unlike that which faces an interpreter of biblical literature; for, like the Bible, there are portions of the Vedas which, in the absence of a tradition of interpretation, appear to be in radical conflict with one another.

Regarding the *Upaniṣads*, while these texts are, in many ways, in continuity with earlier Vedic literature, there are also ways in which these texts appear to serve as a critique of earlier Vedic tradition. While this critique typically does not go as far as those of the Jains and Buddhists, who reject Vedic authority altogether, in some ways it does echo (or prefigure) these. To argue that this apparent division within the Vedic ideology is not a contemporary scholarly projection, it is worth noting that the Mīmāṃsā and Vedānta schools, which debate one another on a variety of topics, are distinguished by which portion of the Vedic literature each regards as taking priority over the other: which 'side' each takes in the internal Vedic divide between action and knowledge.

The primary topic on which the *Upaniṣads* at least appear to part company with earlier Vedic literature is in regard to the ritual of sacrifice. The question here is not whether the sacrifice has any validity or efficacy whatsoever. That would be the more radical critique levelled by Jains and Buddhists. As part of the Vedic tradition, the authors of the *Upaniṣads* take for granted that sacrifice has the powers its adherents claim: that it is, indeed, a technology for tapping into the creative power of the cosmos and bringing about the results desired by those performing it.

The critical question raised in the *Upaniṣads* is not whether the Vedic ritual yields the fruits its adherents claim, but whether these fruits are worthy of pursuit. The fruits of Vedic ritual are effects of karma that must be experienced. Such rituals, performed from desire for their fruits, lead only to temporary goods, and to continued rebirth, and not to the highest good – liberation from rebirth, and thus from suffering – which comes only from the renunciation of temporary things. The *Muṇḍaka Upaniṣad* is particularly pointed in this regard:

The fools who hail that [sacrifice] as the best return once more to old age and death. [They are reincarnated.] Wallowing in ignorance, but calling themselves wise, thinking they are learned, the fools go around, hurting themselves badly, like a group of blind men, led by a man who is himself blind.

Wallowing in ignorance time and again, the fools imagine, 'We have reached our aim!' Because of their passion, they do not understand, these people who are given to rites. Therefore, they fall, wretched and forlorn, when their heavenly stay comes to a close. [They are reborn after their ritually created afterlife ends.]

Deeming sacrifices and gifts as the best, the imbeciles know nothing better. When they have enjoyed their good work [their good karma], atop the firmament, they return again to this abject world.[57]

The fate of inevitable suffering and rebirth experienced by those who pursue the ritual of sacrifice is contrasted with the fate of those who renounce life in society to live as mendicants, ultimately passing, after death, through the 'door of the sun', seen by later commentators as an image for passing into the state of liberation, to true immortality:[58]

But those in the wilderness, calm and wise, who live a life of penance and faith, as they beg for their food; through the sun's door they go, spotless [that is, free from karma], to where that immortal Person is, that immutable Self.[59]

The division highlighted here is that between the path of world-affirmation adhered to by the performer of Vedic rituals, whose aim is long life and prosperity through the attainment of worldly goods and conditions – the path of *pravṛtti* – and the path of world renunciation of those seeking happiness in freedom from the cycle of rebirth – the path of *nivṛtti*.

As we shall see, later Indian thinkers adhere to one or the other of these two approaches to life, while some seek to reconcile them. Such reconciliation is typically effected by cultivating an *attitude* of renunciation even while remaining physically involved in the life of society, with all its responsibilities (*dharma*).

Conclusion

In this chapter, we have explored the philosophies of the *Vedas*. In fact, we have only been able to touch upon a few major themes and currents within Vedic thought, this being an enormous body of literature to which many thinkers, reflecting a variety of perspectives, contributed over the course of more than one thousand years, from at least 1500 to 200 BCE.

We have seen two major currents of thought reflected in this literature: an ideology of ritual action, rooted in the 'action portion' of the *Vedas*, and an ideology of transformative knowledge, rooted in the 'knowledge portion' of the *Vedas* – the *Upaniṣads*. These currents reflect the deeper distinction in Indian philosophy between two orientations towards the world: the world-affirming, *pravṛtti* orientation, emphasizing the achievement of happiness through attainment of concrete goals achieved through action, and the world-renouncing, *nivṛtti* orientation, which sees worldly happiness as a mere shadow, reflection or spark of the infinite joy that transcends life in the realm of karma and rebirth. These two approaches later become the basis for two distinct systems of Vedic philosophy: Mīmāṃsā, reflecting the ideology of ritual action, and Vedānta, reflecting the ideology of transformative knowledge.

Finally, we have seen themes developed in the *Upaniṣads* that are, in some ways, critiques of or departures from earlier Vedic thought. There is the fully developed understanding of the idea of karma and rebirth, in which the desire motivating ritual action comes to be seen as fuelling the process of rebirth from which one eventually wishes to be free. Following from this is the idea that ritual action may be an obstruction to freedom from rebirth, which can only be reached through renunciation of all such acts and obligations, and a single-minded focus on liberation. We shall see these ideas extended further as we examine non-Vedic traditions.

Notes

1   Paul Mus, *Barabudur* (Hanoi: Imprimerie d'Extreme Orient, 1935), p. 100.
2   'The ascetics who have firmly determined their goal through a full knowledge of the Vedānta, have their being purified by the discipline of renunciation. In the worlds of *brahman*, at the time of the final end, having become fully immortal, they will all be

fully liberated.' (*Muṇḍaka Upaniṣad* 3.2.6), Patrick Olivelle, trans., *Upaniṣads* (Oxford: Oxford University Press, 1996), p. 276.

3 This view is articulated by Sri Aurobindo in his work *The Secret of the Veda* (New Delhi: Lotus Press, 1995).

4 Asko Parpola and Simo Parpola, 'On the relationship of the Sumerian Toponym Meluhha and Sanskrit Mleccha',*Studia Orientalia* 46 (1975): pp. 205–38.

5 Some scholars have even questioned whether these characters represent a writing system at all, although the view that it is not is not widely held. See Steve Farmer, Richard Sproat, and Michael Witzel, 'The Collapse of the Indus-Script Thesis: The Myth of a Literate Harappan Civilization', *The Electronic Journal of Vedic Studies (EJVS)* 11–12 (2004): pp. 19–57.

6 Asko Parpola, *The Roots of Hinduism: The Early Aryans and the Indus Civilization* (New York: Oxford University Press, 2015).

7 See Edwin Bryant, *The Quest for the Origins of Vedic Culture: The Indo-Aryan Migration Debate* (Oxford: Oxford University Press, 2004).

8 The seers are traditionally said to have been seven in number and are thus called the *saptarṣi*, or 'seven seers'.

9 Deepak Sarma, *Classical Indian Philosophy: A Reader* (New York: Columbia University Press, 2011), p. 196.

10 See Elisa Freschi and Alessandro Graheli, 'Bhāṭṭamīmāṃsā and Nyāya on Veda and Tradition', in *Boundaries, Dynamics, and Constructions of Traditions in South Asia, Volume III: How to Produce, Construct and Legitimate a Tradition*, ed. Federico Squarcini (Cambridge: Cambridge University Press, 2012). For those who are familiar with Christian theology, the Nyāya view is not unlike that of St. Thomas Aquinas on the necessity of divine revelation.

11 The term *Hindu* is actually ancient, but it refers, in its earliest usages, not to an adherent of a religious tradition, but to a person from the Indian subcontinent: specifically, from beyond the River Sindhu, or Hindu, as the name of this river was pronounced in ancient Persian, which is the source of this word. (See Parpola, *The Roots of Hinduism*, p. 3.) *Hinduism*, an English word, is of much more recent coinage, dating to the period of the British rule of India. The process by which a variety of Veda-affirming systems of thought came to be thought of collectively as forming a singular tradition now known as Hinduism is outlined by Andrew Nicholson in his work *Unifying Hinduism: Philosophy and Identity in Indian Intellectual History* (New York: Columbia University Press, 2013).

12 While Indra's weapon is called a thunderbolt (or *vajra*), it is not literally a thunderbolt, but a solid weapon made out of the bones of the ṛṣi, Dadhichi. According to later sources, Dadhichi offered his bones for the making of this invincible weapon. See Swami Bodhasarananda, *Stories from the Bhagavatam* (Mayavati: Advaita Ashrama, 2014).

13 In *The Secret of the Veda*, Sri Aurobindo argues that Viṣṇu and Śiva were always the central focus of religious devotion in India. He interprets the scarcity of references to these two deities in the early Vedic literature as indicative of the awe in which they were held, rather than as evidence that they held less importance in the Vedic era.

14 *Ṛg Veda* 1.164.46. Stephanie W. Jamison and Joel P. Brereton, trans., *The Rigveda: The Earliest Religious Poetry of India, Volume I* (Oxford: Oxford University Press, 2014), p. 359.

15 *Ṛg Veda* 1.164.6. Raimundo Panikkar, trans., *The Vedic Experience: Mantramañjarī–An Anthology of the Vedas for Modern Man and Contemporary Celebration* (Delhi: Motilal Banarsidass, 1977), p. 660.

16 See Joyce Flueckiger, *Everyday Hinduism* (Chichester: Wiley Blackwell, 2015), pp. 44–5.

17 *Ṛg Veda* 1.1.1, 7–8. Panikkar, *The Vedic Experience*, p. 329.

18 Aurobindo Ghose (Sri Aurobindo), *Secret of the Veda* (Harrisburg, Pennsylvania: Lotus Press, 1995).

19 *Ṛg Veda* 3.62.10. Translation mine.

20 Called, for this reason, by scholar Paul Mus, the *mesocosm*. See Mus, , *Barabudur*.

21 Alfred North Whitehead, *Adventures of Ideas* (New York: The Free Press, 1967), p. 109.

22 One might recall from the introduction that *dharma* is also a term that is frequently used to translate the English word *religion*. What is the connection between the concept of a cosmic order and religion, which is a human activity? One can see the beginning of this link in the idea that human activity is integral to the maintenance of cosmic order. Dharma is therefore not only cosmic order, but also the actions incumbent upon human beings to maintain that order. The connection with religion becomes evident when we realize that an important part of our dharma, as human beings, is our duty to perform ritual: an activity widely associated with religion. We shall see that there is a moral dimension of this as well: both in the fact that performing ritual is an obligation which we take on at birth, by becoming human beings, but also in the understanding that life itself is a kind of ritual. A life well lived, a moral life, lived in accord with dharmic principles, is also part of our duty in upholding the cosmos.

23 Veena R. Howard, 'Toward an Understanding of Dharma: The Questions of Identity, Hybridity, Fluidity, and Plurality', in *Dharma: The Hindu, Jain, Buddhist, and Sikh Traditions of India*, ed. Veena R. Howard (London: IB Tauris, 2017), p. 2.

24 The actual spelling of the name of this community is *Brāhmaṇa*. *Brahmin* is a spelling coined by British scholars in the colonial period. It has, however, become conventional to continue utilizing this spelling because it is useful in differentiating the people designated by this name from the set of Vedic texts that are also known as *Brāhmaṇas* (or 'priestly texts'). They also differentiate a member of this group from *Brahman*, the ultimate reality according to the philosophy of the *Upaniṣads*, as well as from *Brahmā*, the creator deity of the *Purāṇas*. I am following this convention and using the spelling *Brahmin* and *Brahmins* to refer to a person or people from this priestly community.

25 Mus, *Barabudur*, p. 100.

26 *Ṛg Veda* 10.90.13. Jamison and Brereton, *The Rigveda*, p. 1540.

27 *Ṛg Veda* 10.90.12. Jamison and Brereton, *The Rigveda*, p. 1540.

28 Later Hindu literature interprets the Puruṣa of the *Puruṣa Sūkta* to be Prajāpati, later called Brahmā, the god of creation. See Hermann Tull, *The Vedic Origins of Karma* (Albany: State University of New York Press, 1989), p. 63.

29 Frits Staal, *Discovering the Vedas: Origins, Mantras, Rituals, Insights* (New York: Penguin, 2009), pp. 136–7.

30 There is also evidence that early Āyurveda developed in a Buddhist milieu. See Kenneth Zysk, *Asceticism and Healing in Ancient India* (Oxford: Oxford University Press, 1991). No doubt multiple streams of thought contributed to the development of this body of knowledge.

31 Jeffery D. Long, *Historical Dictionary of Hinduism*, 2nd ed. (Lanham: Rowman and Littlefield, 2020a), pp. 424–5.

32 The term *āśrama* later comes to refer also to a stage of life. These are described in the *Dharma Śāstras*, or legal texts of the Vedic tradition. It also refers in the modern period to any place of spiritual retreat: an *ashram*.

33 Tull, *The Vedic Origins of Karma*, p. 120.

34 This is not spelled out explicitly in the early Vedic literature. It becomes explicit only in the *Upaniṣads*.

35 *Mahābhārata* 5:1517, cited in Bhagwan Das, *The Essential Unity of All Religions* (Wheaton, IL: Quest Books, 1932), pp. 316–17.

36 *Ṛg Veda*, 10: 130, 4a (*Nāsadīya Sūkta*).

37 *Bṛhadāraṇyaka Upaniṣad* 4: 4.6a–All citations from the *Upaniṣads* that follow are adaptations of the translations of Patrick Olivelle and Valerie Roebuck. Olivelle, *Upaniṣads*; Valerie Roebuck, trans., *The Upaniṣads* (New York: Penguin: 2004)

38 Ibid, 4: 4.6b–7a.

39 Significantly, the word *upaniṣad* can also mean 'secret connection'). See Patrick Olivelle, *The Early Upaniṣads: Annotated Text and Translation* (Oxford: Oxford University Press, 1998), pp. 24–7.

40 Ibid, 1: 4.10.

41 Carl Sagan, *Cosmos* (New York: Random House, 1980), p. 258.

42 *Chāndogya Upaniṣad* 6: 9–10, 12–13.

43 See Joel Brereton, '"Tat tvam asi" in Context', *Zeitschrift der Deutschen Morganländischen Gesellschaft* 36, no. 1 (1986): pp. 98–109.

44 Olivelle, *Upaniṣads*, pp. 152–6.

45 Olivelle, personal communication at the Association for Asian Studies annual meeting, University of Hawaii, 2010.

46 *Tattva*, or 'that-ness', subsequently becomes an important term in Indian philosophy for the core truth or principle of a thing: its essence or 'being-ness'.

47 Ibid., 6: 1.

48 *Bṛhadāraṇyaka Upaniṣad* 2: 5.

49 Ibid.

50 *Chāndogya Upaniṣad* 3: 14.1.

51 *Taittirīya Upaniṣad* 2: 9.

52 *Bṛhadāraṇyaka Upaniṣad* 2: 3.6.

53 Swami Vivekananda, *Complete Works*, vol. 1 (Mayawati: Advaita Ashrama, 1979), p. 249.

54 Polygamy, though not the norm in ancient India, was certainly not unknown. Polyandry has been practiced in parts of the region as well.

55 *Ṛg Veda* I.164.46. Jamison and Brereton, *The Rigveda*, p. 359.

56 *Māṇḍūkya Upaniṣad* 7.

57 Ibid., 1: 2.7a–10.

58 In the early Vedic period, this image of the door of the sun was not seen so much as a metaphor as a literal gateway to a higher realm: svārga, or heaven. Recall that the aim of some of the early Vedic rituals is a rebirth in heaven. This would not have been seen, as it is in later Vedic thought, as a temporary realm of rebirth or penultimate goal, but as the highest goal that one might attain. See Olivelle, *The Early Upaniṣads*, p. 21.

59 *Muṇḍaka Upaniṣad*, 1: 2.11.

2

Jain and materialist thought

Strivers and sceptics

Introduction

Vedic thought and the culture in which it arose did not exist in a vacuum in ancient India. Other cultures co-existed with the one in which the Vedas were compiled and composed, and there were movements even within the Vedic milieu that did not endorse every facet of its ideology. As we have already seen, the *Upaniṣads* document a movement internal to the Vedic tradition that questions facets of Vedic thought, such as the idea of birth caste as a measure of one's place in the spiritual cosmos, and the act of literal ritual sacrifice (versus the inward 'sacrifice' of meditation).[1]

Significant currents of Indian philosophy emerged not only from the Vedic tradition, but also from traditions that defined themselves in explicit opposition to the authority of the Vedas. These include traditions which share many common beliefs and practices with the Vedic tradition, particularly its *Upaniṣadic* branches: the ideas of karma and rebirth, the aspiration to become free from the rebirth cycle, and the practice of renunciation, believed to be necessary to achieve this freedom. They also include sceptical traditions which accept neither the efficacy of Vedic sacrifice nor the ideas of karma, rebirth or liberation.

Among those traditions whose world views overlap with the teachings of the *Upaniṣads* are two which are practiced today: Jainism and Buddhism. Yet another, the Ājīvika tradition, had, by some accounts, an even wider following in ancient times than Jainism or Buddhism, but it is now extinct. Scepticism, too, remains a strong undercurrent of Indian philosophy.[2] Every thinking person is a sceptic, inasmuch as one evaluates ideas and finds them either wholly unacceptable or in need of modification. *Scepticism* here, though, refers to a thoroughgoing scepticism which not only questions specific ideas, but in some cases questions the very possibility of knowledge.

The strivers: A tradition of renunciation

Simultaneous with the development of Vedic thought, a movement arose in northern India articulating a world view quite distinct from that of the *Vedas* – particularly from that of the earlier, action-oriented portion of the *Vedas*, but with affinities to ideas found in the *Upaniṣads*. Adherents of this movement were known as *Śramaṇas*, or 'those who strive'. The Śramaṇas, as figures of religious authority on par and in rivalry with the Brahmins were well established in India by the time of Megasthenes (roughly 350 to 290 BCE). Megasthenes was a Greek ambassador in India who catalogued his observations in a text called the *Indica* which later became the main source of knowledge about India in Europe (until European explorers went to India themselves in the late medieval and early renaissance periods).

Some aspects of the traditions of the Śramaṇas, like those of the Brahmins, may be traced to the Indus Valley civilization. Indeed, some Jain scholars have advanced the claim that the Indus Valley civilization was a Śramaṇic – and essentially Jain – civilization.[3] As, however, with attempts to see facets of Hinduism in this civilization, such claims remain speculative.

As mentioned in the last chapter, the *Ṛg Veda* refers to wandering groups of naked, long-haired ascetics, thought to have magical powers, and known as *Vrātyas*: 'keepers of vows'. These Vrātyas may represent an early phase of the Śramaṇa movement. In the *Ṛg Veda*, the Vrātyas are viewed with ambivalence, as persons whose ascetic practice has led them to master paranormal abilities. The practitioner of yoga who, by engaging in self-denial and focusing attention fully inward, is able to master such powers (known as *siddhis*, or 'perfections'), is a prominent figure in the Indian imagination. Such persons are viewed with ambivalence because, on the one hand, their ascetic practices enable them to achieve liberating, transformative knowledge, but on the other, these practices also enable them to do things like read minds and inflict curses on those who anger them.[4] This inner mastery and the power it can bring could be seen as rivalling the power available to the Brahmin through Vedic sacrifice.

Such inner mastery could also be seen as a development *from* the Vedic sacrifice. As we have seen, the Vedic sacrifice is a model of the inner and outer universes. The internalization of the sacrifice reflected in the *Upaniṣads* could be seen as a step away from the outward offerings detailed in the earlier, action portion of the *Vedas*, and in the direction of the practices of the yogic masters of later Hindu, Jain and Buddhist literature. Indeed, for much of the history of the study of Indian traditions in the West, this has been the dominant view of the origins of traditions like Jainism and Buddhism: that they developed from the Vedic tradition as the next logical phase after the *Upaniṣads*.[5]

Some scholars, however, argue that the Śramaṇa movement is not an extension of the Vedic tradition – a continuation of the line of critical thinking found in the *Upaniṣads* – but an independent tradition, and that the *Upaniṣads* reflect an incorporation of Śramaṇic elements into Brahmanical thought. The chief proponent of this view has been Indologist Johannes Bronkhorst.[6]

There are merits to both of these views because adherents of these movements were clearly in conversation with one another throughout the process of their development. It is likely that the Śramaṇa movement was a pre-existing tradition which exerted influence on Vedic thought, as has been argued by recent scholarship, but that thinkers in the Vedic tradition also generated insights and contributed to the intellectual conversation in ways which also influenced the Śramaṇas. Much of this 'the-chicken-or-the-egg' debate boils down to technical issues regarding the relative dating of ancient Indian texts to determine who expressed what first. Given the extent to which all Indian traditions passed on their ideas orally long before these attained a final written form and developed their ideas in dialogue with one another, even this method is an uncertain guide to the origins of ideas. To mention just one example, the famous parable of the Blind People and the Elephant has been utilized by Buddhists, Hindus and Jains throughout the centuries. Our first known written sample of it is from a Buddhist source.[7] But do we know for sure that it did not exist previously?

Whatever its origins, the Śramaṇa movement is, above all, an ascetic movement. The term 'one who strives' refers to the exertions involved in Śramaṇic practice: fasting, giving up luxuries (including, in some cases, basic items like clothing), practicing meditation for long periods, often in uncomfortable or difficult-to-maintain postures, and depending on laypersons or householders (non-ascetics) for one's physical sustenance.

The point of all this ascetic exertion is self-mastery. One is stripping away all attachment, all sense of ego, to achieve a state of uninterrupted inner serenity. This state of serenity, in turn, is pursued for the sake of the same goal presented in the *Upaniṣads*: liberation from the cycle of karma and rebirth. This requires freedom from all craving for external objects or conditions. One is peeling back all that is inessential to find one's *true* self. In the *Upaniṣads*, at least according to one prominent school of thought, this true self is Brahman, the absolute reality at the foundation of existence. For the Jains, it is the *jīva*, the soul or life force, while the Buddhists affirm that there is no 'thing' called a 'self' at the core of one's being at all. As a broad movement, not all Śramaṇas followed exactly the same ideas or practices. They were divided into sub-groups: Jains, Buddhists and so on. Each group was focused on living the teachings of its founding figure, who was regarded as having achieved the highest goal.

Among these groups, possibly the oldest, and the one with a following in India today, is the Jains. Another group, the Ājīvikas, had a considerable following at one time, but had died out by the year 1000 of the Common Era. There were probably other such groups as well, but their teachings are either lost to history or were later incorporated into other traditions. Then, there are the Buddhists, whose tradition had largely (though not entirely) died out in India by the year 1300, but not before spreading far and wide across Asia, forming the first world religion, in the sense of a tradition carried by missionary efforts to many regions. By the time Buddhism declined in India, it had become dominant or significant in countries across Asia, including the countries of Southeast Asia, China, Korea, Japan and Tibet, as well as much of Central Asia. It was reintroduced to India in the modern era by a combination of Ambedkarite Buddhists protesting against caste prejudice and Tibetan refugees fleeing the occupation of their country by communist China.

Finally, there were sceptical philosophies whose connection with the Śramaṇa movement is not clear. Some teachers of these philosophies appear to have been ascetics; but it is unclear how they conceived of their asceticism, given that they typically denied the cosmology of karma and rebirth on which groups like the Jains based their ascetic practices. Early Buddhist texts speak of six Śramaṇa teachers who were contemporaries of the Buddha, some of whom are attributed with views which are, at least *prima facie*, difficult to reconcile with ascetic paths aimed at spiritual realization. Pūraṇa Kassapa, for example, is said to have rejected the idea of karma. Sañjaya Belaṭṭhiputta is said to have taught agnosticism. Were these teachers truly Śramaṇas? Bronkhorst, as we shall see, has a provocative theory that at least some of these sceptics might not have been Śramaṇas, but Brahmin cynics.

Jain and Buddhist textual traditions and the question of language

The Jain world view is the oldest and the most complete extant example of ancient Śramaṇic thought which continues to command a community of devoted adherents today. Jainism thereby provides one of our clearest windows into the thought and practice of the Śramaṇa movement.

The earliest available Jain texts were not composed, interestingly, in Sanskrit – unlike most premodern Indian philosophical writings – but in a language which was spoken in the eastern half of the Ganges River valley from roughly the middle to the end of the first millennium BCE. This language, Ardha Māgadhī, is a *Prakrit*. Prakrits are closely related to Sanskrit. They reflect the ways in which language continued to develop in various parts of the Indian subcontinent after the compilation of the *Vedas*. While Sanskrit was spoken in the north-western region of India in the second millennium BCE, in later centuries, in the course of being used as the language of everyday discourse in various regions, it began to diverge from its original form. Each region had its own set of earlier linguistic substrates that affected the way people in those regions spoke Sanskrit: or what had originally been Sanskrit. In time, these 'dialects' of Sanskrit became distinct languages. These languages are the Prakrits.[8]

A similar process can be observed in European history, in the case of Latin. Latin, the dominant language of the Roman Empire, was also spoken in different ways by people in different regions, based on their prior linguistic habits. Each of these Latin dialects developed into what are now regarded as independent languages –Italian, Portuguese, French, Spanish, Romanian and so on. Just as Sanskrit-based languages are called Prakrits, Latin-based languages are now known as *Romance* languages (derived from the language of Rome).

The term *Prakrit* implies a deliberate contrast with *Sanskrit*. *Sanskrit* means 'cultured' or 'refined'. *Prakrit* means 'natural' or 'unrefined'. As Sanskrit fell out of daily use (which it had certainly done by the middle of the first millennium BCE), it continued to be used as the language of 'high' culture: philosophy, literature and other intellectual pursuits. It also came to be 'frozen' in time. Sanskrit grammarians such as Pāṇini (c. fifth century BCE) worked to ensure that Sanskrit usage did not change. This was due to its importance as the language of Vedic ritual. Part of the correct performance of a Vedic ritual is the correct pronunciation of the Sanskrit mantras of the Vedas. As an eternal, *apauruṣeya* (or non-man-made) text, the words of the Vedas could not vary. As a result, and through the efforts of those who adhered to the Vedic belief system, Sanskrit soon became a formal language of ritual, associated chiefly with the Brahmins.

The Prakrits, in contrast, were the languages which people spoke 'naturally', in the course everyday life. The Prakrits gradually evolved into the modern languages spoken in northern India today, like Hindi, Bengali, Marathi, Gujarati and many other regional languages as well. If one studies Sanskrit drama, one can observe that it is not uncommon for the main characters, typically people drawn from the upper classes of society, such as kings and Brahmins, to speak in Sanskrit, but for Prakrit to be used by characters drawn from the wider mass of society, such as servants.

This connection of Sanskrit and Prakrit with different classes of society has fuelled some speculation about the choice of the Jains to present their teachings in a Prakrit, and not in Sanskrit. Like the choice of the early Buddhists to present their teachings in Pāli, another Prakrit language, this choice is sometimes seen as ideologically motivated: as a marker of the Śramaṇa movement's view of itself as being opposed to the Vedic ideology of the Brahmins.

Because Sanskrit was not the language of daily discourse for the average person, but had to be learned specially to study the Vedas, and because it is a difficult language (being regarded as such even in ancient India, and not only by contemporary students in the West), the Brahmins' use of Sanskrit in their discourses can be interpreted as a sign of elitism: that Brahmanical knowledge is special, elite knowledge not intended for everyone. Even the name of the *Upaniṣads*, a word meaning 'secret knowledge', suggests these texts contain knowledge only meant for the initiated few. Rather than seeing this elitism as a matter of chauvinism, snobbery or selfishness, it should be borne in mind that Vedic knowledge was considered by its adherents to be extremely powerful: a key to tapping into the secrets of creation. It was thus not something to be shared lightly.

The contrast here is with the Śramaṇas, who viewed their knowledge as something that *was* to be shared with everyone, regardless of social status: that all beings, suffering under the bondage of karma and rebirth, should be given the 'good news' of how to free themselves from this bondage and escape the rebirth cycle. The Śramaṇas, so the argument goes, presented their teachings in the language of the common people for this reason. This view fits well with the idea that the Śramaṇa movement is akin to a 'Protestant Reformation', paralleling Luther's translation of the Bible from Latin to German, though predating it by some two thousand years: the idea of the Śramaṇas either as rebels against or reformers within the Vedic tradition.

Whatever its merits, this thesis should be approached with caution; for it is often the case that theories developed by scholars of Indian culture involve some amount of projection of those scholars' own concerns and interests onto the past. To the extent that many early Indologists were also committed Protestants, their casting of the Brahmins in the role of the Catholic Church in an ancient Indian 'Protestant Reformation' could involve prejudiced attitudes against Hinduism and the Hindu priesthood, making Brahmins the 'bad guys' and Śramaṇas the 'good guys' in a struggle between oppressive religious elitists and those who would liberate the common people from such 'priestcraft'.[9]

Even if this interpretation of the Śramaṇas as religious reformers who desired to connect with the common people is historically valid, it was not a stance the Śramaṇa traditions maintained for long. After Ardha Māgadhī and Pāli themselves ceased to be languages of everyday discourse in the respective regions of India in which they had been spoken, undergoing the same processes of linguistic transformation that Sanskrit had undergone previously, they nevertheless continued to be the languages of the Jain and Buddhist scriptural traditions. The Jain and Buddhist scriptures were not, in other words, 'updated'. Any Jain or Buddhist scholar who wished to study these texts in depth had to learn the languages in which they were written, just as the Brahmins had to learn Sanskrit to study the Vedas. Ardha Māgadhī and Pāli became, in effect, the technical languages of Jainism and Buddhism, respectively, just as Sanskrit was the technical language of Brahmins.

Interestingly, around the second century CE, Jain and Buddhist philosophers also began to write in Sanskrit, just as Brahmin philosophers did, although many Jain works were still produced in the regional vernacular languages, as remains the case today, with a good deal of Jain literature being produced in Gujarati, Hindi and Kannada (as well as English). Buddhists outside India also translated their works into such languages as Tibetan, Chinese and Japanese.

The shift to Sanskrit by Jains and Buddhists could have been made in order to enable them to participate in the wider Indian philosophical discourse which was then being carried out in this language. Although Sanskrit was not the language of the common people, it was a trans-regional language, known by intellectuals across the subcontinent. Like Latin in Europe, it thus became a medium for trans-regional communication.

It is also possible that this shift occurred because many Sanskrit-trained Brahmins became Jains and Buddhists and continued to think and write in the language that was natural to them for these purposes. The renowned Jain philosopher Haribhadrasūri was, for example, born a Brahmin, as was the famous Buddhist philosopher, Nāgārjuna. Many more examples could be cited. The various schools of thought were not sealed off, watertight compartments. Adherents of various traditions were aware of one another. They studied one another's teachings and, if they found the views of a particular school of thought compelling, they shifted their allegiance to it.

Sources for early Jain thought: The *Āgamas* and the *Tattvārtha Sūtra*

The Jain Ardha Māgadhī scriptures, or *Āgamas*, are considered by most Jains to be accurate authoritative records of the teachings of a figure known as Mahāvīra, a title meaning 'great hero'. Mahāvīra's given name was Vardhamāna. He was born a prince of the Jñātṛputras, a warrior clan from the eastern Ganges region.

According to Jain tradition, Vardhamāna, at the age of thirty, chose to renounce the world and pursue liberation from karma and rebirth. Pulling out his hair and giving up his royal finery, he practiced intense fasting. He refused to harm any living being, even allowing insects to crawl on his body. He observed a vow of silence that he did not violate, even if people would speak to him and become angry when he did not reply, threatening him with physical harm and sometimes even beating him. He offered no resistance to these physical assaults and never complained of his physical discomfort. After twelve years of this difficult asceticism, he attained his goal of *kevala jñāna*, or 'absolute knowledge'. For achieving this extremely difficult goal, he came to be known as a *Jina*, or 'conqueror' – not in a violent, militaristic sense, but as one who has conquered oneself – and as the great hero, Mahāvīra. He freed himself from karmic bondage and spent the remainder of his life – his last in the cycle of rebirth – teaching the Jain path of purification. He established four *tīrthas* – that is, 'fords' or 'crossings' over the river of rebirth, to the other shore of liberation. These four tīrthas consist of four communities: male and female ascetics and male and female householders, or laypersons, who support the ascetics as they pursue the path to spiritual freedom. For making these tīrthas, Mahāvīra also came to be known as a 'tīrtha-maker' or *Tīrthaṅkara*.

According to the Jain tradition, Mahāvīra lived in the sixth century BCE, from 599 to 527 BCE. The Buddha, according to many scholars, lived from 563 to 483 BCE, which would make him Mahāvīra's contemporary. These dates are consistent with both Jain and Buddhist canonical sources, which depict these two figures as having overlapping lifespans.[10] It should be pointed out, though, that there is considerable scholarly debate on the dating of both figures.[11]

By the second century CE, Jain ascetics were divided into two sects called Śvetāmbaras and Digambaras. *Śvetāmbara*, meaning 'white-clad', refers to the simple white robes worn by Śvetāmbara male and female ascetics. *Digambara*, meaning 'sky-clad', refers to the fact that male Digambara ascetics own nothing at all, including clothing. They do not even carry a begging bowl – an otherwise universal feature of Śramaṇa ascetics – but take the one meal they eat in a day in their cupped hands. The Digambara tradition does not accept the *Āgamas* as authentic because these texts depict Mahāvīra engaged in activities that Digambaras do not believe are appropriate for an enlightened being.

Despite their disagreements over ascetic practice, on conceptual issues like the nature of reality and knowledge, Śvetāmbaras and Digambaras are in basic agreement. In the second century CE, a Sanskrit text called the *Tattvārtha Sūtra*, or *Root Text on the Nature of Being* – a summary of the philosophy of the *Āgamas* – was composed by a Jain scholar-monk named Umāsvāti (known to Digambaras as Umāsvāmī). Śvetāmbaras and Digambaras both agree upon the authority of this text and its depiction of the central philosophy of Jainism.

Tīrthaṅkaras ('Ford-makers'), the cosmos they inhabit and the prehistory of Jainism

It might be tempting to see the sixth or fifth century BCE Śramaṇa ascetic Mahāvīra as the founder of the Jain tradition. This is, in one sense, correct; for Mahāvīra established the fourfold Jain community that exists today – the contemporary male and female ascetic and lay communities.

In another important sense, however, strongly emphasized by most Jains with whom one might discuss this topic, Mahāvīra is definitely *not* the founder of Jainism in an absolute sense; for he is not the first, but the twenty-fourth maker of tīrthas to exist in our cosmic era and in our region of the universe. (Even more Tīrthaṅkaras have existed in other eras and cosmic realms.)

Like Vedic and Buddhist cosmology, Jainism teaches that there has always been a cosmos. There is no absolute beginning, before which nothing existed. There is, however, a beginning and an end to the cosmos as we know it: the cosmic cycle in which we exist. As we have seen in Vedic literature, creation is not a 'once and for all' event, but an ongoing process, happening at each and every moment.

However, unlike at least some Vedic traditions, Jainism explicitly does *not* affirm the idea of a creator deity. This tradition – like that of the Ājīvikas and the sceptics whose thought we shall be exploring shortly, as well as that of the Buddhists – is non-theistic in this sense. At the same time, though, Jainism does affirm the existence of a sacred reality – the liberated soul, defined either individually or collectively – to which contemporary Jains give the name 'God'.

The Jain tradition does not see the cosmos as needing a creator. The cosmos has always existed and will always exist. The question of the need for an entity to sustain the cosmic order does not arise, as the cosmic order is taken as simply given. Debates between Jains and adherents of theistic schools of thought in many ways mirror or anticipate contemporary debates between those who believe a divine being must be necessary to explain the existence of an orderly universe and those who believe this is an unnecessary hypothesis. From a Jain point of view, the workings of karma are sufficient to explain events in the universe. A deity who would intervene in history would be seen as either superfluous – doing work karma can already explain – or arbitrary – working against the logic of karma. Also, a creator deity, being motivated by the desire to create, would be less perfect than the liberated soul, which desires nothing and is perfectly self-sufficient.

Again, though, while the cosmos has no absolute beginning point, it does go through cycles that have beginnings and endings. According to Jain tradition, during a cosmic cycle, a total of twenty-four Tīrthaṅkaras, like Mahāvīra, appear in our region of the cosmos. Mahāvīra was the twenty-fourth such being to appear in our world. We are thus near the end of the current cycle – though 'near' is a relative term, the cycles being very long. The cosmos will continue to degenerate until it enters another progressive phase, during which it shall renew itself, and things will improve.

The Jain tradition of the existence of twenty-three Tīrthaṅkaras having lived in our cosmic cycle prior to Mahāvīra is the chief basis for the Jain view that this tradition is not, in fact, a branch of or reaction to Vedic traditions. The Jain history of the universe extends back many billions of years. It was over the course of this vast history, recounted in Jain literature, that the Tīrthaṅkaras prior to Mahāvīra are believed to have appeared.

That this is not simply a pious belief but has some foundation in verifiable sources outside of Jain tradition, is evidenced by references to at least three of the pre-Mahāvīra Tīrthaṅkaras in non-Jain sources.[12] The Vrātyas of the *Ṛg Veda* also suggest the existence of an ancient ascetic tradition to which the Jains are laying claim with their idea of twenty-four Tīrthaṅkaras. It is also pointed out by some Jains that the long-haired figures depicted in some of the artworks of the Indus civilization appear to be in *kāyotsarga*, a standing meditation posture distinctive to Jainism. Again, however, as with other depictions of Indus figures seated in what appear to be yogic postures, these may simply be representations of people standing with their arms at their sides. Overall, though, the evidence seems to point to the existence of an ancient ascetic tradition, certainly in place by the time of the *Ṛg Veda*, which was taken even then to be distinct from the Vedic ideology of ritual sacrifice. This 'proto-Śramaṇic' practice may have been either a direct source or an inspiration for both Jainism and Śaivism.

The term *Jain* itself is a relatively modern Hindi and Gujarati rendition of the Sanskrit word *Jaina*. *Jaina* is derived from *Jina*, or 'conqueror', which is a term by which the Jains refer to those who have attained absolute knowledge and freedom from the cycle of rebirth. The Tīrthaṅkaras are a special subset of this group, distinguished from other Jinas by the fact that they not have not only reached absolute knowledge, but have also re-created the Jain community and re-established its teaching. A *Jaina* is a disciple of all *Jinas*, just as a *Śaiva* is a disciple of *Śiva* and a *Vaiṣṇava* a disciple of *Viṣṇu*. A disciple of the Buddha is similarly called a *Bauddha*; but in this book, we are using the modern term *Buddhist* to avoid confusion (and using the term *Jain* in much the same way, as this is how this community refers to itself today).

Even *Jaina* is not the term by which Jains have always referred to themselves. In the time of Mahāvīra, both Mahāvīra and his disciples were called *Nigganṭhas* (in Sanskrit, *Nirgranthas*), meaning 'those who are without bonds'. This is a clear reference to ascetic wanderers with only the bare minimum of ties to the worldly life.

The use of the title 'great hero', or *Mahāvīra*, is also a somewhat later convention. In his lifetime, he was known as *Nigganṭha Nāṭaputta* (or *Jñātṛputra*, a reference to his clan name, not unlike the Buddha's being referred to as *Śākyamuni*, or wise man of the Śākya clan). Under this name, he is one of the six Śramaṇa teachers contemporary with the Buddha who are mentioned in early Buddhists texts.

The use of military terminology – such as 'conqueror' and 'hero' – to refer to an enlightened being is interesting, given the strong Jain commitment to non-violence. The metaphors of spiritual warfare and the spiritual warrior are, in fact, pervasive in both Jain and Buddhist traditions. It is possible that this reflects the Kṣatriya, or warrior, milieu from which Mahāvīra and the Buddha both came, according to the available sources about their lives. Terms like *saṅgha* and *gaṇa*, used to refer to groups of Jain and Buddhist monks, also have military origins, referring to groups of soldiers. They are the ancient Indic equivalents of terms like 'troop', 'platoon', and 'squadron'.[13] As Jainism scholar Paul Dundas has observed, 'The career of Mahāvīra . . . bears witness to a form of spiritual heroism and struggle which struck an empathetic chord within an ancient Indian cultural world where the martial values of the warrior were widely esteemed.'[14]

The Jinas and the question of theism

As we shall mention again in connection with both scepticism and Buddhism, Jainism is a non-theistic tradition in the sense we have already discussed of explicitly denying the existence of a creator God. It is, however, important to distinguish the atheism of Jains and Buddhists from that which is prevalent in contemporary Western thought. Atheism, in the modern West, is largely a reaction against Christianity, and a denial of specifically Christian claims about the existence of a God believed to have created the universe from nothing at a particular point in time. This denial is generally extended to conceptions of divinity found in other religions as well, on the assumption that these religions affirm essentially the same model of reality as Christianity (which they do not). This is part of a wider rejection of 'supernatural' entities not available to scientific examination.

This is quite different, however, from the 'atheism', of the Jain tradition, which does affirm the existence of realities such as the soul, karma and rebirth, which would typically be rejected by atheists in the Western world. Jain practice also involves veneration of and devotion to Jinas as, for all intents and purposes, deities, though Jains, like Buddhists, distinguish between the highest beings in the universe, the enlightened ones, and deities of a more conventional kind who are seen as superhuman and powerful beings, but still trapped in the cycle of rebirth. In short, although Jainism denies the reality of a creator God, it does affirm the existence of something regarded as sacred, in a religious sense: the liberated soul. Indeed, this author has observed Jains using the English word *God* to refer to the Jinas, and even using expressions like 'God bless you' and 'God be with you'. The Jains are an excellent example of the principle which contemporary 'new atheist' Sam Harris has articulated, that one is only an atheist vis-à-vis some specific conception or conceptions of God: in the Jain case, God as creator. A contemporary Christian might similarly be called an atheist with regard to the ancient Greek deity Zeus. Theism and atheism, Indian philosophy shows us, are relative terms.

For all these reasons – and because the Jains themselves affirm that faith in 'God' (*Dev*) is one of their central principles – Jainism scholar John Cort suggests that it is better not to say that Jainism is atheistic, but that it affirms a distinctive form of theism:

> God, according to the Jains, is any soul who has attained liberation. Some of the terms such as ford-maker [Tīrthaṅkara] . . . indicate that while still embodied the Jinas created the Jain religion, and so showed the path to liberation. But they did not create the universe, nor do they grant liberation.[15]

Cort's last point is particularly significant. God, as the Jinas collectively, shows the path to liberation, but does not bestow it in the way the God of Christianity bestows salvation. Instead, it is the task of each soul to work its own way to the ultimate state of spiritual freedom. In Buddhist traditions, this question of 'self-help' versus help from another becomes a topic of debate and is one of the points which differentiates Theravāda Buddhism from Mahāyāna Buddhism. The Jains, however, have remained quite united on this question.

Jain ontology: A pluralistic realism

What, according to Jain philosophy, exists? What does it mean to exist? What is the place of humanity in the cosmic scheme of things? According to Jain thought, the cosmos is composed of six types of entity, or *dravya*, called *dharma, adharma, ākāśa, pudgala, kāla* and *jīva*.[16]

Dharma, in Jain philosophy, does not refer to the fundamental order of the cosmos, as it does in Vedic thought (though Jains eventually adopt this usage). *Adharma*, similarly, does not refer to chaos, or the absence of order, as it does in Vedic traditions. *Dharma*, in Jainism, refers to the principle of motion: that which makes motion possible in the universe. It could, perhaps, be translated as *dynamism*. *Adharma*, correspondingly, refers to *inertia*, the countervailing force opposed to dynamism. These are essentially principles of physics. It is possible, though, that these Jain principles could also be interpreted in the more ethical sense of *dharma* and *adharma* found in other Indian philosophies, if 'motion' is extended to include a moral sense, as something like ethical and spiritual advancement, and 'inertia' as a kind of moral or spiritual sluggishness.[17] A similar moral or spiritual shading to ostensibly physical concepts of dynamism and inertia can be found, as we shall see, in the Sāṃkhya tradition, which seems akin to Jainism in many respects.

Ākāśa is space. It is divided into the *lokākāśa* and the *alokākāśa*: cosmic space and what might be called a-cosmic, or extra-cosmic, space – space falling outside the boundaries of the cosmos. The cosmos, according to Jainism, is bounded. While vast, it has a definite shape and size. The shape of the Jain cosmos, interestingly, has the appearance of the outline, roughly, of a human body, with the legs extended outward and the arms stretched upward, with the fingertips of the hands touching above the head (much like the posture in which one stands while passing through airport security scanners). It is even called the *lokapuruṣa*, or 'cosmic man', in Jain texts. This suggests some connection with the image of the *Ṛg Veda*'s *Hymn of the Cosmic Man* (*Puruṣa Sūkta*), discussed previously.[18]

Pudgala is matter – the basic stuff of which physical reality consists. *Jīva* literally means 'life' and can perhaps be translated as 'life force'. Jīvas are many in number, there being as many jīvas as there are living beings in the cosmos. These are not infinite but could be called 'virtually infinite'. The Jain term (*asaṃkhyāta*) means 'innumerable'.

In addition to dynamism, inertia, space, matter and life forces, there is, according to the Digambara tradition, a sixth entity: *kāla* or time. These six entities, according to Jainism, make up the sum total of what exists.

In terms of ontology – its account of what exists – Jainism is, in contrast with the dominant line of thought in the *Upaniṣads*, *pluralistic* rather than *monistic*. Monism, the teaching that all that exists is essentially one, characterizes the Upaniṣadic teaching that all is ultimately Brahman. In the Jain view, though, there are many fundamental entities. Dynamism is not reducible to inertia, space, matter, life force or time. Inertia is also not reducible to dynamism, space, matter, life force or time. And so on. Each of the six basic entities is just that: basic. None is reducible to the others. Similarly, individual instances of these six basic types of entity are truly distinct from one another. They are not forms or aspects of some more fundamental reality. The many jīvas, for example, do not make up a 'supersoul', like the Upaniṣadic *paramātman*. This is why one can say Jainism has a *pluralistic ontology*.

It also has a *realist* ontology. In a monistic ontology, whether it is an ontology where the ultimate reality is an infinite consciousness (as in non-dualistic Vedānta), or an ontology in which the ultimate reality is matter (as in materialism), it becomes necessary to explain certain facets of daily, waking experience as not reflecting the ultimate nature of reality. Thus, if one's view is that reality is ultimately an infinite consciousness, then the existence of non-conscious matter in the world must be seen as a projection or illusion (which, as we shall see, is called *māyā* in the Vedānta tradition). Similarly, if one's view is that reality is composed of non-conscious matter, then the experience of consciousness must be explained in physical and chemical terms. Jain philosophy resists both of these forms of reductionism: of the conscious to the non-conscious or of the non-conscious to the conscious.

A realist ontology, like that of Jain philosophy, affirms that the experiences of matter and consciousness both truly reflect the plural nature of the cosmos as consisting of *both* material and spiritual (i.e. conscious) entities, and not one to the exclusion of the other.

In a similar vein, Jainism affirms the reality of the phenomenon of time as one of the basic entities making up existence. What does it mean to exist? According to the *Tattvārtha Sūtra*, to exist is to be 'characterised by emergence, passing away, and endurance'.[19] These are real aspects of existence, and not illusory, according to Jainism. Change – and thus time – is real. This is quite distinct from schools of Indian philosophy which either deny the reality of change or see it as an effect or function of consciousness.

What is the place of humanity in the cosmic scheme of things, according to Jain thought? In early Vedic literature, the central focus was human flourishing. What do human beings need to do to be happy? What is our role? What are our duties in maintaining the cosmic order? The *Upaniṣads* begin to step away from this human-centred focus with their emphasis on the concept of rebirth; for they speak of the possibility that one might be reborn in forms other than the human, such as an animal or plant, or even a natural phenomenon, such as wind, water or sunlight, which are not typically regarded as living beings in Western thought.[20]

The Jain tradition takes a definitive step away from *anthropocentrism* (a stance centred on human beings as the chief location and source of value in the cosmos) with its doctrine of the universality of the jīvas. Jainism affirms that the life forces, like the principles of dynamism and inertia, space and matter, pervade the cosmos. The jīva fundamentally *is* the living being. A given living creature, whether it be a human being, an animal, or a plant, is on one level composed of matter (*pudgala*). This matter is, in and of itself, non-living, or *ajīva*. It is part of a living being only inasmuch as it constitutes a body informed by the jīva, or life force. If the life force leaves the physical form, death occurs, and the matter making up the body of the once-living being is now no different from any other non-living matter, subject to the forces of decay.

The jīva, however, continues its existence and is reborn in a new physical form, the specific type of which is determined by its karma. The new form could be a human body, but it could also be the body of an animal or even a plant. A human being, therefore, is a jīva temporarily inhabiting a human form. The same jīva has inhabited many other kinds of form in the past, stretching back through infinite cosmic time, and is likely to inhabit other forms until becoming liberated from the cycle of rebirth by following the Jain path of spiritual purification. The jīva is our true identity.

The Jain path of purification: Ontology in the service of spiritual practice

Each jīva possesses four characteristics, each to an infinite degree. They are thus called the 'four infinitudes' (*ananta catuṣṭaya*). These are infinite knowledge (*jñāna*), infinite perception (*darśana*), infinite happiness (*sukha*), and infinite power (*vīrya*). While *jīva* essentially means the life force of a living being, the fact that it is also the centre of awareness–of knowledge, perception and happiness – means it would not be inappropriate to translate *jīva* as *soul*: a convention which has become common among both Jain and non-Jain scholars writing about Jainism in English.

As living beings, most of us must wonder, on being told of these four infinite characteristics of the soul – and that the soul is what we really are – why it is that what we actually experience in our lives is merely limited knowledge, limited perception, limited happiness and limited power. We are ignorant of many things. We suffer and die. Why is this? Why are we not experiencing our unlimited potential, if this is something we truly possess, as our true essence?

The Jain response to this question is that the soul, for most beings, does not exist in its pure and unobstructed state. It has been tainted by association with non-living (ajīva) matter. There is, in fact, a specific type of matter which adheres to the soul and causes distortions in its intrinsically pure nature. This bondage of the soul to matter did not begin at any particular time. It has simply always been the case that each soul has been existing forever in a state of bondage to matter. The soul did not 'fall' into this state of bondage through some primordial transgression. It is, though, trying to rise from it. The fact that this bondage had no beginning does not mean it can have no end. There is a way to free the soul from this bondage. This is the path taught by the Tīrthaṅkaras.

Interestingly, the specific type of matter that is bound to the soul is called, in Jain thought, *karma*. As we have seen, in Vedic thought, karma is the principle that each action is followed by a reaction of a similar kind from the cosmos. Jainism, one could say, develops a systematic model – almost a physics – of karma by which this principle of action and reaction is explained. Karmas are seen, in Jainism, as particles of subtle matter (or, one could also say, bundles of energy) which adhere to the soul, being attracted to it by distortions or warps in the soul's pure nature. These distortions are caused by *kaṣāyas*, or 'passions'. The passions are reactions to experiences. The intrinsic, pure state of the soul is one of perfect equanimity or *sāmāyika*. The aim of the Jain path is to cultivate this state of equanimity, which is essential to becoming free from the cycle of rebirth.

According to the *Tattvārtha Sūtra*, there are seven basic principles (*tattvas*) making up the Jain path to liberation. These are *jīva* (the soul), *ajīva* (matter), *āsrava* (the influx of karmic matter into the soul), *bandha* (the bondage of the soul to karma), *saṃvara* (the cessation of the influx of karmic matter into the soul), *nirjarā* (the expulsion of karmic matter from the soul), and finally, *mokṣa* (liberation of the soul from all karmic matter). This list of principles essentially describes the process by which a soul becomes bound to and liberated from *saṃsāra*, the cycle of rebirth.

First, there are the soul and matter, the main elements with which the path of purification is concerned. Matter flows into the soul and becomes bound to it. The process of this karmic influx must be brought to an end and the matter already bound to the soul removed for the soul's infinite potential to be realised and freedom to occur.

Karmic matter is compared, in some Jain texts, to a seed (*bīja*).[21] Like seeds, there are many kinds of karma, which are exhaustively listed in Jain texts dedicated to this topic. Some seeds bring pleasant experiences. These are 'good' karmas. Some seeds bring painful or otherwise unpleasant experiences and are seen as 'bad' karmas. Other seeds yield experiences which are neither pleasant nor painful, but neutral. All these experiences – good, bad and neutral – keep the soul bound to the rebirth cycle.

The kind of seed that will be attracted to a soul depends on the passion within the soul that attracts it. Again, the passions are distortions in the soul which exert a kind of magnetic pull upon karmic matter, drawing it to the soul. The passions themselves are the soul's emotional responses to pleasant, unpleasant and neutral experiences which have been produced by earlier karmas. Pleasant experiences tend to create *attraction*. One wants more of this kind of experience. This craving attracts karma to the soul. Unpleasant experiences create negative craving, or *aversion*: a desire *not* to have certain experiences. Neutral experiences create the passion of *indifference*: the sense that one has not been either pleased or pained by the experience, so is neither drawn to nor averse to it. All passions, depending on their intensity, attract different types of karmic particles.

These particles flow into the soul, where they become embedded. After a period of time whose length depends on both the type of karmic particle and the general environment of the soul – the kinds and intensities of the passions pervading it – the karmic seed will 'sprout', producing an experience of a pleasant, unpleasant or neutral kind.

In response to this experience, the soul will feel a passion, which will attract more karmic particles, and the process will begin again. The karmic 'seed' that produced the original experience leaves the soul upon having its effect of creating a happy, unhappy or neutral effect. It will continue to float through the cosmos as a potential for future experiences until it is again drawn into a soul undergoing the type and intensity of passion that attracts it. These particles, though indestructible, can have their effects negated by ascetic practice.

This is the cyclical process by which karmic matter becomes bound to souls. Karmic matter already present in a soul, having been previously attracted to that soul by specific passions which that soul was undergoing, produces experiences. These experiences evoke further passions, which attract more karmas, which also eventually produce experiential effects, and so on, and so on.

The path to liberation involves a twofold process of stopping the influx of further karmic matter into the soul and expelling the karmic matter already present before it is able to give rise to further experiences.

Again, it is not that simply engaging in action attracts karmic matter (and the karmic effects to which this matter gives rise). It is the passions that attract karma to the soul. If, therefore, one cultivates a state of equanimity and does not respond to experiences with the passions of attraction, aversion or indifference, one will cease to attract karma into one's soul.

This cultivation of equanimity is done through a combination of ethical and meditative practices. According to Jainism, except in the cases of persons who have developed an exceptional degree of self-control through ascetic practice, most of our actions are accompanied by passions. This is true even on an unconscious or barely conscious level. Some actions involve specific passions to such an inevitable degree that committing these actions almost automatically involves passion and the attracting of karma to the soul. Thus, even though it is really the passion and not the action which attracts karma, for all intents and purposes, one may speak in shorthand of certain actions always involving bad karma and certain actions always involving good karma. The worst actions, in terms of being accompanied by passions which attract bad karma, are those involved in harming or destroying living beings: those involved in violence in thought, word or deed. This is why the central Jain ethical principle is *ahiṃsā*, or non-violence: the absence of even the desire to inflict harm on another being.

The oldest of the Jain meditative practices is *samāyika* (also a name for equanimity itself). It involves the recitation of certain Jain texts which recollect the serene state of the liberated beings and serve as affirmations of one's own aspiration to achieve that same state. Many Jain laypersons observe this practice daily for a period of roughly forty-eight minutes.[22]

Another form of Jain meditation, known as *prekṣa-dhyāna*, or simply *prekṣa* ('perception meditation', or 'perception') was developed by the twentieth-century Jain master Ācārya Tulsi. It is presented as a recovery or reconstruction of ancient Jain meditation practices long-ago forgotten and seems to draw upon the wider meditation practices shared across many Indian traditions.[23]

It is important to note that the state of equanimity cultivated in Jain meditation is not to be confused with indifference (which, one may already have noted with some puzzlement, is one of the passions). The state of samāyika is sometimes characterised as being 'alike in joy and sorrow'. One who is in this state of equanimity experiences happiness and unhappiness, joy and sorrow, but does not allow these ephemeral experiences to disrupt one's inner peace. One identifies, mentally, with the serenity which is the true and constant nature of the jīva, rather than with one's changing external circumstances. One thus gradually begins to identify with one's own true nature.

Like the philosophy of the *Upaniṣads*, Jainism teaches that seeking happiness in external objects and conditions leads only, at best, to temporary happiness. Infinite joy is to be found in the jīva, which possesses this joy as one of its four essential traits.

Identifying with the serenity of the inner self – the soul – is quite different from the state of indifference. Indifference is based in the ego and external circumstances. One is indifferent to phenomena that do not bring one either pain or pleasure. Indifference is thus based on whether a particular thing or condition is making me happy or unhappy. I am indifferent, for example, to an airplane flying in the distance outside my window. I might barely be aware of it. If I know this airplane is bringing someone I love to visit me, it will become a source of happiness for me. If it crashes into my house, it will become a source of unhappiness. In each case, it is the external circumstance that gives rise to my inner state.

Equanimity, on the other hand, as a fundamental trait of the soul, is constant throughout all external conditions: happy, unhappy and neutral. Once one has cultivated the state of equanimity, identifying with the true nature of the soul rather than with one's temporary, constantly changing circumstances, one ceases to attract karma. One's soul is no longer 'sticky' with passion. It no longer exerts the magnet-like pull on karmic particles that it exerts when subject to the passions.

From a Jain perspective, though, cultivating equanimity and ceasing to attract karma to the soul is only half of the twofold process of liberation. The other half involves expelling the karma already present in one's soul.

This pre-existing karma, as noted earlier, is much like a collection of seeds. Each is waiting to ripen and bear fruit: to give rise to an experience. The particular type of experience to which it gives rise depends on the type of karma it is. The length of time it takes to do so depends both on its type and the conditions of the soul to which it is bound. It is much like the way the ripening of a seed is affected by the conditions of the soil in which it is planted. Is the soil rocky or fertile? Does it have abundant water and sunlight?

The condition of the soul, by analogy, is a function of the degree of control one exerts over the passions. If the passions run free – if one does not control, but is controlled by, these passions – then the karmas will ripen in their own time. As long as these karmic seeds are in one's soul, in an un-ripened state, one is not yet free.

If, however, one is able to master the passions – cultivating equanimity, as discussed earlier, but also imposing a measure of discomfort upon oneself, through ascetic practice, without allowing this discomfort to disturb one's inner state, this is said to end the process of the slow ripening of one's karmas. In effect, ascetic practice negates one's karmas. This is compared in Jain texts to 'cooking' a seed in the 'fires' of asceticism. A cooked seed cannot ripen. Similarly, karmic seeds bound to the soul of one who practices asceticism find that soul to be a hostile environment to their ripening, and flee from it. They are thus expelled from the soul, much as they eventually would have been in any case, upon having their effect; but under the effects of ascetic practice, these karmas leave the soul more quickly, without producing any binding, passion-evoking experiences. This is how the difficult experiences Mahāvīra underwent during his spiritual journey helped lead to his attainment of absolute knowledge.

The idea behind the Jain path of ascetic purification is that by ending the influx of karma to the soul through cultivating equanimity and expelling the already present karma through ascetic practice, the soul eventually becomes karma free. Its full potentials of infinite knowledge and bliss then manifest. One thus attains kevala jñāna – omniscience, or absolute knowledge. One is then a Jina, or conqueror. The only remaining karma adhering to the soul will be of a kind that does not obstruct the soul's inherent characteristics.

One example of non-obscuring karma is *ayu karma*, or the karma that determines one's life span. One will, in other words, live out the lifespan determined by one's karma at birth. Once this karma has worked itself out, the body will die, and one will leave the body behind, now completely free from the cycle of death and rebirth. Such souls dwell forever at the pinnacle of the cosmos, in a place called the 'realm of the perfected ones', or *Siddhaloka*. This is what happens to beings like Mahāvīra. According to Jain tradition, Mahāvīra attained absolute knowledge, freeing himself of all obscuring karmas, at the age of forty-two. His lifespan-determining karma, however, caused his body to live for another thirty years until, at the age of seventy-two, it ceased to function. The soul known as Mahāvīra then ascended to the Siddhaloka, where it resides today and will reside forevermore, experiencing the bliss of its infinite inherent perfection, no more to experience the imperfections involved in the process of birth, death and rebirth.

Jain ethics

Though all systems of Indian philosophy involve an ethical dimension, and though all, to varying degrees and in varying ways, emphasize the ideal of non-violence, it is fair to say that ethical questions are most central to Jainism, and that non-violence is emphasized in this tradition to a greater degree than in any other Indian tradition.

The centrality of ethical practice to Jainism follows logically from the Jain understanding that freeing oneself from the passions is essential to attaining liberation, and that avoiding certain actions – violent actions – which invariably give rise to destructive passions is vital to this process. In this sense, one can say that Jain practice begins and ends with ahiṃsā.

Violent actions (and words and thoughts) are not, however, the only actions likely to bring bad karma into the soul. The Jain moral code is enshrined in a set of five moral rules called *vratas*, or 'vows'. Although not all Jains formally take these vows, they nonetheless define the basic rules of behaviour expected of observant Jains. They are practiced with greater strictness by the ascetic community, though they inform lay Jain life as well.

As observed by ascetics, these rules are known as the *mahāvratas*, or 'great vows'. They consist of:

1. *Ahiṃsā*: absolute non-violence, observed to the strictest degree humanly possible
2. *Satya*: always telling the truth, avoiding all falsehood
3. *Asteya*: not stealing, not taking anything that is not explicitly given to one
4. *Brahmacarya*: celibacy, observing strict control over sensual desires of any kind
5. *Aparigraha*: non-attachment, owning no personal property whatsoever.[24]

As observed by householders, these rules are known as the *anuvratas*, or 'small vows'. These are:

1. *Ahiṃsā*: avoiding deliberate harm to macroscopic (i.e. visible) living beings
2. *Satya*: abstaining from falsehood, maintaining honesty in business dealings
3. *Asteya*: not stealing
4. *Brahmacarya*: marital fidelity, maintaining restraint with regard to sensual desires

5. *Aparigraha*: non-attachment, avoiding greed or obsessive preoccupation with belongings.

Several interesting points can be made about the Jain vows. First, one can see here a basic pattern common to all Śramaṇa traditions: namely, the division of the community into householder and ascetic groups, each adhering to a different set of expectations. This is a pattern one can see not only in Jainism, but also in Buddhism and in those Hindu communities which include ascetic practitioners. In each case, ascetics, as ascetics, naturally observe a stricter set of norms than those expected of householders. Ascetics are understood to be, relatively speaking, closer to the ultimate goal of liberation than householders who are relative beginners on the path. The practice of ascetics represents the highest embodiment of the tradition's ideals. Householders, though, create the material conditions that make the tradition possible. As ascetics cannot pursue a material livelihood, being wholly focused on spiritual aims, it is householders who feed and clothe them. It is also from the ranks of householders that ascetics are drawn. Ascetics are focused primarily on attaining liberation. For householders, liberation is a more distant goal. The focus, for them, is on attaining positive karma and a good rebirth through doing meritorious works in support of the ascetic community.

It is also interesting to note that the values enshrined in the Jain vows are shared across several Indian traditions and can be seen to constitute the basic moral values of at least most Indian systems of philosophy. The Jain vows are identical to the *yamas*, or moral restraints of the Yoga tradition, and four of the five are identical to the *pañcaśīla*, or five precepts of Buddhism. They also make up *sādhāraṇa dharma*, or 'universal duty', in Brahmanical traditions – the moral duties expected of all people under normal circumstances – as distinguished from *svadharma*, the specific duties that apply to one's station in society and stage of life.[25]

A Jain-Buddhist ethical debate: What is more important, consequences or intention?

What determines whether an action is good or bad? Is it the effect of the action? The joy or suffering the action brings about? Or is it the motivation behind the action? This topic is widely debated across cultures, and Indian philosophy is no exception. Whichever option one chooses is apt to cause discomfort if taken to extremes. Our actions often have unintended consequences. One certainly wishes to distinguish between a person whose actions accidentally lead to a death and one who plots a murder for months. But it is also desirable to see responsibility being taken for the consequences of an action, especially if those consequences are particularly grave.

The fact that passions, not actions themselves, bring karma into the soul is significant if one reflects on later debates between Jains and Buddhists regarding what makes an action morally blameworthy. From a Jain point of view, it is the *effects* of our actions to which we must attend in determining whether an action will bring bad karma to the soul. From a Buddhist point of view, it is not so much the effect of the action as the *intention* motivating it that matters. This is arguably why Jain ascetic practice is so much more rigorous than Buddhist practice, particularly its adherence to *ahiṃsā* or non-violence. Even accidentally ingesting or treading upon an insect, in Jain thought, brings bad karma. Some Jain ascetics even utilize a cloth mouth shield, or *muḥpatti*, to avoid accidentally ingesting and destroying tiny organisms.

According to Buddhism, however, only deliberately destructive acts have negative karmic implications, the intention behind one's acts being the ultimate determinant of their moral quality.

Early Jains object to the Buddhist emphasis on intention, subjecting it to relentless ridicule. One Śvetāmbara *Āgama* text, the *Sūtrakṛtāṅga*, reduces the Buddhist perspective to absurdity (a philosophical strategy known in the West as *reductio ad absurdum*, and frequently used in Indian philosophy as well). This text states that if a Buddhist were accidentally to cook and eat a baby, thinking it was a gourd, this would not be a morally blameworthy act. But if a Buddhist were to cook and eat a gourd, thinking it was a baby, this would be a moral abomination.[26]

For Jains, though, as for Buddhists, it is the passions accompanying an action ultimately form the mechanism by which these actions produce negative karma, and later Jains do give weight to intent. How, then, does one account for the difference in emphasis between the two traditions, at least in their early stages, regarding effects versus the intentions behind an action?

An essential component of Jain practice is cultivating constant awareness of the ever-present existence of tiny life forms. Every point of cosmic space is said to contain infinitesimally small living organisms. The smallest of these are *nigodas*. Having only one sense organ, nigodas are the simplest form of life. Rebirth as a nigoda is the lowest rebirth one can experience: meaning a rebirth at the furthest extreme from that in which one can attain liberation. In addition to nigodas, there are numerous other species of tiny life form, up to and including insects.

The average person is unaware of these tiny life forms, and a Jain layperson could be said to have only theoretical knowledge of them. A Jain ascetic, however, becomes keenly aware of the presence of life everywhere, and thus has a correspondingly heightened responsibility to protect it, exercising extreme caution in moving about. Indeed, this extra care even in regard to sitting and standing – as well as eating, drinking and breathing – constitutes much of Jain ascetic practice. From a Jain point of view, we are committing violence all the time. Our very biological processes are destructive to countless tiny life forms in and on our bodies.

If one's awareness of life forms everywhere has been heightened, then the question of *accidentally* causing destruction becomes moot. In other words, it is more likely for me to see myself as harmless if I do not see the very act of my being alive as doing harm to other living beings. The Buddhist position then makes more sense: that one can avoid doing deliberate harm and thereby remain free from moral blame (and bad karma). The Jain ascetic, however, sees every act as potentially carrying destructive potential. The Jain response to a Buddhist who accidentally causes harm and says, 'I didn't mean to do it'', is to say, 'You should have been more careful!' The carelessness involved in unintentional destruction of life stems, from a Jain perspective, from the passions: from selfish absorption in one's own desires without regard for their potential impact on others, even tiny others. To see one's own life and aims as having greater importance than the lives of other beings is, from a Jain point of view, the ultimate in egotistical craving of the kind that binds one to saṃsāra. Jain asceticism is a process of utter self-abnegation: the eradication of ego by seeing all life, even microscopic life, as no less important than one's own.

If this appears extreme, it should be noted that this is the Jain *ascetic* ideal. Jain laypersons, or householders, live much as practitioners of other Indian traditions do, avoiding any *deliberate* destruction of life, but knowing that should they wish to undertake the path to liberation in earnest, it will require a radical lifestyle change. It could be said that from a Jain ascetic perspective, a Buddhist monk is at the same spiritual level as a householder (as some Jain texts argue).

Implications of Jain ethics for Jain epistemology and ontology: The *Anekānta* doctrine

The overriding concern of Jain ascetics to avoid harming living beings has a major impact on Jain philosophy. Questions arose among early Jain ascetics as they pursued their practice of non-violence. How can I tell if something is alive or not? If there are tiny life forms everywhere, how can I cause the least destruction to them? What is the difference between a living being and a non-living being? Are there beings that are, in one sense, living and in another sense, non-living?[27]

This set of reflections also involved reflection on the nature of the jīva, or soul: that which makes, by its presence or absence, an entity a living or thing or not. It was noted that the soul has some characteristics – the four infinitudes – that are stable and enduring, and some – like incarnation in a particular form and the emotional and karmic states experienced in that form from moment to moment – that undergo constant change.

From these reflections a set of doctrines arose that are quite remarkable and distinctive to the Jains, and that seem to have been poorly understood by adherents of other systems of Indian philosophy who critiqued them. These are the doctrines of the complex, 'multiplex' nature of reality and the relativity of ordinary knowledge (prior to kevala jñāna), as well as the Jain doctrine that a statement is only valid when the conditions under which it may be true are specified.[28]

In terms of ontology, *anekānta-vāda*, the doctrine of the complexity of reality (literally, the 'non-one-sided' doctrine) states that reality is complex: that no phenomenon can be reduced to a single truth. Recall that the basic ontology of Jainism is pluralistic and realist. It rejects the idea that everything can be reduced to, for example, modifications of a unified field of consciousness (the view of Advaita Vedānta, based on the *Upaniṣads*), or a set of modifications to unconscious, non-living matter (the view of materialists in India and the West). Reality has many dimensions. It is complex and 'many-sided' (*anekānta*), and so defies simplistic, reductionist characterizations. This follows from the nature of the soul, as including both stable, unchanging characteristics and states of being that change from moment to moment. Each entity, like the soul, has many aspects, is both living and non-living, and so on.

Related to this conception of being as complex is a corresponding doctrine of knowledge, or epistemology. *Naya-vāda*, the doctrine of perspectives, states that for every aspect of an entity, there is a perspective from which it can be viewed. From the perspective of its intrinsic traits, the soul is unchanging. From the perspective of its changing states, the soul is ephemeral and so on. Each perspective captures a real aspect of the complex nature of the entity.

This epistemology of perspectives gives rise to a distinctive Jain doctrine regarding how one should formulate philosophical propositions. Rather than stating absolutely either that the soul is eternal and unchanging or that it is ephemeral and varied from moment to moment, it is necessary to specify the perspective from which such assertions are made.

In the *Āgama* texts of the Śvetāmbaras, Mahāvīra is depicted as taking this approach to questions widely regarded as *avyākata*, or 'unanswerable', like whether the universe and the soul are eternal or non-eternal (having a beginning and an end or existing perpetually). In a discourse with one of his monks, or *bhikkhus*, named Jamāli, Mahāvīra explains that there is a sense in which the universe and soul are eternal and a sense in which they are non-eternal:

> [T]he Venerable Mahāvīra told the Bhikkhu Jamāli thus: . . . [T]he world is, Jamāli, eternal. It did not cease to exist at any time. It was, it is and it will be. It is constant, permanent, eternal, imperishable, indestructible, [and] always existent. The world is, Jamāli, non-eternal. For it becomes progressive (in time-cycle) after being regressive. And it becomes regressive after becoming progressive. The soul is, Jamāli, eternal. For it did not cease to exist at any time. The soul is, Jamāli, non-eternal. For it becomes animal after being a hellish creature, becomes a man after becoming an animal and it becomes a god after being a man.[29]

Mahāvīra is here explaining that those who claim the cosmos is eternal and those who claim it is non-eternal are both correct, from their points of view. According to the Jain world view, there has always been a cosmos. It is, in this sense, eternal. But it is not static. It undergoes constant change, its character being vastly different during the various phases of a cosmic cycle, known as progressive (or *utsarpiṇi*) and regressive (or *avasarpiṇi*). It is, in this sense, not literally the same universe from era to era.

In a similar vein, the individual soul, or jīva, is also eternal. It has always existed and will always exist. But it inhabits many forms over the course of its journey to freedom. The same soul can be, in one lifetime, a human being, in another an animal and so on. These forms are not eternal. They perish and pass away, to be replaced by another, and another, until liberation. If by 'living being' one is referring to organism that is a composite of body and soul, then this is non-eternal.

Answers to questions like, 'Is the cosmos eternal or non-eternal'"? and 'Is the living being eternal or non-eternal?' depend on whether the questioner has in mind the totality of the cosmos or its current state of affairs, or the jīva as such or the body it currently inhabits. In this way, seemingly incompatible answers to these questions can both be seen to be true. There is that in all of us which is eternal, and that in all of us which will pass away forever. The two are not mutually exclusive.

This approach to seemingly contrary answers to the same question became, in the hands of Jain intellectuals over the course of two and a half millennia, a complex system of logic according to which the views of rival systems of thought could be reconciled into an integral synthesis.

In its fully developed form, *syādvāda*, the Jain doctrine of conditional predication, states that a proposition is only true *syāt* – that is, from a certain perspective, or in a certain sense. From another perspective, the same claim is false. From yet another perspective, the same claim is both true and false. And from another perspective yet again, the truth or falsehood of the claim cannot be determined. It is indeterminate or 'indescribable'. If one adds the non-redundant combinations of these four possibilities, one comes up with a total of seven possible truth values for a given truth claim. This teaching is therefore also known as the *saptabhaṅgi-naya*: the sevenfold (or literally, 'seven-limbed') perspective. According to this teaching:

1. From one perspective, or in one sense, claim X is true.
2. From another perspective, or in another sense, claim X is false.
3. From another perspective, or in another sense, claim X is both true and false.
4. From another perspective, or in another sense, the truth of claim X is indeterminate.
5. From another perspective, or in another sense, the truth of claim X is both true and indeterminate.
6. From another perspective, or in another sense, the truth of claim X is both false and indeterminate.
7. From another perspective, or in another sense, the truth of claim X is true, false and indeterminate.

Using this method, one can integrate multiple perspectives regarding the nature of a thing into a more comprehensive perspective. The most comprehensive perspective of all is that of an omniscient Jina, who has attained absolute knowledge.

What is an example of syādvāda in action? Let us take the example of a clay pot. We can say that a clay pot exists inasmuch as it is actualizing the characteristics we associate with a clay pot at a given time. It is made of clay. It has a particular shape. It can hold water. And so on.

But there are also senses in which the clay pot does not exist. It does not exist *absolutely*, that is, at all times and in all places. It came into being at a particular time, will endure for a while, and will eventually cease to exist as a clay pot (such as if it is broken, in which case it will no longer actualize the characteristics of a clay pot, but of a collection of clay shards). It fills a certain quantity of space in a particular location. It also does not exist as certain other things. It is not a pen: that is, it is not actualising the characteristics of a pen. One cannot write with it, for example, or carry it in one's pocket.

There is a sense in which the clay pot both does and does not exist. It is embodying certain characteristics at a certain time and place and is not embodying these at others.

It is embodying these characteristics and is not embodying other characteristics. And there is a sense in which the nature of the clay pot's existence cannot be captured in words or concepts. There is that which is in the clay pot that makes it an actual entity and not simply a collection of ideas: what we might call its inexpressible *thatness*.

Although these doctrines affirm that simple metaphysical claims should not be made in an absolute fashion and that the truth of a claim is dependent upon – that is, *relative to* – the perspective from which it is made, these Jain doctrines should not be taken to constitute a form of *relativism*, if by that one means the view often found in contemporary discourse according to which there is either no such thing as ultimate truth or no way of knowing what that truth might be. These are not, in other words, sceptical doctrines. On the contrary, they reflect the conviction that when we properly disambiguate our claims by specifying the perspective from which they are made, we are able to capture the truth better than otherwise.

A philosophy of universal inclusiveness or of Jain superiority?

The implications of these doctrines become clearest when one brings Jainism into dialogue with other systems of philosophy. As deployed by Jain thinkers throughout much of the premodern period, these doctrines demonstrate the partial, incomplete character of the views held by adherents of other schools of thought in contrast with the more comprehensive view of Jainism.

With regard, for example, to the question of the basic nature of existence as characterized by either change or continuity, one finds Indian schools of philosophy to gravitate either towards the view that existence is basically a flow of discrete but related events, coming one after the other, and creating the illusion of solid, continuous existence, or towards the view that existence is, at its core, eternal and unchanging, with the flow of events through time being the illusion. The view that existence is a flow of changing events is typically found in Buddhist traditions. The view that existence is made up of fundamentally unchanging substances is predominant in Vedic traditions.

With their logic of anekānta-vāda, Jain thinkers have argued that Buddhists and Brahmins have each captured an aspect of the truth with their respective teachings. Buddhists, for their part, have described the flow of karmically determined events. Brahmins have described the substantive side of existence, such as the unchanging essence of the soul. Each, however, has erred in not attending to the contrary view. This results in a one-sided or absolutist (*ekānta*) philosophy, which fails to capture reality in its full, complex, anekānta richness. Jain thinkers who argue in this way have essentially utilized the doctrines of the complexity of reality and the relativity of perspectives as a polemical tool to argue for the superiority of Jainism, just as thinkers from other schools have argued for the superiority of their points of view.

In the modern period, however, a growing number of Jain thinkers have begun to see these doctrines as a way to argue for pluralism in a different sense: not merely ontological pluralism, but a pluralism of world views, in which many religious and philosophical perspectives can be treated appreciatively, as each capturing a particular aspect of reality, but none capturing it fully. This can be seen as akin to modern Hindu teachings along similar lines, to the effect that many religions are paths to the same ultimate goal.

From a Jain perspective, this openness to varied views can be seen as an extension of the principle of non-violence into the realm of philosophical discourse: as 'intellectual ahiṃsā'.[30]

The key question here is whether Jain thinkers are willing to apply these doctrines to the teachings of Jainism itself: to see Jainism, along with other traditions, as teaching important truths, but as also incomplete and in need of learning from the others. Of course, it is part of the logic of adhering to a point of view that one finds it, in some way, superior to other perspectives. But this need not preclude an openness to learning from others and acknowledging that, as long as one has not yet attained absolute knowledge, there may be important truths not yet in one's possession. Even the teachings of an omniscient Jina, inasmuch as they are conveyed through the imperfect medium of language, require interpretation, and thus remain within the realm of the relative, rather than the absolute (even if they point beyond themselves to that absolute realm).

There is no consensus among Jain thinkers on this topic. There are indications, though, that even in ancient times, there were Jain intellectuals who saw beyond the use of these doctrines as a polemical tool, and could envision them as ways of expressing an appreciative view of other traditions. Kundakunda, a Digambara philosopher who lived around the third century CE, speaks of two perspectives: the ultimate perspective of the enlightened Jina, or *niścaya naya*, and the ordinary perspective of those who have not attained absolute knowledge, or *vyavahāra naya*. This is a Jain version of what is sometimes called the 'two truths' model, versions of which can also be found in the Buddhist and Advaita Vedānta traditions. The ultimate perspective is, according to Kundakunda, beyond what mundane words and concepts can grasp. It is 'above the different perspectives'.[31] This suggests that even Jain teaching is part of the realm of relative knowledge, pointing beyond the limited words and ideas constituting it and towards the *experience* of absolute knowledge. However, it must also be borne in mind that, within the realm of relative knowledge, there are still more and less true views, and that Jains would see their view as superior to others.

Haribhadrasūri, an eighth century Śvetāmbara philosopher, is also noteworthy for his view of non-Jain traditions as ultimately aimed at the same highest truth, and his relatively positive way of describing these traditions. In his *Yogadṛṣṭisamuccaya*, or *Collection of Views on Yoga*, he says the experience of *mokṣa*, or liberation, is essentially one. He explains that it is described differently by the great masters of various traditions who have attained it in order to meet the needs of their disciples and the times in which they lived. The proper attitude, therefore, to hold towards all the founders of various paths to liberation, to whom he refers as 'omniscient ones' – is veneration and respect. Disputation with rival schools is to be avoided as non-conducive to the supreme and common goal of *mokṣa* or *nirvāṇa*.

> The highest essence of going beyond *saṃsāra* is called *nirvāṇa*. The wisdom gained from discipline is singular in essence, though heard of in different ways.

'Eternal Śiva, Highest Brahman, Accomplished Soul, Suchness': With these words one refers to it, though the meaning is one in all the various forms.[32]

Similarly, the seventeenth century Śvetāmbara philosopher, Yaśovijaya, draws upon non-Jain sources such as the philosophy of the Navya Nyāya, or 'New Logic', school of thought which was prominent in his time. In his *Adhyātmasāra*, or *Essence of the Inner Self*, he approvingly cites the *Bhagavad Gītā* as a source-text, and in his *Jñānasāra*, or *Essence of Knowledge*, he utilizes the terminology of Vedānta in talking about the ultimate nature of the jīva, referring to the soul as the *paramātman*, or 'supreme self', and even *parabrahman*, or 'supreme Brahman'. He thus implies, without actually stating, that the supreme goals of Vedānta and Jainism are one and the same.

Kundakunda, Haribhadra and Yaśovjiaya, therefore, each in various ways, anticipates the modern Jain understanding of *anekāntavāda* and its associated doctrines as a philosophy seeking accommodation and acceptance, and viewing other traditions in a positive light, rather a way to show the superiority of Jainism. Certainly, each of these thinkers was deeply committed to the Jain path. Haribhadra, in fact, was a Brahmin convert to Jainism. But they did not view this commitment as requiring them to dismiss all other traditions as wholly false or without value.

While such attitudes have come to the fore in the modern period, they represent a persistent theme throughout the history of Indian philosophy. While there has been argumentation aplenty among adherents of Indian philosophies, the extent to which these traditions the other not as an opponent, but as a fellow traveller heading toward the same final goal, is remarkable. This thread of openness and is evident from the famous verse of the *Ṛg Veda*, 'Though reality is One, inspired poets speak of it in many ways',[33] to the affirmations of modern Hindu teachers that all religions are paths to the highest realization. The Jain re-articulation and re-appropriation of anekāntavāda as a doctrine of religious and philosophical pluralism can be seen as one example of this trend.

A popular way to illustrate the philosophy behind such attitudes of inclusion is the famous story of *The Blind People and the Elephant*. As mentioned earlier, this story has been used by Hindus, Buddhists and Jains to express this way of thinking. The oldest surviving version of it is from an early Buddhist text from the Pāli canon, the *Udāna* which I have paraphrased as follows:

Once, a disciple of the Buddha heard the followers of various schools of thought arguing bitterly with one another about a variety of philosophical topics. Confused, he approached the Buddha and asked him to explain which amongst the adherents of these various views was correct. The Buddha, in reply, told himthis story:

As a joke, a king sent seven blind men to feel an elephant and describe its nature. Each approached the elephant from a different direction, seized a different part, and, being blind, assumed that what he perceived was the whole elephant. One grasped the ear and declared, 'Elephant is like a large fan.' Another grasped a leg and declared, 'Elephant is like a great pillar.' Another found the trunk, and feeling it, proclaimed, 'Elephant is like a snake.' Another grasped the tail and declared,

'Elephant is like a rope hanging from the sky,' while another, grasping only the tuft of the tail, said, 'Elephant is like a broom.' A sixth encountered the side of the elephant and maintained, 'Elephant is like a wall.' The seventh insisted that the others were all wrong, for he had grasped the tusk. He proclaimed, 'Elephant is not any of those; elephant is like a spear.' Each being certain of the truth of his own experience, they began to fight.

A person who could see chanced to come by and found them quarrelling. After listening to their individual perceptions from their different points of view, he gently explained that there was no need for fighting over the issue, for each was partially right. But to have complete knowledge of the nature of the elephant, he said, one would have to be able to be aware of and combine all the different aspects of the creature.[34]

Clearly, this story can be read in two different ways. Is the person who can see the entire elephant the Buddha? Or Mahāvīra? Or a stand-in for whichever philosophical system is held by the person telling the story? If this is the case, then this story illustrates a position called *inclusivism*, in which one is willing to concede that there is at least partial truth in the teachings of other views, but that these partial truths are ultimately included in and superseded by the total vision of truth given in one's own system of thought. Or is the person who can see the whole elephant, rather, a stand-in for a hypothetical omniscient being – maybe the Buddha, maybe Mahāvīra, maybe God – whose perspective cannot be captured by any single, finite, humanly created set of ideas, but is something these limited systems can only, at best, approximate? This interpretation points us to *pluralism*: the view that there are many partially true and partially false systems aiming at ultimate truth. Different Jains, at various points in the history of their tradition, have interpreted their anekānta doctrine in both ways: either as a form of inclusivism or as a form of pluralism. The inclusivist trend has been the dominant one for most of history, but a pluralistic approach is increasingly discernible in the modern period.[35]

The mystery of the Ājīvikas: The lost Śramaṇa tradition

As mentioned earlier, among the various ascetic striver traditions flourishing in northern India during the first millennium before the Common Era, two survive as independent traditions today: Jainism, whose philosophy we have been examining thus far, and Buddhism, to which we will be turning in the next chapter. The Jain community, with a following of approximately five million adherents, is largely to be found in India today, whereas the Buddhist tradition, the fourth largest religion in the world in terms of the number of its followers, is largely practiced in East and Southeast Asia. It had largely vanished in the Indian subcontinent by the thirteenth century of the Common Era, although pockets of Buddhist practitioners still flourished, and continue to flourish today, on the geographical margins of the region, in what are today the nations of Nepal, Sri Lanka, Bangladesh and Bhutan. The tradition has also been reintroduced into India in the modern period.

In the first millennium before the Common Era, though, there were more Śramaṇa or striver groups in India, and many teachers in addition to Mahāvīra and the Buddha who were seen by their followers as enlightened beings. Most of these groups have since vanished from history, with little more than their names or the names of their founders surviving in Buddhist and Jain texts. It is likely these groups did not have large followings and that some of them merged with the emergent Hindu, Buddhist or Jain communities. It is worth noting that clear, sharp boundaries among these traditions did not exist in this early period (and that such boundaries are, in any case, typically porous in the Indian context).[36]

In fact, it may be an error to project the very notion of distinct traditions too far back into the past. One very early text of this period, the *Iṣibhāṣiyaim* or *Sayings of the Seers*, suggests that there may have been a variety of independent teachers, regarded widely as enlightened seers, who were only later, retroactively connected with one tradition or another as the identities of religious communities coalesced. In this remarkable text, the teachings of seers identified in later texts with Buddhist, Jain and Hindu traditions are mixed together, with no indication that they were ever perceived as rivals or representatives of distinct schools of thought. Even the Śramaṇa-Brahmin divide is absent in this text, which includes Yajñavālkya, from the *Upaniṣads*, among the seers whose wisdom it cites. It could well be that distinct communities with identities which we now label as *Jain* or *Buddhist* did not begin to solidify until the third century before the Common Era. And, of course, the widespread Indian attitude of pluralism and mutual inclusion of traditions adds to the difficulty in pinpointing separate, well-defined schools of thought, as there are thinkers and texts that are claimed and shared by more than one system.

A now-extinct school of thought known as the *Ājīvika* tradition commanded adherents and existed as an independent community until the medieval period, at which point it appears to have been absorbed into the Digambara Jain tradition, with which it shares many features.[37]

The name *Ājīvika* may mean 'lifelong', and derives from the vows which Ājīvika ascetics undertook: 'For as long as I live (*ā jīvāt*), I vow to harm no living being', and so on. It appears the Ājīvikas followed four vows identical to the first four of the five vows observed by Jains.[38] This is interesting, from an historical point of view, because, according to the Jain tradition, the twenty-third Tīrthaṅkara, Pārśvanātha, taught this same set of four vows. It is very likely that the Ājīvikas saw themselves as part of a continuous tradition extending back to Pārśvanātha, just as Mahāvīra and his followers saw themselves to be.[39] From an outside point of view, one can see the Ājīvika and Jain traditions as divergent branches of Pārśvanātha's tradition, claiming him as an authority.

According to both Jain and Buddhist texts, the founder of the Ājīvikas was a figure named Makkhali Gosāla. Gosāla is presented as an arch-villain in both Jain and Buddhist sources. In the Śvetāmbara Jain scriptures, Gosāla is a disreputable character who falsely claims to have achieved enlightenment. He also lives with a woman 'under compromising circumstances'.[40] These texts even depict Mahāvīra as engaging in a battle of paranormal powers with Gosāla. Ancient accounts also suggest the Ājīvikas had a large following, rivalling those of both Mahāvīra and the Buddha.

Does communal rivalry perhaps underlie the prejudicial accounts of Gosāla's life and teachings?

Gosāla is attributed by both Jains and Buddhists with a teaching that might help to explain the aversion shown to him in both traditions. He supposedly taught, 'that fate or destiny (*niyati*) was the central motive force in the universe against which no human effort could have any effect'.[41] It is said he carried a ball of string, which he would unwind to dramatize the point of his teaching. This string is said to have symbolized the duration of a being's bondage in saṃsāra, the cycle of rebirth. This bondage would last as long as it was fated to last, and there was nothing one could do about it. No human effort could bring one closer to liberation. It was only a matter of time, of waiting for the string to unwind, for fate to take its course.

Both Jains and Buddhists found such teaching dangerous and inimical to the spiritual path. Why make any effort towards liberation if it is eventually going to happen anyway? Why worry about karma, about doing good and avoiding evil, if all that happens is simply a matter of destiny, beyond our control? This is a teaching that would clearly need to be discredited if people were to take seriously the need to improve themselves and strive for liberation. *Striver*, again, is the very meaning of the word *Śramaṇa*. It may be that stories of Makkhali Gosāla's alleged wickedness are meant to dissuade those who hear them from taking up such a dangerous doctrine.

On the other hand, as Jainism scholar Paul Dundas points out, it is difficult to conceive of such an idea becoming the foundation for a spiritual path. By all accounts (including the Buddhist and Jain accounts), the Ājīvikas were ascetics every bit as rigorous as the Jains, having quite a few affinities with the later Digambara Jain tradition. Why would one practice such strict asceticism if liberation were simply a matter of waiting?

The *Sayings of the Seers* includes Gosāla among the teachers it cites, which suggests that he was not always viewed as a philosophical arch-villain. As presented in this text, Gosāla did not teach a wholly fatalistic doctrine, but instead advocated 'the virtue of imperturbability in the face of the continued change and modification which were seen to be in the world'.[42]

Bronkhorst has argued that the depiction of Ājīvika doctrine as fatalism is a half-truth. His claim is that whereas the Jains teach that one can both stop the influx of new karma and rid oneself of old karma through ascetic practice, Gosāla taught that one could only stop the influx of new karma. The karma one has already accumulated is fixed and must run its course. Ascetic practice can be effective in preventing further karmic influx, which helps explain the otherwise inexplicable fact that the Ājīvikas practiced quite rigorous asceticism. But one must simply accept one's current karma and bear with the experiences it brings.[43] This analysis has the virtue of reconstructing the Ājīvika doctrine in a way that is far more credible in light of available historical data. The ascetic practices of the Ājīvikas make are understandable as an attempt to prevent karmic influx.

Furthermore, the popularity of the Ājīvika doctrine in ancient times, such that it could rival that of both Jainism and Buddhism, also makes sense if this doctrine was really not so radically different from these traditions as its presentation in Jain and Buddhist sources suggests.

Ancient Indian materialist scepticism:
The Lokāyata or Cārvāka school

A common stereotype of Indian philosophy in the West is that it is entirely occupied with spiritual matters. Certainly, as presented thus far, one might see why this stereotype has come to be held so widely. The focus of the Vedic tradition on ritualistic performance, of the philosophy of the *Upaniṣads* on realizing Brahman and achieving transcendence, and of the Jains and Ājīvikas on attaining liberation from the cycle of rebirth: all arguably fit better in the category of 'religion' than 'philosophy'.

Sceptical thought, however, has always been widespread and pervasive in India. Indeed, if we define *scepticism* broadly as the willingness to ask any question, and to leave no assumption unexamined, one can find scepticism in every system of Indian philosophy: even those which may appear, from a modern Western perspective, more akin to 'religion' than 'philosophy'.

As early as the *Ṛg Veda*, one finds expressions of frank agnosticism, questioning whether even the supreme deity knows the answers to all questions, such as the mystery of the source of creation, or whether these questions are beyond even divine knowledge:

> Who really knows, and who here can say, from where this creation was born and from where it comes? The devas came after the creation of this world. Who, then, knows from where it first arose? He, the first origin of this creation, whether he formed it all or did not form it, whose eye controls this world in the highest heaven, he truly knows it . . . or perhaps he does not.[44]

However, despite its widespread and influential character in India, this current of thought receives relatively little attention in most works on Indian philosophy.[45] The system of philosophy most widely associated with scepticism is the materialist system of the Lokāyatas who are also known as the Cārvākas. Like scepticism in general, though, this system has also received relatively little attention from scholars of Indian philosophy.

This is at least partially due to the fact that much like the Ājīvika system, a living, ongoing, institutionalized school of thought which could preserve the texts of this tradition has not survived. As with the Ājīvikas, much of what we know about Indian materialism must be pieced together from texts of rival schools that were seeking to refute it. Indeed, one text that presents some of the thinking of this school begins its presentation with the casual statement that this school is 'difficult to eradicate'.[46] This suggests that some efforts were being made in this regard, and also that these efforts were being resisted.

The fact that so few texts of this tradition have survived suggests that there may have been a deliberate effort to suppress this school thought; although it should be noted that there remain, even today, enormous collections of texts in ancient Indian libraries that remain untranslated and unexamined by modern scholarship. 'Lost' texts of ancient Indian materialism may yet emerge, as well as texts from other traditions whose names we do not even know today.

It is also the case that the ways in which Indian philosophical thought is presented are often shaped by ideological considerations. Scholars often focus on schools of thought with which they feel a particular sympathy or affinity. The most in-depth study of ancient Indian scepticism was undertaken by a Marxist scholar, Debiprasad Chattopadhyay, who saw this tradition as something like an ancient Indian Marxism: a liberating materialist philosophy of the common people rising up in intellectual revolt against the religious obscurantism of the priestly sects that dominated ancient Indian discourse.[47] And we have already mentioned the fact that the Śramaṇa movement has often been portrayed as something like an ancient Indian 'Protestant Reformation' against the 'priestcraft' of the Brahmins. One must be wary of such projections, even if they are, to some extent, inevitable. A great deal of writing on Indian philosophy in the modern period has tended to emphasize the Advaita Vedānta tradition, also because this is a philosophy which has tended to have a large following among influential Indian intellectuals.

The fact that materialism has been a significant presence in Indian philosophy, despite the comparatively scanty surviving remains of actual materialist texts, is evidenced by the fact that adherents of every other system of Indian philosophy have felt obligated to refute it. Even though a formal materialist school of thought did not survive to the modern period, the power of sceptical argumentation more broadly was such as to require adherents of rival systems to address them in presenting their own views of reality, knowledge and the good life.

Comparing and contrasting Indian and Western materialisms

As one begins exploring Indian materialism, it is highly likely that one will be reminded of Western materialism, with which, substantively, it shares much in common. First, both Indian and Western materialism affirm that our primary basis for knowing anything (or *pramāṇa*, in Indian terms) is the data which we receive from our five senses: sight, hearing, touch, taste and smell. In modern times, this data has of course been expanded to include the data we receive from scientific instruments, which are essentially extensions of the senses: telescopes, microscopes and so on. Both traditions, Indian and Western, reject the idea that sacred texts or meditative insight should be seen as valid sources of knowledge, relegating these sources to the realm of superstition or, at best, unreliably subjective knowledge.

Controversially, Indian materialism is said to accept *only* sensory data as a valid source of knowledge, whereas Western materialism, affirming the validity of the scientific method, accepts logical reasoning reflecting on sensory data as an additional knowledge source, albeit one that is dependent on sensory data for its substantive content; although many Western thinkers would also hasten to point out that mathematical propositions and geometric theorems can arguably be derived and deduced through purely logical methods, independent of sensory observation. Two plus two equals four, regardless of whether there are actually two pairs of objects to add to one another. Epistemically, though, from the perspective of how one attains knowledge, it could be argued that in the absence of any sensory experience of concrete objects, mathematical truths, too, would be unavailable to us. Two plus two may equal four regardless of whether there are actually two pairs of objects to add. But will this idea make sense to us without any experience of objects?

Apart from mathematical truths, there are other important concepts, such as causation, the objective reality of which is not *absolutely* verifiable through sensory observation. In the Western philosophical tradition, Immanuel Kant (1724–1804) famously argues that certain basic concepts in the absence of which experience as we know it would be inconceivable are part of the mental apparatus by means of which we perceive the universe, as opposed to being objective qualities inherent in the universe itself – concepts such as space, time and causation. This Kantian move is sometimes called the *subjective turn* in Western philosophy, in which many thinkers ceased to explore metaphysical issues about the objective and absolute nature of reality, with many coming to regard metaphysics of this kind as simply impossible. They instead shifted their focus from ontology to epistemology: from the nature of reality to the nature of knowledge. Indian materialism does not make this move, though as we shall see, the traditions of Buddhism and Vedānta each do something analogous to the extent that they each, in different ways, collapse the questions of the natures of being and consciousness.

In terms of ontology, its view of what exists, Indian materialism is closer to its Western analogue. According to Indian materialism, reality consists of material elements which exist in combination with one another. It attributes the arising of consciousness to accidental interactions of material elements, using the image of how intoxicants affect consciousness to argue for this thesis. If consciousness can be shaped by material forces, so the argument goes, it must itself be a material reality, and not something wholly different, as other schools of thought affirm: a quality of the immortal jīvas of Jainism, or the eternal Brahman or ātman of the *Upaniṣads*:

> [T]he four elements . . . are the original principles; from these alone, when transformed into the body, intelligence is produced, just as the inebriating power is developed from the mixing of certain ingredients; and when these are destroyed, intelligence at once perishes also.[48]

Indian materialism is also atheistic, denying the existence of a creator deity. As we shall see, though and as we already have seen with the Jains and Ājīvikas, this denial is shared by many non-materialist systems of Indian philosophy as well.

Apart from deities, Indian materialism also rejects the idea of other unseen or 'paranormal' forces in the cosmos, such as the efficacy Vedic sacrifice, karma and rebirth, seeing such ideas as tools for deceiving the gullible into providing material support for the Brahmins and the Śramaṇas:

> The *Agnihotra* [Vedic fire sacrifice], the three *Vedas*, the ascetic's three staves [the *triśula*, or triple staff carried by some Indian ascetics], and smearing oneself with ashes [another common ascetic practice]:

[The materialist seer] Bṛhaspati says these are but means of livelihood for those who have no manliness nor sense.[49]

All of this, of course, closely parallels Western materialism, affirming that the universe consists entirely of material processes and denying 'the supernatural'. Western materialism includes consciousness among the material processes, just as Indian materialism does. Both traditions are atheistic, denying that the universe was brought into being by a divine creator. And both tend to perceive religion as a tool for manipulating the naïve masses and controlling society.

Atheism: A point of contrast between Indian and Western thought

An important contrast needs to be drawn, though, between Indian and Western thought on the question of atheism. In Western thought, atheism and materialism typically go hand-in-hand as part of a sceptical world view that is largely a reaction to the dominant Christian tradition.

In Indian thought, however, atheism and materialism need to be kept sharply distinct; for Indian atheism co-exists, in some traditions, with ideas such as karma and rebirth that materialism denies. The materialism of the Indian sceptics, as well as their epistemic dependence upon sensory perception alone, is the primary basis for the rejection of this way of thinking by adherents of other Indian schools of philosophy.

A particularly strong worry of the non-materialist thinkers of India is the materialist denial of such concepts as karma and rebirth, in the absence of which, they argue, it is difficult to conceive how one might justify moral behaviour. Without dharma, without a sense of the order of existence revealed either in Vedic texts or the realizations of enlightened beings like Mahāvīra and the Buddha, people would follow their sensory impulses and there would be chaos.

This is not unlike the argument one finds in the Western world that without religious belief, the foundations for personal morality and social cohesion are undermined. Materialism is also seen by adherents of other systems as undermining spiritual practice. Pursuing *mokṣa* is meaningless if there is no such thing as rebirth.

In both contexts, of course, materialists have recourse to counterarguments. If religious people are themselves immoral – if Vedic ritual and Śramaṇic asceticism are tools for dishonestly and hypocritically duping the gullible – then the morality argument for religion collapses. True joy, according to the materialist school of thought, consists precisely of sensory enjoyment. It would be foolish to forego such enjoyment, according to this view, in the name of an imaginary mokṣa. 'The only end of man is enjoyment produced by sensual pleasures. . . If anyone were so timid as to forsake a visible pleasure, he would indeed be foolish like a beast.'[50] According to this argument, the asceticism practiced by adherents of other schools of thought is unnecessary and unnatural.

The *atheism* of the Indian materalists, though, is not only unproblemlatic to many other schools of thought: it is, in fact, shared by them. As we have seen, from the perspective of the Mīmāṃsā school, it is unnecessary to postulate a divine author of the *Vedas*; for the adherents of this system see the *Vedas* as authorless and eternal. In the philosophy of the *Upaniṣads*, there are theistic and non-theistic currents of thought: some that view Brahman as a personal deity and some that view Brahman as an impersonal, pure consciousness and as the material cause of the universe. Jainism is also non-theistic, in the sense of denying the existence of a creator deity, though theistic, in the sense of affirming a sacred reality in the form of the souls of liberated beings. This was also likely true of Ājīvika thought and is arguably true of Buddhism as well.

The important distinction between atheism in India and the West – atheism, in the sense of the denial of the existence of a creator deity – is that, for most Indian systems of thought, such a denial does not imply the absence of a reality that might be called spiritual or sacred, but only the absence of a creator deity.

In the West, one of these typically implies the other, such that one who denies the existence of God will likely also deny ideas such as the existence of a soul, an afterlife, a cosmic system of reward and punishment (karma), the efficacy of performing religious rituals, and so on.

In fact, even those Indian systems of thought which are theistic, affirming the existence of a divine being who upholds, preserves and coordinates the universe, do not affirm the existence of a creator in an absolute sense. In other words, the theistic systems of Indian philosophy see the act of creation as an ongoing process. The idea that God, or Īśvara, created the entire universe from nothing at a specific point in time is foreign to Indian philosophy. In this sense, if *atheism* means denial of the God of classical Western theism, who creates the universe ex nihilo, then all systems of Indian philosophy are atheistic. Even in Indian philosophies in which there is a robust sense of the existence of a supreme being, this supreme being creates (and re-creates) the universe from eternal, pre-existing material. In some Indian traditions, Īśvara creates the universe from out of his own form. God's body is thus the material from which the cosmos is fashioned. This hearkens back to the *Ṛg Veda*'s *Hymn of the Cosmic Man*, in which the creator's body becomes the universe. The God of theistic systems of Indian philosophy is thus closer to the Demiurge of ancient Greek Platonic and Pythagorean philosophies than the God of classical Western thought, informed by Christian doctrine. It is also close to the neoclassical theism of modern philosophers such as Alfred North Whitehead and Charles Hartshorne.[51]

The objection of other Indian schools of philosophy to the materialist system, again, is not primarily to its atheism, which many of them share, but the utter nihilism which they perceive as necessarily emanating from it. Like many religious persons in the West, the objection of the other schools of thought to materialism is that it leads to a gloomy and pessimistic attitude towards life, in which there is no greater end to work or to look forward to other than death. As one Buddhist text characterizes it:

There is [according to the Materialists] neither fruit nor result of good or evil deeds [i.e. karma]. There is no such thing as this world or the next. . . There are in the world no recluses [Śramaṇas] or Brahmins who have reached the highest point, who walk perfectly, and who having understood this world and the next, make their wisdom known to others. A human being is built up of the four elements. When he dies the earthy in him returns and relapses to the earth, the fluid to the water, the heat to the fire, the windy to the air, and his faculties pass into space. The four bearers, on the bier as a fifth, take his dead body away; till they reach the burning-ground [cremation ground] men utter forth eulogies, but there his bones are bleached, and his offerings [karmas, Vedic rituals] end in ashes. It is a doctrine of fools, this talk of gifts. It is an empty lie, mere idle talk, when men say there is profit therein. Fools and wise alike, on the dissolution of the body, are cut off, annihilated, and after death they are not.[52]

The Lokāyata critique of causation

One of the chief lines of attack by which adherents of other systems of Indian philosophy refute materialism has been to show the absurdities involved in accepting sensory data as the only valid source of knowledge. How, for example, do I know the thing I see right now is the same thing I saw a few moments ago? Some other form of knowing, some way of processing our sensory data, must be involved in the act of even ordinary, mundane grasping of the world around us. It is not that we simply perceive raw data and thereby know everything we need to know to navigate a complex world of objects. We *see* colours and shapes, but we then *interpret* them as chairs, tables, people and so on. Our perceptions are a synthesis of raw sensory data and ideas we have learned from our cultural environment, by acquiring language and associating words with things (or that are, in some cases, according to Kantian thought, 'hard wired' into our minds). Memory, too, plays a role in this process. A memory may be based on sensory data, but the experience of memory is not the same as the experience of actual sensation. If we are literally dependent *only* upon sensory experience for knowledge, then all we can really know is what we are sensing right now. This is what Western philosopher, George Santayana, describes as 'a solipsism of the present moment',[53] the idea that only the present moment is real. Such solipsism is the result of applying sceptical principles to all but our immediate sensory data.

It is, of course, possible that the view of the materialist school of thought in India was more nuanced than its critics have suggested, and that it did not merely affirm that we can know only what our senses tell us in the present moment. The materialist school's affirmation of the *primacy* of sensory perception might have been seized on and exaggerated to create a 'straw man' argument to make this school's perspective easier to refute, just as the Ājīvikas' views on the workings of karma may have been similarly distorted to look like a mechanistic fatalism by their Buddhist and Jain opponents.

At the same time, though, the materialist school of thought raises some probing questions about the limits of logical inference and the knowledge it is capable of yielding. Not unlike David Hume (1711–76), whose reflections sparked Kant's subjective turn, Indian materialists question the concept of causation: a very basic tool that we commonly use in navigating the world around us.

Very much like in modern science, the inferential reasoning that is deployed in most Indian philosophies is based on the idea of cause and effect: the idea that certain factors invariably occur in conjunction with others. This idea of invariable concomitance (*vyāpti*) is a key concept of Indian logic. If one mixes certain chemicals, for example, certain predictable things happen. There is a lawlike regularity to such phenomena. We call the mixing of the chemicals the *cause* of the event which follows it. But is causation itself ever actually *perceived*, or is it *presupposed*? Or is it, as Kant suggests, *superimposed* upon the reality we perceive? What if the chemicals were to behave differently than we expect? Is the fact that they have always behaved a certain way in the past a guarantee that this will invariably be the case, as the principle of vyāpti requires?

The example Indian thinkers most often cite to explain inferential reasoning is the argument for the claim that, 'There is fire on the mountain.' This thesis is supported by the fact that smoke is observed rising from the mountain. The principle is then asserted that smoke occurs wherever there is fire. In support of this assertion, the example is given that one sees smoke accompanied by fire in other situations, such as in the case of a cooking fire. Therefore, the conclusion is reached that there is fire on the mountain.

The weak point of this inference is the assertion that smoke is *always* accompanied by fire. Indian sceptics point out that the smoke on the mountain might be caused by something else, 'for complex, indeed, is the nature of this universe'.[54] The idea of causation is based on the idea that a specific effect inevitably and invariably follows from its cause. But unless someone has observed all the situations in which a cause was present, one cannot know if its effect always follows. Even if, hypothetically, one had observed all such situations, this does not mean the same thing would necessarily happen the next time.

This is the point of Hume's famous example of the billiard balls. One sees a billiard ball struck by another, so the second billiard ball moves. This happens each time one observes one ball hitting the other. But how can one know with *complete certainty* that this will happen the next time one ball is struck by another? Inferential reasoning yields, at best, a high degree of statistical *probability*, but not absolute *certainty*. This, of course, is true of the scientific method as well. From the perspective of the Indian materialists, this sufficiently weakens inference as a means of knowledge to undermine the philosophical systems of their rivals, which are built upon it; for all other Indian philosophies use inference. In the case of science, it means that conclusions are never final, and knowledge must continue to advance as new phenomena are observed.

A mystery: The relationship of Indian sceptics to the Brahmins and the Śramaṇas

Due to their rejection of the authority of the Vedas as a valid source of knowledge and their ridiculing of the notion of the efficacy of Vedic sacrifice, the Indian sceptical tradition tends to be categorized by later thinkers as a non-Vedic, or *nāstika*, system of philosophy, hence its inclusion in this chapter. But the categorization of the different schools of thought as *āstika* and *nāstika* is a much later development than the period with which this chapter has been concerned: the period of the emergence of the striver traditions of the Jains, Ājīvikas and Buddhists. Starting around the tenth century of the Common Era, Brahmanical thinkers began to categorise systems of philosophy based on whether these systems affirmed or denied the authority of the Vedas.[55]

As discussed previously, those systems of thought that affirm Vedic authority have come, in the modern period, to make up what is now known as Hindu philosophy. Those that deny Vedic authority are those of the Jains, Buddhists and Lokāyatas: the materialist sceptics whose thought we have been examining. The terms *āstika* and *nāstika* mean 'affirmer' and 'denier', respectively. 'Affirmative' philosophies affirm the authority of the *Vedas*. 'Denying' or 'negative' philosophies deny it. In the modern era, the terms *āstika* and *nāstika* have come to mean *theistic* and *atheistic*, respectively – or *religious* and *non-religious*. But, as we have seen, to project these meanings back into history is problematic, given that there are systems of philosophy, like Mīmāṃsā, which affirm the Vedas, but which are not theistic, and that Jainism and Buddhism have religious dimensions.

Did the Lokāyata philosophy emerge as part of the wider rejection of Vedic authority found in the striver movement of the first millennium BCE? Does it represent part of a larger, pan-Indian scepticism directed at the claims of the Brahmins? There is some evidence in favour of this claim. Jain and Buddhists sources describe some of the teachers who rival Mahāvīra and the Buddha as sceptics who adhere either to a teaching of *Ajñāna* (agnosticism) or *Lokāyata* (materialism).

Agnosticism is, of course, not the same thing as materialism. Agnosticism is an epistemic doctrine which teaches that attaining certainty is impossible. It could be called *radical scepticism*. It is ascribed in ancient Buddhist sources to a Śramaṇa named Sañjaya Belaṭṭhiputta.

Materialism, on the other hand, is the claim that it certainly is the case that the world is made up, entirely and exhaustively, of material elements: a definite knowledge claim about the nature of the world advanced on the basis of sensory perception. It is attributed in the Buddhist sources to a Śramaṇa named Ajita Kesakambalī.

These two views – agnosticism and materialism – are each attributed to different teachers in the ancient sources, and given different names, as indicated. But the presence of both of these, broadly speaking, sceptical ways of thinking in a Śramaṇa milieu, taught by thinkers identified as Śramaṇas, strongly suggests these sceptical schools were part of the same movement of inquiry as Jainism and Buddhism: interlocutors in a shared conversation, the common thread of which was rejection of Vedic authority.

The name *Lokāyata* itself, which means 'extended throughout the world', suggests that this view was the ordinary, common-sense view of the average person in ancient India. It can also be taken to mean 'philosophy of the people'. This is Chattopadhyay's Marxist interpretation of this system.[56]

According to another interpretation, not exclusive of the others, *Lokāyata* means 'worldly philosophy'. This interpretation contrasts materialism with philosophies aimed at transcending the world and becoming free from the cycle of rebirth (the aim of every other philosophy, apart from Mīmāṃsā, which is aimed primarily at achieving worldly enjoyment through Vedic ritual).

On the other hand, it has long been noted with some puzzlement that the Lokāyata teaching is attributed in many sources to the Vedic sage Bṛhaspati, the guru of the devas, mentioned in the Lokāyata verse cited earlier. This system of philosophy is also sometimes called *Cārvāka*, which refers to sweet or agreeable speech. This is sometimes taken to mean that adherents of this system were effective speakers, easily able to attract many people to their views. But it is also taken to mean that this system was developed by a sage named Carvaka, which is an epithet of Bṛhaspati.

In addition to sources attributing this school to Bṛhaspati, the *Artha Śāstra* of Kauṭilya, a first or second century BCE text devoted to statecraft and political science, mentions the Lokāyata philosophy, along with Sāṃkhya and Yoga, as one of three philosophies based on the *Vedas*.

Given that this philosophy explicitly and strongly rejects Vedic authority and the efficacy of Vedic ritual, it seems peculiar that it would be regarded as Vedic. What is the explanation for this seeming inconsistency? How can a system that appears to reject and even ridicule Vedic ritual be a Vedic system, taught by the divine sage, Bṛhaspati?

Bronkhorst has proposed a provocative thesis that the Brahmins of the late first millennium before the Common Era were culturally divided between those who lived in cities and those who lived in rural areas. It was the rural Brahmins who developed systems of thought such as Mīmāṃsā and put forth great effort to ensure the continuity of the ritualistic Vedic tradition.

The rural Brahmins earnestly performed their Vedic rituals in the belief that this was what was necessary to uphold the cosmic order (with some becoming disenchanted with these rituals and withdrawing to forest retreats to meditate on Brahman and escape the cycle of rebirth, as reflect in the *Upaniṣads*). Meanwhile, however, the more cynical and worldly-wise urban Brahmins knew quite well that the Vedic system was a sham designed to dupe gullible people into providing them with material support.[57]

According to this interpretation, Lokāyata thought is, indeed, Vedic: a conversation among knowing insiders who, with a wink and a nod, promote a ritualistic system for their own livelihood, knowing quite well that it has no basis in reality. This is an inversion of Chattopadhyay's thesis: that the Lokāyatas were something like ancient Indian Marxists, raising a voice of criticism against the mystification of society by the Vedic ritual cult. If Bronkhorst is correct, some of the Brahmins did see their ritual system as a mystifying, world-deluding project: and this was its whole point.

Conclusion

Although less known in the Western world than either Hinduism or Buddhism, the thoughts and practices of the Jains, Ājīvikas and Lokāyatas were enormously influential upon both of these better-known traditions. Possibly representing an ascetic tradition that arose alongside (if not, in fact, prior to) the Vedic traditions, the Jain and Ājīvika philosophies articulate a clear and powerful understanding of the process of karma and rebirth and an ethic of *ahiṃsā*, or non-violence, both of which would become central to most Indian philosophies. It may be due, at least partially, to Jain influence that the adherents of Vedic traditions, in which animal sacrifice was once commonplace, now largely recoil from this practice, with many practicing strict vegetarianism. And while most Indian traditions strongly reject the materialism of the Lokāyatas, this system's sceptical bent of mind helped fuel an intellectual environment in which no question was off limits, and all topics were open for debate. One always had to be prepared to defend one's views from the withering critiques of the cynical materialists, and to ensure that one's views could withstand logical inquiry.

As mentioned earlier, with the stakes so high – the possibility of attaining the infinite bliss and freedom of mokṣa – and with one's philosophy being deeply interwoven with one's most deeply held values and way of life, it was important to 'get it right'. Far from sweeping uncomfortable questions under the proverbial rug, this meant being willing to raise and address any and every conceivable objection there might be against one's view. Ancient India was a vibrant intellectual environment in which views were proposed and brought into creative confrontation.

It was from this vibrant environment, this clash of world views, that there emerged a thinker standing at the confluence of all the tendencies we have discussed: Vedic, Śramaṇic and sceptical. This was the Buddha, to whose thought we now turn.

Notes

1 Upaniṣadic meditation is known as *upāsana*–literally, 'sitting near [to the Self]'.
2 See Ethan Mills, *Three Pillars of Skepticism in Classical India: Nagarjuna, Jayarasi, and Sri Harsa* (Lanham: Lexington Books, 2018) for an example of three prominent Indian philosophers associated with the idea of scepticism.
3 Vastupal Parikh, *Jainism and the New Spirituality* (Lahore: Peace Publications, 2002).
4 See David Gordon White, *Sinister Yogis* (Chicago: University of Chicago Press, 2011).
5 Long, *Jainism*, p. 45.
6 See, for example, Johannes Bronkhorst, *Greater Magadha: Studies in the Cultures of Early India* (Leiden: Brill, 2007).
7 *Udāna* 6.4:66–9, from the Buddhist Pāli canonical literature.
8 See Andrew Ollett, *Language of the Snakes: Prakrit, Sanskrit, and the Language Order of Premodern India* (Berkeley: University of California Press, 2017).
9 See Vishwa Adluri and Joydeep Bagchee, *The Nay Science: A History of German Indology* (New York: Oxford University Press, 2014).
10 See Bhagchandra Jain Bhaskar, *Jainism in Buddhist Literature* (Nagpur: Alok Prakashan, 1972).
11 See Joshua J. Mark, 'The Dates of the Buddha', *World History Encyclopedia*, https://www.worldhistory.org/article/493/the-dates-of-the-buddha/, accessed 18 June 2023. According to Mark, 'The modern scholarly consensus for the dates of the Buddha, since c. 1906 CE, has been c. 563 - c. 483 BCE based on external evidence such as Jain texts, Ashoka's reign, and astronomical calculations as well as probable dates for the founding of Buddhist schools of thought. These dates, however, are also approximations and, even though they are more acceptable to the modern-day sensibilities concerning precise dating, are far from certain. No dates for the Buddha's birth, life events, or death will ever be certain because the first writers to set down the

events of his life, as noted, did not care about precision in dating; they cared about telling a memorable story.'

12 Long, *Jainism*, pp. 41–2, 54.

13 Paul Dundas, *The Jains* (Second Edition) (London: Routledge, 2002), pp. 16–17.

14 Ibid., p. 17.

15 Cort, *Jains in the World*, pp. 92–3.

16 Padmanabh S. Jaini, *The Jaina Path of Purification* (Berkeley: University of California Press, 1979), p. 81.

17 Christopher Key Chapple, personal communication.

18 Indologist Asko Parpola has suggested that the concept of the cosmic man may have roots in the Indus civilisation, perhaps a shared historical source for these Vedic and Jain images See Parpola, *The Roots of Hinduism*.

19 Umāsvāti, *Tattvārtha Sūtra* 5: 9. Translation mine.

20 See, for example, *Kauṣītaki Upaniṣad* 1.2.

21 Jaini, *The Jaina Path of Purification*, pp. 111–12.

22 Cort, *Jains in the World*, p. 123.

23 See Ācārya Tulsi, *Transmutation of Personality through Preksha Meditation* (Ladnun, Rajasthan: Jain Vishva Bharati, 1994).

24 This vrata is the chief point of division between the Śvetāmbara and Digambara branches of Jainism. Digambara male ascetics take it literally and do not even own clothing. Śvetāmbara ascetics, male and female, wear white robes.

25 Rajendra Prasad, *A Conceptual-Analytic Study of Classical Indian Philosophy* (Delhi: Concept Publishing Company, 2008), p. 349.

26 *Sūtrakṛtāṅga* 2: 6.26–8.

27 Piotr Balcerowicz, *Early Asceticism in Jainism: Ājivikism and Jainism* (London: Routledge, 2016), p. 326.

28 Ibid., pp. 174–85; 220–6.

29 *Bhagavatī Sūtra* 9:386. Translation by Matilal. Cited in Bimal Krishna Matilal, *Anekāntavāda: The Central Philosophy of Jainism* (Allahabad: L.D. Institute of Indology, 1981), p. 19.

30 John Cort, 'Intellectual *Ahiṃsā* Revisited: Jain Tolerance and Intolerance of the Other', *Philosophy East and West* 50, no. 3 (July 2000): pp. 324–47.

31 *Samayasāra* 151. Translation mine.

32 *Yogadṛṣṭisamuccaya* 129–30; translation by Chapple. Christopher Key Chapple, *A Collection of Views on Yoga* (Albany: State University of New York Press, 2003), p. 131.

33 *Ṛg Veda* I.164.46. Jamison and Brereton, *The Rigveda*, p. 359.

34 Paraphrased from *Udāna* 6.4:66–9.

35 See Cort, 'Intellectual *Ahiṃsā* Revisited'.

36 John Cort, ed., *Open Boundaries: Jain Communities and Cultures in Indian History* (Albany: State University of New York Press, 1998).

37 Jaini, *The Jaina Path of Purification*, p. 25.

38 See Johannes Bronkhorst, 'The Riddle of the Jainas and Ājīvikas in Early Buddhist Literature', *Journal of Indian Philosophy* 28 (2000): pp. 511–29.

39 Balcerowicz, *Early Asceticism in Jainism*, p. 311.

40 Ibid., p. 22.

41 Dundas, *The Jains*, p. 29

42 Ibid.

43 Bronkhorst, *Greater Magadha*, pp. 38–51.

44 *Ṛg Veda* 10: 130.6–7.

45 A noteworthy recent exception is Mills, *Three Pillars of Skepticism in Classical India*.

46 *Sarvadarśanasaṃgraha*, cited in Sarvepalli Radhakrishnan and Charles Moore, *A Sourcebook in Indian Philosophy* (Princeton: Princeton University Press, 1967), p. 228.

47 Debiprasad Chattopadhyay, *Lokāyata: A Study in Ancient Indian Materialism* (New Delhi: People's Publishing House, 1968).

48 Radhakrishnan and Moore, *A Sourcebook in Indian Philosophy*, p. 229.

49 Ibid., p. 230.

50 Ibid., p. 229.

51 See Whitehead, *Process and Reality* and Charles Hartshorne, *The Divine Relativity: A Social Conception of God* (New Haven: Yale University Press, 1982).

52 *Sāmañña-phala Sutta*, 2: 23–4, Pali Text Society Edition pp. 73–4.

53 George Santayana, *The Letters of George Santayana, Book Eight, 1948-1952* (Cambridge, MA: The MIT Press, 2008), p. 116.

54 Radhakrishnan and Moore, *A Sourcebook in Indian Philosophy*, p. 238.

55 A process described in Nicholson, *Unifying Hinduism*.

56 See Chattopadhyay, *Lokāyata*.

57 Bronkhorst, *Greater Magadha*, pp. 150–72.

3

Turning the wheel of dharma

The Buddha's synthesis

Siddhārtha Gautama: The Awakened One

Like the Jain and Ājīvika traditions, with which it shares a great deal, the Buddhist tradition teaches that there have been many enlightened beings throughout history who have found the way to freedom from the cycle of rebirth. Just as Jainism has the twenty-four Tīrthaṅkaras, Buddhism teaches that there have been many *Buddhas*, or *Awakened Ones*, of whom the most recent is the figure widely known as the historical Buddha: Siddhārtha Gautama.

The Buddha, like Mahāvīra, appears to have been an actual, historical person – though one sometimes sees the claim made that even should he prove to have been wholly mythological, this would not refute Buddhism as a philosophy. Unlike Western religions, like Christianity, and much like the Jain and Vedic traditions, Buddhism is not focused so much on believing certain events occurred in the past as on eternal truth – *dharma* – and its lived practice. If stories of great, inspired figures of the past can help people today understand and live the dharma, then that is a good thing, to be encouraged. But it is ultimately not these stories or figures that matter, so much as the dharma to which they point.

That being said, the Buddha is deeply revered by Buddhists, with a reverence sufficiently intense and thoroughgoing to satisfy most definitions of the term *worship*. As we shall see, there are multiple systems of Buddhism that differ among themselves on the question of what might be called the Buddha's 'divinity'. For the Theravāda tradition, the Buddha is a deeply insightful, important and special being – but ultimately human, and not metaphysically different from the rest of us. From the perspective of many Mahāyāna Buddhists, however, the historical Buddha is a concrete historical projection into time and space of cosmic consciousness, not unlike the *avatāras*, or divine incarnations, of Hinduism. Even more than the historical Jesus, the historical Buddha is someone about whom very few things can be known with certainty, due to the gap between the time of his life and the time of the composition of the first Buddhist scriptures.

There has been considerable debate about when the Buddha lived. One prominent Buddhist tradition from Sri Lanka dates him from roughly 563 to 483 BCE.[1] Both Jain and Buddhist textual sources tell us that the Buddha's and Mahāvīra's lives overlapped, with Mahāvīra living, according to Jain texts, from roughly 599 to 527 BCE. Both figures lived in the same region of India, in the eastern half of the Ganges River valley, and frequented some of the same cities. There is no record of them having met, but there are accounts of them speaking with one another's followers.

The *Buddhacarita*, or *Deeds of the Buddha*, the first full account of the Buddha's life story, by the monk Aśvaghoṣa, was not committed to writing until the second century of the Common Era.[2] It is likely, though, that the core material from which it was composed had been passed on orally for centuries. Much of it may have come from tales recounted to Buddhist pilgrims by guides at sites associated with events from the Buddha's life, like his birth in the forest of Lumbini, his upbringing at the royal palace in Kāpilavastu and his attainment of *nirvāṇa* at Bodh Gaya. It is not clear how much of this material might be historically based and how much is legendary and intended to teach a spiritual lesson, "a blueprint for and a reflection of the lives of Buddhists."[3]

Older than the *Buddhacarita* are the texts making up the earliest canonical literature of Buddhism: the *Tripiṭaka*, or *Three Collections*. Set down in writing around the first century of the Common Era, these texts, too, were passed on orally from one generation of Buddhist monks to the next. Like the Jain *Āgamas*, these texts were composed not in Sanskrit, but in a Prakrit: in this case, Pāli. The 'three collections' are the *Vinaya* (the rule manual for Buddhist monks) the *Sūtras* (the discourses of the Buddha) and the *Abhidharma*, meaning 'further teaching' consisting of early Buddhist philosophy, probably composed after the Buddha's time. All the Buddha says, autobiographically, in these texts is that he grew up rich and spoiled. He then chose to renounce this lifestyle to pursue awakening and freedom from suffering for all beings.[4]

Traditional accounts of the Buddha's life present his biography according to the same basic template one finds in the lives of the Tīrthaṅkaras of Jainism. The life trajectories of enlightened beings across Śramaṇa traditions have certain shared features. Like Mahāvīra, the Buddha is born to a royal family of the Kṣatriya or warrior community. Both Mahāvīra's and the Buddha's births are preceded by visions in which their mothers are informed of the special natures of the children to whom they will give birth. In the case of the Buddha's mother, Queen Māyā, she sees a celestial white baby elephant who announces to her that she is going to give birth to him, and that he will become a great enlightened being, destined to show countless others the path to freedom from the suffering inherent in the cycle of death and rebirth. Both Mahāvīra and the Buddha experience a spiritual crisis which prompts them, around the age of thirty (twenty-nine in the Buddha's case), to renounce the world for spiritual awakening. Both pursue rigorous ascetic practices. In the case of Mahāvīra, this works after twelve years, and he achieves absolute knowledge at the age of forty-two. The Buddha decides excessive asceticism is non-conducive to the spiritual path and develops a more moderate practice known as the *Middle Path*. This works after six years, and he achieves nirvāṇa at Bodh Gaya at the age of thirty-five. Mahāvīra and the Buddha establish communities of ascetic and householder followers. Mahāvīra passes away from his physical existence at the age of seventy-two, and the Buddha does so at eighty. Both are Śramaṇas, or spiritual strivers.

One of the most significant differences between the Buddha and Mahāvīra is that while Mahāvīra received his family's permission to undertake the path of renunciation, the Buddha had to sneak away from his father's palace in the dead of night.

Like Mahāvīra, the Buddha is known to history primarily by an epithet – *Buddha*, meaning *awakened*, although many have translated it as *enlightened*. As one among many awakened beings, he is often referred to as Śākyamuni, the sage of the Śākyas (the community into which he was born and of which his father was a leader, according to traditional accounts of his life). His given name, Siddhārtha, can either mean 'fulfilment of a wish' or 'one whose wish is fulfilled'. Both meanings are, in different ways, appropriate. Siddhārtha was, as a healthy child and male heir, the fulfilment of his father's wish to continue his family's lineage and overlordship of their realm. At the same, time, Siddhārtha's own wish would later be fulfilled when he reached the state of spiritual awakening.

Gautama (Pāli: Gotama) was Siddhārtha's *gotra* name: a name given to a child in Vedic traditions to indicate the child's bond to one of the seers who first uttered the Vedas. The fact that Siddhārtha had a gotra name, as well as his father's disapproval of his aspiration to renounce, may suggest that his family, in contrast with Mahāvīra's, had a closer connection with Vedic traditions than Śramaṇic ones. Many ancient Brahmins disapproved of the path of renunciation.

Siddhārtha is also widely known as *Śākyamuni*: the sage or wise man of the Śākya clan. It is known through archaeological and other sources, as well as Buddhist texts, that the Śākyas were a community who inhabited a region overlapping what is now eastern Nepal and northern India. Siddhārtha's birthplace, Lumbini, and the town where he was raised, Kāpilavastu, are both located in modern Nepal. Siddhārtha's father, Śuddhodana, was likely the Śākyas' hereditary chieftain.

When Siddhārtha was an infant, a Vedic ritual was held to confer his name upon him, celebrate his birth, and introduce him to the community. Many Brahmins were called to perform this ceremony, which was also attended by a renouncer named Asita. Asita predicted Siddhārtha had a great destiny, and that he would follow one of two possible paths. He would either become a *cakravartin* – a world-ruling emperor – or a *buddha*: an awakened being who would show the path to freedom from suffering.

King Śuddhodana wanted his son to become a ruler, like himself, and was thrilled at the prospect that he would one day rule the world. He was somewhat less than thrilled, however, at the prospect of his son becoming a wandering, begging ascetic, even an awakened one. Recall that even today, renunciation is viewed with some ambivalence in Indian culture. If one's child becomes a renouncer, he may become a great spiritual teacher, but he will also not have children or a conventional married lifestyle.

This ambivalence would likely be even deeper – perhaps shading into outright hostility – in the case of a king, who also had a responsibility to pass the leadership of his realm to a worthy heir. Śuddhodana thus understandably asked Asita how to ensure that Siddhārtha would follow the path of a world-ruling emperor rather, not that of a renouncer.

Asita replied that if Siddhārtha were to see four particular sights, these would trouble his mind so much he would feel compelled to renounce his life of privilege and become a wandering seeker. The sights were: sickness, old age, death and renunciation.

If Siddhārtha could be kept from seeing these four things, he would rule the world, rather than renouncing it.

As the story unfolds, King Śuddhodana, mindful of Asita's prophecy, tries to shield his son from even the mention of sickness, old age, death or renunciation: an impossible task. If one takes the story literally, the king seems rather foolish as he tries in vain to shield his son from any of life's unpleasantness to ensure he does not become despondent and renounce. Metaphorically, though, the story conveys a profound message. Parents often shield their children from the harsh realities of life. But we all reach a point in our journey, from childhood to adulthood, where our protective 'bubble' is burst, and we realize there is much in life that is unpleasant and unfair. The point of the king's attempt to shield his son is precisely that it is impossible. This impossibility is underscored by the fact that Siddhārtha's mother, Māyā, lost her life to illness when Siddhārtha was an infant. He was raised by his aunt, a strong, assertive woman named Mahāprajāpatī (who later became the first Buddhist nun). Certainly, the young Siddhārtha would have been aware of his mother's death. And certainly, he would have seen and noted the signs of aging in his father's and aunt's features and would have himself fallen ill at some point during childhood.

Siddhārtha eventually becomes aware of life's sufferings, seeing the four sights after asking his father to allow him to venture out of the palace to see the world outside. Despite Śuddhodana's attempts to ensure Siddhārtha will not, in the course this venture, encounter any of the four sights, Siddhārtha nevertheless sees sick people, elderly people, a corpse being taken for cremation and an ascetic renouncer with his begging bowl, sitting in blissful meditation.[5] Some accounts say the devas ensured Siddhārtha would see these sights so he could fulfil his destiny, after his father sought to ensure that he would not encounter the four sights during his venture outside of the palace grounds.[6]

Siddhārtha's quest

Siddhārtha's decision to leave his father's palace and pursue the life of a wandering ascetic was not easy. Prior to making this decision, he had been married to a beautiful princess named Yaśodharā. They had conceived a son, Rāhula, who was born shortly before Siddhārtha undertook his renunciation. Leaving his wife and child to become a renouncer was a heart-rending choice for the young prince. It is said that he eventually resolved to leave because he realized his wife and child, too, would one day suffer and die and be reborn to suffer and die again. His search for awakening is presented not simply as a personal quest to rid himself of suffering, but as an effort undertaken for the good of all beings, out of compassion for the world. It is also worth noting that he did not abandon Yaśodharā and Rāhula to poor material circumstances. They continued to live and be lovingly cared for in his father's palace, in the hope that Siddhārtha would one day return, which he eventually did do, though not as the crown prince, but as the Buddha. At that time, Rāhula became a Buddhist monk and Yaśodharā a Buddhist nun, along with other members of the Śākya community who opted to join Siddhārtha's monastic order.[7] According to one account of Siddhārtha's journey, Yaśodharā, although she remained in the palace at Kāpilavastu, experienced everything that Siddhārtha experienced, such was the bond of love uniting them. She ate when he ate, fasted when he fasted and so on.[8] On the night of Siddhārtha's departure, a mysterious mist descended on the city of Kāpilavastu, putting everyone to sleep except for Siddhārtha, who thereby managed to elude his father's guards with this bit of help from the devas. He rode out of the city on his horse, Kaṇṭhaka. The devas helped 'by holding the horse's hooves suspended above the ground to prevent the sleeping city from waking'.[9]

After cutting off his hair and giving away his jewellery and royal finery to a passing hunter (who threw it away, for fear he would be accused of robbing the young prince if caught with it), Siddhārtha wandered into the countryside and began to follow the lifestyle of a wandering ascetic.

One may recall from our earlier discussions of the Jains and Ājīvikas that there were many mendicant teachers of the Śramaṇa movement active in northern India in the fifth century before the Common Era: the period of Siddhārtha's lifetime. This was also when the *Upaniṣads* were being composed, and adherents of the Vedic tradition were pursuing their contemplative practices in forest retreats in ways which paralleled the Śramaṇas. It is likely that there was mutual influence among these Vedic and non-Vedic groups. As we have seen, the ancient text, *The Sayings of the Seers*, reflects a milieu in which Brahmin and Śramaṇa teachers shared insights with one another and the rest of society. Over the course of his six years of wandering, the young Siddhārtha mingled freely with these spiritual aspirants, learning what he could from each group and then moving to the next, not unlike many spiritual seekers of the modern world. Traditional accounts of his life detail several of these encounters.

Siddhārtha first studied meditation under a master named Ārāḷa Kālāma. Some speculate that this teacher was affiliated to a tradition related to what would eventually become Yoga school. The *Upaniṣads* refer to meditative techniques and states of consciousness, suggesting that some kind of meditative practice was central to the way of life pursued by Brahmin sages who withdrew from the world to pursue liberation. The *Upaniṣads* do not give detailed or systematic instruction in meditation like that found in later sources like the *Yoga Sūtra*; but it is likely that such instruction was passed on orally from teacher to student and was perhaps regarded as secret knowledge.

According to the Pāli sources, the meditation that Siddhārtha practiced under Ārāḷa Kālāma led him to experience a plane of consciousness known as the 'Sphere of Nothingness'. This would seem to be a state of awareness in which attention was drawn fully inward, away from all sensory stimuli.

Siddhārtha reached this sphere of nothingness quite easily, with relatively little effort. He seems to have been quite a gifted meditator according to our available textual sources: so much so that his teacher wanted him to become his successor and pass on his meditation teaching lineage to Siddhārtha's care.

Siddhārtha, however, though he found the sphere of nothingness peaceful and relaxing, and the concentration skills gained in pursuing it useful, did not find that it led to liberation from the cycle of rebirth, or insight into how it might be broken. It is said he therefore thanked his teacher and took his leave, searching for another teacher who might take him closer to his goal.

He then studied meditation with another master of a similar kind. This master was named Udraka Rāmaputra. It is said that under Udraka Rāmaputra, Siddhārtha reached a meditative state even more profound than the sphere of nothingness, called the 'Sphere of Neither Perception nor Non-Perception'.

Once again, Siddhārtha's achievement was highly regarded by his teacher, who wanted to ordain him his successor. And once again, Siddhārtha thanked his teacher and sought another path, finding he still had not resolved the issue of how to free himself and others from karma and rebirth, but only of how to temporarily withdraw from this realm into a more rarefied state of mind.[10]

Siddhārtha then pursued a different path, joining a group of five other ascetics who were practicing severe forms of self-denial. With these ascetics, 'Siddhārtha turned to extreme forms of asceticism in order to conquer his body's primal demands for food, sleep, sex and sensual enjoyment'.[11] The sectarian affiliation of the five ascetics is never mentioned in Buddhist texts, but in the rigour of their practices, they resemble either Jains or Ājīvikas.

As with his previous spiritual pursuits, Siddhārtha excelled at asceticism, surpassing even the other five ascetics in the rigour of his fasting, seeking thereby to purge his consciousness of its remaining karmas and attain absolute knowledge. In time, however, Siddhārtha realized he was in danger of dying of starvation. He did not fear death itself so much as dying without achieving his goals of awakening and sharing the path to freedom with others.

One day, as Siddhārtha was fasting near a river, a boat went by with two musicians aboard: a teacher and a student. The teacher was explaining to the student how to string an instrument, telling the student, 'If the string is too slack, it will not play. If it is too tight, it will snap.'

This simple statement is said to have awakened an insight in Siddhārtha. The luxurious life of the householder, drowning the mind in sensory pleasures, dulls the mind, making it unable to achieve the insight necessary to escape the cycle of rebirth; but the life of extreme asceticism similarly dulls the mind, making clear thought impossible, while also endangering the life of the body before awakening can be achieved. He therefore adopted what he called the *Middle Way* or *Middle Path*: the moderate path between the extremes of luxury and asceticism. This is why the *Vinaya*, the manual of conduct for Buddhist monks, while certainly strict by the standards of a householder, is considerably less austere than that for Jain monks. The concept of a 'middle path' would also become a productive metaphor in Buddhist philosophy, indicating rejection of extreme positions.

Near death, reduced almost to a skeleton by his fasting, and sitting under a tree, Siddhārtha was approached by a young woman named Sujāta. Siddhārtha was so emaciated he looked barely human. Sujāta, in fact, mistook him for a *yakṣa*, the deity or spirit of the tree under which he sat, and offered him a bowl of rice mixed with sweet milk. He accepted her gift, breaking his fast. In the coming days, he ate more regularly, recovering his health and strength.

See that he had abandoned their path of severe asceticism, the other five ascetics with whom he had been practicing saw Siddhārtha as having fallen back into householder life, away from the path to liberation and they left him. He continued in a solitary fashion, practicing the more moderate asceticism he had discovered. Wandering to a place now known as Bodh Gaya, Siddhārtha sat beneath a pipal tree, a descendent of which still grows at the same location today. Having regained his physical health and mental clarity, he began to meditate, resolving not to stop until he had resolved the problem of suffering.

Siddhārtha's awakening

Sitting under what is now called the Bodhi tree, the tree of awakening, Siddhārtha became, in the course of a single night, the Buddha, the Awakened One.[12]

Entering into meditation, he passed through the various 'spheres' of consciousness he had learned from his masters. Penetrating to the core of his being, he encountered the embodiment of his ego: the personification of death and desire, named Māra. Māra, aware that Siddhārtha was on the verge of freeing himself from his realm assailed the young aspirant with visions both tempting and terrifying. In many ways, the temptation of Siddhārtha by Māra is analogous to the temptation of Jesus by Satan in the desert. Both are offered unlimited pleasure and power if they will but yield. Both ultimately refuse and go on to teach their path to others. Satan, however, is a separate being, distinct from Jesus, seeking to dissuade him from his journey as part of his larger defiance of God's plan for humanity. Māra, however, is seen in some Buddhist texts in a psychological light as the personification of egotism and selfishness within us all.[13]

Having overcome Māra's temptations, Siddhārtha penetrated ever more deeply to the core of his being. He began to remember his previous lives, perceiving how the choices he had made in his various forms led, inevitably, to results, and further rebirths, following the principle of karma. 'He recalled his many various previous existences: one birth, two, three, four . . . ten, twenty, thirty, forty, fifty, a thousand, many thousands . . . many hundreds of thousands.'[14] Meditating even more deeply, he began to perceive the past lives of every being that had ever existed, seeing the deep interconnections uniting all beings, and tying them all together in the cycle of action and reaction.

At last, he perceived the means by which the cycle could be broken and karma escaped. In the words of the *Bṛhadāraṇyaka Upaniṣad*, 'One who is attached goes with his action to that very place to which his mind and character cling. Reaching the end of his action [the exhaustion of the results of his karma], of whatever he has done in this world, from that world he returns, back to this world, back to action. That is the course of one who desires"'.[15] If Siddhārtha freed himself from desire, from attachment to the results of his actions, he would be free from the cycle of rebirth. And this is what he did:

> And he truly realized: 'This is the Noble Truth of Suffering; this is the Origination of Suffering; this is the Cessation of Suffering; this is the Noble Truth of the Way leading to the Cessation of Suffering.' Knowing that and seeing that, he was then released from thoughts inclined to sensual desire, he was released from thoughts

inclined to rebirth, he was released from thoughts inclined to ignorance. And released, he had a realization of his liberation: 'Destroyed is my birth; consumed is my striving; done is what had to be done; I will not be born into another existence!' Thus the Blessed One attained to the highest enlightenment.[16]

It is said that Siddhārtha, now the Buddha, remained in meditation for some time after achieving nirvāṇa. He reflected on whether he ought to remain in this state until the death of his body, at which point he would be wholly free, entering the bliss of 'nirvāṇa without remainder', or *mahāparinirvāṇa*. He was, however, now 'awake'. To say someone is a Buddha, an awakened being, is, of course, an analogy. The Buddha is to a person who is awake in the conventional sense as the awake person is to someone who is sleeping and lost in dreams. As a fully awakened being, the Buddha was no longer subject to the illusion of self, of 'your' awakening and 'my' awakening. He saw all beings as interconnected. It is impossible for such a being to behave selfishly. Seeing the suffering of others as no different from his, which is the definition of compassion, the Buddha resolved to share his teaching with the world, so as many beings as possible could be free from the cycle of rebirth.

The Buddha: Standing at the confluence of Vedic, Śramaṇic and sceptical thought

A close examination of the Buddha's teaching, as well as the path he undertook to achieve his realization, reveals that he drew freely from the dominant intellectual currents of his time. He took what he found worked and revised or discarded what did not, drawing together these currents into his own, distinctive synthesis.

From the thought-world of the *Upaniṣads*, one can see that the Buddha drew a profoundly psychological approach to the question of suffering and freedom from rebirth. That which needs to be adjusted and transformed in order for us to be free from this cycle, and from the sufferings of mundane, day-to-day existence, is our own emotive and conceptual process: the way we relate to our experiences.

In short, do we approach our experiences with grasping attachment, with desire and fear (which is essentially negative desire)? Or do we approach our experiences with serene detachment: observing and being fully aware and mindful of all that happens around us, but with the realization that none of this can make us truly happy or unhappy unless we allow it to do so? Our attachment to our experience is the 'fuel' driving the cycle of karma and rebirth. Our attachment impels us to experience the same things repeatedly, like an addict. Eventually, though, we tire of this process and long for something more substantial, transcending the realm of ephemeral states and objects to which we have become accustomed. In the state of mindful detachment, we are fully aware of our experiences, but not attached to them. We cease to seek happiness in fleeting external objects and conditions.

One could say that in the state of mindful detachment, our experiences do not 'stick' to us. This brings to mind the Jain doctrine of karma as a substance literally adhering to the soul. The Buddha's teaching reflects the influence of Jainism no less than it does that of the *Upaniṣads*. The Buddha uses Jain terminology when describing his experience of nirvāṇa (a term also used by the Jains). When he cuts the thread of attachment binding him to the cycle of rebirth, he says he has 'cut off the *āśravas*'. *Āśrava*, one may recall, is the Jain term for the influx of karma into the soul.

In the Buddha's thought, Jain terminology takes on a distinctively psychological cast. One does not see discussions of literal karma particles flowing into or being expelled from the soul; but one does see this terminology being used metaphorically to describe the process by which one is impelled to have certain kinds of experiences due to mental and emotional attachments and freed from these experiences by freeing oneself from these attachments through cultivating insight and equanimity.

Finally, one also sees the imprint of ancient Indian scepticism in the Buddha's tendency to evaluate his own experiences frankly, and to accept no dogmatic position uncritically or without questioning. The Buddha is not a materialist. He rejects materialist dogma no less forcefully than he does certain dogmas of the Brahmins and Jains. But he interrogates his experiences and the predominant ideas of his culture in a critical fashion that is evocative of materialist scepticism.

While the Buddha draws many elements from other teachers of his era, he also freely rejects or modifies elements he does not find compelling or helpful in eradicating suffering. Like the Jains, he rejects the notion that rebirth as a Brahmin has any bearing at all on one's eligibility for spiritual practice or the attainment of liberation. He also rejects the practice of animal sacrifice, common among many of Brahmins of his time, seeing it as cruel and selfish: cruel because of the suffering it causes and selfish because it is offered to fulfil material desires. At the same time, he rejects the Jain emphasis on severe asceticism. While he accepts the teaching of karma and rebirth and rejects the nihilistic materialism of the Lokāyatas, the Buddha's does not teach the existence of a creator deity. The soul is the topic of one of the most interesting and distinctive Buddhist teachings: that what other traditions call the soul (jīva) or self (ātman) is not a thing, but a process. 'The' soul is therefore not literally the same entity from one moment to the next. There is no unchanging 'self'.

In general terms, one can say the Buddha's teaching has affinities to Vedic and Jain thought while at the same time representing its own highly unique contribution to Indian philosophy. It has resonances with the psychological and meditative emphasis of the *Upaniṣads* but also with the Jain emphasis on morality. While morality is present in the world view of the *Upaniṣads*, being deducible from the principle of reciprocity implicit in the concept of karma, the emphasis of the Upaniṣadic path to liberation is on the realization of Brahman: a psychological process, aided by meditation. Meditation allows one to enter progressively deeper states of consciousness, in effect 'peeling away' the more superficial layers of the self and finally attaining awareness of Brahman within, at the core of one's being. One can see this in the practices of the Buddha's early teachers. Conversely, while Jainism includes meditation, its emphasis is not on meditative states, but the practice of ahiṃsā, or non-violence, and developing control of the passions through asceticism.

The Buddha ties these emphases together. They become two of what could be called three pillars of Buddhist practice: meditation and morality, to which the Buddha adds wisdom, or insight. The aim of meditation and morality, from a Buddhist perspective, is to cultivate direct awareness of the true nature of reality. Meditation is essential to this process, as a means of honing the mind and making it a fit instrument for perceiving reality.

The Buddha is sceptical of meditation's leading to an experience of an unchanging reality, like the Brahman of the *Upaniṣads*, because his meditative experience revealed to him a changing flow of experiences. One eventually does return from the sphere of nothingness and the sphere of neither perception nor non-perception to conventional waking consciousness. Meditation, though, nevertheless sharpens the mind, increasing its capacity for awareness of subtle truths. Morality similarly sharpens one's character, turning it away from the pursuit of selfish desires, for such desires are the source of attachment to the cycle of rebirth, and self is the ultimate illusion one must overcome. By shaping one's character and mind through moral and meditative practice, one can perceive the truth behind one's experiences and gain insight.

The four noble truths and the eightfold pth

After the Buddha decided, out of compassion, to share his insight with the world (a choice made, according to some accounts, at the prompting of the deities Brahmā and Indra), he proceeded to walk from Bodh Gaya to the ancient and sacred city of Kāśi (today called Varanasi or Banaras), on the banks of the holy river Ganges. Even as early as the Buddha's time, Kāśi was an ancient and holy city, sacred to the deity Śiva, and a popular pilgrimage site. It is likely the Buddha went there in the hope of encountering other ascetic wanderers with whom he might share his insights.

On the northern outskirts of Kāśi, there is a deer park located in a village called Sarnath. Here, the Buddha encountered the five ascetics with whom he had previously practiced fasting and self-denial. Sensing something different about this wanderer whom they had abandoned after he had apparently left the spiritual path, they overcame their previous anger and disappointment and gathered around him. He then proceeded to preach his first sermon.

According to Buddhist tradition, this first sermon began with the Buddha's sharing of the 'fourfold noble truth' with the five ascetics, who then became his first disciples, 'taking refuge' in him and in his teaching. This noble truth – more widely known today as the 'four noble truths' – is a summary of the core principles of Buddhism.

The four noble truths are:

1. All conditioned states involve suffering.
2. The cause of this suffering is attachment (to external objects and conditions).
3. It is possible to become free from suffering (by becoming free from attachment).
4. The path to freedom from suffering is the noble eightfold path.

The elegance and simplicity of this formula have been a considerable part of the appeal of Buddhist thought – both traditionally, across Asia, and in the modern period, globally. There is no statement here which requires a major leap of faith. None of these statements is incapable of being examined rationally or tested experientially. If one is willing to accept the first truth, the second one makes sense if one reflects upon it. The third is deduced from the first two. And the fourth is something one can try for oneself.[17]

This formula also does not require one to renounce or give up other beliefs or practices, so long as these are not incompatible with the basic moral thrust of the eightfold path (such as animal sacrifice). Buddhism would spread across Asia, the world's first missionary religion, but without, or at least largely without, the bloodshed or the persecution that have accompanied the expansions of other religious ideologies throughout history. To be a Buddhist, one does not have to cease to be a Daoist, a Confucian, a practitioner of Shinto, or an adherent of any of the shamanic traditions indigenous to South, East and Southeast Asia. Some have even argued, in the modern period, that one can be Buddhist and Christian (though, from the Christian side, the doctrine of rebirth can be seen as problematic, depending on one's theology).[18] While Buddhism does not affirm the idea of a creator God – and there are some Buddhist thinkers who argue explicitly against this idea – the four noble truths, by themselves, are not logically incompatible with it.[19] It has also been argued in the modern period that at least on a particular interpretation, the Buddha's teachings, especially with regard to his analysis of empirical experience, are compatible with Hinduism as well.[20]

'All conditioned states involve suffering'

In the original Pāli text, the first noble truth is phrased simply and clearly: *sabbaṃ dukkhaṃ sabbam aniccam*. 'All is suffering. All is impermanent.'

Certainly, there is suffering in life. The story of the Buddha emphasizes the realities of old age, sickness and death. Life is full of tragedies. Many people do not even get to experience old age because their lives are cut short by illness, accident or murder. If we reach adulthood, we all experience disappointments, from the slightest irritations to the most devastating and life-changing losses. But to say that *all* conditioned states involve suffering seems a bit excessive. One can see why there are critics of Buddhism who argue that it is overly pessimistic. How can the Buddha say that we are *always* suffering?

The second half of the Buddha's statement clarifies the meaning of suffering, or *dukkham*, which it would be wise for us to regard as a Buddhist technical term, rather than as *suffering* in the conventional sense. When the Buddha says, 'All is suffering, all is impermanent', he is equating suffering with impermanence. In the words of the popular song, 'All things must pass away.'[21]

Suffering, in the Buddhist sense – *dukkham* – is not simply suffering as usually understood. *Suffering* is also the fact that happiness is impermanent. *Suffering* means we do not experience permanent, lasting happiness, but a series of ephemeral states. Some are happy states. Some are unhappy states. Some are neutral or indifferent (just as Jainism teaches). A more typical expression of this idea in Pāli is *sabbe saṅkhārā aniccā; sabbe saṅkhārā dukkā; sabbe dhamma anattā*: All conditioned states are impermanent;

all conditioned states are suffering; all conditioned states have no self (no permanent essence or substance).

Dukkha could be translated as *instability* or *unsatisfactoriness*. We look for happiness in external objects and conditions, and sometimes we even experience it – for a while. But then things change. We have to keep seeking to sustain our happiness. Just like Brahmin ritualists, who must keep offering sacrifice to sustain the universe and fulfil their desires, we have to keep engaging in action in order to experience its fruits. We do this hoping it will make us happy. Sometimes this even works . . . for a time. But it does not last.

Can there be lasting happiness? Maybe everlasting happiness? The way the Buddha frames the question is: 'Is there a state of freedom from suffering? Is there a state that is not an effect of previous action, of karma, and therefore not subject to the impermanent, unsatisfactory nature of karmic effects?' Is there a state independent of external objects or conditions? The third noble truth's answer to this question is 'yes'. This means judgements of Buddhism as pessimistic are in error; for they do not look beyond the first noble truth. Before we can become free from suffering, though – or rather, *in order to* become free from suffering–we must first understand why it occurs.

'The cause of this suffering is attachment to external objects and conditions'

If one unpacks the first noble truth, the second noble truth becomes obvious. If experience is a series of changing conditions, attachment to any condition will lead to unhappiness, because the conditions to which we are attached are impermanent. We must change our habit of becoming attached to external objects and conditions.

The most dramatic example of the impermanence of our experiences is, of course, death. All that we do occurs in the shadow of death, of which the Buddha teaches we must be mindful.[22] Our loved ones, our achievements, our activities: all of this shall pass away, as we shall ourselves. There is, of course, rebirth. There is continuity from one life to another. But only rarely is this accompanied by memory of who and what we were in a previous lifetime. Even if one allows for the possibility of past life memory, one is still not, in many important ways, the same being one was in a previous existence. One is living in different circumstances, experiencing with a different body, possibly of a different ethnicity, gender and perhaps even species from what one was before. From a Buddhist perspective, one is not even literally the same being through the course of a single lifetime. Think of how different a person is in adulthood from how they were in infancy, or even over the course of adulthood, especially after a traumatic loss, or after many years of experiencing the ups and downs of life. There being no stable point that one can truly grasp, on what basis can a truly lasting happiness be established?

The answer to this is that one must cease grasping after happiness, because true happiness is not an object. One must cease *pursuing* happiness. Only then, paradoxically, can true happiness, lasting happiness, be achieved. Happiness that can be grasped is suffering, for it is an impermanent product of action. True happiness, or freedom from suffering, is not a result of action. It is, rather, what happens when we do *not* grasp. The central paradox of Buddhism (and, to some extent, of all systems of Indian philosophy which see attachment as the root of suffering) is that the key to being truly happy is to stop *trying* to be happy and just *be*.

'It is possible to become free from suffering by becoming free from attachment'

The third noble truth, the truth of the cessation of suffering, as it is traditionally known, is deduced from the first two noble truths. If there is suffering, and if this suffering is caused by attachment, then if one ceases to be attached, suffering will cease as well. This is the ultimate aim of Buddhism: the 'blowing out of the flame' (which is a literal meaning of *nirvāṇa*) of attachment.

It is important to note that this is not presented as only a theoretical possibility. The Buddha teaches that it is possible to become free from suffering because he has done so. For the Buddha, nirvāṇa is not a theoretical possibility, but an empirical reality.

Because it does not involve belief in a creator God and because some in the modern period have suggested that it is, in many respects, akin to psychotherapy, many argue that Buddhism is not a religion. This, of course, depends upon how one defines *religion* (and how one feels about Buddhism and religion, however defined). But there is certainly a dimension of *faith* involved in the third noble truth. Until one attains nirvāṇa for oneself (or at least makes measurable progress on the Buddhist path), to practice Buddhism involves a conviction that Siddhārtha, or someone, became awakened by following this path. This is what 'taking refuge' in the Buddha means (and in his teaching, and in the ascetics who pass it from one generation to the next). This is the ritual by which one formally becomes Buddhist, reciting: 'I go to the Buddha for refuge. I go to his teaching (*dharma*) for refuge. I go to his community of ascetics (*saṅgha*) for refuge.' One affirms faith in the Buddha, his teaching, and his monks and nuns.[23]

It is also important to point out that nirvāṇa, achieved through non-grasping, is an entirely different order of experience from that with which we are familiar from ordinary life. According to the tradition, it is not even entirely correct to describe it as a state of happiness (as I have been doing), because the word *happiness* typically refers to our experiences of impermanent happiness. Nirvāṇa is not, however, simply everlasting happiness: enjoying oneself forevermore. It is freedom from experience as we know it: that is, limited and unsatisfactory. A popular story illustrates this point. A frog returns to the pond where he used to live as a tadpole. The young tadpoles who are still there gather around excitedly to find out about his adventures on dry land, which they have never experienced. 'Can you float over dry land? Can you swim in it?' The frog, of course, has to answer all their questions with a 'no', making it seem as if dry land is no place at all. This is, of course, not true. But there is nothing in the tadpoles' frame of reference to help them comprehend what dry land might truly be like. They have to experience it for themselves.[24]

Similarly, nirvāṇa is understood in Buddhism to be, ultimately, beyond description. This is why it is difficult to answer questions about what nirvāṇa might be like. What, for example, is the status of beings who die after attaining nirvāṇa? Are they in a heavenly state? They are free from suffering and rebirth. But little else can be said definitely about such beings. If it is freedom from experience as we know it, is nirvāṇa a kind of death? If beings who physically die while in the state of nirvāṇa – who leave their bodies behind – are free from the cycle of rebirth, if they will not return to this world, is nirvāṇa the ultimate suicide: the final death, from which one is no longer reborn? Is nirvāṇa, as some early translators of Buddhist texts unfortunately called it, 'extinction'? Such misunderstandings, based on the fact that nirvāṇa cannot be described, lead some to misread Buddhism as pessimistic, gloomy and life-denying. As the tradition formulates it, a being in the state of nirvāṇa cannot be said to exist, cannot be said not to exist, cannot be said to both exist and not exist and cannot be said to neither exist nor not exist.[25]

The fourth noble truth: The eightfold path

It is, of course, one thing to affirm that we must break the habit of attachment to external objects and conditions and cease grasping after happiness to achieve the absolute freedom called *nirvāṇa*. It is quite another to do so. If we have cultivated the habit of grasping for countless lives through infinite time, it must certainly be a difficult habit to break.

It is not impossible, though, because the Buddha did it (as did other Buddhas before him). In fact, according to the Pāli texts, many others have also achieved this goal, like those who heard the Buddha teach, especially his closest disciples, who became *arhats*. Arhats are 'worthy ones', who attain nirvāṇa by practicing the path taught by a Buddha, a self-awakened being.

The fourth noble truth completes the thought process begun in the first noble truth. It has been established that conventional experience entails suffering. Our unhappiness is a function of our grasping after impermanent experiences in the hope that they will yield lasting happiness. If we cease this grasping, our suffering will end. But how do we do this? By following the eightfold path!

It is important to note, first, that the eightfold path does not consist of eight steps, followed sequentially. One does not complete the first part, then the second, then the third. Rather, one should see the eightfold path as a collection of eight virtues one seeks to cultivate all together, as part of a total way of life. This is illustrated by the eight-spoked wheel which has become a symbol of Buddhism. If one looks at the eight-spoked wheel, the outermost portion, the wheel itself, represents the cycle of suffering and rebirth. Day after day, life after life, we pursue happiness around this wheel, never quite catching it: or rather, sometimes catching it, but then having it slip away and having to pursue it all over again. The eightfold path is the way out of this vicious cycle.

As we take up the eightfold path, we proceed, simultaneously, down the eight spokes from the edge of the wheel to the calm, still point at the centre: the hub, representing nirvāṇa.

The eight mutually supportive virtues making up the eightfold path are often grouped into three sets, each of which represents one of the three 'pillars' of Buddhism: insight (or wisdom), morality, and meditation. The eightfold path can thus be represented schematically as follows:

<u>Insight/Wisdom</u>

- Right Understanding
- Right Motive

<u>Morality</u>

- Right Speech
- Right Action
- Right Livelihood

<u>Meditation</u>

- Right Effort
- Right Mindfulness
- Right Meditation

Insight (or wisdom): Right understanding and right motive

Right understanding is understanding that reality is as the Buddha teaches it to be: a series of momentary events, each arising briefly based on the moment before it and then passing on to make way for the next. To become attached to these moments is to suffer, as each moment passes away and change is inevitable. Freedom comes from detachment. This is the core message of the four noble truths. There are also the doctrines of 'No Self' and interdependent origination, or *Interbeing*, both of which will be discussed in more depth shortly, but both of which essentially teach the insubstantiality of the ego. All these teachings imply one another and point to the idea that the ultimate object to which the self is attached is itself. Self is an illusion, to be renounced if nirvāṇa is to occur. Buddhist teaching is a device for achieving this purpose. Even the dharma is not an object grasp, but a tool to use.

Right motive, sometimes translated as *right thought*, is the thought preceding an action. A right motive is based on right understanding. A wrong motive is based on egotism and greed: on selfish desire. Given that self is an illusion, to act based on the desires of self is to act in a deluded fashion and create more suffering in the world – both for others and for the streams of experience we conventionally call 'ourselves'.

One might recall the discussion in regard to Jainism about the relative weight placed on motive versus the effects of an act by the Jain and Buddhist traditions. Jains and Buddhists both teach that motive is essential in determining if an action is good or evil. One who deliberately runs down a squirrel with one's car, from sadistic delight at causing harm, is more blameworthy than someone who accidentally runs down a squirrel because she is speeding her friend to the hospital for urgent, lifesaving medical care. Jainism, however, is more focused on the outcome of an action, rather than its motive, in determining whether it is good or evil. This is likely because avoiding harm to the life forms pervading the environment is so central to Jain practice. Recall that the Jain tradition focuses primarily on the practice of *ahiṃsā* – non-violence in thought, word and deed – as the primary requirement for liberation from the rebirth cycle.

Buddhism, however, focusing on psychological transformation as the main prerequisite for liberation, focuses more upon the motives behind our actions than upon their outcomes. Harm brought about unintentionally through our actions is tragic, and of course to be avoided if possible. It is not, however, morally blameworthy, so long as it is not due to some gross negligence on our part (such as, for example, drunken or distracted driving, which we know is likely to lead to harm to other living beings, even if we do not directly will it to be so).

Morality: Right speech, right action and right livelihood

Even as Buddhism emphasizes motive over outcome, and even while its overall emphasis is more psychological than moral, at least compared with Jainism, morality is nevertheless a central component of the Buddhist path. For a Buddhist, no less than for a Jain (or a Hindu), liberation requires the transformation of the whole person. This includes how one relates to others through one's actions in the world: one's moral choices.

Moral behaviour, from a Buddhist perspective, is behaviour which undermines the illusion of self, or ego, giving a sense of our deep interconnectedness with all beings. Interconnectedness is the true nature of things. Moral behaviour is consistent with reality as perceived by enlightened beings. While motive is the central determinant of morality, there are patterns of behaviour which, experience has shown, are more conducive to the path than others.

The three virtues right speech, right action and right livelihood making up the morality component of the eightfold path focus on avoiding destructive acts and promotive beneficial habits of mind.

Right speech is not only telling the truth, but also speaking in an edifying and positive way. One can imagine a situation in which one speaks the truth, but nevertheless behaves in an immoral fashion: such as gossiping, or offering criticism in a way that is hurtful, not constructive. Even if true, such speech acts constitute wrong speech. One must speak the truth, but in a constructive, helpful way, not a derogatory or hurtful one.

Like Jainism, Buddhism, as a Śramaṇa tradition, distinguishes between householders, who are relative beginners on the spiritual path, and ascetics, who are regarded as more advanced. Right speech, for Buddhist monks and nuns, refers not only to speech as just described, but to avoiding any unnecessary speech. Buddhist monks are expected to maintain silence rather than 'prattling on': filling the silence with meaningless speech.

Right action refers to morally correct action in general. As a guide to what this means, the Buddhist tradition provides a set of five moral principles, or 'five precepts' (*pañcaśīla*). Part of the formal process of becoming a Buddhist – after one has taken refuge in the Buddha, his teaching, and his community of ascetics – is to take these five precepts. One will note a considerable overlap between these five precepts and the vows of Jainism, as well as the moral restraints of Yoga:

1. Non-violence: to 'refrain from destroying living beings'
2. To refrain from stealing: to avoid 'taking what is not given'
3. To refrain from sexual misconduct
4. To refrain from false speech
5. To refrain from taking intoxicating substances.

Much as in Jainism, the expectations for householders are not as strict as those for ascetic practitioners. Regarding non-violence, householders are expected to do no deliberate harm to living things, but nevertheless engage in the normal activities of householders which might do harm on a microscopic level, like driving vehicles and cooking.

Buddhist monks and nuns are expected to be more observant in this regard, though the level of strictness is less than that expected of Jain monks and nuns. It is worth noting that neither Buddhist ascetics nor laypeople are vegetarian to the extent that Jains are. While Jain ascetics view meat as an impure and inappropriate form of food for them to take, Buddhist monks are expected to take what they are given, even if it is non-vegetarian. The only restrictions are that monks and nuns may not kill animals themselves, nor are any animals to be killed specifically for them. But if there is already meat in the house when Buddhist monks arrive and the householder gives them this meat, the monks are expected to eat it with detachment.

It is noteworthy that the rules surrounding food for Jain ascetics are primarily focused on *nonviolence* – the principle that no harm, or at least the minimal harm possible, should be involved in its preparation and serving – but the rules surrounding food for Buddhist ascetics are primarily focused on *detachment* – that the monks refrain from thinking such thoughts as, 'This food is tasty' or, 'This food has an unpleasant texture.' This difference in Jain and Buddhist dietary rules may reflect the roles of moral and psychological transformation in these two similar, yet contrasting, traditions.

It is also noteworthy that the precept of non-violence, for a householder, does not preclude violence for self-defence or the defence of others–the latter, in fact, being a duty for householders. This is also true of Jainism, interestingly and is consistent with the existence of Jain and Buddhist kings throughout history who engaged in warfare. Warfare is ideally to be purely defensive in nature. Again, the intention is central. Does one fight out of fear or hatred for one's enemy, or to prevent greater suffering from being inflicted?

Refraining from sexual misconduct, for ascetics, involves complete celibacy, as it does for Jain ascetics. For householders, this refers to marital fidelity. In general, it refers to not allowing sexual desire – certainly a powerful potential source of attachment – to become a dominant force in one's life. Indeed, there are meditative practices designed to help those for whom overcoming lust is particularly difficult to achieve greater detachment. These involve meditating on decomposing corpses in order to overcome attachment to beautiful human bodies.[26]

In general, one can say that Buddhism promotes an ethos of adhering strictly and seriously to moral principles, but not being judgmental or censorious regarding the behaviour of others, nor allowing one's principles to prevent one from acting for the greater good, even if this involves the rules being bent. A famous story tells of two Buddhist monks traveling in the forest. They came to a river. Standing on the bank and wanting to cross was a beautiful woman, but she was afraid of the river's powerful current. One of the monks offered to carry her across, which he did, setting her gently on the further shore. The woman then continued on her way, and the monks continued on theirs. The other monk was quite indignant about the behaviour of his companion, for Buddhist monks and nuns are not allowed even to touch a person of another gender. The first monk could tell his companion was agitated and asked what was bothering him. The second angrily reproached the first: 'You should be ashamed of yourself for carrying that woman! We are not even to touch a woman, and you carried her across the river!' The first monk smiled and replied, 'I left that woman on the riverbank. I can see you are still carrying her!'[27]

Among the five precepts, the one most distinctive to Buddhism – and not shared by the Jain and Yoga traditions – is the precept to avoid intoxicating substances. This does not mean Jain or Yoga practitioners are permitted or expected to indulge in these substances. On the contrary, Jains see the fermentation process involved with the manufacture of alcohol to be violent. This leads to the Jain prohibition of alcohol on the grounds not of drunkenness, but of non-violence. Again, the principle operating in the Buddhist case is a psychological one, while the Jain principle is moral. Intoxicants distort the mind's ability to perceive reality correctly. Similarly, in the Sāṃkhya and Yoga traditions, which will be discussed in a later chapter of this book, alcohol is seen as a *tamasic* substance, and is thus forbidden as something which is obstructive to any serious spiritual practice. Intoxication is also conducive, according to all these traditions, to running afoul of the other moral precepts. At the same time, as Buddhism has spread globally, there has been some flexibility about alcohol consumption in practice, with an emphasis on moderation replacing complete abstinence in some Buddhist cultures, at least for householders.

Right livelihood refers to pursuing one's livelihood in ways consistent with and conducive to the goals of the spiritual path. Earning a living by killing animals or making weapons that could be used for other than defensive purposes are most often given as examples of wrong livelihood.

Meditation: Right effort, right mindfulness, right meditation

The 'pillar' of meditation is made up not only of meditation itself, but of three types of mental cultivation – including meditation – essential to attaining nirvāṇa.

The first of these is right effort. On the Buddhist path, one seeks to correct the tendencies of countless lifetimes. This cannot be done easily or all at once. It requires persistence and effort. One must bring a disciplined mind to the Buddhist path. Even when one errs and strays from this path, one must return to one's practice and resolve to do better if one wants to attain the goal.

Right mindfulness can be explained in comparison and contrast with meditation. Looking first at meditation, Buddhist meditation, is much like what is found in other Indian traditions: the systematic calming and quieting of the conscious mind so it enters a state of observant, detached, awareness of its own contents.

The distinctive Buddhist contribution to meditation is captured in the term *vipaśyanā* – or, in Pāli, *vipassanā*. *Vipassanā* is 'insight meditation'. Its aim is to be aware of one's thoughts from moment to moment, and to correct the tendency to follow and grasp at thoughts in an unproductive fashion. Rather than suppressing one's thoughts, in Buddhist meditation, one observes them; but does so in a detached fashion, keeping the attention primarily on the breath. One does not violently push away or repress thoughts – even those which would tend to lead to problematic behaviours if indulged. Nor does one indulge these thoughts, identifying and engaging with them in the old, habitual fashion. One observes them in detail, becoming aware of how they emerge and how they pass away. Not unlike the way in which talking about one's problems with a counsellor leads to reduction in anxiety, mindful awareness of thoughts similarly leads to a lessening in their intensity and, in time, their frequency as well.

The result of this practice is that one gradually becomes aware of one's thoughts as a mental flow distinct from one's vantage point as an observer. We typically identify with our thoughts and the emotions accompanying them. This is reflected in our language. We say things like, 'I'm sad' or 'I'm happy.' During vipassanā, one watches one's thoughts as an objective reality separate from oneself, almost like images in a movie theatre, or like clouds in the sky.

One then realizes that one can become as involved in or as detached from this process as one wishes. Gradually, the hold our thoughts have upon us, our tendency to become worried or desirous or obsessive about particular ideas or memories, becomes reduced. In time, it disappears altogether. At an advanced stage, one may even cut off the flow of thoughts, a state called the 'trance of cessation' (*nirodha samāpatti*).[28] This is a kind of 'practice' for nirvāṇa, in which one has attained complete control over one's tendency to grasp after thoughts. It also makes it possible to place one's full attention and energy where one chooses, without distraction: such as one's daily duties. This brings us to mindfulness.

Mindfulness is bringing the mental control and attitude of detached awareness cultivated in depth during meditation to one's day-to-day existence. Mindfulness is bringing one's awareness fully into the present moment, rather than being distracted by thoughts of the present or future. It is being fully aware of one's internal and external environment. This also enables greater control over one's responses to external stimuli.

It would be a mistake to think the state of mind Buddhism cultivates is coldly indifferent to the experiences – the joys and sufferings – of others or oneself. Indeed, as one pursues the path, and the hold of egotism – of 'self' – is reduced on one's mind, and one becomes more deeply aware of one's interconnectedness with all other beings, the ideal is that one's compassion – one's capacity to feel the sufferings of others as one's own – increases. To be in a state of mindful detachment is not to view oneself or others coldly or clinically, without compassion.

But it *is* to view oneself and others *objectively*, without bias: without attempting to distort the reality we perceive to bring it into harmony with our desires. We become aware of how much of our conventional experience is shaped by our desires for things to happen in one way or another: our attachments to objects and conditions. In the state of mindful detachment, one does not cease to have feelings – including desires and fears. But the ability of these to overwhelm us, to control our lives, is lessened. Their hold on our peace of mind and inner equilibrium is loosened.

One then becomes more effective in practicing compassion. If a loved one were injured and we had called an ambulance for medical assistance, would we rather have medical technicians whose 'compassion' was so great they panicked and fainted at the sight of blood or broken bones? Or would we want a medic who remained calm and cool-headed – in a word, detached – to administer care with the maximum efficiency? The Buddha, in fact, often describes himself as a physician, whose aim is to cure the ailment of worldly existence. True compassion, effective compassion, is not incompatible with, and may even require, detachment. This does not mean one is lacking in love for others. It means one's love is free from the pollution of egotistical fear and craving.

No self: A middle path between materialism and the idea of an *Unchanging* soul

The teaching of No Self is the most distinctive and difficult to grasp of Buddhist concepts. In a Western context, where there is a clash between Christianity and atheistic materialism, if one hears a person deny the existence of a self, a likely assumption is that the person is a materialist, denying the reality of a soul that survives beyond death and affirming instead that consciousness and its contents are nothing but a by-product of physical processes. This, as we have seen, is the view of the Lokāyatas. In the West, this view is sometimes overlaid with a concept of selfhood as a cultural construct. But there is still an assumption that all that might be called a 'self' simply vanishes on the death of the physical body, except perhaps in the memories of those who knew the person while they were alive, or in the artefacts they left behind, or their genetic inheritance.

Coming from this context, the assumption is quickly made that the Buddha, in teaching No Self, held this view as well: that he was a materialist who saw consciousness as a by-product of the body, and self as nothing but a psychological (and by extension cultural) construct. Some contemporary Buddhists in the West seem to take this view, or one close to it. Admiring Buddhist moral teaching and finding benefit from practices like mindfulness and meditation, but accepting materialism, they see concepts like reincarnation as quaint cultural relics, and not essential to the Buddha's teaching, which they take to be something like an ancient Indian secular humanism.[29]

This is not, however, what the Buddha taught. While the Buddha rejected what he called the extreme of 'eternalism', which holds that an eternal and unchanging self exists, he rejected with equal force the other extreme of 'annihilationism': the idea of a destructible, material 'self' found in both the Lokāyata philosophy of ancient India and in contemporary materialisms which look to neuroscience and anthropology for their account of human consciousness.

The Buddha taught, if the accounts of his teaching are a reliable guide, that rebirth is real. This was not so much a doctrine he uniquely promoted as one he took for granted. It was widely held in his environment. But he is also said to have experienced it directly. Traditional accounts of the night of his awakening characterize it specifically in terms of a series of stages which include a recollection of all his own past lives, followed by a perception of the past lives of all beings. In fact, the Buddha is depicted in Pāli and Sanskrit texts as routinely telling stories, called *Jātakas*, about his own past lives and those of his disciples to convey moral lessons.

This is not to say it is impossible to adapt Buddhism to the contemporary world, or that the Buddha himself may not have had his own set of cultural blinders and limitations.[30] Contemporary Buddhists in the West who see the doctrine of rebirth as a dispensable part of their tradition make a good point, and a deeply Buddhist one, when they argue that clinging to views such as belief in rebirth *because one is afraid of death and change* means this belief is an object of attachment and clinging, and thereby a source of suffering. And all such attachments need to severed in order to reach awakening.

Of course, the daily news and human history are full of stories of how fanatical clinging to cherished beliefs causes suffering not only for those who are doing the clinging, but all too often, for those on whom the 'clingers' seek to impose their world view. Buddhism is certainly not about fanatically affirming the doctrine of rebirth.

At the same time, though, the denial of rebirth, or the soul, or any spiritual reality, can itself become an object of attachment, just as much as the affirmation of these things can do. Philosopher David Ray Griffin refers to this as 'negative wishful thinking'.[31] Both believers and deniers have done abundant damage to their fellow living beings in the name of their respective ideologies, their clinging to either materialist or spiritualist views. Communist regimes in the twentieth century, holding to an adamantly materialist and anti-religious ideology, were no less involved in bloodshed than those who have inflicted violence in the name of religion. It is not at all clear that materialist beliefs are less likely to cause damage than non-materialist ones.

It may also be the case that in rejecting the concept of rebirth, one will miss the ways in which this belief radically undermines and transforms our sense of ego in relation to other beings. If it is likely that I have been, in different lifetimes, a being of many genders, ethnicities and even species, then this militates against any kind of prejudice towards others.

The problem, it seems, is not so much with the *content* of a belief as the *attitude* with which it is held. Are they objects of attachment? If so, it is better to let them go than to cling to them. Beliefs need to be held in ways that allow us, and indeed encourage us, to interact lovingly with our fellow beings, and not in ways that create hatred and lingering ill will. It is not our beliefs that are themselves the problem, so much as our inappropriate attachment to them. This, at least, is an ideal Buddhist approach to belief.[32]

The five aggregates

If there is no self, though, as the Buddha teaches, and if there is also rebirth, what, then, is reborn? For that matter, what is it that creates one's sense of personal continuity from moment to moment, from day to day, and from year to year? Without even turning to the doctrine of rebirth, one can see clearly that I, as an adult, am not literally the same being that I was when I was a baby. But there is nevertheless some sense of continuity between that baby and this adult that makes me feel justified in saying I was *that* baby and not another one. If there is no self, what is it that makes that baby 'me'?

The Buddha's answer to these questions is the *pañca skandha*, or five aggregates: form, sensation, perception, habitual tendencies and consciousness.

The Buddha taught that what we falsely call (and then cling to as) 'self' is not really a self at all. It is, rather, a continuum, a flow of events. The word 'self' is like the word 'river'. As a similarly minded Greek thinker of the same period, Heraclitus, tells us, we cannot step in the same river twice. We may try to do so. We may think we are doing so. But the water flowing over our foot the second time we place it in the river is not the same water that flowed over it the first time. That water has already gone downstream. None of us is the same being from moment to moment. The stream of consciousness is constantly flowing, its contents changing, sometimes subtly and sometimes dramatically, from moment to moment and from lifetime to lifetime.

A 'self', on the Buddha's understanding, possesses two qualities which he views as unreal and incoherent: independence and eternality. In other words, a self is something whose existence is unaffected by and unrelated to anything else, and it is something that does not change.

As we have seen, this is how Vedic and Jain thinkers, respectively, characterize ātman and jīva: as something that remains essentially the same as the body changes, passing through old age and death, and then moving on to another rebirth and so on. Jains do speak of the jīva as, in a sense, changing, due to its karmic modifications, but as nevertheless unchanging in its basic, core essence.

According to the Buddha, no such entity exists. All entities, rather, are interrelated and in a state of constant flux. Rather than a unitary, changeless self, the Buddha speaks in terms of the dynamic interplay of the five aggregates. The five aggregates can be seen as five phases or aspects of a single moment in the existence of what adherents of other philosophies would call the 'self'. Each moment of the interplay of these aggregates is unique and unrepeatable. It arises and then passes, with the next moment inheriting some of its characteristics, but with a few subtle changes. The flow from one moment to the next creates the sense of a continuously existing entity; but it is really a series of discrete moments existing in succession.

This succession of moments could be compared to the still photographs that constitute a motion picture. The running together of the individual photographs, each of which is unique and distinct from the ones that precede and follow it, creates a sense of smooth and continuous motion. Only if we slow down the running of the film can we notice each individual photo making it up. Similarly, through the profound states of meditation he experienced, the Buddha observed the fact that what we normally perceive as a continuous flow of experience is made of discrete, individual moments. It is the succession from one moment to the next, the fact that moments exist in what appears to us as a causal sequence, that creates for us the phenomenon of time. Time itself is not real in an ultimate sense. It is the ordering of moments in a particular way – moments that are the fundamental units or 'atoms' of our experience – that gives rise to the phenomenon of time. Time is the sequence of moments as they appear to our experience.

Each moment of our experience is further divisible into the five aggregates which make it up. If we say each moment of experience is like an 'atom' of time, the five aggregates are the 'subatomic particles' making up these atoms. It is the aggregates that flow from death to rebirth.

Each experience is an experience *of* something. This basic content is the aggregate called *form* (*rūpa*). It consists of the objects of the six senses: the five familiar physical senses, but also a sixth sense consisting of the mind. The Buddhist idea of a 'sixth sense' is not related specifically to paranormal phenomena like telepathy or clairvoyance (though traditionally, Buddhist thinkers, like adherents of most systems of Indian philosophy, are open to such possibilities).

The mind as a sixth sense refers to the means by which we 'sense' ideas and emotions: experiential contents that do not fall under the heading of the five physical senses. The objects of the six senses – colours, sounds, flavours, smells, tactile sensations, as well as ideas and emotions – are known in Buddhism as *dharmas*. As we shall see, Buddhist thinkers after the time of the Buddha began to speculate about the nature of these dharmas. At this point, it suffices to think of them as the basic building blocks of any possible experience. One of the dharmas is nirvāṇa: a unique dharma that cannot be reduced to any other experiential form.

It is important to note that unlike the Jain tradition, Buddhism does not posit a sharp duality between the physical and non-physical – ajīva and jīva. Some interpreters of the five aggregates characterize the aggregate of 'form' as consisting of the body, with the other four making up the non-material aspects of one's being. This is not, however, entirely right. The Buddha's approach to experience seems closer to what in Western philosophy, would be called a *phenomenological* approach. Experiences are experiences: whether of sensory phenomena like colours or sounds, or of concepts or emotional states. The contents of all experiences can be seen as examples of 'form'. Characterizing some of these as 'physical' and some as 'mental' is a projection. They are simply dharmas. As we shall see, later Buddhist philosophies will see experience as, fundamentally, a modification of consciousness. But the Buddha's original teaching, at least inasmuch as this is discernible from the Pāli sources, at least seems to be closer to what Western philosophers might call a 'neutral monism', affirming that the basic elements of experience are neither purely material nor purely mental in nature. They just are.

This interpretation of the Buddha as a neutral monist is consistent with the overall picture of the character of his thought given in early Buddhist texts: that he was uninterested in speculating about issues he saw as irrelevant to the path to freedom from suffering. Whether the fundamental forms of our experience are essentially physical or essentially mental in nature or some mix of the two is certainly a good candidate for a question the Buddha regarded as unconducive to spiritual edification.

Out of the range of possible dharmas, in any given moment of experience, only some are acting as objects of *sensation* (*vedanā*): the second of the five aggregates. Sensation is contact between a form and the sensory organ appropriate to it. In an experience of saltiness, for example, the form consisting of a salty flavour comes into contact with the tongue. In an experience of a concept or emotional state, the form which consists of that concept or state comes into contact with the mind. And so on.

After contact comes the third aggregate: *perception* (*saṃjñā*). At any given moment, we are sensing many things that we are not necessarily perceiving because they do not rise to the level of our full attention. If I am walking through Times Square in New York and having a conversation with a friend, I am sensing a multitude of sights and sounds. All these sensations, though, do not take on the same level of importance in my experience. If they did, I would be overwhelmed and unable to function. Of the many things that I am sensing in that moment, I am *perceiving* only a few: my friend, the contents of the conversation we are having, the words my friend is saying, the words I want to say in response and whatever objects are immediately in front of us as we walk.

Moving to a more refined level – from the sphere of all possible objects of experience (the forms), to the selection of possibilities currently in contact with my six senses (the sensations), to the selection of those sensations that attract my attention (the perceptions) – we move to the fourth aggregate, which consists of my responses to my perceptions. These responses occur so quickly – at least until I have cultivated mindfulness and meditation – that they happen in a way that is almost unconscious. These are my *habitual tendencies*.

Known as *saṃskāras*, the habitual tendencies are of three basic kinds: aversion, attraction and indifference. This is also how the kaṣāyas are categorized: the passionate states, enumerated in Jainism, which draw karmic particles to the soul. In Buddhism, the saṃskāras play an analogous role in binding a being to the cycle of suffering and rebirth as the kaṣāyas play in the Jain model of this process. In Buddhism, this process is more psychological, and in Jainism, it is more physical. It is at the level of the habitual tendencies that one can see the eightfold path operating as a therapeutic system for modifying the habits of attachment leading to suffering and rebirth.

The fifth aggregate is consciousness: the awareness of the other four aggregates as making up a moment of experience. If the other aggregates constitute the content of an experience, as well as its emotional tone, it is consciousness that makes this content an object of awareness.

A process self?

One might argue that the Buddha creates unnecessary confusion when he says there is no self. One could say, as some contemporary interpreters have done, that the Buddha is not so much denying a *self* as denying *an entity that is independent and changeless*. Rather than saying 'There is no self', the Buddha could have said, 'There is a changing self.'

In other words, one could say the Buddha is affirming not an essentialist self, but a process self: a self that is interdependent with all other beings and in a state of constant flux. This is a fair interpretation of the Buddha's teaching if one comes from a context where the word 'self' has the pliability to allow for it. One suspects, though, that the Buddha, for whom 'self' implies 'something independent and changeless', would find the idea of an interdependent and changing self to be like a round square or square circle. A 'process self' would likely be, in the Buddha's linguistic and conceptual context, an oxymoron.

This suspicion is borne out by the reaction of other Buddhist schools of thought, after the time of the Buddha, to the group of Buddhist thinkers called *Pudgalavādins*, or Personalists. The Personalists had the same idea of self-as-process that some modern interpreters have proposed.[33] They taught that something called the 'person', or *pudgala*, emerges from the coming together of the five aggregates: a sixth, new entity, not simply identical to the five aggregates, but dependent upon them. Again, this is, at first glance, not an unreasonable way to think about personhood in Buddhist terms. But the aversion to the term 'self' runs deep in Buddhism, and the rest of the tradition rejected this approach.[34]

The Personalists were trying to render the Buddhist teaching of the radically impermanent and momentary character of all phenomena consistent with our daily, common-sense experience of the continuity of phenomena through time: including our sense of being the same entity from one moment, day and year to the next, with such traits as memory and so on. As we shall see, the struggle with the implications of radical impermanence became a major preoccupation of Buddhist thinkers for much of the history of Buddhist philosophy.

'Self', from a Buddhist perspective, is at best a handy, conventional designation. To cite a famous dialogue from the Pāli literature between the Buddhist monk Nāgasena and the Indo-Greek king Milinda, one uses the term 'chariot' to refer to the coming together of certain parts – an axle pole, wheels, a cart and so on. In the same way, one also uses personal terms, such as 'Nāgasena', 'Milinda' and 'Jeffery D. Long' to refer to the coming together of the five aggregates and their flow from one moment to another. But when the five aggregates come together, they do not make a sixth, new thing, as the Personalists affirmed. There is no essence of the person, just as there is no 'chariotness' hiding in the parts of what we conveniently call a chariot. 'We' are nothing other than the coming together of the five aggregates from one moment to the next.

At its worst, 'self' is the ultimate object and locus of all clinging – all attachment – and so of all suffering. This is why it is to be eliminated, and the concept undermined at every turn of the spiritual life. This is why Buddhist thought is so preoccupied with denying any substantial essence or singular existence underlying persons or objects. The idea of No Self is intimately connected with the second noble truth: desire for objects as the cause of suffering.

The Buddha and the philosophy of the *Upaniṣads*: Which self is the Buddha rejecting?

The renowned scholar of early Buddhism, Richard Gombrich, has argued, based on certain turns of phrase attributed to the Buddha in the Pāli scriptures, that he was certainly familiar with at least some portions of the earliest *Upaniṣads*: the *Bṛhadāraṇyaka Upaniṣad* and the *Chāndogya Upaniṣad*. Even if he did not study the actual texts, ideas in them were circulating in his milieu.[35]

In terms of the Buddha's intellectual milieu, the context in which he formulates his way to freedom from suffering, the No Self doctrine certainly sounds, at least at first glance, like a firm rejection of the central teaching of the *Upaniṣads*: that there is a true Self beyond the conventional self, or ego, and that this Self – or ātman – is identical with the unchanging, independent and eternal ground of all being – Brahman. In the philosophy of the *Upaniṣads*, which were being composed during the Buddha's lifetime, we get rid of the lower self to realize the higher Self: our true nature, as opposed to the false ego, which is part of the changing and not entirely real material realm.

It could be argued, as some adherents of this philosophy have done, that the self that is rejected in the No Self doctrine is the lower self that the *Upaniṣads* also teach us to overcome to realize the deeper truth of Brahman, the infinite consciousness that is our true Self. This would mean there is really no deep incompatibility between Vedānta and Buddhism: that both are aimed at realizing the same ultimate truth beyond the realm of changing phenomena.

Consistently, however, at least throughout the Pāli literature widely taken to represent the earliest, most authentic record of the Buddha's teaching, the Buddha simply rejects the term 'self' wherever it arises, saying no such thing is anywhere to be found. Might it be that the Buddha does not truly reject the ultimate reality the Vedānta tradition calls *ātman*, but rather rejects any attempt to reify or objectify it – attempts that result in its becoming an object of attachment, or its conflation with the ego? The *Upaniṣads*, too, contain a current of apophatic thought – the idea that the highest reality cannot be captured in words. Recall that Brahman is that from which 'words recoil', which is *neti, neti*: 'not this, not that'. Does the Buddha's teaching perhaps reflect a thread of Upaniṣadic apophaticism that he encountered in his early wanderings?

One Pāli text on which Vedāntic interpreters of Buddhism have seized in order to show the Buddha's thought to be compatible with Vedānta is *Udāna* 8.3. In this text, the Buddha says:

> There is, O monks, an unborn, unbecome, unmade, unconditioned. If, O monks, there were not that unborn, unbecome, unmade, unconditioned, you could not know an escape here from the born, become, made, and conditioned. But because there is an unborn, unbecome, unmade, unconditioned, therefore you do know an escape from the born, become, made, and conditioned.

While the Buddha does not refer to this 'unborn, unbecome, unmade, unconditioned' as a self, it certainly meets the description an adherent of Vedānta might give of the higher or true Self beyond the ego; for Brahman, too, is 'unborn, unbecome, unmade, unconditioned', and makes liberation possible. It is important to note, though, that the Buddha, adamantly refuses to make this move.

The Buddha also does not identify the 'unborn, unbecome, unmade, unconditioned' with consciousness, which is one of the five aggregates. As an aggregate, consciousness is undergoing constant change and is not, as the Buddha emphatically states on a number of occasions, a 'self'. Vedānta, however, identifies consciousness with the highest Self: with Brahman.

The atomic versus the unitary and unchanging nature of consciousness also seems to be a genuine difference between the teaching of the Buddha and the philosophy of the *Upaniṣads*. And while some correspondences can be drawn between at least a couple of the five aggregates and the five kośas or 'sheaths' encompassing the ātman in the *Upaniṣads*, these concepts are not identical.

On the nature of consciousness, too, though, there is scope for speculation on the potential compatibility of these two philosophies. As both continued to develop throughout the centuries, both focused on cultivation of a state of consciousness 'purified' of the subject and object structure of conventional awareness. As with the issue of self and Self, an adherent of Vedānta might argue that the consciousness making up the fifth aggregate is conventional consciousness, not the non-dual consciousness characterizing nirvāṇa in Buddhism and the *turīya*, or 'fourth state' described in the *Upaniṣads*. This remains a disputed issue today. Buddhist scholar Walpola Rahula, for example, sharply rejects the idea that there is some kind of deeper self (or Self) lurking beneath the surface of Buddhist thought.[36] Scholars of Indian philosophy generally hold that Buddhist philosophies are in opposition to Vedānta and other Hindu systems, despite the many interesting similarities that obtain among them. This is certainly how Buddhist and non-Buddhist thinkers in India tended to see the situation in ancient and classical times, when they wrote polemics critiquing one another's views and sought to gain institutional advantages over one another.

Interbeing

We have seen that what is conceived of as a stable, continuous 'self' in other systems of thought is seen in Buddhism as a process of momentary events. It is not appropriate to see this process as a 'self', according to Buddhism, because of the grasping and attachment associated with this term. The aim of Buddhism as a practice is to cease all such grasping, and in so doing, to enter the state of nirvāṇa.

But what is the nature of this 'process'? What is it that is passed on from one moment to the next as one passes away and the other arises? This question brings us to the Buddha's doctrine of interdependent origination (*pratītya samutpāda*), or dependent co-arising, or – to use a term coined by the modern Buddhist master, Thich Nhat Hanh – Interbeing.[37]

Interbeing is the Buddha's response to the problem of causation, discussed previously in relation to materialist scepticism. One billiard ball hits another and the second one moves. Chemicals are mixed together and a reaction occurs. Fire is lit on the mountain and smoke rises from it. But does one actually ever perceive causation?

Recall that, as opposed to other systems of thought which affirm that the reality of causation can be inferred from repeated observation, Indian sceptics – anticipating David Hume by about two millennia – deny that inference provides reliable knowledge of causation. How do we know, even after many observations, that the billiard ball will move the next time it is struck, that the chemical reaction will occur, or that the smoke on the mountain is from a fire or something else?

The Buddha approaches this issue an ingeniously. If reality consists of discrete moments, occurring one after another, how does one account for the sense of continuity which runs through them and leads to the mistaken sense that we are continuously existing beings, rather than a series of momentary processes? One way to approach this is to say that each moment of experience gives rise to, or *causes*, the next. The causal efficacy of each moment is felt in the next as resemblance to its predecessor.

Each 'still photograph' in the 'motion picture' of existence, in other words, slightly resembles the ones preceding and following it, thus accounting for the smooth flow of experience. The moments do not occur in a chaotic or random fashion, which would make a world impossible. Also, given that Buddhism teaches the reality of karma and the importance of moral behaviour to one's future spiritual state, one must be able to affirm that certain actions *cause* certain results to occur.

On the other hand, conventional Indian accounts of causation, in which certain effects must inevitably arise under certain causal conditions, are also problematic from a Buddhist perspective. If we say fire always, inevitably, produces smoke, we are giving fire a 'self': an unchanging essence that will remain the same under all circumstances, contradicting the selfless, impermanent nature of things that is central to Buddhist thought. If all things are impermanent – if there are not really things, but processes – then to assign 'things' an unchanging essence or nature – to define them in a way which does not allow for change, possibly even radical change, over time – is to construct a potential object of grasping and attachment.

The Buddha addresses the issue of causation by speaking in terms of the *interdependence* of events. From a Buddhist perspective, just as an entity is not an unchanging thing, but a changing process – more like a river, one might say, than a rock (though rocks also change over time) – an entity is also a nexus of *relations*. This particular smoke at this particular time is not the same as other smoke arising at another time, though both may share a number of important features which allow us to refer to them by the same name. But, just as with 'self' – just as with 'Nāgasena' and 'Milinda' and 'Jeffery D. Long' – using the word 'smoke' for all occasions of a particular kind is a matter of convenience: a convention. It does not reflect the ultimate nature of reality.

While it may be the case that, under certain circumstances, fire is followed by smoke, this is not due to some intrinsic and unchanging quality of fire, because no such unchanging entity as 'fire' exists. Causality is a relation. When we say, 'This fire is causing this smoke', we are saying something about both the fire and the smoke. The fire is a cause only in relation to the smoke (or to any other phenomenon that may co-arise with it, like heat or light).

In other words, if it were not for the smoke – if no smoke were present – then we could not say of the fire that it was the cause of the smoke, for the smoke would not be there. In other words, it is just as true to say the fire depends on the smoke as it is to say, in a sense, that the smoke depends on the fire: that is, that the smoke contributes the quality of 'being a cause of smoke' to the fire, which would otherwise be a qualitatively different entity.

This is the meaning of Interbeing, or interdependent origination. One thing does not simply cause another. Cause and effect, rather, exist in relation to one another. They 'co-arise'. Entities do not exist independently of one another. They *inter-exist*. There is no 'being', in the sense of a wholly separate substance, independent of the specifics of the moment. There is Interbeing.

The Buddha's teaching in ancient Indian society and intellectual history

We have seen that the Buddha occupies a distinctive position within Indian philosophy. In one sense, the Buddha is clearly situated firmly within the Śramaṇic stream of Indian thought and practice. The Buddha was identified as a Śramaṇa, as were his followers. Indeed, the Pāli word *śamaṇa*, as a term for Buddhist monks, was exported across Asia, in some parts of which it came to be a generic term for any holy person or religious specialist. It eventually turned into the word *Shaman*, from where the religious category of *Shamanism* takes its name.

At the same time, the Buddha displays a remarkable intellectual independence in drawing ideas and practices from the Vedic stream of thought as well as the Śramaṇic. As presented by early Buddhist literature, he stands at the confluence of the Vedic and Śramaṇic streams. This can be shown in his attitude towards some prominent issues in Indian society of his time.

In regard to the Vedic practice of animal sacrifice, the Buddha is one with his fellow strivers and sceptics in rejecting this practice as having no efficacy and as involving unjustifiable cruelty to innocent living beings. Because the *Vedas* are presented as supporting this practice, he also rejects the idea that these texts are authoritative guides to action and knowledge. The Buddha shares the sceptic's willingness to reject ideas, even ideas venerated by many in his society, when he finds them incoherent or leading to immoral outcomes.

In regard to theism, we also find the Buddha expressing scepticism about the need for a creator deity: something in which many of his Brahmin interlocutors believed deeply, and to which they gave the name *Brahmā*. The necessity of this deity is rejected by the Jains, Ājīvikas and Lokāyatas. Here, too, the Buddha echoes his fellow Śramaṇas.

Conclusion

The story of the Buddha's contribution to Indian philosophy does not end with him. The next chapter will explore how Buddhism transformed from a singular tradition into many schools of thought, each with varying responses to the questions of existence, but each anchored in the vision of Siddhārtha Gautama.

Notes

1 Rita Gross, 'Buddha Dharma', in Howard, *Dharma*, p. 151.
2 Ibid., p. 152.
3 John Strong, *The Experience of Buddhism: Sources and Interpretations*, 3rd ed. (Belmont: Thomson Wadsworth, 2008), p. 2.
4 Ibid., pp. 10–11.
5 Kevin Trainor, ed., *Buddhism: The Illustrated Guide* (Oxford: Oxford University Press, 2004), pp. 28–9.
6 Ibid., p. 28.
7 Zenno Ishigami, ed., *Disciples of the Buddha* (Tokyo: Kōsei Publishing Company, 1990), pp. 57–61.
8 Strong, *The Experience of Buddhism*, pp. 9–18.
9 Trainor, *Buddhism*, p. 31. Siddhārtha left Kaṇṭhaka in the care of 'his faithful charioteer', Chandaka, who had accompanied him during his first ventures outside the palace, when he saw the four signs.
10 Strong, *The Experience of Buddhism*, pp. 18–19.
11 Trainor, *Buddhism*, p. 31.
12 Ibid., pp. 34–5.
13 See, for example, contemporary Zen teacher Jnana Sipe, 'Reflections on Mara', *Urban Dharma*, http://www.urbandharma.org/udharma8/mara.html, accessed 30 August 2022.
14 Strong, *The Experience of Buddhism*, p. 22.
15 *Bṛhadāraṇyaka Upaniṣad* 4: 4.6a.
16 Strong, *The Experience of Buddhism*, p. 23.
17 This is essentially the argument of Robert Wright's *Why Buddhism is True: The Science and Philosophy of Meditation and Enlightenment* (New York: Simon and Schuster, 2018).
18 See Rose Drew, *Buddhist and Christian? An Exploration of Dual Belonging* (London: Routledge: 2013).
19 This logical compatibility has enabled the phenomenon of persons practicing Buddhism in tandem with theistic traditions such Christianity and Judaism. See, for example, Drew, Paul F. Knitter, *Without Buddha I Could Not Be a Christian* (London: Oneworld Publications, 2013), and Rodger Kamenetz, *The Jew in the Lotus: A Poet's Rediscovery of Jewish Identity in India* (New York: HarperOne, 2007).
20 See Swami Ranganathananda, *Bhagavan Buddha and Our Heritage* (Mayawati: Advaita Ashrama, 2001).
21 George Harrison, *All Things Must Pass* (London: Apple Records, 1970).
22 *Dhammapāda* 1: 6.
23 Gross, 'Buddha Dharma', p. 145.
24 Recounted by Ronald Eyre in *The Long Search, Volume 3: Footprint of the Buddha* (Ambrose Video, 1977).
25 Bimal Krishna Matilal characterizes this fourfold formulation, or *catuṣkoṭi*, as the negative equivalent of the Jains' positive assertion that a being, in some sense, exists,

does not exist, both exists and does not exist, and is indescribable. See Matilal, *Anekāntavāda*, pp. 12–18.

26 These meditations and the rationales behind them are described by the fifth century Theravāda Buddhist thinker Buddhaghoṣa in his *Visuddhimagga* (*The Path of Purification*). See Buddhaghosa (Bhikkhu Ñāṇamoli, trans.), *The Path of Purification: Visuddhimagga*, 5th ed. (Kandy: Buddhist Publication Society, 1991).

27 Paul Reps and Nyogen Senzaki, *Zen Flesh, Zen Bones: A Collection of Zen and Pre-Zen Writings* (Tokyo: Tuttle Publishing, 1985), pp. 33–4.

28 See Paul J. Griffiths, *On Being Mindless: Buddhist Meditation and the Mind-Body Problem* (Chicago: Open Court, 1991).

29 See, for example, Stephen Batchelor's *Buddhism without Beliefs: A Contemporary Guide to Awakening* (New York: Riverhead Books, 1998).

30 Buddhism scholar and Buddhist feminist Rita Gross, for example, points out in her work that the Buddha seems to have accepted certain conventions of the patriarchy of his cultural context, despite the tensions that exist between the teachings of Buddhism and the maintenance of gender-based institutional inequities. He is attributed, for example, with stating that the sangha would decline more quickly if women were allowed to join it, but that he nevertheless acquiesces to the rest of his aunt to establish a women's sangha so that she might achieve nirvāṇa. 'The equality and common humanity of women and men was not the Buddha's major perception about gender, even after his enlightenment. Differences between women and men and the tensions that arise from their close proximity seem to have been much more evident to him. In short, seeing the negativities of androcentrism through women's eyes simply was not his issue. It took persistent women, fueled by their own experiences of suffering caused by patriarchy, to challenge him to do something unconventional and out of the ordinary regarding gender arrangements. This perhaps could be cited as a shortcoming of the Buddha, a limit to his omniscience, but it is also the unfortunate truth that women, not men, are usually the ones who push for non-patriarchal gender arrangements. This is not necessarily due to ill will on men's part, but simply to lack of experience and consciousness.' (Rita Gross, *Buddhism After Patriarchy: A Feminist History, Analysis, and Reconstruction* (Albany: State University of New York Press, 1993), pp. 34–5.

31 David Ray Griffin, *Parapsychology and Spirituality: A Postmodern Exploration* (Albany: State University of New York Press, 1997), pp. 26, 151.

32 I say 'an ideal Buddhist approach to belief' because, of course, Buddhists are human beings and can be just as inclined to attachment, and even to violence, as adherents of other traditions. As Stephen L. Jenkins notes, 'Falsely branding Buddhism as pacifist has been harmful in a number of ways. It sets Buddhism up as a false pole of comparison to other faiths. It currently supports misunderstandings of Burmese, Thai, and Sri Lankan uses of force. It undermines Buddhist cultures' ability to apply their own moderating values in conflict and to understand their own histories.' (Stephen L. Jenkins, 'Buddhism and Nonviolence', in *Nonviolence in the World's Religions: A Concise Introduction*, ed. Jeffery D. Long and Michael G. Long (London: Routledge, 2021), p. 41.

33 See, for example, Nicholas F. Gier, *Spiritual Titanism: Indian, Chinese, and Western Perspectives* (Albany: State University of New York Press, 2000) pp. 55–7, 175.

34 Indeed, Buddhism scholar Steven Collins refers to the No Self doctrine as a 'linguistic taboo' for early Buddhists. See Steven Collins, *Selfless Persons: Imagery and Thought in Theravāda Buddhism* (Cambridge: Cambridge University Press, 1982), pp. 12, 77, 136, 149, 183.

35 Richard Gombrich, *What the Buddha Thought* (London: Equinox Publishing, 2009).
36 See Walpola Rahula, *What the Buddha Taught* (New York: Grove Press, 1974).
37 Thich Nhat Hanh, *Interbeing: Fourteen Guidelines for Engaged Buddhism* (Berkeley: Parallax, 1987).

4

The Buddhist conversation unfolds

Dharmas, emptiness and non-dual consciousness

Introduction

The Buddha sparked a conversation that continues to unfold today, as Buddhists continue to encounter new belief systems, new cultures and new phenomena which they seek to interpret based on the core insights the Buddha revealed. This chapter will not explore Buddhist thought to the present. It will confine itself to some of the ways in which Buddhist philosophy developed in India up to the point when it largely ceased to exist in the Indian subcontinent around the thirteenth century of the Common Era. The further development of Buddhism, until the modern period, has occurred mainly outside of India, in Southeast Asia, East Asia and Tibet.

Early Buddhist history: Aśoka's adoption of Buddhism and the Nikāya schools of thought

One may recall that the first collection of Buddhist texts consists of the *Vinaya*, the manual of right behaviour for Buddhist ascetics, the *Sūtras*, or the discourses of the Buddha, and the *Abhidharma*, or further teaching. These texts were not committed to writing immediately but passed on orally from one generation of Buddhist monks to the next, beginning with the first generation: the living disciples of the Buddha during his time on earth. According to Buddhist tradition, the Buddha's teachings were first recited by his disciples at a council held shortly after his death: his passage into 'nirvāna without remainder', or *mahāparinirvāṇa*.

In the roughly one and a half centuries that followed, Buddhist monks carried their master's teachings and way of life far and wide across the Indian subcontinent. In time, and as groups of Buddhist ascetics became geographically isolated from one another, differences emerged in their teachings and practices (though all agreed on the basic ideas explored in the last chapter: the Four Noble Truths, No Self and Interbeing). By the middle of the third century BCE, roughly eighteen to twenty forms of Buddhism were in practice across India. Some of the differences among these Buddhist traditions were minor and related to issues of ascetic observance. But others were more philosophically significant.

In 262 BCE, an event occurred which was to have a momentous impact on the fortunes of Buddhism: namely, its adoption by the ruler of, at that time, the largest kingdom to have emerged in the history of India. This was Aśoka, the third ruler of the Maurya dynasty. The Maurya Empire, at its height, encompassed most of the Indian subcontinent, excluding its southernmost regions, but including areas extending even beyond the modern-day Republic of India, such as portions of Nepal, Pakistan and Afghanistan. In 262 BCE, Aśoka completed the expansion of the empire of his father, Bindusara, and his grandfather, Candragupta Maurya, with his conquest of the kingdom of Kaliṅga, in what is now the state of Oḍiṣa in modern India. According to later accounts – as well as his own inscriptions left in sites throughout his empire – Aśoka felt great remorse at the suffering and the loss of life involved in his conquest of Kaliṅga. It is said that seeking atonement for the suffering that he had caused, and under the influence of his wife and her guru, the Buddhist master Upagupta, Aśoka renounced violence and adopted Buddhism as his path.

It is worth noting at this point that the various systems of Indian philosophy were, to a great extent, dependent on a system of patronage, in which they were supported by wealthy laypersons – householders – to pursue their philosophical reflections and their spiritual practices. The patronage of kings was especially prized, as it was seen to ensure the survival and security of one's school of thought so long as it held royal favour. Rulers and other influential persons in Indian society provided adherents of the various traditions with such material essentials as food, clothing (except for those sects, like the Ājīvikas and Digambara Jains who did not use clothing on principle) and dwelling places which eventually became elaborate monastic complexes. In return, it was widely believed that providing patronage and material support to holy persons was a source of religious merit: of *punya*, or good karma. Laypersons across India therefore fed and clothed ascetics and gave them shelter.

It is also important to note that such patronage was often not exclusive. In other words, a king or another wealthy person might support Buddhists, Jains, Ājīvikas, Hindu renouncers and the householder Brahmins whose sole employment was the performance of Vedic rituals. In some cases, exclusive support might be given to just one tradition, such as if the patron was particularly devoted to it. However, most often – and this also seems to have been the case with Aśoka – a patron would have a primary commitment to a particular tradition but would still give support to other schools of thought as well. Aśoka, in fact, specifically commends, in one of his inscriptions, learning the teachings of many schools of thought and respecting all.[1] This reflects a pluralistic ethos found in many phases throughout Indian history, both among philosophers and in the wider community of laypersons.

Aśoka's embrace of Buddhism therefore did not lead to banning or persecution of other traditions in his empire (though there are some contested accounts of his having persecuted specific groups of Brahmins at one point).[2] It did, though, lead to an era of ascendancy for Buddhism as a preferred and privileged tradition, with resources at its disposal it did not previously possess.

One result of Aśoka's conversion was the formalization and commitment to writing of the Buddhist canon. Some of the branches of Buddhism that had emerged since the time of the Buddha had their own versions of the *Tripiṭaka*. The oldest of these collections to survive is the Pāli canon of the Theravāda tradition. Theravāda ('teaching of the elders') is the only ancient, early school of Buddhism to survive to the present. The rest died out when Buddhism as a whole disappeared in the subcontinent (with the exceptions noted earlier). Theravāda survived because, having been favoured by Aśoka, Theravāda missions were sent outside of India. The most successful of these was led by one of Aśoka's sons, Mahinda – who became a Buddhist monk. Mahinda established a Buddhist community in Sri Lanka, which remains today the oldest continuously existing Buddhist society on earth. From Sri Lanka, Theravāda Buddhism was transmitted to Southeast Asia. The Theravāda traditions of Sri Lanka, Thailand, Burma and other countries of this region were not affected by the invasions which led to the demise of the other early schools of Buddhism in India.

The *Tripiṭakas* of the other early systems have in some cases been lost and, in some cases, recovered in translation, having been rendered into non-Indic languages like Chinese, Tibetan or Japanese, as they were transmitted across Asia. In other cases, fragments exist, often as quotations in texts of rival schools seeking to refute them on one issue or another. Scholars sometimes refer to these early Buddhist systems as *Nikāya* Buddhism, given their adherence to the authority of the *Nikāya* texts that make up the *Sūtra* section of the *Tripiṭaka*. Older scholarly writings refer to these early systems as *Hīnayāna*. As we shall see, though, this is a pejorative term that developed out of intra-Buddhist debates and does not reflect the understanding of adherents of these schools.

Abhidharma and its discontents: Conflicting interpretations of the dharmas

The *Vinaya* and *Sūtra* sections of the *Tripiṭakas* of the various Nikāya schools do not differ dramatically. However, their *Abhidharma* sections – the further teachings added after the time of the Buddha – differ substantially in their interpretations of the implications of his teachings. Specifically, they differ on the nature of the dharmas: the building blocks of experience mentioned in our discussion of the five aggregates and No Self. The Abhidharma debates among the Nikāya schools mark the beginning of Buddhist philosophical reflection after the Buddha. They also help fuel a radically different understanding of Buddhism that would eventually become a movement called *Mahāyāna*, with a set of views distinct, in many ways, from all the Nikāya schools. It is the Mahāyāna systems that eventually spread north into Central and East Asia: to China, Korea and Japan.

From what we can glean from his statements in the early Buddhist suttas, the Buddha himself was not overly fond of philosophical speculation for its own sake. He saw his purpose as relieving the suffering of living beings. If he thought a question was irrelevant to that purpose, he often refused to answer it, responding with silence. Consequently, the early Buddhists' only guide, when philosophical questions emerged, were the Buddha's teachings on topics he viewed as relevant to the path to nirvāṇa. Exploring the implications of these teachings was left to the community, whom the Buddha taught to 'be a light unto themselves'.

The primary issue Buddhist thinkers were left to contemplate was the seeming continuity and smoothness of experience in light of the Buddha's teaching of radical impermanence. It is here that the idea of dharmas comes to play a central role. It was in their respective *Abhidharma* literatures that adherents of early Buddhist schools of thought worked through these questions and issues, engaging in debate with one another when becoming aware of one another's views.

The Theravāda *Abhidharma* is neutral on the nature of dharmas. In fact, these texts largely consist of lists of dharmas. The Theravāda *Abhidharma* attempts to list, comprehensively, every possible object of experience: all visual, auditory, tactile, olfactory, gustatory and mental forms. The attempt to break experience down to fundamental building blocks and then list them seems to have a played an important role in early Buddhist meditation practices. A Buddhist monk or nun would gaze with great concentration at an object, committing its every detail to memory. That object would then be re-created and visualized in the mind of the meditator. Gradually, each characteristic of the object – its colours, textures, shapes and so on – would be mentally removed. The object as visualized would be deconstructed, down to its basic components or dharmas. The aim of such meditation exercises is to cultivate a state of detachment towards all objects, creating a sense of their constructed, unreal nature: the idea that 'no thing' exists, only dharmas.

Other Buddhist schools of thought, however, speculated about the nature of the dharmas. There was also debate about what, precisely, should belong in the list of dharmas. We have seen, for example, that the Pudgalavādins, or Personalists, were criticized by other Buddhist schools of thought for asserting that a new entity – the *pudgala*, or person – arises as the five aggregates come together. This was rejected by other Buddhists as too closely resembling the idea of a self.

Another early Buddhist group, the Mahāsaṅghikas, or 'Members of the Great Assembly', engaged in speculation about the nature of the Buddha himself, asserting that he was not, as the Theravādins affirmed, a human being who had discovered the path to freedom from suffering and rebirth, but a divine being with supernormal powers, like the ability to be in all places at once.[3]

This view of the Buddha as something like a divine being is another element which fuelled the rise of the Mahāyāna movement. It is not clear precisely how many Buddhists in ancient India held these views; but the name of the Buddhist community that endorsed them – the Mahāsaṅgha, or 'Great Assembly' – suggests that they may have been many in number. These views applied not only to the historical Buddha, but to all Buddhas, all awakened beings, throughout cosmic time.

Yet another group of Buddhists, the Sautrāntikas, or 'Adherents of the *Sūtras*', saw the speculation in which other Buddhists were engaged in their *Abhidharma* literatures and viewed it as deviating from the spirit and substance of the Buddha's teaching: his single-minded focus upon the path to freedom from suffering. In their own *Abhidharma*, the Sautrāntikas sought to reorient the Buddhist discourse back towards this central concern.

In terms of the further development of Buddhist philosophy, though, the Nikāya system whose views proved to be most provocative and productive of responses from other thinkers was the Sarvāstivādin school. Meaning 'Those who Teach that Everything Exists', the Sarvāstivādins proposed that dharmas, as possible objects of experience, exist always and everywhere: in the past, present and future. The dharmas are eternal.

The Sarvāstivādins made, one could say, the most systematic and serious attempt to address the issue of the continuity of experience in a world of impermanent events. They were also trying to address the fact, attested in the *Sūtras*, that the Buddha perceived events that had occurred in the past (such as his own and others' past lives) and future (such as his prediction of the coming of the next Buddha, Maitreya). One does not even have to turn to the question of past lives to raise the issue of memory. How is it that we perceive events that have occurred in the past, if those events no longer exist? One could, of course, argue that those events still exert causal efficacy in the present, due to their being part of the chain of events leading to the present moment (which is one response to the Sarvāstivādins' position). But what about future events? Aspiration, as much as memory, is able to exert a causal influence, one could say, upon the present. How can this happen if the future also does not, in some sense, exist?

Recall that dharmas are the basic building blocks making up any possible experience. The basic premise of the Sarvāstivādins is that while the moments making up our experience are, just as the Buddha taught, radically impermanent, the dharmas exist perpetually, flashing into and out of the atomic moments of experience making up our lives.

One could compare the Sarvāstivāda Buddhist idea of the dharmas as perpetually existing possibilities for experience with the teaching of the Western philosopher, Plato, that the forms we experience in the world of concrete existence are the shadows or manifestations of true and perfect forms existing in a pure, perfect, eternal realm of ideas. Each dharma exists according to its own nature, or *svabhāva*, without changing. But the dharmas also constantly manifest in the world, becoming actualized in the ephemeral moments of experience. Just as we earlier compared the moments making up our experience to the still photographs making up a motion picture, one might also compare dharmas to the colours of the pixels making up an image on a television or computer screen. The images we see are made up of a vast multitude of pixels. Each pixel retains a particular colour for a brief moment in time. A pixel that is part of an image of the sky might be blue. But as the scene changes to a view of a forest, that particular pixel might turn brown or green. 'Blue', 'brown' and 'green', however, as possibilities, have not been destroyed. The fact that the pixel has ceased to be blue and has become brown does not mean it might not, at some point, turn blue again. Or other pixels might turn blue. 'Blue' remains a possible state – a dharma – which a pixel – a small piece of a moment in time – might instantiate. The difference between a presently occurring dharma and a dharma existing in the past or the future is that the presently manifesting dharma is exerting its power of activity or function (*karitrā*).[4]

In short, the Sarvāstivādins address the question of how to reconcile the smooth continuity of our experience with the radically impermanent nature of each moment by asserting that while the particular arrangement of the fundamental building blocks of our experience does indeed shift from moment to moment, the building blocks themselves – the dharmas – are constant and enduring.

Each dharma has its own nature (*svabhāva*) which does not change. The dharmas can thus act as a foundation for our experience, the metaphorical rug on which the furniture of our existence rests.

Pulling the rug out from under our existence: Nāgārjuna's doctrine of emptiness

The objection, as one might expect, to the Sarvāstivādin attempt to account for continuity in the midst of change with recourse to perpetually existing dharmas with unchanging essences is that this concept seems to meet the very definition of a 'self' which the Buddha says does not exist.

Theravādins and adherents of some of the other early Buddhist schools of thought (like the Sautrāntikas) objected, on this basis, to the Sarvāstivādin concept of eternally existing dharmas. The most radical critic of this idea, however, was a Buddhist thinker of the late second to the early third century of the Common Era named Nāgārjuna.

Although he does not mention the term *Mahāyāna* in any of his extant writings, Nāgārjuna is undoubtedly the most renowned Mahāyāna Buddhist philosopher in history. His work served to establish the Mahāyāna movement on a firm intellectual footing and helped to grant it legitimacy in the eyes of mainstream Buddhists. Nāgārjuna achieved this goal by arguing for Mahāyāna views on the basis of universally accepted Buddhist teaching, rather than on the basis of the Mahāyāna *Prajñāpāramitā* sūtras, which would have been viewed by other Buddhists as idiosyncratic texts not bearing the authority of *Buddha-vacana*: the word of the Buddha.

The emergence of Mahāyāna Buddhism: Multiple causes of a complex phenomenon

The first textual evidence of Mahāyāna Buddhism is a vast collection of literature known as the *Prajñāpāramitāi* or 'Perfection of Wisdom' sūtras. The earliest of these texts date from the first century of the Common Era. One common trait which these texts share is profound sense that language is at least as much a barrier as a guide to the true nature of reality. The ultimate truth is beyond words, and words and logic can become a trap which keeps one away from awakening. This point is made by employing the Buddha's concept of the Middle Path as indicating a refusal to be pulled into accepting any verbal statement as the full truth. This is typically done in this text through the positing of a particular position, which is followed by a discussion of the inadequacies of this position, which is then followed by a discussion of the inadequacies of the first position's opposite. In other words, these texts show that the rejection of one perspective does not necessarily entail the acceptance of its opposite. All views tend towards extremes which are to be rejected by one on the path to awakening.

This rejection is not mere intellectual scepticism. It is pursued in the name of achieving a higher realization, a deeper level of insight, than mere words and concepts allow. As scholar John Strong explains these texts:

> *Prajñāpāramitā* literally means the 'wisdom gone beyond,' and engaging in this literature is somewhat like playing a game of transcendental leapfrog in which the hurdles come in binary pairs. As soon as one jump is made beyond, say, the assertion of something, it is time to make the next jump, beyond its negation. This is a campaign against stumbling at the barriers of thoughts, things, words.[5]

The *Prajñāpāramitā* sūtras form the background for two major systems of Mahāyāna philosophy: that of Nāgārjuna – the Madhyamaka system – and the Yogācāra or Vijñānavāda system.

Before turning to the specifics of these two systems, we need to ask what Mahāyāna is and how it came to be. *Mahāyāna* literally means 'great vehicle'. It is a system of Buddhism in which one cultivates the virtues of a *Bodhisattva*, or 'awakening being': that is, one who will eventually become a Buddha, an awakened being. As recounted in the Perfection of Wisdom literature, this is a far more ambitious aim than the more conventional Buddhist aim of becoming an *arhat*, or 'worthy one': that is, attaining nirvāṇa by following the path taught by a Buddha. Just as in Jainism there are enlightened beings, the Jinas, but only a few of these, the Tīrthaṅkaras, create a path to help others attain absolute knowledge, similarly, not all beings who reach nirvāṇa are called Buddhas. It is the Buddhas who set the 'wheel of dharma' in motion, enabling other beings to reach nirvāṇa as well.

The scholarly consensus at the present is that this movement was a complex phenomenon with no single origin and with fairly fluid boundaries. Rather than a single cause or point of origin, it is best to think of the Mahāyāna and its beginnings in a Buddhist fashion: as arising from the coming together of multiple causal factors. These factors include, as noted, a reaction against the philosophizing of the Abhidhārmikas (thinkers from the various Nikāya schools who engaged in speculation like that of the Sarvāstivādins), an idea of Buddha as a cosmic presence with multiple manifestations in the world of time and space (as in the teaching of the Mahāsaṅgha) accompanied by an increase in Buddhist devotionalism, the idea of the transfer of merit (or good karma), criticisms of excesses on the part of the monks, and reflection on the implications of the Buddha's teachings of No Self and Interbeing.

The Mahāsaṅghika teaching that all Buddhas are supernormal beings possessing godlike powers, motivated by boundless compassion, coincides, historically, with an increase in Buddhist devotional practice. In Buddhist literature, the Buddha often refers to himself in the third person as 'the *Tathāgata*'. In the Theravāda tradition, this is interpreted to mean 'one who has gone thus' (*tathā gata*): one who is no longer present in the realm of saṃsāra, the cycle of rebirth, because he has gone to the realm of nirvāṇa. The absence of the Buddha from the world of time and space is depicted in early Buddhist art with symbols like an empty throne or footprints. Artistic depictions of the Buddha as a human being are a later development.

It is clear, though, that by around 200 BCE, when the first Mahāyāna texts began to emerge, many Buddhists had come to think of the Buddha not as absent, but as *tathā āgata*, another possible reading of *Tathāgata*, meaning not 'one who has gone thus', but 'one who has come thus': that is, a universal, cosmic presence. The Buddha has not gone. He has arrived, now being one with all.

The Buddhas, like the Tīrthaṅkaras of Jainism, represent the ideal to which their adherents aspire. Conceptually, they may appear to be remote figures. A classic scholarly work on the idea of the Tīrthaṅkara, *Absent Lord*, by Lawrence Babb, captures this idea in its title.[6]

One might recall that, in Jainism, the Tīrthaṅkaras show the way to liberation, but they do not bestow it upon their followers, such as through a blessing or act of divine grace. At least one prominent strand of Theravāda Buddhism shares a similar sensibility about the Buddhas. These beings show the way, but it is up to the individual to follow the path they have presented. It should be noted, though, that even in Theravāda Buddhism, there is an understanding that the presence of a Buddha, an arhat, or even a monument containing the relics of such a being can greatly multiply the effects of spiritual one's efforts.

Religious devotees typically want to draw near to their ideal, to experience it not as remote or absent, but radically *present*. Some scholars have argued that one factor in the rise of Mahāyāna Buddhism may have been just this very aspiration on the part of Buddhists. It is probably not a coincidence that during this same period, a movement of *bhakti*, or devotion, also emerges in the traditions now seen as making up Hinduism. The Brahman of the *Upaniṣads*, like a Jina or Buddha, can be seen as a remote, abstract ideal. If this ideal can be conceived as taking on personhood – not merely existing as an impersonal cosmic principle, but becoming present to human awareness as the Supreme, and supremely loveable, Lord – then a path to realization through devotion is possible.

The bhakti movement of Hinduism and the Mahāyāna movement of Buddhism seem to be manifestations of the same impulse emerging among practitioners of these traditions in the same period: the last couple of centuries before the Common Era. Devotionalism remains a current in Jain life and practice to the present, and possibly emerged in this period as well. Early Jains, like early Buddhists, often showed devotion to ancient teachers by building and paying their respects at *stūpas*: dome-shaped reliquaries which contain the material remains of a Jain or Buddhist saint. Jains and Buddhists eventually moved to the practice of constructing realistic *mūrtis*, or images, of their respective sacred figures to help facilitate a sense of the presence of these beings to their worshipers. Some have speculated that the movement towards creation of realistic depictions of Buddhist and Jain figures (as well as Hindu deities) might have been fuelled by the arrival of Greek culture in India. With the exception of the period of the Indus Valley civilization, divine or sacred beings were not typically depicted in a realistic artistic form in India – or if they were, they were not made of materials that have survived to the present, though there are a few literary references to wooden images. The Greeks, however, had long sculpted their deities in stone, and depicted them as idealized human beings. When Greeks in India began practicing Buddhism, it was quite natural for them to do the same with the Buddha.

The idea of the transfer of merit also begins to be attested in this period, not so much in the formal texts of philosophical traditions, but in inscriptions made by householders to commemorate gifts to the Buddhist saṅgha, or community of ascetics. The idea of the transfer of merit is that one can do a good deed and, by an act of will, dedicate the resulting *puṇya*, or good karma from that act to another person – like a beloved deceased relative – in order to facilitate that person's journey to nirvāṇa. This is comparable to the practice in the Roman Catholic Church of sponsoring a mass for one who has died, the idea being that the merit of this act could reduce the deceased person's time in purgatory.

Finally, one begins to see growing criticism during this period – from householders, but also from within the saṅgha – of corruption and laxity on the part of Buddhist monks. There is a certain historical logic to this development. A few decades previously, the emperor Aśoka – and, following his lead, numerous wealthy donors throughout his empire – began to lavish material wealth on the saṅgha. Buddhist monasteries became beautiful architectural achievements, full of art treasures.

In a reaction to this trend, a tradition begins around this time, which continues to the present in Theravāda Buddhist countries, of forest-dwelling monks. These are renouncers from *within* the community of renouncers. Monks who dwelled in elaborate monasteries in urban areas came to be seen by some of their colleagues, and perhaps by some of their lay followers as well, as little better than householders in terms of their lifestyle. From owning no wealth at all, many monks had begun to live lives that were, in some ways, even more luxurious than those of householders. The luxurious lives of many Buddhist monks came to be an occasion for scandal in the community. The forest dwellers are an attempt, one could say, to return the Buddhist tradition to its Śramaṇic roots, when ascetics genuinely gave up worldly goods and contacts for the single-minded pursuit of liberation.

Even more relevantly to the rise of Mahāyāna Buddhism, there was another reaction to the perceived corruption of the saṅgha. This was the idea that a Buddhist householder, by cultivating the right virtues and pursing the path with diligence and sincerity, might become more spiritually advanced than a monk. The paradigmatic example of this idea is found in a Mahāyāna text called the *Vimalakīrti Nirdeśa Sūtra*. In this text, the Buddha sends his disciples to a householder named Vimalakīrti. Vimalakīrti is not only a householder, but a wealthy merchant, and thus someone who might be expected to be full of worldly attachment. The Buddha, though, sends his disciples to Vimalakīrti, not to teach him, but to be taught by him: to learn the Bodhisattva path.

In fact, all these concepts – the Buddha as a universal presence, Buddhist devotionalism, transfer of merit and the idea that a layperson might be as enlightened as a monk – culminate in the ideal of the Bodhisattva, the central concept of Mahāyāna Buddhism. If a Buddha is an awakened being who has, through his own efforts, attained freedom from rebirth, and if an *Arhat*, or 'worthy one' – as many of the Buddha's original disciples are designated – are beings who have attained this state by following the path laid out by a Buddha, a Bodhisattva, or 'awakening being', is one who resolves not merely to attain nirvāṇa, but to remain in the cycle of rebirth and accumulate the merit needed to liberate as many beings as possible: to become a Buddha.

Mahāyāna Buddhists basically see liberation as a collective and collaborative, rather than individual, project. Older, mainstream, Nikāya forms of Buddhism (like Theravāda), following the earlier model of Jainism, operate on the assumption that we are each responsible for our own karma and our own spiritual path. Another being can teach one or can lead the way by example. But it is up to us to activate our own spiritual potential and put the path into practice. Mahāyāna, however, sees the cosmos as filled with Buddhas willing, out of their boundless compassion, to help us on the path. It also adheres to an account of karma that sees this energy as transferable to others. Most centrally, it affirms that we are all capable of doing more than 'merely' attaining nirvāṇa. We are in a position to help others do so as well. If our wisdom has been perfected, if our compassion is without limits, this is what we shall do, even if this means it will take longer – perhaps even many lifetimes – for us to reach the goal ourselves.

Indeed, this is the idea behind the term *Mahāyāna*, which, again, literally means the 'great vehicle'. The image being conveyed is of a great ship, carrying as many beings as possible across the river of saṃsāra to the further shore of nirvāṇa (just as the *tīrthas*, or 'fords' created by the Jain Tīrthaṅkaras enable their followers to cross the river themselves). In a deliberate contrast with the 'lesser vehicle', or *Hīnayāna*, taught in mainstream Buddhism – which can be compared to a tiny life raft, conveying only one being at a time across the river – the path of Mahāyāna, the path of the Bodhisattva, aims at conveying as many beings as possible – and ultimately, all beings – to the other shore.

It is important to note that Mahāyāna was not conceived as a new school of Buddhism, in addition to the twenty or so which already existed, which had come into being largely through the diffusion of Buddhism to many areas, not through any effort to divide the community. Mahāyāna Buddhists were, in fact, aware of the fact that creating a division, or schism, in the saṅgha is one of four transgressions against the *vinaya*, or code of conduct meriting permanent expulsion from the order. (The others are murder, major theft and sexual misconduct.) Mahāyāna, rather, was a way of conceptualizing the Buddhist path which co-existed with mainstream understandings in the individual Buddhist traditions. In other words, a typical Buddhist monastery in ancient India might include monks who saw themselves as Mahāyāna Buddhists practising the Bodhisattva path, alongside monks who saw their practice in more conventional terms. It also seems to have been a movement among householders, who undertook Bodhisattva vows and practices as well.

Implications of the Mahāyāna for Buddhist philosophy

Philosophically, what made Mahāyāna defensible as a Buddhist practice was its rootedness in the Buddha's original teachings of No Self and Interbeing. If one were to argue to a Mahāyāna Buddhist that the Bodhisattva path is incoherent because merit cannot be transferred (as some modern Buddhists have argued), or that each of us is responsible for our own spiritual path, a Mahāyāna Buddhist could reply that such a stand is incompatible with the doctrines of No Self and Interbeing. It is the Mahāyāna Buddhist, on this view, who is most true to the Buddha's original teaching.

Why would this be so? If one thinks in terms of 'my nirvāṇa' and 'your nirvāṇa', or 'my karma and your karma', one is still attached to a residual sense of self. One is not appreciating the degree to which all beings – or rather, all the processes we see, in our conventional understanding, as separate beings, or 'selves' – are interdependent and existing in a state of mutual causation. The Buddha's compassion, which consists of seeing the sufferings of others as no different from one's own, is fully realized when one is aware that the distinction between 'self' and 'other' is unreal. The most logical response to suffering in a universe in which all beings are interdependent and interpenetrating is to address *all* suffering, not only one's own.

To be fair, practitioners of mainstream forms of Buddhism in ancient India, and Theravāda Buddhists today, do not see themselves as placing their interests above those of the rest of the universe. They certainly do not refer to themselves as practicing the 'Hīnayāna', or 'lesser vehicle'. One can say that Nikāya Buddhists do not see Buddhism as undercutting, in quite the same radical way, our conventional sense of a world of distinct subjects and objects as Mahāyāna Buddhists do.

It was important for Mahāyāna Buddhists to establish their practice on a firm footing, in the teachings of the Buddha, lest they be seen as 'heretics', and as deliberately deviating from the word of the Buddha (*buddha-vacana*). While other Buddhists may not have found their arguments persuasive, by making them on a Buddhist basis – by taking their stand on No Self and Interbeing – adherents of Mahāyāna established themselves as part of the Buddhist tradition. Their views might be seen as idiosyncratic to other Buddhists, but they were still recognizably Buddhist views, and not attempts to divide the community.

Nāgārjuna on the emptiness of all dharmas

This is where Nāgārjuna enters into Buddhist – and Indian, and global – intellectual history. In philosophical writings aimed, at least partly, at the Sarvāstivāda view that dharmas are eternal and possess an unchanging nature, or svabhāva, Nāgārjuna argues for the Emptiness (*śūnyatā*) of all dharmas. He, in effect, pulls the rug from under the Sarvāstivāda view of reality. In place of the idea that impermanent moments rest upon a foundation of unchanging possibilities, Nāgārjuna teaches that reality is Interbeing at every level, even at its supposed foundation.

Nāgārjuna's term *Emptiness* is as susceptible to misunderstanding as the Buddha's *No Self*. Indeed, Nāgārjuna was misunderstood even by his fellow Buddhist interlocutors. Just as No Self does not mean there is nothing that reincarnates or that can be described as a centre of subjective awareness at a given moment, but rather that our language for talking about these phenomena is not adequate to the ultimate nature of reality, Emptiness similarly does not mean 'nothingness' in the sense of 'absolute non-existence'. As Nāgārjuna repeatedly affirms, *Emptiness* refers to *Interbeing*, or dependent co-arising: the fact that a thing is not a 'thing', an essence or substance in the conventional sense, but the coming together in a given moment of the factors constituting it. Reality is made up not of changeless essences, but intertwining and ever-changing nexuses of relations. It is not nothingness, but 'no thingness'.

Though the term *Emptiness* is most closely identified with Nāgārjuna's school of thought – the *Madhyamaka*, or 'Middle Way' school – it first appears in early Buddhist literature. Again, Nāgārjuna is seeking to present himself not as an innovator, but an adherent of the true, original meaning of the Buddha's teaching. *Emptiness*, in early Buddhist literature as well as in the early *sūtras*, or root texts of the Mahāyāna movement, and in the works of Nāgārjuna, has a variety of meanings. In addition to being synonymous with Interbeing, it also refers to the fact that words and philosophical theories are incapable of fully capturing truth. It is possible, in this sense, to identify Emptiness with *relativity*: that the truth captured in words is 'empty'. It is relative, not absolute. This does not mean words and doctrines do not capture truth at all. Just as Emptiness does not mean 'nothingness' in the sense of 'absolute non-existence', when it is applied to doctrinal claims, it also does not mean absolute falsehood. Nāgārjuna is sometimes mischaracterized as a sceptic because his meaning of *Emptiness* as *relativity* is not fully grasped.

Finally, the term *Emptiness* also refers to a meditative state in which the mind is clear from or 'empty of' obstructions in the form of false beliefs and the cravings they sustain. All these meanings are at play in Buddhist thought: the Emptiness of a phenomenon (its interdependently originated nature), of a view about that phenomenon (its relativity), and of the mind in relation to that phenomenon (its freedom from craving).

The Sarvāstivādins seek to make sense of the persistent, continuous nature of much of our experience in light of the Buddha's teaching of radical impermanence by positing that the basic components of our experience – the dharmas – do not change, except in the sense that they move back and forth from potential to manifestation. There is a universe of potentials for experience, of eternal essences – like, for example, the colour blue – which manifest at particular points in time and space, as characterizing particular moments in the causal chain, and then return to their potential state. But they always exist, even if they are not manifesting concretely at every moment.

Nāgārjuna challenges this concept, arguing that an entity that does not change in its essence is an incoherent concept. No Self teaches that we are not literally the same entity from moment to moment. One cannot step into the same river twice. The 'I' of the present moment is different from the 'I' of a few moments ago and from the 'I' that will exist a few moments hence. These differences are due to subtle differences in the infinitesimally small units of time making up the experience of 'me'. The effects of these subtle differences are demonstrated – and magnified – if we expand the scope of our examination. 'I' am most definitely different in the present moment from the 'I' who was an infant of the same name, and from the (hopefully extremely old) man who will one day leave the complex of processes that I call 'my body'. And 'I' am even more dramatically different from the 'selves' of my past lives.

A Sarvāstivādin might object that yes, while I am indeed a different 'I' from the one I was in the past, or that I will be in the future, I did see the colour blue in the past. I am seeing it now. And I am likely to see it again. This same colour blue, this dharma, is an ever-existing possibility available to my experience. How can one otherwise explain the continuities of our experience, of the fact that things like colours, shapes and sounds, occur repeatedly?

In response, Nāgārjuna says that just as we use the same name – Nāgārjuna, or Jeffery D. Long – to describe what is really a series of distinct, discrete moments of experience, knowing this is just a conventional designation that does not reflect the ultimate nature of reality, similarly, the colour blue I experience in the past, present and future, is a *different* colour blue each time. Resemblance, even close resemblance, is not absolute identity.

The word 'blue' perpetuates the illusion of sameness across time. In fact, these varied blues arise due to different conditions. The blue in the sky at a given moment, due to the presence of nitrogen in the atmosphere, of sunlight shining through this atmosphere, of this sunlight entering my eye and then being interpreted by my brain as the colour blue, is different from the sky blue of a crayon, which is 'blue' due to a chemical process of crayon manufacturing, followed by a similar process of light (different light now) bouncing off the crayon and into my eye and being interpreted by my brain as blue. Even the blue of the sky, from moment to moment, is not the *same* blue. The air has moved. The sunlight that previously entered my eye and appeared to me as blue is already several light seconds away, moving through space and so on. My eye and brain are not even the same eye and brain, the atoms and molecules making up these organs cycling into and out of my body as I consume energy and replace it with food. And, of course, my sense of these organs even being 'mine' is a construct.

Nāgārjuna, in short, argues that there is no 'ground', no changeless essence, anywhere in our experience. It is Interbeing all the way. When Nāgārjuna calls this *Emptiness*, he means all entities are *empty* of – that is, free from – an unchanging essence. This is not an assertion of nihilism. Nāgārjuna's Buddhist opponents argue against him that if all dharmas are empty, there can be no nirvāṇa, no spiritual path. This is because they take *Emptiness* to mean *non-existence*. Nāgārjuna argues in reply that it is precisely *because* all dharmas are empty that a spiritual path and its fruit are possible. An entity is able to have an impact on the world around it – to affect the universe of change – only if it is able to be related to it in a meaningful way. According to Nāgārjuna, an entity that does not change is not an entity at all, because it cannot connect with the field of our changing experience.

What does this mean? Again, by a Buddhist account, I am a constantly changing entity: I am not technically the same 'I' from one moment to the next. Why is this the case? Let us say that, at a given moment, I am standing. Part of what makes up the 'I' of that moment is the fact of being an entity who is standing. Let us say, shortly afterwards, I sit down. I am now different from the being who was standing, if for no other reason than that I am now an entity who is sitting down.

There is nothing here thus far to which a Sarvāstivādin would necessarily object. It is basic Buddhism. But now, let us imagine that I am gazing at a painting. It affects me. Its beauty creates an emotional impact. I leave the experience transformed and go to do something else. I have, of course, changed. But what about the painting? Has my experience of it transformed it in any way, or has this been a one-way exchange? The painting, in this case, might be analogous to the dharmas as understood by the Sarvāstivādins, who would say the painting remains unchanged as a possibility for future experiences. Other people may yet come and look at it, and be transformed by it: including future versions of 'me'.

Nāgārjuna, however, would emphasize that the relations of causation making up a moment of experience are mutual. It is incorrect to think of 'the painting' and 'me' as independent entities who have briefly come into contact. One, rather, needs to look holistically at the entire experience of 'me looking at the painting'.

In other words, it is not that the painting is a purely external object that can be experienced by me in one way and by another person in another way: which is our conventional way of thinking of these things, and is the way the Sarvāstivādins think of dharmas. Each experience of the 'same' painting is actually a distinct moment of reality. This is true whether we are thinking of two people looking at the painting simultaneously, or the 'same' person looking at the painting at two different times. It is not only the persons who change through time. The painting changes as well.

For Nāgārjuna, this is important. Dharmas that cannot change cannot be related. Let us say I look at the painting on a day when I am feeling happy and have one experience, and then I look at it on another day when I am feeling sad and have a different experience. The painting has to be related to me in such a way that it is capable of being experienced in these differing ways. If the painting was unchanging and eternal, it could not accommodate my changing nature in this way. It would have to remain static. It would not be accessible to the experience of a changing being. Similarly, Nāgārjuna argues, even nirvāṇa, to be a real possibility, must be empty. It must be part of the continuum of Interbeing, not some separate, unchanging 'other' realm. Relations, for Nāgārjuna, are always mutual. No being is related purely externally to another.

Another way to put the matter is to say that the act of dividing an experience into a separately existing, independent subject – me looking at the painting – and a separately existing and independent object – the painting itself – is mistaken. The factors constituting the moment co-arise. They together go into making up the unique experience of the moment. There is no passive object being witnessed by an active subject. There is a moment of experience which is uniquely what it is because of the relations, in that moment, of the factors constituting it. These factors are not the same from moment to moment. Each is unique to the moment in which it occurs. The entire basis of the grasping which causes suffering, according to the second noble truth, is the notion of subject and object: the grasper and that which is grasped. In affirming the Emptiness – the dependent co-arising – of both, Nāgārjuna has undermined the false conceptual foundation on which our suffering is built. A more Nāgārjuna-like way to phrase the matter is to say there is no painting and there is no viewer of the painting. There is only the ephemeral nexus of relations which we conventionally call 'viewer-looking-at-painting'. The reality is Emptiness.

Emptiness as relativity: The 'Middle Way' between opposite extremes

Nāgārjuna calls his approach to philosophy the 'middle path'. He deliberately employs this ancient Buddhist image as a metaphor for avoiding the extremes to which philosophical views lead. The Buddha took the 'middle path' between the lifestyle of the householder and that of the ascetic. In a similar way, Nāgārjuna takes a middle way between the mistaken view that entities essentially exist and the mistaken view that all entities are essentially non-existent. He says that he has no view regarding the essential existence or non-existence of entities. From this perspective, the silence of the Buddha in response to some questions is not merely a rhetorical device to show that the question was ill formed or inappropriate. The silence of the Buddha, rather, is the truest response to these questions: the middle way of neither affirming nor denying a mistaken view or its equally mistaken opposite.

The Buddha had long ago affirmed the danger of becoming attached to views. In keeping with this sensibility, Nāgārjuna argues that it is not only objects, and not only dharmas, which are empty: free from a self or essence. This is also true of philosophical positions.

In much of his writing, Nāgārjuna shows how a wide array of philosophical views current in his time – Buddhist and non-Buddhist – lead to self-contradiction and are ultimately inadequate to describing the true, ultimate nature of reality.

Just as *Emptiness* means Interbeing or dependent co-arising, it also means *relativity*. A view may have utility to a certain extent; but no view is the final truth. The Nāgārjuna scholar Jay Garfield argues that Nāgārjuna's approach to views can be compared to the way in which modern scientists view theories. They are useful tools for interpreting a set of phenomena, but they are not the ultimate truth of existence, and it is assumed that they will eventually be superseded by other theories and that this process will never end in any final or definitive way.

The scholar of Indian philosophy, Bimal Krishna Matilal, argues that Nāgārjuna's dialectic is a 'negative' version of the 'positive' dialectic of Mahāvīra, which evolves into the Jain doctrine of the complexity of reality (anekāntavāda). Just as anekāntavāda teaches that all views reflect a partial grasp of the complexity of reality, and are thus only partially true, Nāgārjuna's teaching is that all views are ultimately inadequate. They are not true, if by 'true' one means absolutely and perfectly true. This is also not dissimilar to the apophatic teaching of the *Upaniṣads* that 'words recoil' from the ultimate Brahman, which is *neti, neti* – 'not this, not that'. Reality is finally beyond description. It cannot be described fully, but must be realized directly:

> Consistent with the attitude of the Buddha, who refused to be dragged into the quicksand of philosophic disputations, the Mādhyamika rejects most philosophic positions by exposing their inherent contradictions and anomalies and points out that *tattva* (truth) is not to be arrived at through such philosophic disputations, for it is only revealed to the *prajñā* or insight.[7]

Though the focus of Nāgārjuna is generally on the *inadequacy* of philosophical views– the senses in which they are false – it is also true that in the fully developed philosophy of anekāntavāda, the claim that all views are, in a sense, false, is affirmed as strongly as the claim that all views are, in a sense, true.

Furthermore, as Matilal points out, 'It should . . . be noted that Nāgārjuna's position was not always expressed through negation or rejection.'[8] For a view to be 'empty' is not for it to be *wholly* false, but rather for it to be ultimately inadequate to the task of describing reality in a full and comprehensive way. Views are not wholly true or false, but both true and false in relative and partial ways. The truth and falsehood of statements can admit of degrees. Substantively, then it does not seem that Nāgārjuna's approach and anekāntavāda are as different as a characterization of one as 'positive' and the other as 'negative' might suggest. Both finally teach relativity.

What differentiates Nāgārjuna's teaching of relativity from the Jain approach is that in the case of Nāgārjuna, there is no attempt to establish his own, independent position. The approach of the Jains, as Matilal explains, is to 'try to overcome partiality and one-sidedness and search for the totality of outlook, for omniscience'.[9] Nāgārjuna, however, does not seek to integrate all of the partial or relative visions of truth in all other schools of thought into a larger view. Nāgārjuna understands that being a linguistic construct, any such 'super philosophy' would itself become one more empty, relative and ultimately inadequate way of trying to capture a reality that is finally beyond words. This insight is not absent from Jainism. Recall, for example, that one of the seven values of a truth claim in Jain philosophy is that its truth is finally 'inexpressible'. The Jain philosopher, Kundakunda takes a 'two truths' approach which affirms that linguistic expressions of truth ultimately fall short of reality as revealed in the experience of absolute knowledge. But the overall trend of Jain thinkers is toward integrating the 'partial' and 'relative' views of other traditions into their own, which they see as the most comprehensive and complete view.

Nāgārjuna affirms that even his own position is empty. It is not simply that he does not claim to have a superior view. He claims to have no view at all. Emptiness, Nāgārjuna says, is empty. Truth is beyond words. 'The victorious ones have said that Emptiness is the relinquishing of all views. For whomever Emptiness is a view, that one has accomplished nothing.'[10]

Emptiness is the middle way because it avoids the tendency for a view to create its opposite: its antithesis. If one posits any philosophical view, one can immediately generate its opposite by simply saying 'not that'. The cosmos originated in time. No, it didn't. There is a creator deity. No, there isn't. The soul is everlasting. No, it isn't. And so on. From a Jain perspective, each of these views captures a piece of the truth. It is not that Nāgārjuna would dispute this; but he would assert that nirvāṇa is not a 'view'.

The non-duality of Saṃsāra and Nirvāṇa: The coalescence of relative and absolute

Another radical implication of Nāgārjuna's teaching is that if all entities are empty, and if this includes nirvāṇa and saṃsāra, then nirvāṇa and saṃsāra are not ultimately different. He says, 'There is no distinction whatsoever between saṃsāra and nirvāṇa; and there is no distinction whatsoever between nirvāṇa and saṃsāra. The limit of nirvāṇa and the limit of saṃsāra: one cannot find even the slightest difference between them.'[11]

If Nāgārjuna is saying what he appears to be saying, this would seem to undermine the Buddhist path. Is not the aim of Buddhism to escape saṃsāra, the cycle of rebirth, and enter nirvāṇa, the state of freedom from karma, rebirth and suffering?

What Nāgārjuna is saying, though, applying the dialect of Emptiness to this set of opposites just as he does to various opposing views is that it is wrong to think of saṃsāra and nirvāṇa as different 'realms'. One does not 'go' anywhere when one goes to nirvāṇa. One's consciousness is transformed. The world experienced as a cycle of suffering and rebirth – as saṃsāra – is the same world experienced as a state of perfect freedom – nirvāṇa – if one's consciousness is purified of false constructs and the impulse to grasp after them. Saṃsāra and nirvāṇa are not *identical*. Such a claim would, indeed, be antithetical to the Buddhist path. But the relationship between them is one of *non-duality*. They are not identical, but neither are they fundamentally different, in such a way that one could not account for the transition from one state to the other.

Both these implications of Nāgārjuna's teachings – the ineffability of truth and the non-duality of saṃsāra and nirvāṇa – are realized with particular vividness as Buddhism is transmitted, in the course of the first millennium of the Common Era, into East Asia. In the Zen traditions of Japan, the central emphasis is on attaining a realization that cannot be described in words.

Awakening, or *satori* in Japanese, can at best be evoked, but not 'taught' in a conventional sense. Similarly, the non-duality of saṃsāra and nirvāṇa is expressed in artworks that use nature as a vehicle to express the ideal of ultimate freedom. Nirvāṇa is not 'escaping' the world. It is seeing it with a mind free from delusion. Thus, it is seeing the world in its truest, most intense, ineffable and ephemeral beauty. To evoke at least a glimpse of this experience becomes the aim of Japanese art and aesthetics, which seek to cultivate an experience of *mono no aware*, or 'tragic beauty' – the beauty of the impermanent, unrepeatable, empty moment.

Nāgārjuna in a wider Buddhist context

Early Buddhist philosophy was, broadly speaking, realist in much the same sense in which Jainism is realist in its ontology: its teaching about the nature of reality.

Realism, one might recall is the affirmation that the basic features of reality are not radically different than that given in our experience: that time, matter, consciousness and so on, are, in some sense, *there* as elements of the world. We have seen that Jainism is realist as well as pluralist. It does not seek to explain (or explain away) basic features of our experience through reductionism. It does not say, therefore, that consciousness is really an effect of matter (as the Lokāyatas do), or that matter is a mere projection of consciousness. It also takes for granted the reality of time (*kāla*), affirming that it is one of the fundamental entities (*astikāyas*) that make up existence.

Early Buddhism is not, however, ontologically pluralistic in the way that Jainism is. The Buddha, at least as portrayed in the Pāli canon, seems to have adhered to a neutral monism on the question of the nature of phenomena. Are dharmas physical or purely mental? Neutral monism takes the position that the basic 'stuff' of reality can be experienced as 'mind' and 'matter', and cannot be reduced to either. For the Buddha, it seems, the dharmas are 'objects of experience', with no comment being made about 'what' they otherwise are or might be, because this question is not relevant to the aim of showing living beings the path to freedom from suffering.

In not taking a stance on this issue the Buddha is, one can say, a realist, not a reductionist. Reality just is, and we experience it in ways that we call physical and mental.

The issue of whether reality is physical, mental or both is the kind of question Nāgārjuna sees as generative of relative views that do not finally capture the truth. One can see Nāgārjuna's method as making explicit the method already implicit in the Buddha's teaching: that views may have utility at a certain point along the path to awakening, but that one does not finally awaken to a view. One awakens to reality itself, which no view expressible in words can encompass or grasp. The early Buddhists did not see this, according to Nāgārjuna, because they were still too wedded to the use of conventional categories like subject, object and essence as a way of explaining reality at a deeper level where these categories do not apply.

The charge of Nihilism and the two truths doctrine

Nāgārjuna's Madhyamaka or 'Middle Path' was a powerful way for Mahāyāna Buddhists to articulate their view – or non-view – of reality. No view can capture ultimate truth. The truest thing one can say about reality is that it is empty – free of self, free of independent self-existence and interdependently arisen. Nāgārjuna's dialectic was also a powerful tool for refuting the views of others without having to establish his own position.

As mentioned earlier, Nāgārjuna's teaching was easily misunderstood as nihilistic and as undermining any positive attempt to make assertions about the nature of reality. It was certainly taken to be an assault on the project of the Abhidhārmikas: to catalogue and describe the nature of dharmas. If dharmas have no nature, then this would certainly appear to be a fruitless project. To be sure, Nāgārjuna nowhere actually states that Abhidharma is a wrong or un-Buddhist activity. Rather, it is the attribution of an essence (svabhāva) to dharmas to which he objects.

But if Nāgārjuna asserts that no 'view' is wholly true, what about Buddhism itself? The objection from other Buddhists to which one sees Nāgārjuna make frequent reference in his works, and that one could well see as a worry raised by his approach, is that he seems to be pulling the proverbial rug out from under not only false views that any Buddhist might regard as incompatible with the Buddha's teaching, such as the idea of an unchanging self, but even from under Buddhism itself.

Nāgārjuna proposes an important distinction between the 'relative' or 'conventional' truth (*saṃvṛti satya*) and the ultimate truth (*paramārtha satya*). The relative truth is the truth that can be captured, albeit inadequately, in words. It includes the teachings of Buddhism, inasmuch as these can be transformed into a theory or conceptual model (of the kind the Sarvāstivādins attempted). But it points beyond itself to the ultimate truth, which cannot be captured in words, but can only be experienced in the state of nirvāṇa. Saṃsāra is reality as perceived from the perspective of conventional truth. Nirvāṇa is the same reality perceived from the perspective of ultimate truth. Ultimate truth can only be realised if one has ceased trying to capture it in an empty collection of thoughts and words. Discursive philosophy ends in the silence of meditation.

A popular Mahāyāna image for what Nāgārjuna is trying to communicate with his idea of the two truths is that of a thorn used to remove another thorn that has become lodged in one's skin. When the thorn – representing false views – that is causing suffering is removed by the other thorn – the 'empty' teaching of Buddhism – then both can be thrown away. Another one, popular in the Zen tradition, is of a person pointing with his finger at the moon so his friend can see it. The moon is ultimate truth. The finger is Buddhist teaching. Once one's friend has seen the moon, one may lower one's finger. Teaching is not ultimate truth. A map is not the territory it depicts.

It would not be accurate to characterize Nāgārjuna as a sceptic in the sense of the Ajñāna, or agnostic school of thought, and it would most definitely not be accurate to characterize him as a Lokāyata materialist. The Lokāyata affirmation of the ultimately material nature of reality is, for Nāgārjuna, just one more relative view, to be refuted by its opposite.

Nāgārjuna should instead be seen as a highly original thinker who successfully pressed a sceptical methodology into the service of a transcendentalist, spiritually oriented path. If a sceptic were to argue that there is no basis for accepting the reality of paranormal phenomena, like past life memory or the existence of deities, Nāgārjuna would likely reply that matter and self are of a similarly unestablished nature. Neither a sceptic nor a believer is able to capture the full truth in a view. Nirvāṇa occurs when one is free from all limiting concepts. It is not attained by engaging in conversations based on polarizing dichotomies.

The consciousness school: Vijñānavāda

Roughly two hundred years after Nāgārjuna, another system of Mahāyāna thought arose that sought to correct the trend toward extreme negativity or nihilism that arose from misreadings of Nāgārjuna and his project of showing the inadequacy of views. Specifically, this new system sought to rehabilitate the more ancient Buddhist project of Abhidharma, but on a Mahāyāna basis, taking Nāgārjuna's important criticisms of earlier versions of this project into account.

Around the year 400 of the Common Era, two brothers from the north-western part of India became Buddhist monks. These brothers, named Asaṅga and Vasubandhu, together developed a system of Mahāyāna thought known variously as *Yogācāra*, *Vijñānavāda* and *Cittamātra*.[12] Each of these names gives some idea of the emphasis of this system. *Yogācāra*, or 'Practice of Yoga', points to the fact that the founders of this system sought to re-establish Abhidharma on its original basis as an aid to meditation. *Vijñānavāda*, or 'Teaching of Consciousness', and *Cittamātra*, or 'Mind Only', on the other hand, emphasize the tendency of this system toward what is called, in the West, 'idealism'.

As Buddhism scholar John Strong points out, though, to characterize this school of thought as 'idealist' is not entirely correct:

> Vijñānavāda is sometimes called a philosophically 'idealist' school, implying that it does not believe in the reality of the external world, that it sees the world

and everything as being somehow 'unreal' – nothing but a projection of our consciousness. [This is the traditional meaning of *idealism* in Western philosophy.] Vasubandhu would probably have found such a statement bizarre and still based on a mistaken subject-object dualism. He is not trying to show the *unreality* of the world but rather to analyse its *reality*. That reality is characterised by the absence of subject-object dualism.[13]

The reason this school of thought is sometimes mistaken for a form of idealism, as this is known in the West, is the fact that it emphasizes that consciousness alone makes up the nature of reality. This is different from Western idealism, which claims the world around us is a projection of our consciousness, *and thus unreal*, because Western idealism is still contrasting this projection of consciousness with an idea of 'reality' as subsisting in material objects, to which the existence of consciousness is irrelevant. From a Buddhist perspective, though, this way of putting the matter is flawed. To say the world is a projection of consciousness *and therefore not real* is to operate with a false conception of reality: that 'to be real' involves a separate, independent existence. As Nāgārjuna has established, no such separate, independent reality exists. To say the world is a projection of consciousness is therefore, from a Buddhist point of view, simply to describe what the world is. As Strong, again, explains:

> One of the preoccupations of this school was the analysis of consciousness. For the Vijñānavādins, that was equivalent to an analysis of reality-as-we-know-it, because like all Buddhists they believed that we know reality only through the consciousnesses [the moments of dependently co-arising consciousness] that come with our senses and our minds.[14]

Essentially, the Yogācāra/Vijñānavāda/Cittamātra school re-centres the conversation about the nature of dharmas and reality itself in consciousness.

Recall that the Sarvāstivādins conceive dharmas in realist, conventional subject and object, terms: 'I' the changing stream of awareness, of the five aggregates, which is mistaken for a 'self', experience a field of intrinsically unchanging eternal dharmas which flash into and out of 'my' awareness, manifesting their potential as objects of experience. These dharmas are not changed by the process of entering and leaving the stream of awareness, like a painting unaffected by being gazed upon. Nāgārjuna problematizes this model, based on the fact that an eternal essence of dharmas violates the principle of No Self, and on the fact that, to see dharmas as operating in an independent sphere, wholly unaffected by the process of becoming objects of experience, violates the principle of Interbeing.

It is not, therefore, that there are some unchanging entities being observed or experienced by changing ones, but that the experiencer and the experienced, the subject and the object, co-arise as elements of a singular moment of experience. One could say, as mentioned earlier, that the act of dividing an experience into a separately existing and independent subject, like me gazing at a painting, and a separately existing and independent object, the painting itself, is mistaken. The factors constituting this moment co-arise. The painting enables me to become a gazer, and I turn the painting into the object of my gaze. These two factors together make up the unique experience of the moment. This is the ontological meaning of Emptiness.

Although Nāgārjuna does not, himself, specifically mention the division of the experience into subject and object, one can see this as an implicit part of his criticism of thinking of dharmas as unchanging objects, unaffected by their interactions with the world of change. This implication of Nāgārjuna's teaching is drawn out and made explicit in the teaching of the Vijñānavāda school. As Strong says, 'In a sense, subject-object dualism is the "villain" for Vasubandhu the way inherent self-existence [svabhāva] was the 'villain' for Nāgārjuna.'[15]

In its re-articulation of dharmas in line with Nāgārjuna's principles, the Vijñānavāda school makes a move comparable, in some ways, with Kant's transcendental idealism (briefly mentioned in our discussion of Lokāyata materialism). If, as in Hume's critique of causation, Nāgārjuna can be seen as problematizing the idea of dharmas as independently existing realities, one can see the Vijñānavādins, much like Kant, affirming that dharmas are not features of the world, as a realist would affirm, independent of consciousness. They are, rather, features of how we perceive the world. Unlike Kant, however, the Vijñānavādins, following Nāgārjuna, have also dispensed with the notion of a world of independent objects. Substantively, Vijñānavāda is closer to the process thought of Alfred North Whitehead than to that of Kant. Rather than draw a distinction between the world 'as it is' and the world as we experience it, the idea of the world 'as it is' is dispensed with as a (not very useful) fiction.

How does Vijñānavāda re-articulate the dharmas? Recall that, in the earliest versions of the *Abhidharma* literature, the dharmas are not given a particular nature, as such. They are simply 'there': the objects making up the fundamental building blocks of experience. This reflects what we have been calling, somewhat inexactly, the Buddha's neutral monism.

It is then the Sarvāstivādins who assert that the dharmas have essences and persist through all the phases of time – past, present and future – manifesting, or being 'active', only in the present. This is the view Nāgārjuna then rejects, saying dharmas do not exist independently, but co-arise dependently from moment to moment. Just as I am not the same 'I' from moment to moment, each occasion of the colour blue is a unique, dependently co-arising occasion – a fact obscured by the fact that our conventional habit of using the same word to describe occasions of a similar kind.

The Vijñānavādins, though, much like the Sarvāstivādins and other Buddhist philosophers, are concerned to explain why it is that there is so much similarity, so much continuity, that we are able to have a smooth, coherent set of experiences – so much so as to give rise to the illusion of a permanent self. While Nāgārjuna corrects the tendency towards excessive 'eternalism', it could be argued that he thereby sets the stage for a movement toward 'annihilationism' and nihilism. Of course, Nāgārjuna rejects nihilistic philosophies no less than he does eternalist ones. This is part of his 'middle path'. But it is a misreading to which his seeming rejection of *all* views, including Buddhist views, is vulnerable. The Vijñānavādins, one could say, see themselves as engaging in yet another course correction to ensure that Buddhist thought indeed does remain on the middle path between the extremes of eternalism and annihilationism. One could argue (though not all scholars nor all Buddhists would agree) that it is not Nāgārjuna's actual teaching from which the Vijñānavādins depart so much as the potential misreading of it, from their perspective, in a too-nihilistic direction.

The *Saṃdhinirmocana Sūtra*, a major early Vijñānavāda text, suggests that this philosophy is the 'third turning of the wheel of the dharma'. The first turning, 'Hīnayāna' (early Buddhism) under-negates. The second turning, Madhyamaka, over-negates. Vijñānavāda is presented as being the middle way between these two.

The solution, briefly, that the Vijñānavādins propose is quite brilliant. True, as Nāgārjuna has reminded us, the dharmas are empty of self-existence. But one cannot deny that something that can reasonably be called 'the colour blue' emerges repeatedly in the field of our experience. Why do dependently co-arising moments have causal efficacy of a kind which enables similar objects to appear to our consciousness again and again?[16]

Recall that Kant asserts that certain persistent phenomena, like space, time and causation – categories without which we would be unable to have a coherent experience – do not exist 'out there', in the world beyond our minds (as conventional realist thinking suggests). These necessary, or *transcendental*, categories are elements of our mental structure. They are, one could say, 'hard wired' into our consciousness.

The Vijñānavādins similarly affirm that dharmas are not independently existing entities, as Nāgārjuna has shown they cannot be, but they *are* part of the structure of the field of consciousness that is reality itself. As possibilities that may come to fruition, they are compared to seeds. These seeds exist, metaphorically speaking, in what the Vijñānavāda philosopher Vasubandhu calls a 'granary' or 'storehouse' (*ālaya*). This 'storehouse consciousness' (or *ālayavijñāna*) contains an impression of everything that has happened in the past and the seeds of everything which may yet happen in the future. It is to this consciousness that one awakens when one becomes Buddha, an awakened being. To one who has not awakened, this consciousness is experienced as a universe, as the realm of saṃsāra, of karma and rebirth, and suffering. But to one who has awakened, it is experienced as infinite possibility, infinite creativity and infinite joy: nirvāṇa. Saṃsāra and nirvāṇa are not two separate realms, as Nāgārjuna has shown, but different ways of experiencing consciousness. To be caught in the 'dream' of worldly life is to experience through a modality that divides the one interconnected reality of mind into illusory and insubstantial (*empty*) subjects and objects. Awakening is the experience of non-duality: of going beyond the bifurcation of being into subject and object.[17]

Unlike Kant, who, in keeping with much of Western thought, affirms that there is a 'real' world beyond our consciousness, whose nature we can never know, Vijñānavāda teaches that the world just is that which appears to our consciousness. Kant refers to the unknowable 'things in themselves', as they are, independent of our awareness of them, as *noumena*. This is in contrast with the *phenomena* that we experience. Vijñānavāda, in effect, collapses this distinction, along with rejecting the duality which it implies.

Buddhist 'Theology': The three bodies of Buddha

It is in the Yogācāra idea of an awakened cosmic consciousness that Mahāyāna philosophy most closely shows its affinity with the early Buddhist Mahāsaṅghika teaching that the Buddha is akin to a deity, characterized by unlimited awareness, power and benevolence, and manifesting in the world as many different beings: the Buddhas and Bodhisattvas of the Mahāyāna tradition.

Over the course of the development of Mahāyāna thought, the nature of the cosmic Buddha came to be elaborated in what could be called a Buddhist theology. Specifically, Mahāyāna texts discuss something known as the *Trikāya*, or 'three bodies' of Buddha.[18]

The distinction between the physical and spiritual forms of the Buddha is present in the Theravāda tradition. It is sometimes said of monumental statues of the Buddha in Sri Lanka that they represent the physical form of the Buddha in their appearance. But in their enormous height, they represent the height of his virtues – his spiritual greatness and pre-eminence.[19] One also finds references in the Pāli scriptures to the *Dhammakāya* (Sanskrit, *Dharmakāya*), or 'teaching body' of the Buddha: the 'body' consisting of the truth the Buddha taught. This is contrasted with the impermanent and limited physical body of the Buddha as a living being. The Buddha asks one of his disciples who has come to see him, 'Why do you want to see this filthy body? Whoever sees the Dhamma sees me; whoever sees me sees the Dhamma.'[20]

In Mahāyāna Buddhism, the Dharmakāya is the sum total of metaphysical truths. It is, at the highest level, identical to cosmic consciousness, viewed from the perspective of nirvāṇa. It is also the foundation of our existence, as living beings within the cosmic process. It is the one reality which might be said, in Buddhism, to be permanent, because it is the sum total of the eternal truths – the dharmas – forming the framework in which the cosmic process occurs. This sense of *dharma* is also the closest that Buddhism comes to the Vedic sense of *dharma* as cosmic order. It may be that it is to this unchanging framework of existence that the Buddha refers when he says:

There is, O monks, an unborn, unbecome, unmade, unconditioned. If, O monks, there were not that unborn, unbecome, unmade, unconditioned, you could not know an escape here from the born, become, made, and conditioned. But because there is an unborn, unbecome, unmade, unconditioned, therefore you do know an escape from the born, become, made, and conditioned.

The Dharmakāya is the body of Buddha as seen from the perspective of a fully awakened consciousness. Seen from the perspective of conventional consciousness, it appears in two distinct modes: the other two bodies of Buddha.

It manifests to ordinary consciousness as the physical form of an awakened teacher, such as Siddhārtha Gautama. This conventional physical body – the form in which the Buddha lived and breathed and walked the earth for eighty years, and ashes of which, after his cremation, were kept in various stūpas – is the 'least real', the most ephemeral, of the Buddha bodies. It is known as the *nirmāṇakāya*, or 'transformation body'.

According to Theravāda and other Nikāya forms of Buddhism – like in Jainism, with its many Tīrthaṅkaras – there have been many awakened beings, many Buddhas, in the past, and there will be many more such beings to come in the future. The next awakened being, who is currently a Bodhisattva residing in one of the heavens, is named Maitreya. Whenever these beings are incarnate in their last lifetime – the lifetime in which they will attain awakening and become Buddhas – the body each inhabits is an example of a 'transformation body'. Whenever Maitreya is born next as a human being and attains full awakening, his physical form will be a transformation body.

According to Mahāyāna Buddhism, there are also numerous cosmic Buddhas and celestial Bodhisattvas residing in heavenly realms all of the time. While Theravāda Buddhism tends think in terms of a temporal series of Buddhas appearing in our world, the Mahāyāna tradition teaches that Buddhas and Bodhisattvas exist simultaneously in parallel realms. Some of these realms, such as the 'Pure Land' of the Buddha Amitābha, are described as heavenly paradises where one can be born if one has practiced diligently, with great devotion. An entire sect of Mahāyāna Buddhism in East Asia is based on the idea of being reborn in the Pure Land of Amitābha by putting faith in this Buddha's benevolence. The ethereal bodies of the cosmic Buddhas and Bodhisattvas, depicted in beautiful and colourful works of art and described vividly in Mahāyāna Buddhist texts, are called 'enjoyment bodies', or *saṃbhogakāya*.

The three bodies of Buddha thus refer to the physical bodies of living awakened beings, such as Siddhārtha when he walked the earth, the bodies of celestial or cosmic Buddhas living in heavenly realms (often while simultaneously projecting physical forms, or transformation bodies, into realms like ours, such as the Bodhisattva Avalokiteśvara's incarnations as the Dalai Lamas of Tibet), and the Dharma body, or teaching body, consisting of infinite truth and cosmic awareness itself. The Dharma body is sometimes depicted in an anthropomorphic form as a Buddha whose body makes up the entire cosmos – not unlike the Supreme Lord or Īśvara of Hindu thought). This cosmic Buddha is named Vairocana or Mahāvairocana – meaning 'sun' or 'great sun', the light of awareness that illumines the cosmos. He has been depicted, anthropomorphically, in monumental art as a massive Buddha (*daibutsu*) at the Todaiji temple in Nara, Japan.[21]

The two truths revisited: The three Svabhāvas

Nāgārjuna, in his two truths doctrine, expands upon a concept already present in such Pāli texts as the *Milindapañha*, or *Questions of King Milinda*, in which, one might recall, Nāgasena, a Buddhist monk, teaches a king named Milinda the No Self doctrine using the metaphor of a chariot. The idea is that 'chariot', like 'self', is simply a conventional designation for a collection of parts.

In terms of the two truths, idea is that there is a realm of conventional truth in which it is appropriate to speak of chariots, and even 'selves', to use personal names and so on. But we must be aware, if we are intent on nirvāṇa, that ultimate truth is not captured by such words or concepts.

The Vijñānavāda tradition expands upon this insight with its *trisvabhāva*, or 'three natures' teaching, developed by the philosopher Vasubandhu (c. fourth to fifth century CE), the brother of Asaṅga. *Svabhāva* here does not refer to the independent self-existence of a thing, rejected by Nāgārjuna, but rather a mode of understanding things as they truly are (*tathatā*). As characterized by Buddhism scholar Jonathan C. Gold, the 'three natures' are:

> three vantage points on . . . reality. Very briefly, the 'dependent nature' (*paratantra svabhāva*) is the process viewed from outside – a causal description of the arising of an erroneous duality. This is likened to the magical construction of an illusory appearance of an elephant. The 'constructed nature' (*parikalpita svabhāva*) is simply the appearance itself – ordinary, erroneous (dual) experience. This is likened to the elephant that appears to exist. The 'perfected nature' (*pariniṣpanna svabhāva*) is a fact about the constructed nature: that it is 'empty' of reality, that it does not exist as it appears. This is likened to the non-existence of a real elephant in the locus of its appearance.[22]

The first two of these modes could be said to correspond to Nāgārjuna's 'conventional truth' and the last to his ultimate truth. The 'constructed nature' is the deluded way in which beings view the world: namely, as being made up of more or less permanent objects, persons and so on. It is a product of false concepts projected onto reality. The 'dependent nature' is a description of how the constructed nature, the appearance of a solid entity, comes to be: or rather, *appears* to be. The perfected nature, corresponding to Nāgārjuna's ultimate truth, is the truth of the matter.

The constructed nature is the way an ordinary person perceives the world. The dependent nature explains how the constructed nature comes to appear to a mind that has not become purified of its old mental habits of clinging to objects and conditions and functioning on the basis of subject–object duality. The perfected nature, finally, is the way a Buddha perceives reality, free from false, dichotomizing constructions. The world that appears to most of us is, according to Vasubandhu, neither real nor unreal. It is an appearance (*ākṛti*). Significantly, for Vasubandhu, the idea is not that there is some deeper reality (like the Brahman of Advaita Vedānta) beyond appearance, but that reality *is* appearance: an interplay of dynamic appearances.

The Buddha's skilful means

It should, however, be noted that Mahāyāna Buddhism also has a doctrine called *upāya kauśalya* – a Buddha's 'skilful means' – according to which a Buddha, knowing precisely what a being needs to be taught in order to be brought most quickly to awakening, is able to use a variety of ideas – even ideas that may appear to contradict one another – in the relative, conventional realm in order to show beings the way truth.[23]

In one text, the Buddha Śākyamuni is presented as stating that, 'To the ones who are attached to a self, I have taught no self. To those who are attached to no self, I have taught self.' In the *Lotus Sūtra*, the Buddha is represented as a father whose children are playing in a burning house. The children are so caught up in enjoying their toys that they do not realize they are in danger. When the Buddha calls out, 'Children, you are in danger! Come out of the house!' they ignore him. Being a wise father, though, he intuits how he can save them, and says, 'Look at all these wonderful toys that are outside! They are so much better than the toys inside!' Their curiosity peaked, the children leave the house and reach safety. As suffering, unenlightened beings, caught up in all of our varied attachments, we do not immediately recognize the truth of existence when it is taught to us in the clearest, most straightforward way. It needs to be couched in terms we find acceptable at our current level of awareness. Similarly, according to Mahāyāna Buddhism, many religions and philosophies exist because each is addressed to the needs of those who follow them. Some need a benevolent personal deity. Some need strict moral teaching and so on.

The idea that truth can admit of degrees – that there is no absolute truth that can be put into words, but rather, claims that can be 'more true' or 'less true' – makes this possible. This allows pluralism to flourish within Mahāyāna Buddhism, and for contemporary Mahāyāna Buddhists to affirm that there is truth and goodness in all religions and world views. But it also indicates that some claims are, in the final analysis, truer than others and that some claims are completely false and delusory. Buddhism thus avoids radical relativism. To say there are different 'levels' of truth and that none is wholly without value, is not to say that all teachings are *equally* true or of *equal* value: that 'anything goes'.

Buddha nature: Our universal potential for awakening

According to Mahāyāna Buddhism all beings bear the potential for awakening. The infinite, awakened consciousness of the universe is in all of us. The difference between an ordinary being and a Buddha is that a Buddha has awakened to this true, awakened nature that was actually always there. We are all potentially Buddha. This idea of a potential for awakening in all of us is called the *tathāgatagarbha*, or 'Buddha embryo' teaching of Mahāyāna Buddhism. Each of us is an embryonic Buddha, awaiting maturation to our fully developed, awakened state. This idea that each living being is a 'Buddha embryo' – or, as it is phrased in East Asian Buddhist traditions, that we all have 'Buddha Nature' – is the basis for East Asian forms of Mahāyāna, such as Zen, whose aim is to break down conceptual thought and realise one's original nature in an experience of awakening or enlightenment, known in Japanese as *satori*.

Buddhism in the context of Indian philosophy

With Aśoka's endorsement of Buddhism, this tradition received what could be called 'most favoured tradition status' in ancient India, attracting numerous patrons from the wealthy classes of society. This patronage, combined, it is fair to say, with its intrinsic appeal, put this tradition in a position to have a major impact on Indian thought: an impact felt long after there had ceased to be actual Buddhist practitioners in most of the subcontinent.

Vedic traditions, for their part, responded with their own criticisms of Buddhism and their own incorporations of dimensions of Buddhist thought and practice into their understandings and views of reality. Vedānta, particularly its non-dualist school, drew quite liberally from Buddhism: indeed, to such an extent that it was taken to task by adherents of other Vedic philosophies.

Remarkably, one finds that the adherents of the various Indian philosophical systems, both Vedic and non-Vedic, despite their many criticisms of one another's views, were open to learning from one another. As the participants in the Indian dialectic engaged with one another, they honed their arguments for their own views, but also, often in ingenious ways, adapted these views to include the insights of others, through such conceptual devices as, in the Mahāyāna Buddhist case, upāya kauśalya, or, in the Jain case, anekāntavāda.

Conclusion

The Buddhist tradition remained an ascendant force in Indian intellectual life for several centuries after the reign of Aśoka – well into the first millennium of the Common Era. Over time, though, the adherents of Vedic thought re-asserted themselves until eventually, to cite the title of a recent work by Johannes Bronkhorst, 'the Brahmins won', with their tradition, known today as Hinduism, becoming dominant in the subcontinent.[24] The re-ascent in the first thousand years of the Common Era of Vedic traditions, combined with foreign invasions in the tenth to the thirteenth centuries, spelled the end of Indian Buddhism; but not before this tradition had made its influence felt on both Indian and world philosophy, an influence that continues to be felt even today.

Notes

1 Aśokan inscriptions.
2 Johannes Bronkhorst, *How the Brahmins Won: From Alexander to the Guptas* (Leiden: Brill, 2016).
3 Strong, *The Experience of Buddhism*, pp. 132–3.
4 Ibid., p. 131.
5 Strong, *The Experience of Buddhism*, p. 151.
6 Lawrence Babb, *Absent Lord: Ascetics and Kings in a Jain Ritual Culture* (Berkeley: University of California Press, 1996).
7 Matilal, *Anekāntavāda*, p. 31.
8 Ibid.
9 Ibid., 30.
10 Nāgārjuna, *Mūlamadhyamakakārika* 8: 8, Jay Garfield, trans., *The Fundamental Wisdom of the Middle Way* (New York: Oxford University Press, 1995), p. 212.
11 Strong, *The Experience of Buddhism*, p. 150; *Mūlamadhyamakakārika* 25:19–20.
12 According to Tibetan tradition, Asaṅga learned this system of Buddhism directly from the bodhisattva Maitreya, who will eventually be reborn on the Earth and become the

next Buddha of our world. 'The saint [Asaṅga] strove for many years to have a vision of the celestial Bodhisattva Maitreya, at that time residing in the Tuṣita ['happy'] heaven awaiting his time to return to earth as the next Buddha. Despairing of the results of his meditation Asaṅga gave up, but when, full of compassion, he stooped to help a suffering dog by the roadside that dog became Maitreya himself. Maitreya is always there, but he is only seen through the eyes of compassion and holiness.' (Paul Williams, *Mahāyāna Buddhism* (London: Routledge, 1989), p. 80.

13 Ibid., p. 153.

14 Ibid.

15 Ibid.

16 Indeed, the Vijñānavādins accept the self-existence, or *svabhāva*, of mental dharmas, though not physical dharmas. For Vasubandhu, emptiness specifically means the absence of subject and object, not the absence of self-existence.

17 See Brianne Donaldson, ed., *Beyond the Bifurcation of Nature: A Common World for Animals and the Environment* (Cambridge: Cambridge Scholars Publishing, 2014).

18 Paul J. Griffiths, *On Being Buddha* (Albany: State University of New York Press, 1994).

19 Eyre, *The Long Search, Volume 3.*

20 Etienne Lamotte, trans., *Śūraṃgamasamādhisūtra* (Delhi: Motilal Banarsidass, 2003), p. 49.

21 The more famous *daibutsu* of Kamakura is a depiction not of Vairocana (Japanese: Birushana), but of Amida.

22 Jonathan C. Gold, 'Yogācāra Strategies against Realism: Appearances (*ākṛti*) and Metaphors (*upacāra*)', *Religion Compass* 1 (2006): pp. 3–4. doi:10.1111/j.1749-8171.2006.00014x.

23 Some Buddhist texts have even argued that a Bodhisattva can even resort, on the basis of the principle of skillful means, to actions that would normally be considered morally wrong from a Buddhist perspective, if doing so will lead beings to nirvāṇa. If nothing has self-existence, then nothing can be *inherently* immoral (as nothing is *inherently* anything). Therefore, nothing is forbidden in an absolute sense. The use of violence, intoxicants or sex may in some situations be part of a Bodhisattva's activity. See Charles Goodman, *Consequences of Compassion: An Interpretation and Defense of Buddhist Ethics*, Paperback Reprint (Oxford: Oxford University Press, 2014).

24 Bronkhorst, *How the Brahmins Won.*

5

Vedic thought revisited

Śāstras, epics and the 'Orthodox Systems'

Introduction

In the year 180 BCE, after a period of decline, the Maurya Empire was disbanded. India then came to be ruled, as it has often been throughout its history, by a collection of kings, each in control of a relatively small territory. By the fourth century CE, though, a royal family called the Gupta dynasty managed to become the predominant power. Under its emperor Candragupta I (not to be confused with Candragupta Maurya), it became the chief power in India, remaining dominant until the sixth century, after which it was itself succeeded, like the Mauryas, by regional powers.

Just as the Mauryas, through giving patronage to Buddhism, aided its ascent as one of the most influential systems of belief and practice in ancient India, the Guptas similarly favoured the Brahmins and promoted Vedic – now known as Hindu – traditions.

The Brahmins were not inactive during the era of Buddhist ascendancy. It may be argued that their literary activities during this period laid the foundation for their resurgence under the Guptas. The period from the third century BCE to the fourth century CE, the same period which saw the rise of the Mahāyāna Buddhist philosophies, also saw prodigious literary activity on the part of Brahmins. While the Vedas remained the special preserve of Brahmin teachers, a massive literature was also compiled at this time that made Vedic thought available to a wider audience, aiding in Brahmin ascendancy.

Religious and philosophical allegiance in ancient and classical India

To convey a clear idea of what it means to refer to the relative 'ascendancy' or 'decline' of various schools of thought in India, it should be noted again that Indian systems of philosophy traditionally thrived under a system of patronage not unlike that of medieval Europe, in which artists and literary figures were enabled to pursue their work with the financial support of wealthy patrons.

Philosophy and theology in the European context, however, were largely the preserve of the Church. It was from the Church that one who wished to pursue these fields received support. No single organization, however, comparable to the Church existed in India, which has long been home to many traditions. In India, those who pursued philosophy were either renouncers – members of a Jain, Buddhist or Brahmanical ascetic community – or, in the case of householder Brahmins, priests whose livelihood came from performing Vedic rituals. All this activity, whether ascetic or ritual in nature, required support from the lay community: householders involved in regular occupations. The lay community, for its part, appears to have had multiple, co-existing and overlapping views regarding support for religious and philosophical activity. In other words, some laypersons were exclusive in their allegiances, supporting exclusively either Jain monks and nuns, or Buddhist monks and nuns, or renouncers adhering to Vedic philosophy, or Brahmins practicing Vedic rituals. And, until the tenth century, there were the Ājīvikas as well. It seems to have been far more common, though, for laypersons to have multiple allegiances and to give liberally either to all 'holy persons' whom they might encounter, or, as seems to have been the case with Aśoka, to have a primary allegiance (in Aśoka's case, Buddhism), but nevertheless support adherents of other systems as well, in a spirit of *inclusivism*: seeing other traditions in a generally positive light, even if not as at the same level of one's preferred tradition, as teaching 'lesser truths', or as steps on the path to the highest truth.

Relations among philosophical schools were not always peaceful. As Alexis Sanderson, however, notes, "Indian and Southeast Asian states generally propagated tolerance in matters of religion . . . . . .[T]he religions that flourished during the early mediaeval period in the Indian subcontinent and Southeast Asia enjoyed in many regions an enviable degree of peaceful co-existence." But there is "evidence of sporadic outbreaks of intolerance and persecution." Inter-religious violence occurred in India, but it was the exception rather than the norm.[1]

Vedic pluralism

In addition to the diversity of Indian religious and philosophical traditions, there was also diversity internal to the Vedic tradition. The fact that, today, it has become conventional to identify these traditions as *Hindu*, and as streams within a larger movement called *Hinduism*, can obscure the fact that in ancient times, these traditions, though sharing a basic orientation of respect towards the Vedas, were quite diverse, and, as we shall see, often opposed to one another on various topics. It should be born in mind that during the period when the Vedic systems emerged, they were seen by their adherents as distinct from one another, and often debated one another on a wide array of philosophical topics, no less than they did adherents of non-Vedic schools of thought like Jainism and Buddhism.

Śāstras and epics

Before discussing individual Vedic systems or schools of philosophy, we should address a considerable body of literature which is, broadly speaking, Vedic in orientation, but which cannot be identified with any one school of thought. This is the literature which goes under the heading either of *Śāstra* – authoritative writing – or *Itihāsa* – history. These could be called 'pan-Vedic' or 'pan-Hindu' texts.

Śāstras are texts that present an authoritative Vedic perspective on a topic. These include topics ranging from political science and statecraft (the *Artha Śāstra*), to song, dance and drama (*Nāṭya Śāstra*), to architecture and the ordering of space (*Vastu Śāstra*), to sensory enjoyment (*Kāma Śāstra*), to justice and the good life (*Dharma Śāstra*). And this is not an exhaustive list. The Śāstras are essentially 'how to' guides on the whole range of human activity, written on the assumption that there is a 'right' way to do all these things.

A remarkable quality of much of this literature is its pragmatic, non-judgmental approach to the topics it addresses. Two texts, in particular, have produced reactions of shock on the part of earlier generations of Western scholars, and even some indigenous commentators: Kauṭilya's *Artha Śāstra* and Vātsyāyana's *Kāma Sūtra* (one of many texts in the *Kāma Śāstra* genre).

Kauṭilya is often identified with Cāṇakya, who was, according to tradition, a Brahmin who advised the young Candragupta Maurya. Following Cāṇakya's advice, Candragupta rose to the heights of political authority, establishing the first dynastic power to hold sway over most of the subcontinent. The *Artha Śāstra*'s attribution to Cāṇakya suggests this text conveys the essence of his philosophy, though most scholars place its authorship to a later era (about the first or second century BCE, or one to two centuries after Cāṇakya's lifetime) as well as differentiating its author, Kauṭilya, from Cāṇakya.[2] Often compared to Machiavelli's *The Prince*, a political text also seen as quite scandalous in its time, the *Artha Śāstra* gives a great deal of pragmatic advice to rulers and would-be rulers. Some of it, however, has been condemned as violating the ideals of dharma, such as its recommendations about when and how to go about assassinating one's enemies, or the recommendation that it is best to disguise spies as holy men (monks or Brahmins) because they can go anywhere without fear of harassment, and people tend to ignore them, speaking their secrets freely in front of them without fear.

Similarly, the *Kāma Sūtra*, probably taking its current form around the second century of the Common Era, describes a wide array of sexual positions and activities, including homosexual activities, without passing judgement or taking on a moralistic tone. There is even advice on how to go about seducing the wives of important men so these women will help one to win political favour with their husbands.

Even the *Dharma Śāstras*, which focus on what is and is not considered morally acceptable conduct, display a refreshing understanding that it is not always practically possible to observe ideal moral strictures. Though affirming moral absolutism, especially regarding the authority of the *Vedas*, there is simultaneously a situational ethic operating in these texts. As Hinduism scholar Wendy Doniger explains:

> Manu says: priests should study the Veda, and commoners should trade; in extremity, however . . . a priest can engage in trade; but he is not allowed to trade *all* the things that commoners trade; he cannot sell sesame seed, for instance; but he *can* sell sesame seed under certain circumstances; and, finally, if he does sell it in the wrong circumstances, he will [be reborn as] a worm[3]

The *Dharma Śāstras* are not 'law books' in the Western sense, but explorations of the ideal of dharma and the ways in which it becomes attenuated in practice. 'Good' and 'evil' are poles, and most human behaviour falls somewhere in the middle.

In the *Dharma Śāstras*, the duties of the various groups making up society are presented: the *varnas* or 'castes', as well as the *jātis*, or heredity 'sub-castes' making up the varnas. This conservative ideal for society has never been uncontested in India; but, for those who accept and promote it, the *Dharma Śāstras* serve as their chief source of authority.

In addition to the varna system, the *Dharma Śāstras* also lay out a system of stages, called *āśramas*, which track the course of the life of an individual male. These stages begin around the start of adolescence, when a male is expected to leave home for his studies in a forest retreat. After his education is complete, he will marry and become a householder. After his children are grown and married, he and his wife will enter a state of retirement. Or he may become a renouncer.

The first three āśramas pertain to worldly life, and are, in a sense, universal. All societies involve a phase of training for youth, an active and economically productive phase maintaining a home and family, and a retirement phase, in which one rests, passes on one's wisdom to the next generation and prepares for death. The fourth āśrama, renunciation, is not for everyone, but only for those who feel a strong aspiration for liberation from the cycle of rebirth.

Varna and āśrama form, one could say, two axes along which one might plot the duties of a human male at any given time in his existence. For this reason, the dharma taught in the *Dharma Śāstras* is often called the *varṇāśrama* or *varṇāśrama dharma* – the 'ordering of life into stations and stages'. The duty of a Brahmin male in the householder stage will be different from his duty in the student stage. His duty as a student is to obey his teacher and study what is taught. His duty as a householder is to perform Vedic rituals, providing economic security to his family. Similarly, the duty of a Kṣatriya male in the householder stage will be different from that of a Brahmin: not to perform Vedic rituals, but to defend, and perhaps administer, a political unit, like a kingdom (*rāṣṭra*).

For women, *varṇa* traditionally translates into marrying a man of the same varna and performing her role as a wife and mother in the household. The system of *varṇāśrama* is most definitely patriarchal, like religiously based systems of morality that have developed around the world.

One of the distinctive features of dharma, as understood in the *Dharma Śāstras*, is the fact that it involves both a general understanding of the duties pertaining to all human beings – a universal morality akin to those found in traditions from other parts of the world – but also a focus on the specific duties pertaining to where one is in the *varṇāśrama* matrix: whether one is a Brahmin householder, a Kṣatriya student and so on. Universal or general morality is *sādhāraṇa dharma* (general, common or universal dharma). It consists of the moral restraints and injunctions known as *yama* and *niyama* (which will be discussed when we come to Yoga philosophy). In contrast, the duties specific to one's varṇa and āśrama are known as *svadharma* (literally, one's 'own dharma'). If the general principles and specific duties come into conflict with one another, moral reasoning is needed, to which the *Dharma Śāstras* are an aid.

The *Itihāsa*, or historical literature, is also frequently characterized as having the teaching of dharma as its primary intent. Like the *Dharma Śāstras*, but through the medium of stories rather than enumeration of rules and exceptions, this literature illustrates the moral ideal and the various ways human beings fall short of it. Meaning literally, 'thus it was', the *Itihāsa* texts are typically referred to among scholars as 'epics', given their resemblance to this genre of literature as found in other cultures: lengthy heroic poems with many characters, usually involving warfare, as well as adventure, daring escapes and rescues and heart-rending tragedy.

The two most famous *Itihāsas* are the *Rāmāyaṇa*, or *Life of Rāma*, and the *Mahābhārata*, or *Great Tale of the Bhāratas*. In terms of dharma, the *Rāmāyaṇa* represents the ideal. The main character, Rāma, is a prince of the northern Indian city-state of Ayodhyā. Rāma's father, King Daśaratha, is forced by one of his wives, Kaikeyī, to fulfil two promises he had made to her long ago when she had saved his life by carrying him away from a battlefield when he had been knocked unconscious.

Daśaratha is on the verge of naming his eldest and favourite son, Rāma, as his successor to the throne. Rāma is the son of Daśaratha's eldest wife, Kauśalyā. (Polygamy is traditionally rare in India, but it was historically common among rulers who needed to ensure male heirs to succeed them.) Kaikeyī forces Daśaratha to name her son, Bharata, the next king, and banish Rāma to the wilderness for a period of fourteen years.

Rāma, the paragon of dharma, rather than becoming angry at either Kaikeyī or his father, reasons that a king must keep his promises, or the order of society will break down. Without any complaint, he accepts Kaikeyī's request and voluntarily goes into exile, accompanied by his wife, Sītā, and his faithful brother, Lakṣmaṇa.

During this period of exile, Sītā is abducted by a wicked *rākṣasa*, or monster, called Rāvaṇa. Rāvaṇa is the ruler of Laṅkā – today identified with the island of Sri Lanka – which is a land of rākṣasas, not yet tamed by the teaching of the Buddha. Rāma rescues Sītā with the aid of an army of intelligent apes, led by a general named Hanumān. Rāvaṇa and many other rākṣasas are killed in the course of the battle. In the end, Rāma and Sītā return home to rule Ayodhyā in peace.

Though, on the surface, a great adventure story, the *Rāmāyaṇa* is full of moral lessons and role models. In many ways, it illustrates the ideals of dharma. The story also has theological dimensions, particularly when it is revealed that Rāma is an *avatāra*, or incarnation, of the deity Viṣṇu, the preserver of dharma, who maintains the cosmic order in part by periodically taking form in the world to destroy beings of chaos, such as rākṣasas and *asuras*, or demons. Sītā is also an incarnation of Viṣṇu's wife, the Goddess Lakṣmī, and Rāma's brother, Lakṣmaṇa, is the cosmic serpent, Śeṣa, on whom Viṣṇu reclines while floating on the ocean of consciousness in his infinite, cosmic form. Hanumān, too, is a deity in his own right – the embodiment of *bhakti*, or devotion to God (in this case, God in the form of Viṣṇu). According to one Vaiṣṇava tradition, Hanumān is an incarnation of the deity Śiva, taking form on the earth to assist Viṣṇu.

One can clearly see, illustrated in this popular story, Vedic ideals like adherence to dharma and beliefs of the increasingly popular theistic devotional tradition of Vaiṣṇavism.

The other Hindu historical epic, the *Mahābhārata*, is a massive text, made up of eighteen books (compared to the *Rāmāyaṇa*'s seven). In contrast with the *Rāmāyaṇa*, the *Mahābhārata* is a more complex depiction of human beings struggling – and often failing – to uphold dharma. It narrates a conflict between two sets of cousins – branches of a royal family in another northern Indian kingdom: that of the Kurus. Likely rooted in historical events, this text is a treasury of ancient Indian literature and philosophy. It includes numerous discourses on a variety of issues, usually incorporated as dialogues between one character and another. Probably the most famous of these dialogues is the *Bhagavad Gītā* – the *Song of the Blessed Lord* – in which Arjuna, a prince of the Pāṇḍavas (the heroes of the story), questions the purpose of existence on the eve of the final battle with his cousins, the villainous (but also, in their own ways, heroic) Kauravas. Arjuna's friend and charioteer, Kṛṣṇa, is, like Rāma, an *avatāra* of the Supreme Lord, Viṣṇu (and is, on some accounts, such as that of the *Bhāgavata Purāṇa*, not a mere incarnation, but nothing less than the Supreme Being).[4] In advising Arjuna, Kṛṣṇa draws on a wide range of Indian philosophical systems and incorporates them into a distinctive synthesis.[5]

In addition to the Śāstras, the *Rāmāyaṇa*, and the *Mahābhārata*, a set of eighteen scriptures known as the *Purāṇas*, or *Ancient Lore*, were also compiled from the period just preceding the rise of the Gupta Empire and continuing into the second millennium of the Common Era. While there is much of philosophical interest in the *Purāṇas*, these texts are more generally regarded as being in the realm of religion, focusing, as they do, on the deeds of the major deities that are the focus of the bhakti movement: Viṣṇu, Śiva and the Mother Goddess, called Śakti or Devī. These deities remain the central focus of devotion among most Hindus to the present day, and the centrepieces, respectively, of the Vaiṣṇava, Śaiva and Śākta traditions of Hinduism.

Hindu tradition categorizes all this literature as *smṛti*, or 'remembered'. This is in contrast with the *śruti*, or 'heard' literature, consisting of the *Vedas*. The contrast is between a set of texts regarded as the direct revelation of reality (or the Supreme Being) to the seers of the past and a secondary set of texts whose authority is derivative from the first. A good comparison might be with the distinction made in the Roman Catholic faith between scripture and tradition – the Bible, regarded as the word of God, and church tradition, which is authoritative, but not as authoritative as scripture, on which it is based. In both cases, the original scriptures – the *Vedas* and the Bible – are seen as infallible and unchanging – but the sources of derivative authority – the *smṛti* and church tradition – are relevant for particular times and places.

The central premise of the smṛti literature – and the main principle by which these texts are categorized – is the concept of the four *puruṣārthas*, or 'aims of humanity'. According to this idea, articulated in both the *Dharma Śāstras* and the *Itihāsas*, there are legitimate four aims for human beings to pursue. The *Śāstras* are guides to pursuing these:

1. *Dharma*: righteousness, goodness, justice, duty; to live well and in accord with morality; the 'good life'. This goal helps to regulate the other three.
2. *Artha*: wealth, power; the means to live well.
3. *Kāma*: sensory enjoyment.
4. *Mokṣa*: liberation from all limitation, from suffering, from the cycle of rebirth; nirvāṇa.

The concept of the aims of humanity is sometimes shocking to those who associate Indian traditions exclusively with ascetic, otherworldly aims, such as transcendence and liberation. One needs to recall, though, that two paths are laid out in the *Vedas*: the path of *pravṛtti*, or affirmation of the world, and the path of *nivṛtti*, or renunciation of the world. Renunciation is for those whose goal is liberation. Most people, however, are not ready for such radical self-discipline and ascetic commitment. The first three aims of humanity – duty, wealth and enjoyment – are for the majority of people: householders. Householders, by definition, are on the path of *pravṛtti*, and, for them, enjoyment of the world is perfectly acceptable. Dharma is there to ensure that one does not pursue enjoyment in an immoral fashion, leading to bad karma.

There is nothing wrong, however, with enjoying the good things of this world according to Vedic tradition. In fact, Vedic rituals are designed precisely to ensure such enjoyment, and doing so is sometimes even described as something akin to a duty, at least for householders. The allure of sensory enjoyment is only a problem if one wishes to reach mokṣa. Then, and only then, does it become necessary to sever one's social attachments. For most Hindus, as for most Buddhists and Jains, the aim of mokṣa is seen as distant and likely to occur only after many lifetimes. The more immediate goal is a better rebirth, secured through good, or meritorious, action (*puṇya karma*).

At the same time, though, it is important to note that during the period of the compilation of the smṛti literature, a third option emerges, which integrates the worldly life of pravṛtti with the spiritual aims of nivṛtti. This is the Hindu analogue, one could say, of Mahāyāna Buddhism, which emerges around this time as well. This is the path of *bhakti*, or devotion to a deity, a personal form of the supreme being, as a way to liberation. This is effective even for householders, and can be cultivated by anyone, of any caste, gender or nationality. An Indo-Greek king of the second century BCE, Heliodorus, is known to have become a devotee of Viṣṇu, and in the modern period, devotional forms of Hindu practice have been exported around the world, including followers from many national and ethnic backgrounds.

The 'Classical Systems' of Hindu philosophy

Just as there are *Dharma Śāstras* written to instruct people in dharma – in how to pursue the first and most important of human aims – and *Artha Śāstra* and *Kāma*

Śāstra to guide people in the pursuit of wealth and pleasure, there are also *Mokṣa Śāstras*, whose purpose is to guide persons on the path to liberation. These are the *sūtras*, or root texts of the *darśanas*, the systems of Vedic philosophy.

How many such systems are there? For centuries, it has become conventional for traditional Indian thinkers and many modern scholars of Indian philosophy to refer to the *ṣaḍ darśanas*, or 'six systems' of philosophy. There are, however, many more than six systems of Indian philosophy, and even of Vedic philosophy, depending upon how one divides them.

Many indigenous scholars who have written about six darśanas have used this number, it seems, as a convenient way to limit the purview of discussion to what they regarded, in their particular times and places, as the major systems of thought at that time seen as making serious claims about the nature of reality: claims which any thinker worthy of the name needed to consider and reflect upon (even if ultimately accepting only one of them).

Probably the earliest Indian thinker to write about six darśanas was the Mahāyāna Buddhist philosopher, Bhāviveka, who lived in the fifth century CE. In addition to his own Madhyamaka system, Bhāviveka engages with six other systems, which he lists as Nikāya Buddhism (which he labels collectively as *Śrāvakayāna* – the 'vehicle of the listeners', the Buddha's earliest disciples – or as *Hīnayāna*, 'lesser vehicle'), Yogācāra, and the Vedic systems of Vaiśeṣika, Sāṃkhya, Vedānta and Mīmāṃsā. (One will note that, as an adherent of Madhyamaka, Bhāviveka does not list Madhyamaka as one of the six systems, or 'views.' This may be because Madhyamaka claims not to be a view.) An early sixth century Tamil Buddhist text lists the six darśanas as the Lokāyata, Bauddha (or Buddhist), Sāṃkhya, Nyāya, Vaiśeṣika and Mīmāṃsā. The eighth century Jain thinker, Haribhadra, lists them as Buddhist, Nyāya, Sāṃkhya, Jain, Vaiśeṣika and Mīmāṃsā.[6] Clearly, there was long no consensus about which darśanas made up 'the six systems.'

Again, the basis for classifying a darśana as one of the 'six systems' in these works seems simply to be the fact that it is well known to the author. By the tenth century, though, the Advaita Vedānta thinker, Vācaspatimiśra, had articulated another way of conceptualizing the six darśanas. This system had become commonplace by the nineteenth century, and is presupposed, for example, by the renowned teacher of modern Vedānta, Swami Vivekananda.[7]

According to Vācaspatimiśra's categorization, although there are certainly many more than six schools of Indian philosophy, only six are regarded as *āstika*, a word which is often translated as *orthodox*.

The precise meaning of *āstika*, though, has shifted over time. Today, it most often refers to belief in *Īśvara*, the Supreme Being, with a *nāstika*, the opposite of an *āstika*, being an atheist. In fact, *nāstika*, or *nāstik*, is probably the most common term for an atheist in modern Indic languages, such as Hindi. For the Jain thinker Haribhadra, *āstika* refers to belief in the principle of karma, the cycle of rebirth and the possibility of liberation. As a Jain, Haribhadra would, of course, be an atheist vis-à-vis the Vedic Īśvara, as well as a denier of the authority of the Vedas. But he does not regard himself as a nāstika; for he affirms the reality of karma and rebirth and is devoted to the Jinas as the embodiments of his highest ideal, the liberated soul. Regarding the categorization of the six systems which has become standard today, though, *āstika* means 'affirming the authority of the *Vedas*'. Because affirming Vedic authority is definitive of Hindu identity, the six *āstika* systems of philosophy refer to what are now called the Hindu systems of philosophy: though, again, a perception of these systems as forming part of a unity does not apply to the ancient period, when these were independent, and often contesting, schools of thought. The idea of these systems as forming something like a collective unit arose gradually, mainly since Vācaspatimiśra's time.

The ṣaḍ darśanas, according to this categorization, are Sāṃkhya, Yoga, Nyāya, Vaiśeṣika, Mīmāṃsā (Pūrva Mīmāṃsā) and Vedānta (Uttara Mīmāṃsā). Left out of this categorization are systems of philosophy that do not affirm the authority of the *Vedas*, such as the various Buddhist systems, Jainism and Lokāyata. Though Buddhism and Jainism affirm the principle of karma, the cycle of rebirth and the pursuit of *mokṣa* (and are therefore, from Haribhadra's Jain perspective, *āstika*), they reject Vedic authority. And of course, the Lokāyata system rejects Vedic authority and the cosmology of karma, rebirth and liberation, as well as the existence of Īśvara, affirming only the reality of the material world.

Character and historical background of the 'Six Systems'

The six systems of Hindu philosophy can be further categorized into a set of three pairs, based on certain assumptions and affinities shared across them. These pairings are: Sāṃkhya-Yoga, Nyāya-Vaiśeṣika and Mīmāṃsā-Vedānta.

Sāṃkhya and Yoga share a largely common worldview and terminology. Nyāya and Vaiśeṣika share so much that they eventually became a single system, known as Nyāya-Vaiśeṣika. The first members of these two pair can be seen as having a relationship to the second of theory to practice. That is, there is a sense in which Yoga is applied Sāṃkhya, and Vaiśeṣika applied Nyāya. Mīmāṃsā and Vedānta share a focus on the *Vedas*. Mīmāṃsā, however, focuses on the earlier *Karma Kāṇḍa*, the action portion of the *Vedas*, concerned with ritual. Vedānta is focused on the later *Jñāna Kāṇḍa*, or knowledge portion of the *Vedas*: the *Upaniṣads*.

It should be noted, before we proceed to examine these systems, that we shall, by necessity, be exploring them at a high level of generality. Individual authors adhering to these traditions often display great creativity and originality in articulating their views, and do not always adhere strictly to their system's 'party line' on every issue. This is also true, of course, of the systems we have already explored. It should not be thought that these systems were monolithic, and that the texts produced within them simply reproduce in a robotic fashion the same views and arguments.

That being said, the self-understanding of the adherents of these systems, typically, is that they are not, in fact, saying anything novel in their writings, but that they are re-stating and further unpacking the implications of the eternal wisdom contained in the original root texts, or *sūtras*, on which each is based. The preferred genre of writing for the scholars who identify with these systems is the *bhāṣya*, or commentary. Each commentary claims to explain the understanding of reality presented in teachings of the system's founding seer.

It should also be noted that participation in these systems was not mutually exclusive. A thinker known as an adherent of one particular system could and would write commentaries on the root texts of other systems. There have been Vedāntins who have written commentaries on the *Yoga Sūtra*. Yaśovijaya, a Śvetāmbara Jain, wrote on Nyāya (the Navya Nyāya, or 'new logic' school that was prominent in his time). Many more such examples could be cited. When composing a commentary on the sūtra of a particular school, commentators would typically adhere to the norms of that school: its assumptions and norms of argumentation.

Although the sūtras on which the six systems are based were compiled in their current form in the last couple of centuries before the Common Era, each of these systems represents an ancient thread of thought – 'thread', interestingly, being the literal meaning of *sūtra*, cognate with the English word *suture*. Elements of each system can be found in literature extending back to the *Ṛg Veda*. This does not, of course, mean these systems existed in their developed form as early as the *Ṛg Veda*. It does suggest, though, that numerous currents of thought in play since at least the Vedic period gradually coalesced in the first millennium before the Common Era and were organized and systematized into formal schools of thought by the time that era had begun. As in our earlier discussion of the *Upaniṣads* in relation to non-Vedic schools of thought, there has also been speculation among scholars that non-Vedic ideas have also influenced the development of these schools of thought, particularly the Sāṃkhya and Yoga systems, which bear strong resemblances to Jainism, particularly in their affirmation of a strong dualism of spirit and matter, as well as in the moral principles they enjoin.

The six systems can be represented schematically in the following way:

System	Founding Seer/Author of Sūtra	Worldview/Emphasis
Sāṃkhya	Kapila	Spirit and Matter Dualism/Liberation
Yoga	Patañjali	Spirit and Matter Dualism/Liberation
Nyāya	Gautama	Pluralistic Realism/Logic
Vaiśeṣika	Kanāda	Pluralistic Realism/Ontology
Mīmāṃsā	Jaimini	Vedic Ritualism
Vedānta	Bādarāyaṇa/Vyāsa (?)	Realization of Brahman/Liberation

The remainder of this chapter will be devoted to an exploration of the first five of these systems. Historically, Vedānta became the predominant school of Indian philosophy, as Vedāntic commentators incorporated dimensions of other systems into their own world view and as Vedānta became the chief mode of theological discourse, particular in the Vaiṣṇava religious tradition.

Sāṃkhya

Sāṃkhya is a very ancient system of thought, traced to a seer named Kapila (for whom the city of the Buddha's upbringing, Kāpilavastu, is named). Kapila therefore certainly predates the Buddha. Scholars place his lifetime around the sixth or seventh centuries before the Common Era.

Coming from the same region and period as emergent Jainism, it would not be surprising to find that Sāṃkhya shares a number of affinities with this tradition, which it does. Like Jainism, the ontology of Sāṃkhya is dualistic. It affirms, like Jainism, that there are two fundamental types of elements of which reality consists. These are *puruṣa*, or spirit, and *prakṛti*, which means nature or materiality. This is not unlike the division of existence into *jīva* and *ajīva* in Jain ontology. Like Jainism, Sāṃkhya teaches that spirit has been forever entangled with matter. Like Jainism, the aim of Sāṃkhya, as a spiritual path, is the disentanglement of spirit from matter for the sake of attaining *mokṣa* or liberation from the cycle of rebirth.

The details, however, of spirit's entanglement with matter are quite different in Sāṃkhya from in Jainism. One may recall that in Jainism, jīvas are bound to a particular type of ajīva, or matter, called karma, which exists as particles in cosmic space. Karma particles become attracted to jīvas by passions, which are affective by-products of experiences produced by the fruition of previously embedded karma particles. The Jain path consists of preventing further influx of karma particles into the soul by practicing equanimity – not allowing experiences to arouse karma-attracting passions – and expelling already present karma particles through ascetic practice.

According to Sāṃkhya, there is no literal association of puruṣa with prakṛti. The issue is not physical entanglement. The problem is that puruṣa – which, like jīva, is pure consciousness – has misidentified itself with prakṛti. It has fallen prey to the illusion that it is a physical body inhabiting a material world. This is a deluded perception. In reality, all puruṣas – all souls – are not associated with materiality at all. They exist in a passive state in a realm of pure consciousness. Puruṣas do not literally 'do' anything. Prakṛti, however – material nature – is dynamic and in a state of constant flux. Souls have become enraptured by observing the changes of the material world and now identify with it.

The Sāṃkhya path of purification is thus deeply psychological – not unlike Buddhism. For Sāṃkhya, liberation does not involve removing or blocking any literal, material karma, of the kind affirmed in Jainism. It involves reversing a cognitive error. As in Buddhism, which teaches that bondage to saṃsāra is due to forming a false idea of self, identifying with that idea, and then grasping after objects and circumstances for the benefit of that self, Sāṃkhya teaches that our bondage is due to a false identification of our true self – the soul, or puruṣa – with the elements of the material world. Like the jīvas of Jainism, there are as many puruṣas as there are living beings. Like jīvas, they are numerically many. Their nature, however, is one: pure consciousness.

It is interesting to note that the Sāṃkhya term for the soul – *puruṣa* – which literally means 'person', is the same term used in the *Ṛg Veda* for the cosmic being from whom the cosmos has sprung. In theistic traditions, such as Vedānta, this Vedic concept becomes the basis for the idea that the cosmos is the body of Īśvara, the Lord, who is overseeing the process of cosmic creation, preservation, destruction and re-creation. The apparent diversity of the puruṣas is a product of God's creative activity – also known as *māyā* – by which the one Lord takes on the appearance of being the many entities that make up the universe. Some forms of Vedānta, like Advaita, see this diversity as only apparent, while others, in a more realist vein, affirm that the divine puruṣa actually does *become* the universe, as stated in the *Vedas*.

Sāṃkhya, though, is not theistic in a Vedāntic sense. It teaches, like Jainism and Buddhism, that prakṛti – the material world – does not need any outside explanation to account for its existence or its ordered nature. Sāṃkhya has therefore been categorized by many scholars as atheistic, like Jainism and Buddhism.

However, one may recall that neither Jainism nor Buddhism is atheistic in the modern sense of denying any kind of spiritual or sacred reality. For Jains, the Jinas, collectively, are God (*Dev*), as is any liberated soul, and contemporary Jains are happy to use the English word *God* to refer to it. While Buddhists have not embraced theistic language to the degree that Jains have, Buddhism also incorporates a clear sense of sacrality into its discourse about and iconic imagery of Buddhas and Bodhisattvas.

Among the systems of Indian philosophy, only the Lokāyatas are atheists in the modern sense, affirming the reality only of the material world and explicitly denying the existence not only of a creator deity in the absolute sense (which the systems of Indian philosophy are also happy to deny), but also of souls, karma, *siddhis* (paranormal powers arising from meditation practice, such as past life memory and telepathy) and so on.

In what sense is Sāṃkhya theistic? Are the liberated puruṣas divine for the adherents of this tradition, as the liberated jīvas are for the Jains? Andrew J. Nicholson, has presented the following argument against conventional representations of Sāṃkhya as atheistic:

> There are three possible accounts for God in the Sāṃkhya and Yoga systems: (1) a God who is completely passive, (2) a God who is not creator of the world but is an active agent in the world [which is essentially the God of at least some forms of Vedānta], and (3) a God who is creator of the world. [Sāṃkhya] arguments . . . are designed to prove the nonexistence of the third type of God and would also seem to apply to the second, since any action by God would require some prior desire. [This, one might recall, is a Jain argument against the existence of a creator God as well: that, even if such a being exists, it is inferior to the liberated souls, who are beyond desire.] However, these arguments are not targeted at the first sort of God, a completely passive God. This suggests that the existence of a completely passive God remains a theoretical possibility for the Sāṃkhya[8]

Sāṃkhya scholar Gerald Larson has argued that Sāṃkhya is not entirely uniform regarding the question of the existence of Īśvara, but that even in those passages from Sāṃkhya texts that do affirm the existence of Īśvara, this Īśvara is irrelevant to the liberation of the soul – a position in keeping with the traditional Jain view:

> It is true, of course, that some Sāṃkhya passages . . . are clearly theistic. It is also true that many other Sāṃkhya passages are set in a framework which espouses the old Upaniṣadic notions of *ātman* and *brahman* . . . Most important to note, however, are the several passages in which a *non-theistic* doctrine seems clearly

implied . . . Salvation is the realization that the *puruṣa* . . . is distinct or apart from *prakṛti* or essential material reality. *Īśvara*, if it exists at all, is considered to be a part of the material nature and thus is irrelevant from the point of view of salvation. In other words, the problem of salvation is viewed in non-theistic terms. Whether or not *Īśvara* exists makes little difference. Only the knowledge or realization that the *puruṣa* . . . is apart from all else including the *Īśvara* can lead to salvation.[9]

As presented by both modern and traditional commentators, the view which one finds most commonly is that Sāṃkhya and Yoga share the same basic ontology, but they differ on the question of Īśvara. The Īśvara of Yoga is typically presented – as Nicholson presents it – as 'a completely passive God'.[10] One of the practices of Yoga is *Īśvara-praṇidhāna*: 'contemplation of God'. God, in this context, is a puruṣa, a soul, who has never been bound to the cycle of rebirth.

This is not unlike the role of the Jinas as God in Jainism: beings who do not grant salvation, but embody it. The Jinas are not part of the salvation process, apart from their important role of showing the way to it. But the process itself is described in impersonal terms as the cessation of the influx of karmic matter and expulsion of karmic matter from the soul. This is something one does oneself. It is not granted by a deity. (We saw, similarly, that in Theravāda Buddhism, one also is responsible for putting into action the path taught by the Buddhas, and that this is in contrast with Mahāyāna Buddhism, where one can hope for a transfer of merit from a Bodhisattva and eventually 'pay it forward' by becoming a Bodhisattva oneself.) As the Jains state, and as Larson asserts in his account of Sāṃkhya, even were an active Īśvara in charge of coordinating the events of the universe to exist, such a being 'is irrelevant from the point of view of salvation'. The Īśvara of those Sāṃkhya authors who affirm its existence – and of the related Yoga tradition – is not such an active Īśvara. An Īśvara who acts is an Īśvara who desires. From the point of view of Sāṃkhya and Yoga (and Jainism and Buddhism), an Īśvara, or Lord, who desires is not God. It is not the highest ideal of these traditions, whose value is complete detachment from the changing processes of the material world. Without detachment, liberation is impossible.

The main difference on the question of theism, then, between the Jain tradition, on the one hand, and Yoga and theistic forms of Sāṃkhya, on the other, is that the Jinas were all previously bound to karma. The Tīrthaṅkaras were exceptional souls who found the path to liberation and made it available to others, and the remaining Jinas are beings who followed this path successfully, joining the Tīrthaṅkaras in the realm of the perfected ones (*Siddhaloka*). Īśvara, on the other hand, as affirmed in Yoga and in at least some of the texts of Sāṃkhya, is a puruṣa who has always been liberated.

Īśvara is, one could say, the perfect puruṣa, never bound to the cycle of rebirth by confusing itself with material nature. When a regular puruṣa, however, becomes free by realizing its true nature as pure consciousness, it becomes (or rather, it realizes it always was) no different, in its intrinsic essence, from Īśvara. It is then, in the words of one Sāṃkhya text, *anīśvara*, or 'having no Lord'.[11] It has no Lord; for it *is* the Lord, in essence.

This being 'one with the Lord' of classical Sāṃkhya should not be confused with merging into a loving union with Īśvara, as found in theistic forms of Vedānta, such as

Vaiṣṇava traditions. It is a oneness of essence: a realization that one already was what God has always been, the only difference being that one did not know this of oneself, whereas God has always known it.

How have the puruṣas become bound to material nature? Again, much like Jainism and Buddhism, Sāṃkhya does not posit a beginning to this process, in terms of a temporal point at which it began. It is, like the bondage of the jīvas to karma, a beginningless process. In terms of the mechanism by which it occurs, though, this, again, has to do with the puruṣas' identification of themselves with the dynamic process of the material world. The puruṣas themselves and prakṛti, material nature, have always existed. There is not, in Sāṃkhya, a creation story which accounts for their emergence as separate entities. They are eternal realities.

It should also be noted that puruṣa is not literally bound. It simply misidentifies itself with the material world. The 'bondage' of the puruṣa to saṃsāra is therefore merely apparent. To use a Buddhist image, it is like a dream from which one may awaken. In a passage reminiscent of the Mahāyāna teachings of Emptiness and No Self, a core text of Sāṃkhya, the *Sāṃkhya Kārikā*, states that, "No one, therefore, is bound, no one released, likewise no one transmigrates. (Only) *prakṛti* in its various forms transmigrates, is bound, and is released."[12] Nature goes through its various changes, but the puruṣa, in reality, remains ever the same. They are not truly related.

As Larson elaborates:

[T]here is an absolute separation between *prakṛti* and *puruṣa*. The *puruṣa* is never in fact bound to the world. It only appears to be bound due to the lack of discrimination. Thus, *prakṛti* and *puruṣa* are always only in proximity to one another, never in actual contact. This is a puzzling notion if one thinks of *prakṛti* and *puruṣa* as two things . . . [H]owever, *prakṛti* and *puruṣa* are two realities of a completely different order. The one [prakṛti] includes in itself the potentiality of all things in the manifest world, both mental and physical. The *puruṣa*, however . . . is something like the simple fact of consciousness. Hence, it is not a thing of the manifest world, but rather a presence in the midst of the world. The *puruṣa* is *in* the world but not *of* the world.[13]

The puruṣas, presences of pure consciousness, passively observe the operations of dynamic prakṛti, or material nature. Prakṛti is in constant motion, oscillating through three modes of being, or qualities, called *guṇas*. These guṇas are known as *sattva*, rajas and tamas. They are used both to describe the qualities of what is conventionally regarded as the material world, but also spiritual and emotional states, which are also, for Sāṃkhya, part of material nature.

Rajas is the active quality. It could be translated as dynamism. Tamas is inertia. Sattva is a peaceful state of equilibrium between these two. From a spiritual perspective, to be tamasic is the worst state to cultivate, in which one makes no progress, nor has any interest in doing so. A tamasic person – one in whom tamas is predominant – could be called a 'couch potato'.[14] The predominance of rajas causes one to be active: a better state than tamas, but nonetheless one in need of transcendence. The best of the guṇas is sattva, a calm but alert state in which one can view reality with more objectivity than the desire-driven states of rajas and tamas. Even sattva, though, needs to be transcended; for the ultimate goal of Sāṃkhya philosophy is liberation of the puruṣa, which has become so transfixed with the activities of prakṛti that it has falsely identified itself with them. The most obvious example of this is our identification with the physical body, which is a bundle of prakṛti.

It is interesting to note that the terms for the two main principles of Sāṃkhya philosophy, *puruṣa* and *prakṛti*, are, respectively, a masculine and a feminine noun in the Sanskrit language. Indeed, *puruṣa* is one of the words for a *man*, a male person, in Sanskrit (although the more neutral *person* is the closest English cognate to this word).

The genders of these terms for spirit and matter, respectively, are significant because in Tāntric thought, as we shall see, these two come to be personified as the male and female principles underlying reality and are embodied as the God and Goddess Śiva and Śakti. Śiva embodies pure consciousness, and Śakti, creative power. This pairing of the Father and Mother deities as embodiments of cosmic principles may be very ancient. It is one element of Hindu thought that scholar Asko Parpola traces to the Indus Valley civilization, as is the Puruṣa of the *Ṛg Veda*.

Prakṛti is also identified in Vedānta with *māyā*, the creative power of Īśvara, utilized in the creation, maintenance, destruction and re-creation of the cosmos. Prakṛti is a dynamic, energetic reality, not the 'dead matter' of some forms of materialism, both Indian and Western. Indeed, in those Sāṃkhya texts which are non-theistic, the dynamism of prakṛti is seen as sufficient to account for the phenomena of the material world. All phenomena can be explained in terms of the interplay of the three *guṇas*. For this reason, Sāṃkhya, even more than the materialist Lokāyata system of Indian philosophy, is a promising conversation partner for contemporary materialists in the West, who, in light of the ongoing discoveries on the boundaries of physics, are coming to see materiality much less in terms of 'dead', self-contained particles that are inert until acted upon by an outside force, but in terms of a more dynamic conception of matter as energy, as demonstrated by Einstein.

As a path to liberation, Sāṃkhya is, as Larson describes it, a path of knowledge rather than a path of action. How is this knowledge achieved? It comes from the study of the *tattvas*, or principles, of Sāṃkhya: puruṣa, prakṛti, the guṇas and other principles arising from the (apparent) association of puruṣa and prakṛti, such as *manas* (mind), *buddhi* (intellect) and *ahaṃkāra* (ego, the sense of individual selfhood) and others. In fact, the term *Sāṃkhya* means 'enumeration', referring to the enumeration of these principles. 'From the study (or analysis) of the *tattvas* . . . the knowledge arises, 'I am not conscious; consciousness does not belong to me; the 'I' is not conscious.'[15]

Clearly, though, more than simple cognitive awareness is meant here by knowledge–*jñāna*. If simply being taught the truth of Sāṃkhya, that one's true identity is not the body, mind, intellect or ego, but a pure consciousness beyond all these, were sufficient to give rise to liberation, then one could achieve liberation by reading this book. Would that it were so simple! By 'knowledge', however, a deeper, more transformative knowledge is meant. As Larson explains:

> Even though this 'knowledge' arises from the study or analysis of the *tattvas*, this
> does not mean that one can achieve this realization simply by learning the number

and function of the various evolutes or emergents of the system. Much more is involved. *Jñāna* or 'knowledge' is one of the *bhāvas* and thus a basic striving or possible orientation in man's [human] nature . . . Thus the 'study of the principles' implies much more than ordinary study. It implies, rather, a fundamental change in the basic orientation of man [humanity]. It implies a kind of intuitive realization or discrimination which separates out pure consciousness from everything that is not consciousness . . . All notions of 'I,' all strivings, all thought, all the processes of ordinary existence are radically eliminated, and one is left only with the pure fact of consciousness.[16]

One will likely note that this elimination of the 'I' – the realization that there is no 'self' in any of the places we would normally locate it – is reminiscent of Buddhism. But one will likely also ask the question of *how*, precisely, this 'intuitive realization' arises. According to Sāṃkhya, it is knowledge, and knowledge alone, that constitutes liberation. It is not a result of action. How, then does one go about achieving it? It involves studying the tattvas, but it is not simply a matter of listening to a teacher or reading a book. Is a transformative practice available to cultivate a mental state conducive to this intuitive awareness? This is the question to which Yoga is addressed.

Yoga

A beginning student of Indian philosophy is likely to puzzled and perhaps even shocked to find that Yoga is a system of Indian philosophy. In the contemporary world, and especially in the West, the word *yoga* is associated not with philosophy, but with physical exercise. It is generally known that it comes from India. And some systems of yoga are quite clear about their rootedness in a spiritual and philosophical vision of reality. But the dominant view of yoga today is that it is a system of postures, or *āsanas*, and exercises practiced for promoting physical and mental health.

This picture of yoga, however, is far from complete. The word *yoga* itself is derived from the Sanskrit verbal root *yuj*, meaning 'yoke'. The aim of yoga is to 'yoke' the mind to its true nature or source. The practice of meditation – also strongly associated with contemporary yoga – thus comes to mind when one reflects on the meaning of this term. What, precisely, this practice refers to, though – what it means in pragmatic terms to practice yoga – is not thus illuminated. Does it refer to a system of postures, to meditation, to both of these together, or to something else?

Interestingly, the root meaning of *yoga* as being yoked or tied back to one's true nature or source is not unlike the root meaning of *religion*. The Latin *religio* is derived from *religare*, which means something like 'to yoke' or 'to tie back' to one's source, to one's higher reality. Yoga and religion are thus closely connected in their original meanings. As it develops through the course of the history of Indian philosophy, *yoga* comes to refer to any spiritual discipline or practice. This includes the kinds of things one associates with yoga today – breathing exercises, meditation and postures – but also things like devotional practice (*bhakti yoga*) or doing good works (*karma yoga*) or cultivating the kind of knowledge at which Sāṃkhya is aimed (*jñāna yoga*). In the

Jain tradition, *yoga* is often used synonymously with terms like *darśana*. In this usage then, the various systems of Indian philosophy can also be known as yogas – as, for that matter, can the world's religions.

What, then, is the Yoga system of Indian philosophy? How did the contemporary sense of the word *yoga* develop and come to be so pervasive?

Yoga, as mentioned earlier, could be seen as a practice built on the Sāṃkhya model of the nature of reality. The Yoga darśana accepts the Sāṃkhya world view, but adds an eight-step, 'eight-limbed' (*aṣṭāṅga*) practice aimed at liberating puruṣa from prakṛti. In contrast with the emphasis on liberating knowledge (*jñāna*) that characterizes Sāṃkhya, the emphasis of Yoga is on a *practice* that transforms the mind into an environment conducive to the intuitive insight at which Sāṃkhya aims. From a Sāṃkhya perspective, the practice of Yoga could be seen as a preparatory discipline to make study of the tattvas effective.

Yoga, as a system of philosophy, presupposes Sāṃkhya. It uses Sāṃkhya vocabulary and concepts and makes presuppositions which are consistent with the teachings of this school.

As a practice, however, Yoga appears to be 'exportable', in the sense that one can envision adherents of multiple philosophical orientations adopting and adapting this practice to their own ends, so long as these are compatible with the basic values and aims of the Yoga tradition. In other words, we have already seen something akin to Yoga in the Buddhist eightfold path.[17] One can easily envision a Jain following the Yoga philosophy with little or no incompatibility (and indeed, Haribhadra, in his *Yogadṛṣṭisamuccāya*, or *Collection of Views on Yoga*, makes a case for this very thesis). And in later centuries, adherents of the various systems of Vedānta wrote commentaries on the *Yoga Sūtra* and assimilated Yoga to their practices and aims, a process which continues to the present. When Islam became part of Indian culture in the medieval period, Sufis incorporated elements of Yoga into their practices and philosophies as well. In the contemporary period, there have been numerous (and controversial) attempts to develop a 'Christian Yoga'. It may be debated whether the metaphysical assumptions and ethos of the Abrahamic traditions are as compatible with the Yoga tradition as Indian philosophies like Buddhism, Jainism and Vedānta, which share far more of the original Sāṃkhya vision of reality than non-Indian traditions do. The point, though, is that the fact that Yoga has been *perceived* to be as adaptable as it has helps to underscore what a powerful and effective system for personal transformation it presents, such that persons even from traditions with values, aims and world view which diverge from it in certain important ways nevertheless feel drawn to tap into it and make it their own. Even an adherent of a purely secular, materialist world view may feel drawn to take up the practice of Yoga in pursuit of the mental and physical health benefits it has been shown, empirically, to cultivate.

Not unlike the eightfold path of Buddhism, Yoga involves eight practices aimed at making the mind an environment conducive to liberating realization. However, unlike the eightfold path, which consists of eight habits cultivated simultaneously – as portrayed visually with the image of the *dharmacakra* or 'Wheel of Dharma' – the Eight Limbs of Yoga form a series of steps or stages, to be undertaken more or less in sequence. This does not mean that one gives up the earlier steps as one progresses to the later ones, but rather, that each step builds upon the one or the ones that precede it.

These eight steps are enumerated by the seer Patañjali in his *Yoga Sūtra*, the root text of this system. Just as Kapila is the *ṛṣi*, or seer, to whom the Sāṃkhya tradition is traced, Patañjali is the seer of the Yoga tradition. There is some debate among scholars over the precise identity and date of Patañjali. A Sanskrit grammarian of the second century BCE was named Patañjali. Some scholars affirm that this grammarian and the author of the *Yoga Sūtra* are the same person. Most scholars, however, see them as two different people who happened to have the same name, with the Patañjali of the *Yoga Sūtra* probably having lived between the second and fifth centuries CE. As with many Indian traditions, though, it is likely that the Yoga philosophy presented by Patañjali did not originate with him, but that he compiled and put into a systematic form the teachings of a pre-existing school of thought which may be quite ancient indeed. One may recall that there have been speculations that this school – or a precursor of it – may trace to the Indus Valley civilization. Given its pairing with Sāṃkhya, whose concepts have a similarly ancient pedigree, this is not an entirely implausible hypothesis, though it remains speculative.

The eight limbs of Yoga are as follows:

1. *Yama*: ethical restraints; five moral rules identical with the *vratas* of Jainism
2. *Niyama*: ethical injunctions; an additional five moral rules
3. *Āsana*: literally 'seat'; correct posture for the practice of meditation
4. *Prāṇāyāma*: breath control; breathing correctly for the practice of meditation
5. *Pratyāhāra*: withdrawal of the senses; moving from an outward to an inward orientation
6. *Dhāraṇā*: concentration; focusing the attention on just one object
7. *Dhyāna*: meditation; focusing the mind on one's desired ideal – the *puruṣa*
8. *Samādhi*: absorption; becoming completely identified with the object of one's meditation.

The first four of the eight stages involve external, physical preparation for the inwardly directed practices of the latter stages, though the first two, Yama and Niyama, also entail moral preparation.

Yama and Niyama are ethical restraints and injunctions one must master before one begins the process of meditation. The Yamas, identical to the Jain vows, or vratas, are:

1. *Ahiṃsā*: non-violence
2. *Satya*: telling the truth, avoiding all falsehood
3. *Asteya*: not stealing, not taking anything that is not explicitly given to one
4. *Brahmacarya*: not indulging sensual desires
5. *Aparigraha*: non-attachment

As has been mentioned previously, 'chicken-or-the-egg' questions about which school of thought came up with which idea first and which was influenced by the other are extremely difficult to answer in Indian philosophy. It is likely that neither the Jains nor the Yogins borrowed their moral principles from the other, but that both emerged from a shared context in which these principles were commonly accepted. It is fairly certain, though, that the Buddha innovated in his articulation of the Five Precepts by replacing aparigraha with non-consumption of intoxicants, and that the shared list of the Jain and Yoga schools is the older system.

The Yamas are moral restraints. They focus upon behaviours one should avoid if one wants to cultivate knowledge – violence, lying, stealing, indulging the senses, and attachment. The Niyamas, in contrast, are injunctions: behaviours one should cultivate to prepare one's mind for the transforming knowledge that leads to liberation.

The Niyamas are:

1. *Śauca*: purity, cleanliness, both inward and outward
2. *Santoṣa*: contentment
3. *Tapas*: asceticism
4. Svādhyāya: study
5. *Īśvarapraṇidhāna*: contemplation of God

As we have seen, according to traditional accounts of Sāṃkhya and Yoga, affirmation (or not) of the existence of Īśvara is the primary difference between these two philosophies. We have also seen, though, that the idea of an entirely passive Īśvara is compatible with Sāṃkhya. This Īśvara is an ever free being, a puruṣa never bound to prakṛti; and contemplation of Īśvara is one of the practices Yoga commends for attaining liberation.

This contemplation of a passive, ever free Īśvara is akin to the Jain and Buddhist practice of contemplating enlightened beings to emulate the liberated state which they embody and represent. The only difference between this Īśvara and the Jinas or Buddhas is that there was a time when the Jinas and Buddhas were bound to the cycle of rebirth, whereas Īśvara has always been free. And of course, according to Sāṃkhya, even we ourselves were never truly 'bound' in a literal sense. Our 'bondage' consists of our lack of awareness of our freedom: of the fact that puruṣa has never really been tied to prakṛti at all.

Interestingly, Yoga scholar Edwin F. Bryant has made a fascinating and detailed argument, drawing on a variety of sources, that the Īśvara of the Yoga system is not simply the passive ever free puruṣa of some varieties of Sāṃkhya, but that this Īśvara might refer specifically either to the deity Viṣṇu or the deity Śiva, from the wider religious environment Patañjali inhabited.

Bryant's argument does not simply amount to the assertion that Yoga is 'exportable' in the way mentioned previously, such that adherents of theistic systems of practice focused on devotion to a particular deity can adapt this system to their needs, with *Īśvara* – the Lord – being a convenient placeholder into which any specific conception of the Godhead can conceivably be inserted. It is on such a basis, for example, that contemporary forms of 'Christian Yoga' operate, using reflection on Jesus as their 'Īśvarapraṇidhāna'. Patañjali uses the term *iṣṭa-devatā*, drawn from the *Upaniṣads*, to refer to the use of a particular (Vedic) deity as one's means of access to the infinite Brahman. The infinite Lord assumes finite forms to become available to devotees, to enable their path to liberation. Bryant argues that there is evidence that either Viṣṇu or Śiva was probably Patañjali's *iṣṭa-devatā*.[18]

After Yama and Niyama, *Āsana*, or 'seat', refers to the posture in which one meditates. Patañjali tells us the only absolute requirements for posture are that one practice in a clean and comfortable place and keep one's back straight (to aid breathing).[19]

It is interesting, given the emphasis on posture in much contemporary yoga practice, a good deal of which is nothing but *āsana*, that Patañjali says so little about this aspect of yoga. As Bryant points out, this does not mean Patañjali did not think posture was important. There is evidence that several postures for meditation already existed in his time, so he may have either presupposed these or did not feel the need to comment on them. A complex system of postures is developed in the later Yoga tradition: a system called *Haṭha Yoga*. It is this system that has been adopted and adapted in the modern period to the needs and interests of contemporary practitioners and is the reason so many people think of physical postures when they hear the word *yoga*. For Patañjali, the point of correct posture is to aid meditation. All the limbs of Yoga are, for Patañjali, in service of its primary aim: *citta-vṛtti-nirodha*, the calming and eventual cessation of the modifications of consciousness, the stilling of the flow of thoughts that distract us from realizing our true nature.

Prāṇāyāma is control of breath, another essential element in the practice of meditation. It should be understood that this is far more central in the practice of Yoga than it might appear at first glance. The way that one breathes both reflects and also influences the way in which the mind works. It is commonly known, for example, that pausing for a moment and taking several deep breaths after one has been provoked to anger can have a calming effect on the mind. Prāṇāyāma builds an entire system for concentrating the mind upon this insight. As scholar Edwin Bryant has explained:

> [C]oncentration on one's object of meditation has to accompany the practice of *prāṇāyāma*. One must clear the mind of *vṛttis* [distracting thoughts] in conjunction with suspending the breath, not just devote oneself to suspending the breath alone . . . [Y]ogic *prāṇāyāma* in turn, done properly, reciprocally helps to arrest the *vṛttis* of the mind and make it one-pointed. Thus, this practice can lead the mind toward *samādhi*. In any case, without such arresting of the mind, *prāṇāyāma* is not *yoga* but merely a physical feat.[20]

The next limb of Yoga, after Prāṇāyāma, is Pratyāhāra. With Pratyāhāra one deepens one's focus upon the inner dimensions of Yoga, building upon the foundation established by the first four limbs. Pratyāhāra is control of one's response to external stimuli. One gradually withdraws attention and from the outer realm of prakṛti and directs it inwardly, towards the puruṣa: one's real identity.

Dhāraṇā consists of concentration on a single object. Any ordinary object can be used as the object of such concentration. This is in preparation for Dhyāna, or meditation, in which the object of one's focus becomes the puruṣa. The word *dhyāna*, interestingly, comes to be pronounced as *chan* in China, when this practice is taken there by Buddhist monks, and when *chan*, in turn, is taken to Japan, it comes to be pronounced as *zen*.

The culmination of Dhyāna, is Samādhi, or complete absorption in the object of meditation: the puruṣa. Samādhi itself has two modes: *savikalpa samādhi*, where there is a residual awareness of the distinction between subject and object, and *nirvikalpa samādhi*, where this distinction has gone completely. Just as in Yogācāra or Vijñānavāda Buddhism, one is aimed at achieving a state of awareness free from the dichotomy of subject and object. Awareness of any duality between the practitioner and the puruṣa is eliminated. There is no longer the puruṣa as object of meditation. There is only the puruṣa.

Nyāya

We have seen that contrary to popular perceptions of Indian philosophies as paradoxical and transcendentalist, many systems of Indian thought are realist, in terms of the ontologies they affirm. Jainism is realist, affirming that the world which we perceive really exists more or less as we perceive it – that our basic categories for understanding are not fundamentally in error. It affirms that we ultimately want to become free from this reality, to achieve transcendence by freeing our essentially blissful and omniscient soul from obscuring karmic matter. But it does not say the world is unreal. Sāṃkhya, Yoga and early Buddhism are also realist in their understanding of the world around us, though with the twist that what we normally take to be our self is not our true self at all, and that liberation comes from fully internalizing this knowledge. With Mahāyāna Buddhism, we begin to see assertions that we fundamentally misconceive reality by perceiving it as made up of independent objects in space. And, of course, the Lokāyatas, while in many ways at one with contemporary materialists in their denial of entities falling beyond the range of the senses–deities, souls and karma – are also deeply at odds with common-sense understandings of reality as including such phenomena as causation, because they affirm sensory perception alone as a valid basis for knowing.

The next two systems of philosophy we shall explore are also strongly realist in their way of conceiving the world and our knowledge of it. Both are also Vedic systems, seeing the *Vedas* as an authoritative guide to realities beyond the range of normal human perception. But they do not see these texts as *conflicting* with such perception, which is the standard they employ in making the affirmations they do about the world. Nyāya and Vaiśeṣika consist of the use of reason for understanding the world around us. The focus of Vaiśeṣika is the nature of the world, and that of Nyāya is reason itself. Like Sāṃkhya and Yoga, these two systems are traditionally paired, with the first member being in a relation to the second of theory to practice. Nyāya is a system of logic focused on attaining valid knowledge (or *epistemology*). Vaiśeṣika applies this system to the description of the physical world (or *cosmology*).

Developed by the seer Gautama (not to be confused with Siddhārtha Gautama, the Buddha), Nyāya is focused upon establishing a firm foundation for knowledge. How do we know what we know? How do we support the truth claims we make? This system was formulated shortly before the start of the Common Era and then systematized by Gautama, the author of the *Nyāya Sūtra*, around the second or third century CE. The word *Nyāya* literally means 'rules'. In the words of Indian philosophy scholar Bina Gupta, 'The Nyāya school likely had its origin in its attempt to formulate canons of argument for use in debates.'[21]

It should be underscored that Nyāya, like most systems of Indian philosophy, has as its ultimate aim the attainment of the highest good. Though it may appear obsessively preoccupied with questions of logic, and thus akin to the relatively denaturalized and disembodied discipline of analytic philosophy in the West, the *Nyāya Sūtra* asserts at the outset that its main concern is the path to mokṣa.[22] Nyāya is an excellent example of the principle that even if a system of thought and practice is aimed at some ideal of the highest good that might be regarded as, in contemporary terms, 'religious', this does not mean it lacks logical rigour and strict standards of proof and argumentation. It has become a commonplace in the contemporary era to associate any kind of belief in a transcendent reality with irrational, or even fanatical, 'blind faith'. This is not an accurate description of the adherents of the philosophies of ancient India. As mentioned previously, precisely because the stakes are so high – the possibility of one's attainment of limitless, infinite bliss through realizing the true nature of reality – followers of these ancient schools of thought see it as essential that their views be built on a firm foundation.

In Indian philosophy, one's basis for making a knowledge claim is a *pramāṇa*. Adherents of the various systems of Indian philosophy accept different sets of pramāṇas. In fact, the lists of specific pramāṇas acceptable in the systems of philosophy is one of the bases for distinguishing one system from one another.

One principle of Indian philosophy accepted by all schools is that when one debates an adherent of another system, one should only use pramāṇas the other accepts. If, for example, one is an adherent of a Vedic system debating with a Buddhist or Jain, citing the authority of the *Vedas* as the basis for one's claims will carry no weight with one's interlocutors. To be persuasive, one needs to cite sensory experience or inferential logic – both of which Buddhists and Jains accept – as elements of one's argument. Similarly, in Western philosophy, if a Christian is debating an atheist, the fact that a claim is supported by the Bible will not be persuasive to the atheist. 'What difference does it make if your claim is written in an ancient book'?' The Christian will need to put forward evidence the atheist can accept, such as scientific proof.

Nyāya accepts four pramāṇas: sensory perception (*pratyakṣa*), inferential logic (*anumāna*), verbal comparison, or analogy (*upamāna*) and 'word' (*śabda*), which refers to the speech of an authoritative person or text (like the *Vedas*). Two additional pramāṇas that are not part of Nyāya system, but found in other systems, are 'implication' (*arthāpatti*) and non-perception, or 'negative proof' (*anupalabdhi*). The latter two are typically rejected in Nyāya as redundant with inference.

Pratyakṣa – sensory perception – is the only pramāṇa accepted by all Indian systems, including the Lokāyata system (which accepts *only* this pramāṇa). As explained by Gupta:

> For the Naiyāyikas [adherents of Nyāya], perception is cognition that is produced (*janya*) from the contact of the sense organ with an object; it is not itself linguistic, is not erroneous, and is well ascertained. The self [*ātman*], the mind [*manas*], sense organs, objects, and a particular kind of contact between them, are necessary conditions for perception. The contacts take place in a succession: the self comes in contact with the mind or *manas*, the *manas* with the sense organ concerned, and the sense organ with the object. This operation produces a cognition of the sort 'this pitcher is blue.' All knowledge is revelation of objects, and the contact of the senses with an object is not metaphorical, but literal.[23]

This explanation of the Nyāya account of perception draws attention to several aspects of Nyāya as a whole and the world view and approach to knowledge it affirms. A number of comments can be made by way of comparison between Nyāya and the views of other systems.

First, Gupta notes that in an act of perception, the self, or ātman, comes into contact with the mind. The clear contrast here is with Sāṃkhya, in which the self, or puruṣa, never has any real contact with any element of the material continuum, or prakṛti, of which the mind is a part. This contact is, in Sāṃkhya, only apparent, and is precisely the primordial misapprehension that needs to be corrected for liberation to occur. On a spectrum, then, one could say Nyāya is a more realist approach to philosophy than Sāṃkhya, which relegates our sense of relationality or actual contact with the objects of the world to a realm of misapprehension (though Sāṃkhya is nonetheless realist in the important sense that it affirms the reality of prakṛti, and thus of the world).

Another contrast is, of course, with Buddhism, which rejects the concept of self entirely, and accounts for perception purely in terms of the contact of the mind aggregate with the sensory organ aggregate, and the sensory organ aggregate with the sensory object (or 'form') aggregate. There is no deeper 'self' processing all this. (Early Buddhism, though, is realist in the sense of not denying reality to the sensory objects or the mind's relations with them, but only to the idea that either objects or mind have a permanent, enduring, independent existence.) As might be expected, Buddhists and adherents of Nyāya debated extensively in the classical period of Indian philosophy.

Second, Gupta notes that, 'All knowledge is revelation of objects, and the contact of the senses with an object is not metaphorical, but literal.' This is hard-core realism. Objects are not dependently co-arising realities, dependent upon a perceiving subject for their existence; nor is the relationship of subject and object an illusion to be overcome by perception of a deeper oneness. Objects really are 'out there'. When we experience ourselves as perceiving them, it is because we really are perceiving them (unless we are dreaming or deluded).

Inferential logic, or *anumāna*, typically takes the form, in Indian philosophy, of a five-step syllogism. This is distinct from the three-step syllogism of Western philosophy, attributed to Aristotle. The Western three-step syllogism is often illustrated with the following example:

1. All men are mortal. (Major premise)
2. Socrates is a man. (Minor premise)

3. Therefore, Socrates is mortal. (Conclusion)

The Western syllogism begins with a statement that a universal principle applies to a category. ('All men are mortal'.) It then proposes a particular case of that category. ('Socrates is a man'.) It then concludes that the universal principle applies to the particular case, due to this case being a member of the category to which the universal principle applies. ('Therefore, Socrates is mortal'.) The three-step syllogism essentially works from combining the major and the minor premises.

The Indian syllogism includes five steps which come to define how logic is done in India, just as the Aristotelian syllogism has come to define logic in the West. As presented by Matilal, the five-step syllogism is illustrated with the following example:

1. There is fire on this mountain.
2. For, there is smoke there.
3. Smoke goes with fire always (or, in all cases, or in all places): witness, kitchen.
4. This is also a case of smoke.
5. Therefore, there is fire there (on the mountain).[24]

Matilal represents this structure schematically as follows:

1. A (or, A applies here).
2. Because B (or, B applies here).
3. B goes with A always, or in all cases, or in all places; witness case C.
4. It is a case of B.
5. Therefore, it is a case of A.

As Matilal points out, logically speaking, this five-step syllogism 'can be transformed to fit into Aristotle's . . . But, such transformations, though certainly permissible and legitimate, disregard certain important and specific characters of the model of arguments examined by the Indian logicians'.[25]

Rephrased in Indian terms, the Western three-part syllogism proceeds in the following way:

1. Socrates is mortal.
2. Because he is a man.
3. Mortality always goes with being a man: witness, Abraham Lincoln.
4. Socrates is an example of a man.
5. Therefore, Socrates is mortal.

According to Matilal, whereas the Western syllogism is presented in a 'subject-predicate form', the Indian syllogism is presented in a 'property-location form'. In other words, the Western-style argument focuses on the subject (Socrates) and seeks to affirm something true about him (that he is mortal). The Indian argument, on the other hand, focuses on the property (mortality) and seeks to establish that it is occurring in a particular location (Socrates). Substantively, the conclusion is the same: Socrates is mortal (or, mortality is a property of Socrates). Both forms of argumentation reach the same final point, given their premises. But Matilal's analysis reveals that Western and Indian approaches to logic begin from subtly different starting points. Western logicians want to know if *Socrates* is mortal. Indian logicians want to know if *mortality* is present in Socrates. Again, the conclusion is substantively the same. But the emphasis is distinct.

Probably the biggest difference between the Indian and Western syllogisms rests with the third step of the Indian syllogism: the *udāharaṇa*, or example of the general rule which one wishes to prove is applicable to the particular instance under consideration (such as, 'Mortality always goes with being a man: such as, Abraham Lincoln'). The Western syllogism establishes that a statement is formally true – that is, *valid*. The conclusion follows logically from the premises regardless of whether the premises themselves are true. The Indian syllogism seeks to establish not only that a statement is valid, but that it is *sound* – that is, that it is at least highly likely to be true, because other instances of the same principle being applied in the syllogism can be found elsewhere. The Indian syllogism requires the premises with which one begins to be true.

Verbal comparison, or analogy (*upamāna*) refers to knowledge gained from knowing the meanings of words. If one has never seen a cow, but has heard a cow described, then, when one actually does see a cow, in addition to the knowledge of the particular creature that comes from direct observation – such as its being brown, having horns, and making a 'moo' sound – one will also have the realization, 'This is a cow.' According to Nyāya, this is a distinct form of knowledge, so it comes from a distinct pramāṇa. It is not sensory knowledge. One does not see the word 'cow' printed on all cows. Many other schools, however, see it as reducible to, and so redundant with, other pramāṇas. Buddhists, for example, see it as a combination of perception (seeing the cow) and verbal testimony – having heard about cows from someone else. The Mīmāṃsā and Advaita Vedānta schools accept upamāna as a pramāṇa.[26]

Verbal testimony – literally, 'word', or *śabda* – is one of the most controversial pramāṇas. It is controversial on two levels. On one level, there are thinkers who raise doubts about its validity at all. Verbal testimony essentially means one knows something because a reliable person has conveyed it through the medium of language (the spoken or written word). But how does one know a person is a reliable authority? Even if someone has been established as a reliable authority, how does one know that one has correctly understood what that person said? As Gupta elaborates, ' . . . [I]t is not enough that the testimony be reliable; it is contingent upon understanding the meaning of the sentences uttered by an *āpta* [authoritative] person.'[27] On another level, among those schools of thought which do accept this pramāṇa, there is the question of *which* authority is reliable.

Lest one reject the concept of the *śabda pramāṇa* out of hand as an unreliable and wholly subjective faith commitment (as the Lokāyatas do) it should be borne in mind that much of what is widely regarded in the contemporary world as 'knowledge' has not arisen from direct observation. There are scientific principles that many of us regard as true, either by explicit assent, or implicitly, through our actions (such as getting inside an airplane that is about to take off). Most of us have not personally studied the physics behind internal combustion or aerodynamics, nor carried out experiments to verify for ourselves that these things are true. We take the *word* – we accept the authoritative testimony – of those we trust to have done these things: scientists, authors of science textbooks, schoolteachers, professors and so on.

One might point out that the difference between a religious faith of the kind involved in accepting the word of a sacred scripture, like the Vedas, the Buddhist *Tripiṭaka*, or the Jain *Āgamas* as true, and the kind of 'faith' involved in accepting the word of scientific authorities, is that the claims of science are, in principle, available for anyone to verify for themselves. It is unlikely that we will all go out and get doctoral degrees in physics and engineering in order to fly in an airplane or ride in an automobile. But if wanted to, we could. There is no *fundamental* barrier to our doing so, though there are likely to be many practical ones.

Interestingly, however, many systems of Indian philosophy anticipate this objection – and this is one reason many scholars and practitioners are uncomfortable with characterizing these traditions as 'religious'. From a Buddhist or Jain perspective, anyone can, in principle, practice the Buddhist or Jain paths and discover for oneself whether the teaching of the Buddha or Mahāvīra is reliable. We shall see that in the modern period, the same claim has been advanced for the teachings of the Vedic seers. If one follows the path these sages have presented, one can discover for oneself, on a pragmatic basis, whether their claims are true.

In the premodern period, though, it was more often the case, among the adherents of Vedic schools of thought, that the *Vedas* were not seen so much as constituting knowledge one could verify for oneself, but as something akin to a special revelation, as found in Abrahamic religions, which one needed simply to believe.

Different Vedic traditions take different approaches to this question of establishing a basis for Vedic authority. The two main approaches are those of the Mīmāṃsā school and that of the Naiyāyikas.

The Nyāya approach to Vedic authority is to treat the *Vedas* as being like all authoritative speech. That is, speech is authoritative if spoken by a trustworthy, reliable person. From a Nyāya perspective, no one is more trustworthy than God – Īśvara. The *Vedas* are a trustworthy source of knowledge because they are the word of God.

For this argument to work, of course, the existence of God must be established on a basis other than the Vedas; otherwise, it will suffer from the logical flaw of circularity. One can imagine the following argument:

'Why do you believe in God?'
'Because the scripture tells me that God exists.'
'Why do you believe what scripture says?'
'Because it is the word of God.'
'But how do you know that the scripture is the word of God?'
'Because it says so.'

To establish that the Vedas are a valid source of knowledge because they are the word of God, one first has to establish, independently of the Vedas, that God exists.

This is not unlike the project of 'natural theology' pursued by many Christian thinkers. Analogously to the Naiyāyikas, Christian thinkers, such as St. Thomas Aquinas, believe God has revealed important truths which are not available through other means, like observation and reason. For Christians, these are teachings such as that Jesus died for humanity's sins and rose from the dead, as well as the doctrine of the Trinity, which explains how God can be both Father in Heaven and Son living and suffering and dying on Earth. For the Naiyāyikas, these are teachings such as the reality of the ātman and its relationship with Brahman and the path to liberation.

According to both traditions, however, the existence of God as such, apart from the more specific details the scripture is believed to reveal, can be arrived at through observation and logical argumentation.

Adherents of Nyāya, over the course of several centuries, developed several ingenious arguments for the existence of God, most of which are variations on what in Western theology, is called the *cosmological argument*: an argument from the existence of order and coherence in the world to a divine orderer. It is interesting to point out the differences, though, between Western variations of this argument and their Nyāya counterparts. One might recall that in Indian thought, God is not the absolute creator of the universe from nothing. God, rather, 'creates' or 'orders' the world from pre-existing material. Nyāya, operating with the cosmology of the Vaiśeṣika system with which it is paired, affirms that the universe is made up of intrinsically inert atoms. Unlike the internally dynamic prakṛti of Sāṃkhya, the atoms of Nyāya and Vaiśeṣika, much like those of classical Greek philosophy, require some outside force to set them into motion to create an ordered universe. This outside force, according the Naiyāyika theistic arguments, is God (Īśvara).

Though occupied principally with logical argumentation, Nyāya is finally aimed at placing God – and therefore, the *Vedas*, as God's word – on a firm footing of knowledge. Logic functions, as we have seen with other Indian philosophies, in the service of a way of life aimed at the highest good: in this case liberation. This is an excellent example of why it is difficult, and arguably not appropriate, to try to fit Indian philosophy as a whole into a Western category of being 'spiritual', 'mystical', or 'religious' in nature as opposed to being 'secular', 'naturalistic' or 'scientific'. It encompasses both categories, whose sharp separation is largely foreign to it. Is Nyāya a rigorous system of logical argumentation, such as those found in modern Western philosophy? Or is it an intellectual practice in the service of what a Westerner might call a 'spiritual' or 'religious' goal? It is both. Or rather, it is neither, in any exclusive sense.

Vaiśeṣika

Though it was eventually subsumed under the Nyāya system of philosophy, with which it is paired, Vaiśeṣika is one of the most ancient systems of Vedic thought. As Gupta states, 'The Vaiśeṣika is a very ancient system, most probably pre-Buddhist, whose earliest systematization was made by Kaṇāda in the *Vaiśeṣika Sūtra* which antedates most of the extant *sūtras*.'[28]

Vaiśeṣika is a realist account of the universe revealed to our common experience. Unlike Nyāya, it is not so much an epistemology, raising questions of how we know what we do, as a cosmology. It describes the types of entity making up the world revealed to human experience. Just as the main focus of Nyāya is the pramāṇas – the means of valid knowledge – the main focus of Vaiśeṣika is the *padārthas*: the categories of entity making up the world.

The categories are six in number:

1. Substance (*dravya*)
2. Quality (*guṇa* – though here bearing a different meaning than in Sāṃkhya-Yoga)
3. Activity (*karma* – not referring to the law of cause and effect, but to action in general)
4. Universality or generality (*sāmānya*)
5. Particularity (*viśeṣa* – from which the Vaiśeṣika system of philosophy derives its name)
6. Inherence (*samavāya* – the relation between a quality and a substance)

Some later Vaiśeṣikas add a seventh category of absence, or non-being (*abhāva*).

As Gupta points out, while the term *dravya* is often translated as *substance*, its meaning in Vaiśeṣika is different from the meaning of this term in Western philosophy, where it usually has the connotation of something unchanging and eternal. However, 'A *dravya*, according to the Vaiśeṣika, may change, or may last for some time and then cease to be, or may be eternal.'[29] In Vaiśeṣika thought, a dravya is defined not by its permanence or lack thereof, but by serving as the locus of *qualities* and *activities*. Dravya, in short, is that which is characterized by qualities and activities.

There are nine dravyas. They are:

1. Earth (*pṛthvī*)
2. Water (*ap*)
3. Fire (*tejas*)
4. Air (*vāyu*)
5. Ether (*ākāśa*)
6. Time (*kāla*)
7. Space (*dik*)
8. Soul (*ātman*)
9. Mind (*manas*)

These nine dravyas are further categorized as *atomic* or *non-atomic*. The first four dravyas – which correspond, in contemporary science, not to elements, but to states of matter: solid, liquid, plasma and gas – are atomic. They are made up of particles which are the smallest possible unit of a substance, the Sanskrit term for which is *paramāṇu* (literally, 'supremely small'). Paramāṇus combine to form larger particles, much in the way atoms, in contemporary chemistry, combine to form molecules. *Atom* in Vaiśeṣika does not refer to the atoms of contemporary science, but to the smallest possible particle of a dravya. There are earth, water, fire and air atoms.

The objects of daily life, on a human scale, are composed of atoms of these four varieties, combining with one another in various proportions. Hard objects contain a high proportion of earth atoms. Objects are hot or cold to the extent that they contain fire atoms. Soft, 'squishy' objects are a mix of earth and water atoms and so on.

When Gupta states that dravyas can change or even cease to exist, she is referring to the combinations of these atoms – composite entities – which are also called *dravya*. A table is thus an example of a dravya, as are the atoms of which it is made. It is a composite or compound dravya.

The atoms themselves, though, are indestructible and eternal. One can see why this must be. If an atom is defined as the smallest possible particle of a certain type, if it were to be destroyed, it would have to be broken down into smaller particles; but this is a contradiction.

This is a contradiction because anything which can be broken down further is not, by definition, an atom: a paramāṇu. The basic dravyas, then, of which larger composite dravyas are composed, are eternal and indestructible.[30] In this sense, *dravya* is not unlike the Western concept of a substance.

Ether, time and space are non-atomic substances. There is only one of each of them, and they are each all-pervasive, filling the entire cosmos. Ether is the medium by which sound travels. Time and space are understood essentially as they are on a common understanding as, respectively, the succession from one moment to the next and the universal 'container' in which all things exist and through which they move. Vaiśeṣika, again, is realist, so the question of either time or space being an illusion or projection of consciousness does not arise. Because time is one, it is not atomic in the Buddhist sense. Talk of 'one moment to the next' is metaphorical. The Vaiśeṣika concept of space is close to that of Newtonian physics in the West: that in which all objects, or dravyas, are located, and through which they move.

The soul, or ātman, is also non-atomic. It is also – like ether, time and space – all-pervasive. In this sense, the ātman of Nyāya and Vaiśeṣika is like the puruṣa of Sāṃkhya. Like the puruṣas of Sāṃkhya and the jīvas of Jainism, there are as many souls, according to Vaiśeṣika, as there are living beings in the universe. But Vaiśeṣika is more like Jainism in its affirmation that souls really are present in the universe, in a spatial sense, whereas in Sāṃkhya the puruṣas are only 'in' the material universe in a 'virtual' sense, there being no actual relations between puruṣa and prakṛti. Unlike Vaiśeṣika, however, Jainism teaches that souls are located in those specific parts of space in which their bodies reside and are in fact spatially co-extensive with their bodies. A liberated soul even retains the basic shape of the last body in which it was incarnate when it ascends to the Siddhaloka. Vaiśeṣika teaches that all souls pervade the entirety of the cosmos, sharing the same cosmic space. They do not, as in Jainism, literally 'inhabit' bodies, but rather, as in Sāṃkhya, identify with them.

The mind, though, according to Vaiśeṣika - as in Sāṃkhya-Yoga - is distinct from the soul. It is an atomic substance, located in the body of a living being. However, unlike the other atomic substances–earth, water, fire and air – mind does not combine with other atomic substances to form larger substances, though it does experience contact with the substances making up the body.

Why is the mind atomic? According to Gupta: 'The Vaiśeṣika argues that if the mind were not of an atomic size, then there could be simultaneous contact of its different parts with many senses leading to many different perceptions at the same time, which, however, is not the case.'[31]

A dravya, or substance, again, is a locus of qualities and actions. Qualities are of a great many kinds. They are the medium by which we perceive substances. I can see a thing because it has a certain shape and colour. I can see it, hear it, feel it and so on, because it has qualities I can see, hear and feel. Through its qualities, I know of its existence.

The qualities are not limited to physical qualities. Because the dravyas include the mind and soul, the qualities include characteristics particular to these substances. The *Vaiśeṣika Sūtra* lists twenty-four such qualities.[32] This listing might remind one of the *Abhidharma* lists of Buddhism: the lists of all possible objects of experience. The resemblance is more than superficial; for the qualities of the Vaiśeṣika philosophy, like the dharmas of Buddhism, represent what it is possible to experience, at least in a direct fashion, through the senses (including the mind). Substances, again, are known through their qualities. If a fire, for example, did not possess the qualities of light and heat, as well as the ability to cause pain when touched, one would not be aware of its existence. We know the mind can have qualities such as pleasure, pain and desire, because we experience them directly.

The main difference, of course, between the Vaiśeṣika qualities and the Buddhist dharmas can be found in the ontologies affirmed by these systems of philosophy. For Vaiśeṣika, a quality is always a quality *of* some dravya. A quality belongs to a substance. There are no 'free floating' qualities.

For the Buddhist, of course, it is precisely the opposite. There are no 'things'. There are only combinations of dharmas experienced at a point in time. And, of course, whether the dharmas themselves, as possibilities for experience, persist over time or are dependently co-arisen in a given moment – their names and natures being but a conventional fiction – depends upon which Buddhist one asks.

In addition to qualities, a dravya is also a locus for action, or *karma*. Again, *karma* does not refer, in this context, to the law of moral causation. Rather, '*karma* in this school is taken to signify movement of a thing from one place to another'.[33] The all-pervasive substances–ether, time, space and soul – are not capable of motion. This category only pertains to atomic substances. Action is distinguished from quality by the fact that, 'While quality is a passive attribute, *karma* is dynamic.'[34]

The next category – the universal, or general, known as *sāmānya* – refers to 'entities which though one and eternal, inhere in many'. Universals, 'account for an infinite number of particulars appearing to be alike, though otherwise different. . . . It is because of the universal that we designate different particulars by the same name'.[35]

As with qualities, the Vaiśeṣika affirmation that universals are real is problematic from a Buddhist perspective. In fact, this category is even more problematic for a Buddhist than the category of qualities. As we have seen, there are realist schools of Buddhism which are willing to see dharmas as enduring possibilities – like the Sarvāstivādin school, which affirms that dharmas are eternal. But no Buddhist school of thought is willing to see a composite entity as anything other than the momentary coming together of its component parts at a given time. We saw that Nāgasena affirmed that 'chariot' is merely a conventional designation for the coming together of parts in a particular way. There is no 'chariotness' – in other words, there is no 'self' of the chariot.

The Vaiśeṣika tradition, however, affirms that there is such a thing as 'chariotness'. Gupta explains this in the following way:

> It is because of the universal that we designate different particulars by the same name, however, unlike many Western realists, the Vaiśeṣika does not believe that the universal 'cowness' is [just] the meaning of the word 'cow'. The Vaiśeṣika argues that if that were the case, then the sentence 'bring a cow' would mean 'bring cowness', which is absurd; it rather means a particular that is characterized by the appropriate universal, a cow characterized by cowness in this case.[36]

From a Buddhist perspective, 'cowness' is a fiction – an effect of the way we use language to describe what are really different entities, using a single term to indicate that they resemble each other in some fashion.

As realists, the Vaiśeṣikas have a ready response to this situation. We see cows because there *are* cows, and we can call them cows and understand what the word 'cow' means, because there is such a thing as 'cowness' – the quality of being a cow which inheres in the beings we (therefore) call cows.

The importance, from a Buddhist perspective, of affirming the non-reality – or the merely conventional reality – of categories like 'cowness' is that this understanding mitigates our tendency to grasp after and become attached to such entities as cows (seen in ancient India, interestingly, as symbols of wealth).

From a Vaiśeṣika perspective, though, it is as important to affirm the reality of the categories of our ordinary experience as it is for the Buddhist to deny it. It is not a coincidence that Gupta elucidates the concept of the universal with the sentence, 'bring a cow'. In the *Vedas*, there are numerous such instructions – instructions such as 'bring a cow' – making up the Vedic ritual, which, one might recall, is viewed as essential to maintaining the cosmic order. If cows are not real – if our categories do not refer to something actually existing – then this undermines a commitment to ritual practice as having a real effect, as well as the authority of the Vedic texts, which are made of sentences of this kind.

The foregoing discussion reveals that although Vaiśeṣika may appear, on its surface, to be akin to an ancient Indian science – which, in many ways, it is – it is also, like Nyāya, a philosophy pursued in the service of Vedic religion. It is as important, from a Vaiśeṣika point of view, to affirm the reality of the world and our categories for understanding it – to support the *Vedas*, which consist of affirmations about the world – as it is, from a Buddhist point of view, to undermine these categories as upholding potential objects of grasping and attachment.

The next category, particularity, or vi, is the category from which the Vaiśeṣika system takes its name – which essentially means 'the investigation of the particulars of things'. Viśeṣa is what differentiates one entity from another – an essential characteristic of a realist understanding of the universe, which is made up of many distinct entities.

Substances are differentiated from one another by their qualities. Composite entities are distinguished by the universals defining them. Similarly, individuals are defined by their particularities.

What does this mean? A human being is a composite substance. This means human beings have certain qualities, such as intelligence. Other beings may also have intelligence, but we know that a particular being is a human being when that being has all the characteristics possessed by human beings. These qualities are how we recognize that a particular being is a human being, and not, say, a cow or a table. These are what Western philosophy would call *essential* qualities of the substance known as *human*.

All these qualities make up the universal known as *humanness*. When we recognize a being as human, we are recognizing that being's humanness. We perceive the universal directly, according to Vaiśeṣika. But no particular human being *is* humanness. We are each human. But we possess humanness. Humanness inheres within us.

Particulars are those qualities specific to a certain human. They differentiate that human from all other humans. So I, for example, possess human qualities such as intelligence and being a biped. These are generic human qualities. But I also happen to have brown hair and green eyes. These are not generic human qualities. They are my *particulars*. In Western philosophy, they would be called *accidental* qualities: not part of my participation in the universal *humanness*.

Inherence – *samavāya* – is the relationship between a quality and a substance, and between a universal and a particular. Qualities *inhere* in substances. Universals *inhere* in particulars. Qualities are not substances and universals are not particulars. But these things are closely related to one another in such a way that they cannot be separated. That relationship is called, in Vaiśeṣika, *inherence*.

Buddhists and Jains attacked the Vaiśeṣika idea of inherence mercilessly. From a Buddhist perspective, there are no substances in which a quality might inhere, and no universals which might inhere in particulars. Such concepts are fictions, projected on the momentary experiences making up life. The specific argument the Buddhists and Jains used to critique inherence was to raise the question, 'If a relation of inherence is needed to explain why a quality is present in a substance, or why a universal is present in a particular, what is it that connects the relation of inherence to the two elements which it connects?' In other words, if it is not the case that a 'substance' is simply what we call the presence of certain qualities at a certain place and time – which is the Buddhist understanding – and if these separate entities, substance and quality, require an external relationship to connect them, what is it that connects that external relationship to the substance and the quality? Are there two additional 'inherences'? One that connects the original inherence to the substance and another which connects it to the quality? And if that is the case, would we not also need more inherences to explain these inherences' connections to one another? This is an example of what is called, in the West, *reductio ad absurdum* – trying to show the position of one's opponent is absurd by deriving unacceptable conclusions from it. What is, of course, really at issue between the Buddhists and the Vaiśeṣikas are different conceptions of reality.

A seventh category, 'absence', or *abhāva*, is added by later adherents of this school to the original Vaiśeṣika list of six. Absence is the non-presence of a quality; for it is not only part of the definition of a substance that certain qualities inhere in it, but also that certain other qualities do not inhere in it. A human is not only (at most) two-legged, but is also not four-legged. The absence of being four-legged is therefore part of what it means to be human.

This should remind one of the Jain teaching of the complexity of existence, and that there is a sense in which a being can be said both to exist and not to exist. A Vaiśeṣika would find this way of speaking incomprehensible and ridiculous – and Vaiśeṣika critics of Jainism did not hesitate to express their views in this regard. But the deeper meaning of this Jain teaching is very much in keeping with the Vaiśeṣika concept of abhāva: that a particular entity is made up of the presence and absence of specific qualities at a specific point in time.

Nyāya and Vaiśeṣika realism was a powerful philosophical voice of classical Indian thought. Adherents of these two schools (and both together, when they eventually merged) were among the sharpest critics of Buddhism during the period of Buddhist ascendancy in India. Their views, though, were also distinct from those of other Vedic systems, such as Sāṃkhya and Yoga and, as we are about to see, Mīmāṃsā and Vedānta – though, as they did with other schools, we shall see that adherents of Vedānta drew upon and made use of Nyāya-Vaiśeṣika ideas and in the formulation of their own positions in later centuries.

Mīmāṃsā

The final two schools making up the six systems of Vedic philosophy are Mīmāṃsā and Vedānta. The term *mīmāṃsā* means 'exegesis' or 'interpretation'. These schools are also known as *Pūrva Mīmāṃsā* and *Uttara Mīmāṃsā*. These terms, respectively, mean 'earlier interpretation' and 'later interpretation'. 'Earlier' and 'later' here refer not so much to the historical priority of the schools themselves as to the traditional ordering of the texts they interpret from the Vedic canon. Pūrva Mīmāṃsā is focused on the interpretation of the earlier portion of the Vedas (the *Karma Kāṇḍa*) concerned with ritual action. Uttara Mīmāṃsā, or Vedānta, is focused on the interpretation of the later portion of the Vedas (the *Jñāna Kāṇḍa*), also known as the *Upaniṣads*, concerned with knowing Brahman. The name *Vedānta*, by which the second of these schools gradually came to be known, and which is the term we shall use to avoid confusion, refers both to the fact that the *Upaniṣads* are literally the 'end of the *Veda*', the final portion of the Vedic literature to be studied traditionally, and that the knowledge of Brahman this literature teaches is the ultimate goal or 'end' of *Vaidika*, or Vedic, thought and practice.

How did these two schools of thought emerge? Vedic tradition has always been internally diverse. The Vedic literature itself, from the *Ṛg Veda* to the *Upaniṣads*, was composed, according to contemporary scholarship, over the course of more than a thousand years, by seers having a wide variety of philosophical views. We have already seen how some of these threads of thought, or *sūtras*, evolved after the Vedic period into distinct and coherent schools like the ones we have been exploring in this chapter. Even elements of non-Vedic traditions, such as the Jain, Buddhist and Lokāyata schools of thought, can be found at some point or another in the Vedic literature.

Among those thinkers who regarded the Vedas as authoritative, some saw these texts as a guide to right action – typically understood as ritual action. Others, however, saw the Vedas as a guide to right knowledge. This, at its most basic, is the essence of the difference between the two dominant systems of Vedic interpretation, Mīmāṃsā and Vedānta.

For some Vedic thinkers, the central focus of the Vedas was always the yajña – the ritual of sacrifice. These thinkers regarded later Vedic writings, such as the *Upaniṣads*, as elaborations on what made the yajña work. But the yajña itself was always the main point. Those who followed this line of thinking eventually formed Mīmāṃsā. Prominent contributors to this school of thought include Kumārila Bhaṭṭa and Prabhākara, both of whom lived around the eighth century of the Common Era, as well as the traditional founder of the system, Jaimini, who lived around the fourth century BCE and authored the *Mīmāṃsā Sūtras*.

One of the characteristics of Mīmāṃsā is a strong emphasis on the correct performance of Vedic ritual and a corresponding focus on the correct pronunciation of the Sanskrit verses of the Vedic hymns during ritual performance. Though not yet called by the name *Mīmāṃsā*, the various texts on Sanskrit grammar composed from the fifth to the fourth centuries BCE which systematized the use of this language are generally understood to be part of the same basic movement of thought. These grammatical texts are regarded as authoritative by the later Mīmāṃsā tradition, as are the other *Vedāṅgas*, or 'limbs of the Veda': various bodies of knowledge mastered because of their necessity to correct ritual performance. The Vedāṅgas, which are traditionally listed as being six in number include phonetics, grammar, metre, etymology, ritual and astronomy.

While both Mīmāṃsā and Vedānta take the Vedas in their totality to be *śabda pramāṇa* – an authoritative and valid foundation for knowledge – the differences between these two systems are not inconsequential. For Mīmāṃsā, the Vedas are primarily a guide to human flourishing here and now, in the material world. The yajña is essential to the maintenance of cosmic order, and specific Vedic rituals have been revealed to enable human beings to enjoy their existence in this life and ensure a pleasant existence in a heavenly realm after death. For Vedānta, the Vedas are, as the Mīmāṃsakas say, a guide to all these things, but also, and ultimately, a guide to attaining freedom from the bondage of material existence. It is not that Vedānta rejects the Mīmāṃsā world view; but it sees the material enjoyments to which Mīmāṃsā points as penultimate, as merely preliminary to the infinitely higher bliss of mokṣa. Similarly, though Mīmāṃsā does not uniformly deny the possibility of mokṣa (although some Mīmāṃsakas do), its adherents, were not typically concerned with liberation so much as with the attainment of worldly (*laukika*) ends through correct performance of the Vedic ritual. One could say the world views of the Mīmāṃsā and Vedānta systems do not differ so much as their value systems do: their sense of what is most important in the Vedic literature the adherents of both systems affirm and cherish.

A central emphasis of Mīmāṃsā is language – again, given the importance of the correct usage of Sanskrit in Vedic practice – and epistemology: specifically, how the words of the *Vedas* give rise to true, reliable knowledge. In addition to language, regarding ritual itself, the entire structure–what one might call the 'grammar' – of Hindu ritual is based upon Mīmāṃsā principles.

It is probably not possible for a Western reader to appreciate fully the thought of Mīmāṃsā without recalling the extent to which the English language, as spoken today, would not exist without the works of William Shakespeare and the King James Bible. The *Vedas* are similarly definitive of Indian culture, especially northern Indian culture, in the ancient and classical periods, and remain so to a great extent even today. This cultural situation is the starting point of Mīmāṃsā philosophy.

Scholar Dan Arnold contrasts the Mīmāṃsā approach to knowledge with a stance present in Western philosophy, which he discerns in Buddhism as well, known as *foundationalism*.[37] The paradigmatic example of foundationalism in modern Western philosophy is probably the work of René Descartes (1596–1650). A predecessor of David Hume, in terms of approaching the question of knowledge from a sceptical stance, Descartes tried to set aside all concepts that might not be justified. He viewed even sensory perception sceptically; for one's senses are capable of being deluded, and, hypothetically, it might be the case that all we perceive is an illusion presented to us by an evil demon. A contemporary version of this sceptical model is the 'brain in a vat' scenario, in which we are not really having the experiences we believe we are having. We are all disembodied brains in vats in the laboratory of a scientist who is experimenting on us by stimulating our brains to make us believe we are living the lives we believe we are living and having the experiences we believe we are having. A great dramatization of this scenario can be found in the film *The Matrix*, in which many human beings have been plugged into an enormous computer in a dystopian future. The computer is utilizing the humans' neural energy, essentially using them as batteries. It keeps them passive by showing them an elaborate virtual reality, in which they believe they are living lives, pursuing careers and so on. The question for the audience is: how do we know *we* are not in the Matrix?

Descartes famously concluded that the only thing of which he could be certain was the fact that he was thinking. Based upon this certain *foundation*, Descartes developed an entire system of philosophy. His first step was deducing from the fact that he was thinking that he, the thinker, must exist. *Cogito ergo sum*, he famously wrote in Latin: 'I think, therefore I am.'

The Buddha, with his No Self doctrine, arguably takes foundationalism even further than Descartes. The Buddha would not say, 'I think, therefore I am.' What, after all, is this 'I'? It is not a thing directly perceived, but an assumption imported into one's experience by habit. In place of 'I think, therefore I am', the Buddha would likely assert, 'Thought is occurring here and now.'

Foundationalism, as a style of doing philosophy, is pervasive in both Indian and Western thought. The distinction of Mīmāṃsā is its rejection of the foundationalist approach to knowledge. As such, Mīmāṃsā is arguably the most realist of Indian system of philosophy. Yet, this realism leads adherents of this system to make claims that are counter-intuitive and idiosyncratic from a standard (that is to say, a foundationalist) philosophical perspective.

Foundationalism is attractive to many thinkers because it holds out the hope that one might establish one's claims on a non-arbitrary basis. Building one's claim on an established tradition, whether it be Christian, Islamic or Vedic, seems random, if one is seeking universal truth. If one were born in a different culture, where a different text was authoritative, one's views might differ considerably from what they currently are. The foundationalist seeks to transcend this situation.

The problem with foundationalism, from a Mīmāṃsā perspective, is that we are not brains in vats. We are not free-floating minds or centres of consciousness with no prior experiences to shape our perceptions. We are not being deceived by an evil demon. Even if we are, how could we ever know otherwise?

What we are, according to Mīmāṃsā, are beings 'thrown' – to cite Martin Heidegger – into a pre-existing cultural and linguistic setting in the absence of which coherent thought would not be possible. Even granting that we have certain pre-linguistic intuitions (including, but certainly not limited to, sensory perceptions), thought and knowledge, as we typically experience them, are inconceivable in the absence of language. And language is not something we craft *a priori*, from some disembodied space, like a brain in a vat. Language is given to us. We start talking and *then* we start thinking, at least with any depth or seriousness, about any complex problem. A language is not a 'neutral' medium. It has a history. Again, think of Shakespeare and the King James Bible, and all the numerous sayings from the daily lives of English speakers drawn from these cultural resources, these wellsprings of the language we use and the thoughts we think. Our language, whatever it may be, bears within it the assumptions of the literatures and mythologies, the poems and songs, and the daily uses that have fed into making it what it is today.

This, in fact, is why some scholars of Indian thought are extremely cautious about how terms are translated from Sanskrit to English. To render *Īśvara*, for example, as *God* is to create the possibility that unwarranted assumptions will be made about the concept of *Īśvara* based on assumptions the word *God* has accumulated throughout its history as part of the English language. It has been necessary, for example, to stipulate that Īśvara is *not* seen as having created the cosmos from nothing, unlike the God of classical Western theism, and so on. *Īśvara* both is and is not *God*.

As it relates to Mīmāṃsā, the point is that this tradition sees the *Vedas* as the repository of all knowledge relevant to *dharma*: to the performance of right action in the world. To see this as nothing other than an act of 'faith' – of belief unwarranted by evidence – is, on some level, to miss the point; for this a judgment formed based on foundationalism. It is based on the view – a view the Mīmāṃsā tradition sees as profoundly mistaken – that there is an alternative, in the quest for knowledge, to utilizing the received wisdom of one's cultural inheritance as one's starting point. We never begin, as it were, at the beginning – at the foundations of knowledge – however much we may wish to do so. We always walk into a conversation already in progress, which has already been going on for hundreds, perhaps thousands, of years. We do not even choose which conversation we are going to join (unless we have done so in a state between lives). We are already inducted, as it were, the moment we learn a language and are taught by our elders what to do and not do.

Even if we grant that it is possible to strip away our assumptions and cultural trappings through a deconstructive meditative process, like that taught in Buddhism, we will still begin our process of inquiry from an historical and cultural starting point.

The very urge to seek an unbiased foundation for knowledge is itself a product of (foundationalist) cultural conditioning.

Mīmāṃsā anti-foundationalism should not be taken to imply that, philosophically, one can only repeat what has been stated in one's sacred texts. The texts are complex, and their elucidation within a set of basic logical rules still allows for considerable latitude of interpretation. Kumārila and Prabhākara, for example, did not agree on all topics, though both adhered to this system.

Mīmāṃsā, again, is a strongly realist system. It affirms, like the Nyāya-Vaiśeṣika system, the reality of the world affirmed in the *Vedas* and of the person as a doer of action: specifically, of ritual action. In the words of scholar of Indian philosophy Sue Hamilton:

> [The Mīmāṃsakas] held that the uttering of a word indicates [or presupposes] the existence of that which it designates. This assisted them as they sought to demonstrate the reality and nature of the plural world, which included a plurality of independent and autonomous 'selves' as performers of the sacrifice . . . [T]he Mīmāṃsakas stated [that] the nature of selfhood is conscious agent (and therefore active ritualist). As Kumārila said in his *Ślokavārtika*: 'The injunction that one has a duty to understand the self does not have a goal of liberation. Such self-knowledge is clearly intended to motivate performance of ritual.'[38]

Again, in a realist vein, not unlike Nyāya-Vaiśeṣika and Jainism, Mīmāṃsā affirms that we typically do perceive the world around us correctly. We are not fundamentally misconceiving our reality, as taught in Buddhism and Advaita Vedānta:

> For the Mīmāṃsakas, cognition represented a fundamentally valid and reliable means of knowledge, both of the world around us and of individual 'selves' as knowers. The act of knowing 'reveals' the external 'transcendentally real' existence of both known and knower: neither of these, that is to say, is in any way dependent on the operating of the cognitive process. Rather, cognition brings about a state of 'being known' in the object of knowledge, and a confirmation of the existence of the autonomous knower. The process of knowing therefore reveals 'truth,' and in this case confirms the worldview of the eternal *Veda*.[39]

The idea of an autonomous knower and an object of knowledge that is 'in no way dependent on the operating of the cognitive process' is radically different from the view of the Buddhist thinker Vasubandhu, for whom knower and known are mutually related and dependently co-arising.

Previously, we had occasion to discuss the Mīmāṃsā doctrine of the authorless and eternal nature of the *Vedas*. This, for many, counter-intuitive concept has interesting resonances with postmodern literary theory, such as that of Roland Barthes, in which the idea of the author of a text is shown to be problematic, and ultimately irrelevant to textual interpretation.[40] Once a text exists, according to Barthes, the author has no special authority over the interpretation of its meaning and can essentially be treated as a non-entity.

Bhartṛhari

An important Indian thinker often discussed in relation to Mīmāṃsā, though it is not clear if he was an adherent of this system, is Bhartṛhari. Bhartṛhari lived around the fifth century CE. His connection with Mīmāṃsā is his focus on language and the ways in which language serves to make meaning. This is of course a central concern for Mīmāṃsā because of the importance of the Vedas to this system of thought. Understanding how the Vedic sentences are able to convey their import is vital to the ritual process, particularly those sentences which include injunctions to action. Like the Mīmāṃsakas, Bhartṛhari's starting point in his reflections on language are the works of Sanskrit grammarians, such as Pāṇini and Patañjali.

One element of Bhartṛhari's thought that differentiates it from Mīmāṃsā and brings his approach closer to Nyāya-Vaiśeṣika and Vedānta, is his emphasis on liberation. As Hamilton explains:

> Bhartṛhari put forward the view that the understanding of the relationship between the classical language of Sanskrit and reality was not just a way of defending first principles – in his case the validity of the *Veda* and the world it represented– but was also a way of gaining liberating insight . . . His claim was that through understanding the way Sanskrit was correlated with the manifest world, by means of Vedic utterances, one could arrive at knowledge of the universal absolute (Brahman): language itself is, in a very real sense, the sound of reality.[41]

Bhartṛhari's view thus hearkens back to the *Upaniṣads*, and the teaching of works like the *Māṇḍūkya Upaniṣad* that the sacred sound *Om* is the original vibration – Brahman in the form of sound – from which all other sound, and all of reality, has emerged. His view that Sanskrit, uniquely among all languages, correlates directly with the elements of the world it describes is a Mīmāṃsā view as well. It was relentlessly criticized by the Buddhists, who regarded the relations between words and things, in any language, as arbitrary conventions.

Finally, Bhartṛhari is known for his *sphoṭa* theory of language, according to which it is not sufficient simply to know a word to know its meaning. It is necessary to know the entire context of the sentence in which the word is functioning. For Bhartṛhari, it is sentences, not words, that bear meaning.

Conclusion

The āstika or 'orthodox' systems of philosophy differ widely on a variety of topics, such as the nature of knowledge, the soul and the means to liberation. There are also numerous areas in which they are mutually supportive, and even convergent. Some *did* converge historically, essentially becoming one school, such as Sāṃkhya-Yoga and Nyāya-Vaiśeṣika. While differing on the topic of Īśvara and Īśvara's role in Vedic revelation, Mīmāṃsā and Nyāya-Vaiśeṣika are mutually supportive in affirming the authority of the Vedas. Both also affirm the validity of our common-sense categories for perceiving and navigating the world and stand against the idealist tendencies of such traditions as Mahāyāna Buddhism and, later, Advaita Vedānta.

As the history of Indian thought has unfolded since approximately the tenth century of the Common Era, it is the Vedānta traditions which have come to be dominant, with internal Vedāntic debates tending to preoccupy many Indian thinkers in the second millennium; for Vedānta is itself an internally diverse tradition. Adherents of the various Vedāntic systems, though, have drawn from the five systems explored in this chapter in the process of developing their positions.

The systems of thought explored in this chapter, though, are interesting not only inasmuch as they have contributed to the subsequent development of Vedānta. Each is insightful in its own right, and each could, on its own, occupy a lifetime of study for one with the desire to delve into its texts and traditions. These systems continue to command adherents today, and literature is still written from the perspectives of these darśanas.

We turn now, though, to the Vedānta traditions which have increasingly defined the Indian philosophical landscape over the course of the last millennium.

Notes

1 Alexis Sanderson, 'Tolerance, Exclusivity, Inclusivity, and Persecution in Indian Religion During the Early Medieaval Period', in *In Honoris Causa: Essays in Honour of Aveek Sarkar*, ed. John Makinson (Northwood, Middlesex: Allen Lane), p. 159. See also Nicholas F. Gier, *The Origins of Religious Violence: An Asian Perspective* (Lanham: Lexington Books, 2014).

2 See Mark McClish, *The History of the Arthaśāstra: Sovereignty and Sacred Law in Ancient India* (Cambridge: Cambridge University Press, 2019), pp. 43–6.

3 Wendy Doniger and Brian K. Smith, trans., *The Laws of* Manu (New York: Penguin, 1991), p. lv.

4 It is important to note that the word *avatāra* (literally 'descent') does not actually appear in the *Bhagavad Gītā*. However, this text contains two verses which are widely held in the Hindu tradition to be the classic statement of the *avatāra* doctrine: 'Whenever dharma declines and chaos (*adharma*) arises, then do I manifest myself. To protect the good, destroy evil, and restore dharma, I appear age after age.' (*Bhagavad Gītā* 4:7–8, translation mine).

5 Because of its relevance to Vedānta, the philosophy of the *Bhagavad Gītā* is explored in the next chapter.

6 Prem Pahlajrai, 'Doxographies–Why <u>six</u> *darśanas*? Which six?', p. 3, http://faculty.washington.edu/prem/Colloquium04-Doxographies.pdf.

7 Vivekananda, *Complete Works*, vol. 3, pp. 397–8.

8 Nicholson, *Unifying Hinduism*, p. 105

9 Gerald James Larson, *Classical Sāṃkhya: AnInterpretation of its History and Meaning* (New Delhi: Motilal Banarsidass,2011)., pp. 125, 126.

10 This characterization, however, is debatable. *Yoga Sūtra* 1:26, for example, speaks of the teaching activity of Īśvara, which is difficult (though not impossible) to reconcile with a wholly passive being. Vaiṣṇava interpreters of the *Yoga Sūtra* take Īśvara to

be identical with Kṛṣṇa, who does engage in activity, and who manifests in physical forms in order to teach and to destroy evil, or *adharma*.

11 Ibid., p. 125.

12 Ibid., p. 172.

13 Ibid., pp. 172–3.

14 For anyone unfamiliar with this term, it's an American idiom which refers to a lazy person.

15 Ibid., p. 204.

16 Ibid., pp. 204–5.

17 Which likely influenced the Yoga system in a variety of ways. See Karen O'Brien-Kop, *Rethinking Classical Yoga and Buddhism*, Paperback ed. (London: Bloomsbury, 2023).

18 Edwin Bryant, *The Yoga Sūtras of Patañjali: A New Edition, Translation, and Commentary* (New York: North Point Press, 2009), pp. 87–99.

19 Ibid., p. 283.

20 Ibid., p. 290.

21 Bina Gupta, *An Introduction to Indian Philosophy: Perspectives on Reality, Knowledge, and Freedom* (London: Routledge, 2011), p. 171.

22 *Nyāya Sūtra* 1.1.1 See Matthew Dasti and Stephen Phillips, trans., *The Nyāya-sūtra: Selections with Early Commentaries* (Indianapolis: Hackett Publishing Company, 2017), p. 9.

23 Gupta, *An Introduction to Indian Philosophy*, p. 174.

24 Bimal Krishna Matilal, Logic, Language, and Reality (New Delhi: Motilal Banarsidass, 2008), pp. 5, 6.

25 Ibid., p. 6.

26 Gupta, *An Introduction to Indian Philosophy*, p. 180.

27 Ibid.

28 Ibid., p. 156.

29 Ibid., p. 158.

30 Wilhelm Halbfass, *On Being and What There Is: Classical Vaiśeṣika and the History of Indian Ontology* (Albany: State University of New York Press, 1992), p. 93.

31 Gupta, *An Introduction to Indian Philosophy*, p. 160.

32 Ibid., p. 161.

33 Ibid., p. 164.

34 Ibid.

35 Ibid., p. 165.

36 Ibid.

37 Dan Arnold, Buddhists, Brahmins, and Belief (New York: Columbia University Press, 2008).

38 Sue Hamilton, *Indian Philosophy: A Very Short Introduction* (New York: Oxford University Press, 2001), p. 122.

39 Ibid., p. 123.

40 Roland Barthes, *The Death of the Author*, cited in Laura Seymour, *An Analysis of Roland Barthes's The Death of the Author* (London: Macat International, 2018).

41 Ibid., pp. 119–20.

6

Vedānta and Tantra

The interplay of duality and non-duality

Introduction

Athāto brahma jijñāsa. "Now, an inquiry into Brahman." These words form the opening verse of the *Brahma Sūtra*, a root text of the Vedānta tradition. *Brahma jijñāsā*, or inquiry into Brahman, is an excellent definition for Vedānta, a system of thought and practice aimed at elucidating and realizing Brahman, the ultimate reality at the basis of existence, according to this system. What is Brahman's nature? How can it be known? How is it related to the cosmos as a whole, to us and to our lives? The various forms of Vedānta provide answers to these questions, some of which overlap with one another and some of which differ, sometimes sharply. But all are united in the aim of inquiring into Brahman, advancing understanding of the nature of reality and leading spiritual aspirants to liberation.[1]

Vedānta is, apart from Buddhism, probably the best-known system of Indian philosophy. Just as Mīmāṃsā is based on interpretation of the ritualistic portion of the Vedic literature, Vedānta is based on interpretation of the *Upaniṣads*. Vedānta consists of many diverse schools of thought, each with its own concept of the relationship of Brahman to the self and the world. Advaita Vedānta, whose best-known exponent is Śaṅkara, affirms the non-duality of Brahman and the world. *Sarvaṃ khalv idaṃ brahma*: all this, indeed, *is* Brahman, in the words of the *Upaniṣads*. Viśiṣṭādvaita Vedānta, developed by Rāmānuja, affirms the relationship of non-duality between Brahman and all of existence, but does not see the distinctions between self, world and Īśvara as a mere appearance, or *māyā*, but as reflecting real differences *within* Brahman. Dvaita Vedānta, established by Madhva, affirms strong distinctions among Īśvara, living beings (or jīvas – the same term used in Jainism) and the world.

In addition to these three, there are a variety of Vedāntic systems – systems of 'difference-and-non-difference', or Bhedābheda – which aim to affirm both the unity of existence as Brahman, and the reality of the diversity of the world and the distinction between Brahman and the realm of our daily existence, much in the way that Rāmānuja's Viśiṣṭādvaita Vedānta seeks to do.

A particularly strong characteristic of Indian philosophies from the time of the decline of Buddhism – roughly 1000 to 1300 CE – to the modern period is an increased focus on theism in a sense more closely resembling Western theism than has been seen in most of the systems examined thus far. It has been mentioned previously that no system of Indian philosophy corresponds precisely with classical Western theism, in the sense of seeing God as the creator deity who brought the cosmos into being from nothing. The Lokāyata system, of course, denies the existence of any kind of deity, or what might be called a 'sacred', 'spiritual', or 'paranormal' reality, like the soul or the cycle of karma and rebirth. The Jain and Buddhist systems are not theistic in the sense of affirming the reality of a presiding deity over the cycles of existence. But liberated beings – Jinas and Buddhas – are regarded with profound reverence, to the point that the Jain tradition uses the term *God* (*Dev*) to refer to such liberated beings, either as individuals or as a collective. And the cosmic consciousness that dwells in all beings as the Buddha Nature in Mahāyāna Buddhism plays a role akin to that of the coordinating deity of the more strongly theistic Vedic systems. Sāṃkhya and Yoga are similar to Jainism in affirming the reality of a passive divinity – Īśvara as the ever-liberated puruṣa, or soul. Nyāya-Vaiśeṣika is more fully theistic, in a way that would be recognized by Western thinkers, affirming the definite reality of Īśvara as the coordinator of the cosmic order – the mover of the otherwise inanimate atoms making up the material world – and the revealer of the *Vedas*. As we have seen, though, Mīmāṃsā, while affirming the authority of the *Vedas*, sees this literature as eternal and authorless (*apauruṣeya*, or 'not man-made') and is thus non-theistic.

Vedānta, however, as it has developed over the course of the last millennium, has absorbed much of the sensibility of the popular *bhakti*, or devotional movements that began to emerge just prior to the start of the Common Era. These movements are focused chiefly upon the deities Viṣṇu, Śiva and Śakti. Each of these movements sees its chosen deity as the supreme being, Īśvara.

Many of the non-Advaitic systems of Vedānta are closely related to Vaiṣṇava traditions. Indeed, many could be characterized as forms of Vaiṣṇava theology: as faith in the Supreme Lord Viṣṇu, seeking manifestation in the form of intellectual argument and elucidation. Others are less directly related to Vaiṣṇava thought and practice but are nevertheless connected with it through the use of shared foundational texts, such as the *Bhagavad Gītā*.

In addition to Vedānta, this chapter will also explore a set of systems which have emerged during the same period and are known collectively as *Tantra*. Although distinct from Vedānta in many ways, Tantra shares much of its theistic sensibility. While most systems of Vedānta (though not all) lean in a more Vaiṣṇava direction, Tāntric systems have been focused more upon Śiva and Śakti as their preferred objects of devotion.

Another theme, in addition to, and in relation to, theism which is prominent in the systems of both Vedānta and Tantra is the question of *duality* and *non-duality*. *Duality* here refers not to the dualism of matter and spirit that we have seen at play in such systems as Jainism and Sāṃkhya, though it could be said to include it. *Dualism* refers to the idea that differentiation as such is part of the nature of reality. *Non-dualism* sees such differentiation as not ultimately real, much as Mahāyāna Buddhism does.

Vedānta: The end of the *Veda*

Vedānta, traditionally numbered among the six *āstika darśanas* – the systems of Indian philosophy which affirm the authority of the *Veda* – is really a collection of different philosophical systems, all of which aim to elucidate the ultimate meaning of Vedic texts. This is one meaning of the word *vedānta*: the end – in the sense of *aim* or *purpose* – of the *Veda*. While the systems of Vedānta disagree on many issues, and there is a long history of debate among their adherents, all agree that the *Veda* is the highest spiritual authority and that understanding its meaning is necessary for the realization of the aim of spiritual practice: *mokṣa*. One meaning of the term *veda* – apart from the body of texts that go by this name – is *wisdom*. Given its aim of mokṣa, Vedānta can be seen as the end or aim of all wisdom. This idea becomes even more prominent in the modern era, when Vedānta is seen as the science of divine realization.

Three foundational texts: The Prasthāna Traya

All systems of Vedānta take three texts to be foundational authorities. These include the *Upaniṣads*, as well as two other texts: the *Brahma Sūtra* and *Bhagavad Gītā*. The *Brahma Sūtra*, also known as the *Vedānta Sūtra*, is a summary of the teachings of the *Upaniṣads*, presented as a collection of brief and cryptic aphorisms. The *Bhagavad Gītā* – a portion of the *Mahābhārata* – is a dialogue between Kṛṣṇa, the Supreme Being, and the hero Arjuna. The *Bhagavad Gītā* is seen by many Hindus, particularly in the modern period, as equal in authority to the *Upaniṣads*, a stance reflected in its sometimes being referred to as an *Upaniṣad* in its own right: the *Gītā Upaniṣad* (*Gītopaniṣad*). Technically speaking, however, the *Upaniṣads*, as part of the Vedas, are śruti, and the *Bhagavad Gītā*, as a portion of the *Mahābhārata*, is smṛti.[2]

Each system Vedic philosophy has a foundational text, or *sūtra*. These sūtras – like the *Yoga Sūtra*, the *Pūrvamīmāṃsā Sūtra*, the *Nyāya Sūtra* and the *Brahma Sūtra* – consist of brief, cryptic verses. It is likely that this style aided memorization. The various schools of philosophy were taught through a process involving memorization of the school's root text, followed by further elaboration by a teacher. Over time, teachers in various schools of thought began to commit their interpretations to writing. *Bhāṣyas*, or commentaries, on these root texts subsequently became the dominant mode of philosophical writing in classical India.

Through their commentaries, Indian philosophers propagated their interpretations of their sūtras through space and time: to students far and wide across India and to future generations of scholars. Commentaries widely seen as capturing and expressing well the meaning of the sūtras became authoritative texts in their own right, with their authors regarded as *ācāryas*, or special teachers who served as guiding lights to their respective traditions.

Reading the *Brahma Sūtra*, or any sūtra of any system of Indian philosophy, without the aid of a commentary or teacher goes against the grain of Indian traditions. It is understood in these traditions that the text is a guide to right knowledge, and in many cases, spiritual illumination. Only a spiritually illuminated and intellectually adept teacher, whose mastery of the texts and the way of life they commend, can give a student the guidance needed to understand them fully and deeply.

In the case of the *Brahma Sūtra* in particular, beyond the fact that it goes against the grain of tradition, reading this text without the aid of a commentary is also incredibly difficult. The text is of a highly terse, compact nature, rendering its meaning cryptic or even opaque, without the aid of a teacher or commentary. For example, the verse of the *Brahma Sūtra* held to refute the Jain teaching of the multi-faceted nature of reality (*anekānta-vāda*) reads *naikasmin asambhavāt*, or "Not in one, because it is impossible."[3] In other words, it is impossible to affirm that a single entity possesses contrary qualities (like being and non-being). There is no way of knowing that this is what this text means, however, or even that it is directed specifically at refuting Jainism, in the absence of a scholarly commentary or teacher to explain it. Nothing in the sūtra alone explains the meaning of the statement, "Not in one, because it is impossible."

The *Brahma Sūtra* is attributed to the seer Bādarāyaṇa, sometimes identified with Veda Vyāsa, who is, in turn, regarded as the author of the *Mahābhārata* and the compiler of the *Veda*. Academic scholarship locates the *Brahma Sūtra* in the period of the composition of the root texts of the other schools of Vedic philosophy, between the fifth century BCE and the second century CE. This text may be mentioned in the *Bhagavad Gītā*, which says of its own teaching: "It has been sung in many ways by the seers, in various poetic meters and at many times, and in the words of the *Brahma Sūtra*. It has been argued extensively and is now well established."[4] It is not clear if this text, specifically, is being mentioned here, or if the reference is to a tradition of discourse on the meaning of the *Upaniṣads*, perhaps begun by Veda Vyāsa, that may be reflected in the text we have today. It is possible, though, that this text, or at least some version of it, predates the *Bhagavad Gītā*, which scholars trace to the end of the same period, from about the second century BCE to the second century CE.

The *Bhagavad Gītā*, as part of the *Mahābhārata*, is also attributed to Veda Vyāsa. And as the compiler of the Vedas, this figure (or someone functioning in this role) would also be seen, from a traditional perspective as responsible for putting the *Upaniṣads* in their current form. Veda Vyāsa could thus be seen as the foundational figure for the entire tradition of Vedānta and indeed of all Vedic traditions. One meaning of the name *Vyāsa* is *compiler*. One possible implication of this is not that a single person authored all these texts in their totality (such as the character who goes by this name in the *Mahābhārata*), but that the wisdom of many seers was collected and gathered into them.

Each of the texts of the *prasthāna traya*, the triple foundation of Vedānta, can be interpreted in several ways. The *Upaniṣads* consist of many texts: one hundred and eight in total, although about a dozen of these are typically taken as the principal *Upaniṣads* and seen by scholars as dating back to the period of the first millennium before the Common Era. The *Brahma Sūtra*, as mentioned, is notoriously difficult to read without the aid of a commentary. Each commentator's interpretation differs, sometimes radically, from the rest. The *Bhagavad Gītā*, while a fairly short text, and far more accessible to a reader, stylistically, than the *Brahma Sūtra*, also incorporates a variety of systems of thought into its presentation, such that this text, too, lends itself to diverse interpretations.

After the compilation of its foundational texts, a process likely completed by about the second century CE, the variety of interpretations to which these texts lend themselves leads to the history of Vedānta becoming a history of many schools of thought, each offering a distinctive vision of the meaning of the *Veda*. Each of these visions is based on the insights of the founding ācāryas of the Vedāntic systems and later commentators building on those insights. One can thus see the history of Vedānta as being divided into an 'early' phase, whose thought is reflected in the texts of the *prasthāna traya*, and a 'later' or 'middle' phase characterized by the work of the great ācāryas and the systems built on it. The modern era is a third phase, in which the ability of individuals to understand and interpret Vedānta for themselves, outside of a traditional framework, is increasingly affirmed (even as the earlier schools continue to exist and thrive).

Before examining the interpretations of the Vedāntic ācāryas, let us explore the philosophy of the *Bhagavad Gītā*. This text begins, among other things, to integrate various movements that we have seen as distinct schools of Indian philosophy into a single vision. This vision becomes foundational for Vedānta, and for much of Hinduism, drawing together elements of the thought of the *Upaniṣads*, Sāṃkhya, Yoga, the bhakti movement, Buddhism and Jainism – as well as elements that are critical of Buddhism, Jainism and Lokāyata materialism, and of Mīmāṃsā ritualism.

Philosophy in the *Bhagavad Gītā*

The *Bhagavad Gītā*, or *Song of the Blessed Lord*, is an eighteen-chapter dialogue in which Kṛṣṇa, an incarnation of Īśvara, the Supreme Lord, instructs Arjuna on how to attain mokṣa. It is, in effect, a summary of early Vedānta. As a portion of a highly popular epic tale, the *Mahābhārata*, the *Bhagavad Gītā* provides a summary of the *Upaniṣads* for the common person. As one might recall, until the modern era, it was relatively rare for non-Brahmins to have direct access to Vedic texts, including the *Upaniṣads*. Smṛti texts such as the *Mahābhārata* and *Rāmāyaṇa*, though, were available to all. As Bronkhorst has recently argued in a book titled *How the Brahmins Won*, the incorporation of Vedic themes into ancient Indian popular culture – in appealing stories such as the epics – aided the Brahmins in advancing their ideals at a time when non-Vedic philosophies like Buddhism and Jainism were predominant. The *Bhagavad Gītā* is an important component of this popular presentation of Vedic thought.

For those familiar with the *Upaniṣads*, the *Gītā*'s style of presentation would be familiar. Like most of the *Upaniṣads*, this text is presented as a dialogue between a teacher – Kṛṣṇa – and his student – Arjuna. Images in the text also evoke the *Upaniṣads*. These include its setting on a battlefield, with Kṛṣṇa acting as Arjuna's charioteer. The *Kaṭha Upaniṣad* includes a famous image of a chariot as a metaphor for the body, with the horses drawing it representing the senses, the driver the mind and the rider, the Self or ātman. The *Gītā* also includes a verse (the nineteenth verse of its second chapter) almost identical to the nineteenth verse of the second chapter of the *Kaṭha Upaniṣad*:

> Whoever thinks that this one here is a killer, or who thinks that he has been killed, in both cases he is wrong. For indeed he does not kill, nor is he himself killed.[5]

Killing and being killed are very much on Arjuna's mind in the *Gītā*'s setting: a battlefield where he and his cousins are about to engage in their climactic struggle for control of their ancestral land. Perhaps the evocation of the *Kaṭha Upaniṣad*, with its metaphor of the chariot, at this point in the text is a signal that the battlefield of the *Gītā* is a metaphor for life. Indeed, later in the text, Kṛṣṇa proclaims quite openly that the field is the body.[6] Such metaphorical reading of a text in which Kṛṣṇa is encouraging Arjuna to fight the battle before him has enabled interpreters of the *Gītā* such as Mohandas K. Gandhi in the modern period to see it as a guide to a non-violent path, despite the martial context in which it is set.[7]

When Kṛṣṇa says, 'Whoever thinks that this one here is a killer, or who thinks that he has been killed, in both cases he is wrong', he is elaborating upon the first philosophical doctrine the *Gītā* presents: the doctrine of the immortality of the essential soul or self and the rebirth of the self in many forms over time.

> [I]n fact there never was a time when I did not exist, nor you . . . And there never will be a time when we do not exist.
>
> Just as the embodied one experiences childhood, youth and old age, in this body, in the same way he enters other bodies. A wise person is not disturbed by this.[8]

In keeping with the philosophy of the *Upaniṣads*, the ultimate aim of life, according to the *Bhagavad Gītā*, is liberation from the cycle of rebirth. Like the *Muṇḍaka Upaniṣad*, the *Gītā* is critical of those who perform Vedic rituals to achieve worldly ends:

> Some people please themselves by debating the *Vedas*. They recite the florid Vedic chants, but they have no insight, while ever saying that only the *Vedas* matter!
>
> In their hearts, they are driven by desire and are eager for heaven [the heavenly realm achieved after death through Vedic ritual, as opposed to the eternal bliss of liberation]. Their words promise rebirth as the fruit of their actions. Their talk is all about their elaborate rituals whose purpose is to gain pleasure and power [kāma and artha]. [This seems to be a reference to the Vedic ritualists.]
>
> They are obsessed with pleasure and power! The words of the *Vedas* deprive them of good sense. They lack the insight that is based on firm resolve, and they do not gain insight even when engaged in intense concentration.[9]

Rather than being attached to the experiences of this world, which are products of the action – that is, karma – Kṛṣṇa encourages Arjuna to focus upon the infinite ātman within. External objects and conditions do not bring the true happiness that comes only with liberation:

> The world of the *Vedas* is the natural world with its three conditions [the prakṛti of Sāṃkhya philosophy, with its three guṇas]. Arjuna, live in the world that is beyond this one, free of its conditions and dualities. Remain always within this true world, free from both the exertion for wealth and the enjoyment of it. Remain within the Self.[10]

The *Vedas* – which here to refer to the ritualistic action portion of these texts – do not show the path to liberation. One with true insight into reality does not need them:

> As useful as a water tank when there is flooding in all directions, that is how useful all of the *Vedas* are for a Brahmin who has true insight.[11]

Statements as sharply critical of traditional Vedic learning and practice as those found in the *Gītā* would not be out of place in a non-Vedic work, like a Jain or Buddhist text. It is not the case, though, that Arjuna is being dissuaded from the traditional Vedic way of life, nor even from Vedic ritual. Kṛṣṇa enjoins Arjuna to perform the required rituals, but to do so without desire for a result: with detachment. In keeping with an Upaniṣadic understanding, 'ritual' here includes all required action, including the duties associated with one's station in life: one's dharma.

> Focus your mind on action alone, but never on the fruits of your actions. Your goal should never be the fruits of your action, nor should you be attached to non-action.

> Practice yoga and perform the actions that you are obliged to do, but, Arjuna, don't be attached to them. Treat success and failure alike. This kind of even-mindedness is called yoga.[12]

This is one of the central teachings of *Bhagavad Gītā* and is called *karma yoga*: the discipline of action.

Arjuna is instructed here to practice detachment from the fruits of action. This is a standard teaching, as we have seen, of ascetic traditions like Jainism and Buddhism, and the *Upaniṣads*. But Arjuna, significantly, is *not* instructed to renounce in the literal sense of becoming a wandering ascetic. He is to do his required actions, his duties as a householder and a warrior. He is not to be 'attached to non-action'. And he is enjoined to remain even minded, to 'treat success and failure alike'. This is the state of equanimity cultivated in Buddhist, Jain, Sāṃkhya and Yoga traditions. Karma yoga, in summary, is a path to liberation for householders. It requires one not to literally renounce, but to cultivate an *attitude* of renunciation: of detachment.

As the *Gītā* explains further, simply taking up the external lifestyle of an ascetic is not any guarantee that one will in fact, inwardly, be practicing renunciation. Being an external renouncer while still inwardly attached to the things of the world does no good at all. One may note here an echo of the Mahāyāna Buddhist critique of early Buddhist asceticism: its sense that a householder who cultivates an attitude of detachment is superior even to a monk who lives a life of luxury or who is inwardly attached even if outwardly living as an ascetic. Also, the *Gītā* notes, even the strictest ascetic cannot help but engage in activity. One must eat and breathe and sustain one's physical existence:

> One does not go beyond action by merely avoiding action, nor does one achieve spiritual success by renunciation alone.

> For no one exists even for a moment without performing actions. Even if unwillingly, every one of us must act, due to the forces of nature.[13]

One may see in these verses a subtle critique of Jain and Ājīvika attempts to reduce all action to a bare minimum, and to avoid harming living beings even by accidentally ingesting them in the acts of eating or breathing. Action is inevitable. Yet action leads to rebirth. How, then, can one become free from rebirth? How can one be liberated? It is not just any action, but action infused with *desire* – with *craving* and *attachment* – that leads to rebirth. One cannot help but act. But one can act with detachment:

> This world is in bondage to action except when it is performed as a sacrifice. You should remain unattached, Arjuna, and continue to perform action that is intended as sacrifice.[14]

As we saw when exploring the philosophy of the *Upaniṣads*, all of life is seen as a Vedic ritual. All of life is sacrifice. If one acts accordingly, offering all one's actions as sacrifice, rather than performing them for selfish gain – for pleasure or power regarded as ends in themselves – then one's actions are not binding. They do not 'stick' to the soul (if we may evoke the Jain image of karmic matter adhering to the jīva). Action performed as sacrifice is as good as renunciation and is a path to liberation.

In addition to the karma yoga, the *Bhagavad Gītā* also commends the paths of wisdom and meditation – *jñāna yoga* and *dhyāna yoga* – as found in the philosophies of Sāṃkhya and Yoga:

> Some sacrifice material objects, others practice austerities, and still others practice yoga. Some sacrifice through their knowledge and their study of the *Vedas*. These are all devout men committed to keeping their sacred vows.[15]

One topic on which later commentators debate is the relative role of each of these paths in relation to the attainment of mokṣa. Is there finally one, true yoga, for which the others are preparatory? Or are there multiple valid paths to the ultimate goal, each appropriate to a different type of person?

In addition to the paths of action, knowledge and meditation, the *Gītā* commends the path of devotion, or *bhakti yoga*, in which one surrenders oneself fully to the grace of Īśvara: to Kṛṣṇa, who is seen in this text as the supreme embodiment of the Lord, or even as the Lord himself.

Arjuna asks Kṛṣṇa at one point which path is superior: the path of knowledge, in which one is focused upon the impersonal Brahman, beyond form or manifestation, or devotion, in which one focuses lovingly upon the Lord as the supreme reality. This is a topic which would become a major issue of contention among the various systems of Vedānta. Kṛṣṇa responds that practitioners of both paths reach their goal, but that the path of knowledge is more difficult:

I consider them to be the best disciplined who focus their minds on me, who, constant in their discipline, worship me with the greatest faith.

But those who worship the imperishable, the unmanifest, which is beyond words, which is found everywhere and is inconceivable, sublime on the mountaintop, unmoving and firm, who have gained complete control over the senses and equanimity toward all beings, rejoicing in the welfare of all beings, they also attain to me.

There is greater distress for those who have set their thoughts on the unmanifest because it is difficult for those who are embodied to reach a goal that is itself unmanifest.

But those who surrender all of their actions to me and who are focused on me alone, who meditate on me with yoga, and worship me, I lift them up out of the ocean of the cycle of death and rebirth, Arjuna, once they have set their thoughts on me.[16]

As indicated in these verses, the *Gītā* presents Kṛṣṇa as having a manifest form and an unmanifest aspect. This is consistent with the *Upaniṣads*, which also speak of Brahman both in impersonal terms, as the infinite field of potential from which the cosmos emerges, and in personal terms, as a loving deity directing the process of creation. The *Gītā* also includes, in seed form, the teaching that the supreme lord appears in the world periodically, to maintain cosmic order. This is developed in subsequent texts, such as the *Bhāgavata Purāṇa*, into the doctrine of the *avatāra*, or 'descent', of the divine, the doctrine of multiple divine incarnations:

Whenever dharma declines, Arjuna, and adharma [chaos] arises, then I manifest myself into the world.[17]

Finally, the *Bhagavad Gītā* includes a suggestion that adherents of many traditions are not excluded from Kṛṣṇa's grace:

In whatsoever way human beings approach me, thus do I receive them. All paths, Arjuna, lead to me.[18]

Advaita Vedānta: Non-dualism

Śaṅkara, the founder of the Advaita, or non-dualist, system of Vedānta, is widely believed to have lived from about 788 to 820 CE. Śaṅkara's interpretation of Vedānta does not arise in a vacuum, but builds upon the work of his guru, Govinda and Govinda's guru, Gauḍapāda, who is the author of an important commentary on the *Māṇḍūkya Upaniṣad*, the *Māṇḍūkyopaniṣad Kārikā*, where Gauḍapāda develops his position of *ajātivāda*.

The *Māṇḍūkya Upaniṣad* focuses on interpreting the sacred mantra *Oṃ*. This text differentiates the sounds that make up this mantra – *a, u, ṃ*, and the silence which follows – and connects them symbolically with the four states of consciousness: the waking state, the dream state, the state of dreamless sleep and the 'fourth state' of awakening, where one becomes liberated from saṃsāra. *Oṃ* is held in the subsequent Vedānta tradition to be Brahman in the form of sound. It is the original sound from which all other sounds have emerged. Symbolically speaking, this is analogous to the way all beings have emerged from Brahman. Just as sound is a vibration, each element making up the universe is a 'vibration' or modification of the original consciousness at the basis of reality: Brahman.

Gauḍapāda articulates *ajātivāda*, the 'doctrine of non-arising'. Gauḍapāda's view shares features with Nāgārjuna's Madhyamaka philosophy.[19] Nāgārjuna affirms that no 'thing' has ever truly arisen. One might recall that according to a realist understanding of Buddhism, entities co-arise interdependently. Because of the Emptiness of all dharmas, though, no 'entity' actually exists, as something which could be defined independently of the moment in which it emerges. Even the phenomena of space and time are not wholly real, but part of the realm of conventional truth.

Gauḍapāda takes this deeply Buddhist interpretation of phenomenal experience and gives it a Vedāntic twist. The only true reality: meaning the only reality that is not empty and ephemeral, is the eternal, unchanging Brahman.[20] Brahman does not arise or pass away. It simply is. Recall from Buddhism that nothing that arises or passes away – or that appears to arise or pass away – has any substantial reality. The aim of the spiritual life is to overcome attachment to the impermanent phenomena of our experience. Gauḍapāda adds to this that when one has overcome attachment in this way, one realises Brahman as the sole reality: as infinite being, consciousness and bliss. This realization is the essence of liberation.

Buddhism is, of course, also aimed at an awakening to the true nature of reality. One might ask, 'To what does one awaken?' When one realizes the phenomena of this world are insubstantial and dreamlike, what is reality? The Buddhist answer to this question, one might recall, is silence. Nirvāṇa cannot be described in words or captured in concepts. Gauḍapāda answers the question, 'To what does one awaken?' by saying, 'Brahman, the unconditioned, infinite reality.' Brahman is the answer to the ancient prayer of the *Upaniṣads*: 'Lead me from the unreal to the real. Lead me from darkness to light. Lead me from death to immortality.' We have noted that the Buddha affirms the reality of an 'unborn, unbecome, unmade, unconditioned' but does not give it a name or identify it with a self (though later Buddhist thinkers, especially in the Mahāyāna tradition, do seem to make this move, or something like it, with ideas like Buddha Nature and the Dharmakāya). Gauḍapāda takes the Buddha's teaching in an unambiguously Vedāntic direction – essentially recruiting Buddhism in the cause of Vedānta – by identifying the Buddha's 'unborn, unbecome, unmade, unconditioned' with the Brahman of the *Upaniṣads*.

There is precedent for Gauḍapāda's move in the *Bhagavad Gītā*, which refers to the state of the highest realisation, the realisation which leads to liberation, with the term *Brahmanirvāṇa*, or 'absorption in Brahman':

> One who abandons all desires, who goes about free from cravings, for whom there is no talk of 'mine!' or 'me!' – that one finds peace.

> This, Arjuna, is the divine state of Brahman. Having attained this, one is no longer confused. When one abides in this state, even at the moment of death, one attains Brahmanirvāṇa.[21]

> Such a person contains his pleasure and his joy within himself. His light is within himself and nowhere else. Such a one is a yogin who has become one with Brahman. He has reached Brahmanirvāṇa.

> Seers who destroy their sins, who cut through all doubt, who have achieved self-mastery, attain this Brahmanirvāṇa, delighting in the welfare of all beings.

> Brahmanirvāṇa is always present for those devotees who have freed themselves from desire and anger, who have tamed their minds and have come to know themselves.[22]

Śaṅkara – by all traditional accounts, a child prodigy and highly gifted Vedic scholar – builds Advaita Vedānta on a reading of the *Upaniṣads* that shares much with Gauḍapāda's understanding of these texts. For Śaṅkara, Brahman is ultimately an impersonal (perhaps a better term might be *transpersonal*, beyond categories of personal and impersonal) reality, finally beyond the ability of any limited concept to encompass. He expresses this negatively, saying that Brahman is *nirguṇa*, or without qualities or conditions. Brahman, in this sense, is 'empty'. Brahman is not dependently co-originated but is free from limiting concepts.

Śaṅkara approaches the various views of reality given in the prasthāna traya using some basic interpretive principles. First, in keeping with Mīmāṃsā interpretations of the Vedas, Śaṅkara affirms that the Vedas are entirely self-consistent. If contradictions appear in the text, these must be resolved through logical principles. One must decide what the central message is that the Vedas seek to convey. This enables one to determine what in the Vedic text is to be taken literally and what can be interpreted as illustrative or symbolic of this central message. Śaṅkara sees the essential meaning of the Vedas in a few core statements called *Mahāvākyas*, or 'great statements'. These include such statements as *prajñānaṃ brahma* ('Brahman is consciousness'),[23] *ayam ātmā brahma* ('This Self is Brahman'),[24] *tat tvam asi* ('You are That'),[25] *aham brahmāsmi* ('I am Brahman')[26] and *sarvaṃ khalv idaṃ brahma* ('All this, indeed, is Brahman').[27] These statements, as understood by Śaṅkara, affirm the ultimate non-duality of Brahman and all existents, including the individual self. The aim all Vedic practice, on this understanding, is the realization of the ultimate identify of Self (*ātman*) and Brahman. The relationship of Brahman to world is one of non-duality, which is the meaning of *advaita*. Brahman is, in the words of another Mahāvākya, 'one alone, without a second', or *ekam evādvitīyam*. The diversity of phenomena is an appearance, or *māyā*. It is neither real nor unreal. It is how Brahman appears to unenlightened consciousness.

Śaṅkara does not, in most of his writings, teach that the world is an illusion, in the sense of something that does not exist, though an important text attributed to him, the *Vivekacuḍāmaṇi*, famously states *brahma satyaṃ jagan mithyā*, or 'Brahman is truth. The world a delusion.' Recent scholarship on Śaṅkara suggests he can be interpreted as a realist, affirming not that the world is unreal, but that the world does not present the *fullness* of the reality of Brahman.[28] Following Gauḍapāda, he compares the world to a stick one mistakes for a snake. The snake is not real inasmuch as there is no snake there, but a stick. But it is also not wholly unreal. It is based in the reality of the stick. The *appearance* of the stick gives rise to the perception of a snake. This perception, so long as it lasts, has causal efficacy. One's heartbeat and blood pressure rise due to the apprehension one feels on seeing this snake. Similarly, the world is not fully real, but it has reality so long as one has not perceived Brahman. As explained by Swami Tyagananda:

> The snake's reality may have been pseudo, but the snake wasn't totally unreal. A little of the reality showed itself in the snake. How else did I see the snake? The 'existence' of the snake I saw was really the existence of the rope percolating through the veil of my ignorance. It's just that it had become distorted: the existence of the rope was showing itself as the existence of the snake. Even when I saw the snake, I was really seeing the rope *but not as rope* . . . In the same way, I perceive myself *but not as the ātman*.[29]

The subsequent commentarial tradition of Advaita Vedānta, which seeks to elaborate upon Śaṅkara's insights, leans towards seeing the world as an illusion. This reading of Śaṅkara provoked an array of reactions by Vedānta scholars who saw the reality of the world as fundamental to the spiritual path. Recall that other Vedic philosophies, like Mīmāṃsā and Nyāya-Vaiśeṣika, are strongly realist, and see their realism as integral to affirming the truth of the *Vedas*. It is on the basis of the question of the relationship of Brahman to the world that later systems of Vedānta arise, disputing Śaṅkara's affirmation that the world, finally, is identical to Brahman, and that our common experience of separate entities is an appearance. Of central concern to these systems of Vedānta is the reality of Īśvara, the supreme lord, in relation to His devotees.

Īśvara has a central role in Śaṅkara's worldview; but in the end, even the Supreme Being is, for Śaṅkara, but a manifestation – albeit a very important one – of Being Itself, of Brahman, which Śaṅkara takes to be beyond all personal qualities. One might say that Śaṅkara's *cosmology*, his account of the universe revealed to our experience, is realist, and in many ways consistent with other realist systems of Vedic philosophy. Nyāya-Vaiśeīka theism, the Sāṃkhya analysis of experience in terms of the three guṇas, the Yoga tradition's system for calming the modifications of consciousness and experiencing one's true nature, and the Mīmāṃsā tradition's understanding of the correct way to go about practicing Vedic ritual: all are available to an adherent of Vedānta in accounting for and navigating the world of conventional truth. This, in part, is what has enabled this system to become dominant in India over the last thousand years: its ability to assimilate the central insights of other systems of philosophy. But in Śaṅkara's *ontology* he is different from the other Vedic realists, and more akin to the Yogācāra tradition of Buddhism, in affirming that reality, at its core, consists of consciousness, which *appears* as a material world for those who do not perceive its true nature. In another nod to Buddhism, Śaṅkara also accepts Nāgārjuna's distinction between conventional and ultimate truth: the relative truth of common experience (*vyavahārika satya*), and the absolute truth (*paramārthika satya*) of Brahman.

How does Śaṅkara know the world of conventional experience is an appearance and the reality is Brahman? In terms of epistemology – his understanding of how knowledge is acquired – Śaṅkara accepts all the pramāṇas of the Nyāya system, as well as 'implication' (*arthāpatti*) and non-perception, or 'negative proof' (*anupalabdhi*).

Of greatest significance to the content of his overall worldview, though, is the way in which Śaṅkara interprets the śabda pramāṇa – which, for him, of course refers to the *Vedas*, especially the Mahāvākyas of the *Upaniṣads*. What is particularly noteworthy about Śaṅkara's approach to the pramāṇas is, first, his insistence that each pramāṇa must yield a distinct type of knowledge. This is one of the ways the pramāṇas are distinguished from one another: which type of knowledge does a given pramāṇa reveal?

This idea is not unique to Śaṅkara and was indeed affirmed long before by the Naiyāyikas. As it applies to the śabda pramāṇa, however, it is particularly interesting because of the possible approach it suggests to issues of conflict between science and religion in the contemporary world.

For Śaṅkara, the truth unique to the *Vedas* – the truth which makes them the śabda pramāṇa – is their teaching of the nature of Brahman. The *Vedas* do not exist, in other words, to teach us about the material world: knowledge we can gather from other pramāṇas, like sensory perception and inferential logic (i.e. science). Śaṅkara famously states that when the *Vedas* conflict, or appear to conflict, with either sensory perception or reason, then one is either misinterpreting the Vedic text, or, if the topic at hand is not something over which the *Vedas* are uniquely authoritative, one must defer to sensory perception and reason. According to Śaṅkara, if the *Vedas* state that fire is cold or does not give off light, this statement will be false:

> The infallibility [of the *Vedas*] is admissible only in regard to matters not confined to the sphere of direct perceptions etc. . . . Even a hundred statements of śruti to the effect that fire is cold and non-luminous won't prove valid. If it does make such a statement, its import will have to be interpreted differently. Otherwise, validity won't attach to it. Nothing in conflict with the means of valid cognition or with its own statement may be imputed to śruti. [In other words, the *Vedas* cannot be read in a way that either conflicts with other pramāṇas, like sensory perception and logic, or that conflicts with itself – that is self-contradictory.] [30]

The mere fact that a statement can be found in the *Vedas* is not enough to make it true. The *Vedas* are true when talking about things which cannot be known in any other way: not the nature of the material world, but the nature of Brahman and the path to liberation. If they appear to conflict with other established knowledge, or to be self-contradictory, they are not being read correctly. They may be speaking symbolically, or metaphorically, or poetically.

This is not unlike the teaching of the renowned medieval Christian theologian, St. Thomas Aquinas (1225–74), who distinguishes the domain of reason from the domain of faith. Scripture exists to reveal the nature of God. For understanding the material world, we have reason and the ability to observe with our senses: again, science. No real conflict can exist between these two.

Śaṅkara's and Thomas Aquinas' approach to knowledge suggests that conflicts between religion and science are a result of misapplying one's pramāṇas. Scripture can be seen as a reliable guide to transcendental realities, but not to the nature of the material world, which is the realm of science. Science, similarly, is a reliable guide to the nature of the material world, the understanding of which continues to unfold, but questions such as the nature of Brahman or of God, or the path to liberation or salvation, are not of a scientific nature.

A hard-core sceptic, of course, might argue that questions that are not of a scientific nature are not legitimate questions. The *Vedas* are a guide to Brahman and the Bible a guide to God, just as *The Lord of the Rings* is a guide to Middle-earth. This does not mean any of these things are real. An anti-foundationalist, however, might reply that for one embedded in a way of life defined by these texts, to raise the question of their validity is not even a meaningful act, unless one finds a contradiction one cannot resolve, or some life issue the tradition is unable to address: the kind of situation that philosopher Alasdair Macintyre calls an 'epistemological crisis'.[31]

An anti-foundationalist may also argue that the search for an objective basis for knowledge that we might claim as the starting point of our inquiry, as opposed to a starting point in an already established text or tradition, is misguided. In the words of Paul J. Griffiths, the search 'for the foundations of knowledge, for a place to stand upon the desirability of which all reasonable people can agree . . . cannot be realized, and is a direct outflow of the pride that turns from God and toward itself'.[32]

Viśiṣṭādvaita Vedānta: Non-dualism with difference

The next great ācārya to establish a system of Vedānta, Rāmānuja, was born in the eleventh century of the Common Era and died in the twelfth. Rāmānuja, a devout Vaiṣṇava, establishes his interpretation of Vedānta in part to affirm the centrality of *bhakti*, or loving devotion, to the path to liberation. His philosophy becomes foundational to the Śrī Vaiṣṇava tradition of Hinduism.

Initially a disciple of a Vedānta teacher named Yādava Prakāśa, Rāmānuja is famously said to have felt despondent when his teacher interpreted the *Vedas* in a way that seemed disrespectful toward Īśvara. For Rāmānuja, bhakti is the *sine qua non* of liberation. Without love and devotion, the study of the *Vedas* is a dry and meaningless intellectual exercise.

While bhakti is certainly important, according to Advaita Vedānta, mokṣa is nevertheless, according to this tradition, essentially a matter of *jñāna*, or knowledge: of realisation. In particular, it is a matter of realizing the non-duality of the Self (ātman) and Brahman. Ritual and ethical action performed without attachment – *karma yoga* – and the cultivation of devotion to the Supreme Lord–*bhakti yoga* – are important for purifying the mind and preparing it for the highest realization. But they do not, in the end, confer the saving knowledge – *jñāna* – which Śaṅkara sees as constitutive of liberation. In support of this view, one could cite the *Bhagavad Gītā*:

> Arjuna, the sacrifice of knowledge is higher than the sacrifice of material things. All action without exception culminates in knowledge.[33]

Rāmānuja, however, sees bhakti as absolutely central to the path to realization. In fact, for Rāmānuja and later Vaiṣṇava ācāryas, bhakti is *constitutive* of liberation in much the same way that jñāna is constitutive of liberation for Śaṅkara. Liberation, in other words, *consists of* devotion to the Supreme Lord. This position, too, can find support in the *Bhagavad Gītā*:

> I consider them to be the best disciplined who focus their minds on me, who, constant in their discipline, worship me with the greatest faith.[34]

From this perspective, the relegation of the Supreme Being, Īśvara or Viṣṇu, to the status of a mere appearance of a Brahman that is inherently *nirguṇa*, or without any differentiating qualities, is to de-centre the One to whom our loving devotion is essential for liberation. Śaṅkara's approach to Brahman as an impersonal reality, or as beyond such categories as impersonal and personal, strikes Vaiṣṇava interpreters of Vedānta as strikingly close to the non-theistic views of the Buddhists and Jains, who have long been regarded as antagonistic to the Vedic path. It is seen as a position which undermines devotion.

Indeed, the degree to which Advaita Vedānta appears to owe a considerable philosophical debt to Mahāyāna Buddhism for some of its assumptions and forms of argumentation fuels the allegation in Vaiṣṇava circles that Śaṅkara is a 'crypto-Buddhist', lacking in the theistic devotion seen by these critics as the culmination of Vedic religion.[35]

As an interpreter of the *Upaniṣads*, though, Rāmānuja must address the many places in the text where the unity of Brahman with the world and with all beings is affirmed. Can Brahman be both a distinct, personal being with whom one may enter a loving relationship *and* one with all?

Rāmānuja claims the unity of Brahman and the world does not, as Śaṅkara claims, mean only Brahman is real and the world a mere appearance. It is, rather, an organic unity. Īśvara and the world, including all the souls, or *jīvas*, occupying the world, are related in the way that a soul is related to the body it inhabits in a given lifetime. In the words of theologian Michelle Voss Roberts: 'Rāmānuja uses the self-body analogy to indicate the inseparable relationship of God with the world, the dependence of the world on God, the reality of the world, and the accessibility of God' to devotees.[36] For Rāmānuja, God (Viṣṇu) is the soul of the world, and the world is the body of God.

Brahman, the One, is then the single, overarching entity made up of these two, God and the world, united in an eternal, loving embrace. *Brahman* is the name for God and the world as an organic unity: the *theocosm*.[37] This interpretation of Vedānta and the school based upon it is called *Viśiṣṭādvaita*, or 'non-duality with difference', which is also translated as 'qualified non-dualism'. The strength of this interpretation is that it enables a reader of the *Upaniṣads*, the *Brahma Sūtra* and the *Bhagavad Gītā* to see the verses of these texts that affirm both unity and duality – the unity of the Self and Brahman and a robust theism that affirms the distinction between God and the world, the deity and the devotee – as wholly true, and not merely symbolic or metaphorical. Purely non-dualist or purely dualist interpretations require some of these verses to become metaphors.

Rāmānuja's system of philosophy is again, foundational to the Śrī Vaiṣṇava tradition of Hinduism. A good deal of its appeal rests with its concern with the direct and loving relationship between the individual devotee and the Supreme Being. For Rāmānuja, liberation – mokṣa – is not something that one 'attains' by oneself, through self-effort alone. It requires the divine grace. God, for Rāmānuja, is a being of infinite love, possessing not only transcendence (*paratva*), but also accessibility (*saulabhya*). This is depicted in Śrī Vaiṣṇava literature with the image of an elephant and a lame man:

> The elephant is so high that the lame man has no accessibility to its neck by any effort of his. But the tall elephant can kneel down, and the lowly lame man can easily get upon it.[38]

The elephant in this image remains an elephant, just as the Supreme Being maintains the state of divine transcendence. The basic nature of the elephant as an elephant, like the transcendental nature of God, does not change. But the ability and the willingness of the elephant to kneel down to allow the lame man to climb upon him illustrates not only that God has the freedom and the power to act as agent with influence upon the world and the willingness to do so out of love for suffering beings. At the same time, while the kneeling of the elephant represents the bestowal of divine grace, it is also significant that the lame man still needs to make some effort to climb onto the elephant's neck. Divine grace is required for liberation, but those who desire liberation need to ready themselves for this grace through devotional practice and moral observance.

Dvaita Vedānta: Dualism

The *ācārya* Madhva, living from 1238 to 1317 CE, takes the Vaiṣṇava reaction to Śaṅkara even further than Rāmānuja does. Madhva affirms that duality, and not non-duality, is the essential characteristic of existence, and the principle of interpretation one should utilize in interpreting the Vedic texts. His system of Dvaita, or dualism, affirms the eternal distinctness of Īśvara, the world, and the jīvas eternally inhabiting the universe. In this system, affirmations of the oneness of Brahman are taken in a monotheistic sense as affirmations of the uniqueness of God, and not as saying that only Brahman exists and that all else is mere appearance. Dvaita, in other words, does not affirm *monism*, as most systems of Vedānta do, but *monotheism*, in something closer to a sense found in the Abrahamic religions. Madhva's Īśvara, however, still bears the traits of other Vedic conceptions of God, such as not being the absolute creator *ex nihilo* of the cosmos. Also, Madhva's Īśvara is not all-powerful. Jīvas, having free will, can defy the will of Viṣṇu.[39]

Madhva's emphasis on duality points even more urgently to the centrality of bhakti than does, arguably, Rāmānuja's philosophy of qualified non-dualism. The appeal of Madhva's system lies at least in part in its insight that *bhakti*, devotion, is a relationship, and a relationship can only obtain between two distinct entities. One can of course speak of a relationship of identity, but that is arguably mere wordplay. I am not 'related to' myself, I *am* myself. But I am related to those I love, those on whom I depend and those who depend upon me. This is a better characterization of the relationship between individual jīvas and God, according to Madhva, than even Rāmānuja's vision of organic non-duality, and certainly than Śaṅkara's distinction-effacing non-dualism.

Attempts to harmonize duality and non-duality

Other Vedāntic ācāryas lean, much as Rāmānuja does, in the direction of affirming that the relationship between Brahman and the world is, in different senses, dual and non-dual. This approach to Vedānta is called *bhedābheda*. It affirms difference (*bheda*) and non-difference (*abheda*). Indeed, it could be argued that this is the true import of the *Brahma Sūtra*, read in the abstract (although, as already noted, reading a text of this kind in isolation is not the traditional method for approaching it). As mentioned previously, the texts which make up the prasthāna traya lend themselves to many interpretations precisely because many views on duality and non-duality can be found in them. A non-dualist interpretation, like that of Śaṅkara, sees non-duality as the core Vedic message and reads dualistic parts of the text as metaphors or illustrations of the deeper truth of non-duality. A dualist interpretation, like that of Madhva, sees duality as the core Vedic message and reads non-dualist portions of the text, similarly, as metaphorical, or as referring to a singular deity rather than to reality as a whole.

Bhedābheda interpretations, though, affirm duality *and* non-duality as essential features of our experience, and of the relationship between Brahman and the world. In the Dvaitādvaita, or dualist and non-dualist system of Nimbārka (who lived around the twelfth or thirteenth century), duality and non-duality are equally central aspects of the relations between Īśvara and the world. This is in contrast with Rāmānuja, who sees non-duality as the more encompassing category. The Śuddhādvaita system of Vallabha, who lived from 1479 to 1531, affirms a non-duality of essence between Īśvara and individual jīvas. Unlike Śaṅkara, however, who affirms that duality is merely an appearance, Vallabha affirms a part-whole relation between the individual souls and God, using the analogy of sparks and fire. There is numerical duality – many souls distinct from one another and God – but unity of spiritual essence. Finally, the Acintya Bhedābheda of Caitanya, who lived from 1485 to 1533, affirms, as its name indicates, that the simultaneous duality and non-duality of God and the world is inconceivable – the meaning of *acintya*. Rather than being conceptualized, it must be felt in the experience of bhakti. It is ultimately not philosophizing about difference and non-difference, but in surrender to the divine beloved who is both one with us and utterly beyond us that one can truly be liberated.

Tantra: Another approach to duality and non-duality

During the same period that saw the rise of the schools of Vedānta – roughly the eighth to sixteenth centuries CE – another system of thought and practice also addressed questions of duality and non-duality, and was also, in most of its iterations, deeply theistic. Tāntric systems are quite diverse philosophically, affirming both the duality and the non-duality of the spiritual and material realms. Non-dualistic Tantra sees the material as the expression of and the means to realising the spiritual and can be distinguished from Advaita Vedānta by its positive embrace of materiality and sensory experience.

Tantra is a style or repertoire of spiritual practice, elements of which can be found in many Indic traditions. The texts called *Tantras* are primarily drawn from the Śākta and Śaiva traditions and may have precedents dating back to the worship of a Divine Mother and Father in the Indus Valley civilization. But Tantra is also present in the Vaiṣṇava tradition, Mahāyāna Buddhism and Jainism. It is a practice with enormous flexibility, not a rigid or dogmatic system incapable of compromise or transfer across ideological boundaries. In this sense, it is much like Yoga.

But Tāntric philosophy also presents a contrast with what might broadly be called the Yogic thread of Indic spirituality. This style of spiritual practice, represented pre-eminently by Patañjali's Yoga system, but also present in Vedānta, Buddhism and Jainism, involves withdrawal of attention from the senses and sensory objects in favour of an inward focus: on the mind, and eventually beyond the mind, on consciousness itself – the ātman, jīva, puruṣa, or Buddha Nature.

How this process of inward concentration is conceived varies depending on the tradition in which the practice occurs. Patañjali's system, which, as we have seen, shares the basic vocabulary of the Sāṃkhya system of philosophy, conceives the centre of pure consciousness as the puruṣa, which one seeks to differentiate from prakṛti, or material nature. Advaita Vedānta sees the basis of pure consciousness as Brahman, the ground of being. In Buddhism, the practitioner is to see the ultimate unreality of the individual self and realize the truth of No Self (*anātman*). In the Jain tradition, one seeks to realize the pure nature of the *jīva* – the soul or living being – free from the limitations of materiality. In the theistic forms of Vedānta, the practitioner aims at a loving union of the individual soul, or jīva, with God, who shares the same spiritual nature as the jīva, but who is nevertheless distinct from it, since the loving relationship of bhakti is only possible between two distinct entities.

For all these iterations of Yogic practice, materiality and the senses are problematic. They are that which is to be escaped in favour of the realization of a non-material reality or principle. All the various practices associated with the Yogic spiritual style are built on this ultimate aim of finding the highest truth through an experience of intense inwardness, shutting out the realm of the senses as a distraction. One closes one's eyes, focuses on the breath, allows distracting thoughts to melt away, shuts these thoughts out, engages in one-pointed concentration and so on.

Tantra, by contrast, can be seen as the path of transcending the senses not by shutting out or denying the senses, but *by means of* the senses. Unlike the Yogic style of practice, which sees the desires evoked by sensory objects as obstacles to be overcome, Tantra sees these desires as energies that can be redirected productively towards the aim of spiritual liberation.

This ultimate aim is shared by practitioners of both Yogic and Tāntric spiritualities, which are not to be seen as necessarily opposed, but as differing paths to the same ultimate end.

From a Yogic perspective, one can understand why Tantra is often taken to be a dangerous path. In practice, there is a fine line between utilising the desire for sensory objects as a source of spiritual energy to use on the path to liberation and simply indulging such desire. Tāntric traditions themselves are aware of this danger, which is why serious Tāntric practice requires initiation by an experienced teacher and is often shrouded in secrecy. It is not a practice for which everyone is deemed fit.

At the same time, practitioners within Yogic traditions became aware, around the middle of the first millennium of the Common Era, of the spiritual heights that could be attained by means of Tāntric practice and began to integrate elements of Tantra into their own systems. It is at this point that one begins to find Tāntric practices and sensibilities infusing traditions like Vaiṣṇavism, Buddhism and Jainism. The use of mantras, meditation on geometric patterns like yantras and maṇḍalas, and the construction of beautiful, intricate, awe-inspiring temples designed to recreate physically the inward journey to higher realms become features of practice within these traditions during this period.

Among these traditions, Buddhism was probably the most transformed by its integration of Tāntric elements and philosophies, giving rise to what is sometimes seen as an entirely new *yāna*, or vehicle for attainming awakening: the Vajrayāna. Tāntric Buddhism, philosophically, is an extension of Mahāyāna Buddhism. It incorporates the Tāntric practice and sensibility into the Bodhisattva path. The name of this tradition, Vajrayāna, is an indication of this sensibility. The term *vajra* has a double meaning. A vajra is a thunderbolt – the weapon of the Vedic deva Indra – but it is also a diamond. This double meaning conveys the qualities of the state of awakening to which Vajrayāna is intended to lead. Such awakening comes in a flash, like a thunderbolt, rapidly transforming the one who pursues this practice. But it is also a steady, unshakable state: a concept evoked by the image of the hardness of a diamond.

In some texts, this path is also known as the Mantrayāna, which highlights the importance of mantras in this practice. It is by this name that it is known in Japan, where it has been rendered as *Shingon*, or 'sacred word'.

The importance of Vajrayāna in the wider Buddhist world is shown by its prominence in particular regions. The dominant forms of Tibetan Buddhism, historically, have all been Tāntric; and Vajrayāna is the Buddhism of Nepal, Bhutan and the Himalayan regions of India as well. Tāntric Buddhism was also transmitted into China, Korea and Japan. Two of the major systems of contemporary Buddhism in Japan, Shingon and Tendai, are thoroughly Tāntric.

The incorporation of Tāntric elements into Vaiṣṇava practice was eased, no doubt, by the fact that Vaiṣṇava traditions are already deeply rooted in bhakti – the cultivation of intense devotion to the personal form of the Supreme Lord. Bhakti, like Tantra, channels human emotions toward a spiritual end – in this case, emotions of intense love and devotion. In their focus on cultivation, rather than suppression, of emotional energies, as well as their disregard for traditional strictures relating to social status or caste, the traditions of bhakti and of Tantra could be seen to share a common sensibility.

The tradition that was most resistant to Tantra was Jainism. The eighth century Śvetāmbara Jain philosopher, Haribhadra, who is, one might recall, best known for his broad-minded religious pluralism and openness to seeing the truth in a variety of spiritual paths, was uncharacteristically critical of Tāntric practice.[40] The centrality of cultivating moral purity and restraint of sensory desires in the Jain path made it difficult to reconcile with Tantra's embrace of the sensory realm as the expression of higher realities. Nevertheless, even Jains incorporated Tāntric elements into their practice in the first millennium of the Common Era, in the form of beautiful and elaborate temples, the use of spiritual diagrams such as yantras and maṇḍalas, and the recitation of mantras, including bīja mantras.

Like Jainism, the Theravāda tradition of Buddhism was more resistant to Tāntric elements than Mahāyāna. As with Jainism, Theravāda conservatism, with its emphasis on a close adherence to the path of the Buddha, did not lend itself to the incorporation of Tantra on a large scale. But even in Theravāda-practicing countries, one can find Tāntric elements in the culture.

The traditions which have the strongest associations with Tantra, though, are the Śaiva and Śākta traditions. Indeed, Śākta traditions are, for all intents and purposes, synonymous with Tantra. The traditions we have been discussing which absorbed elements of Tantra also absorbed a focus on Goddesses as objects of devotion and embodiments of divine, universal energy: which is the central focus of the Śākta traditions. The sacred texts known as the *Tantras*, from which the Tāntric tradition takes its name, are overwhelmingly Śākta texts. The Śākta traditions are of course centred on the worship of Śakti, the Mother Goddess, who embodies the power (*śakti*) of creation. Indeed, one reason for the speculation that Tantra might be traced to the Indus Valley civilisation is the fact that Goddess worship seems to have been a prominent part of the religion of that ancient culture. Because the deity Śiva is the husband of Śakti, the Śaiva and Śākta traditions share many things in common, including a deeply Tāntric sensibility. In addition to the Śākta traditions, the Kashmiri Śaiva tradition, too, could be considered a purely Tāntric system of thought and practice, systematized by the Śaiva philosopher, Abhinavagupta, in the late tenth century CE.

At the heart of much (although not all) Tāntric philosophy is the idea that Śakti is not only the power of creation, but that all of existence is Her manifestation. This is the Tāntric version of non-dualism or *advaita*. In contrast with Advaita Vedānta, in which Brahman is real and the world is, in comparison, an illusion, Tantric advaita teaches that the world is a real and true manifestation or transformation of the Divine

Mother. *Māyā* is seen in Tantra not as a deluding illusion, but as a creative power by which the Mother Goddess brings all things into being, thus giving expression to Her infinite glory. Māyā is deluding if one fails to see the Divine Mother within all things, but conducive to liberation if one sees the world as nothing but the reflection of Her beauty. A similar concept of māyā exists in Vaiṣṇava traditions as well, where māyā is Viṣṇu's power of creation through illusion.

In non-dualistic forms of Tantra, the material realm is non-different from the realm of awakening. This is the Tāntric version of the 'two truths' doctrine of the Mahāyāna Buddhist master Nāgārjuna and the Advaita Vedānta master Śaṅkara. Reality as perceived through the lens of ignorance is saṃsāra, the cycle of rebirth. The same reality, perceived truly, is nirvāṇa. Reality itself is one and non-dual. In the most radical forms of Tantra, known as *Vāmācāra*, or 'left-hand' Tantra, this non-duality is celebrated through antinomian practices.

The modern teacher of Vedānta, Sri Ramakrishna, who was deeply influenced by Tāntric thought, expresses this Tāntric sensibility when he invokes the distinction between *vidyāmāyā* and *avidyāmāyā* – which mean, respectively, the 'māyā of wisdom' and the 'māyā of ignorance'.

> This universe is created by the Mahāmāyā of God. Mahāmāyā contains both vidyāmāyā, the illusion of knowledge, and avidyāmāyā, the illusion of ignorance. Through the help of vidyāmāyā one cultivates such virtues as the taste for holy company, knowledge, devotion, love, and renunciation. Avidyāmāyā consists of the five elements and the objects of the five senses – form, flavor, smell, touch and sound. These make one forget God.[41]

The aim of Tāntric practice is to bring about a revolution in the awareness of the practitioner – to shift the practitioner from the state of avidyāmāyā, perceiving a world of persons and objects which are separable into 'pure' and 'impure', to the state of vidyā-māyā, or wisdom, in which God is all and all is God.

This is the conceptual basis not only for mainstream Tāntric practice, but also for the more 'scandalous' practices mentioned earlier. The aim is to embody one's transcendence of mundane categories of purity and impurity in a state of non-dual awareness.

Tāntric subtle physiology: Kuṇḍalinī Śakti and the system of Nāḍīs and Cakras

One of the most distinctive features of Tantra is its subtle physiology. According to Tantra, co-existing with the physical body (the *sthūla śarīra*, or 'gross body'), and also occupying the same space, are various subtle bodies (*sūkṣma śarīra*). The idea of subtle bodies is of course an ancient one and is shared with Vedānta. An early version of it can be found in the *Upaniṣads*, as the idea of the *kośas*, or 'sheaths', surrounding the *ātman*, or Self.

Tantra, however, adds considerably to this picture, describing a highly complex subtle body made up of 72,000 *nāḍīs*, or nerve channels, which fill almost the entire space of the physical body, and which, when depicted visually, appear a great deal like the physical nervous system as it is known to medical science. Much like the physical nervous system, the complex of nāḍis connects to a central channel, the *suṣumnā nāḍī*, which corresponds to the spinal cord.

Located along the suṣumnā nāḍī are seven subtle energy centres known as the *cakras*. Each cakra is associated with different emotional and spiritual states. In most persons, a powerful subtle energy lies coiled in the cakra at the base of the spine. This energy is the immanent presence of Śakti, the Mother Goddess. The aim of much Tāntric practice is to awaken this coiled or *kuṇḍalinī* śakti and cause it to ascend through the suṣumna nāḍī. As the kuṇḍalinī energy ascends the spinal column, it activates the cakras in succession, unleashing the energies associated with them. At the top of the head is the *sahasrāra* cakra, or thousand-petal lotus. In some texts, the illumination of this last cakra is equated with awakening and liberation.

Śaiva theology

Tantra, particularly in its Śaiva manifestations, makes important contributions to Indian theism. A consistent criticism of the concept of Īśvara from traditions like Buddhism and Jainism (and from Vedic traditions like Mīmāṃsā and Sāṃkhya, which either reject the concept of Īśvara or conceive of Īśvara in purely passive terms) relates to karma. If the cosmos operates on the basis of a consistent law of moral causation (for which the Jain tradition has even developed a quasi-physical explanation, in the form of karma particles), then, from a moral perspective, what is the need for God? If God dispenses grace – that is, compassion or *karuṇā* – to those who do not deserve it, does this not violate the principle of karma? And if it is possible to explain the events of this world through karma alone, is God not superfluous? In the words of P. S. Jaini, 'If karma is relevant in the destinies of human beings, then God is irrelevant; if he rules regardless of the karma of beings, then he is cruel and capricious.'[42]

Some Śaiva traditions – traditions which conceive of Īśvara as the deity Śiva – respond to this concern by conceiving of Śiva as the answer to the question, 'How is karma guaranteed?' In other words, how is it ensured that the actions which beings commit are followed by appropriate results? How is this process of 'cosmic justice' reconciled with the idea of divine compassion? As scholar Surendranath Dasgupta explains:

> Ordinarily the idea of grace or karuṇā would simply imply the extension of kindness or favour to one in distress. But in the *Śaivāgamas* there is a distinct line of thought where karuṇā or grace is interpreted as a divine creative movement for supplying all souls with fields of experience in which they may enjoy pleasures and suffer painful experiences. The karuṇā of God reveals the world to us in just the manner as we ought to experience it. Grace, therefore, is not a work of favour in a general sense, but it is a movement in favour of our getting the right

desires in accordance with our *karma*. Creative action of the world takes place in consonance with our good and bad deeds, in accordance with which the various types of experience unfold themselves to us. In this sense, grace may be compared to the Yoga philosophy, which admits a permanent will of God operating in the orderliness of the evolutionary creation . . . for the protection of the world, and supplying it as the basis of human experience in accordance with their individual *karmas*.[43]

The non-dual Śaiva traditions also present a distinctive concept of the process of creation with their idea of *spanda*, or 'vibration', as the mechanism by which God creates and orders the world. Śiva is the original unity: the ground of being, identical to the Brahman of the *Upaniṣads*.

From this original unity, *Sadāśiva*, evolves two differentiated realities. One is Śiva as pure consciousness, who is the male principle, not unlike the puruṣa of Sāṃkhya philosophy. The other is Śakti, or pure creative energy, which is a close analogue, as the female principle, to the prakṛti of Sāṃkhya, the material continuum. From the proximity of Śiva and Śakti, their intense and loving relationship, emerges the original vibration which gives rise to creation. The cosmos is the love play of Śiva and Śakti. Each element of existence can be seen as manifesting a different vibration in the dynamic material of existence, the omnipresent form of the Divine Mother, responding to the infinite consciousness which is Śiva. The pairing of the male and female divine principles is sometimes represented as *Ardhanārīśvara*: Śiva and Śakti combined into a single deity.

Conclusion

It might be tempting to see the various systems of Vedānta as conflicting schools of thought hopelessly locked in irreconcilable conflict over their differing views of reality. This is the way in which these traditions are typically viewed by scholars of Indian philosophy. A Vedic theologian, however, in keeping with the ancient Vedic teaching that 'Truth is one; the wise speak of it in many ways', might be better see the various Vedāntic systems as articulating, each in its own way, a particular facet of the total, complex vision of the *Vedas*. Tantra, too, contributes substantially to the philosophical conversation in India, starting in the latter centuries of the first millennium of the Common Era, when the first texts titled *Tantras* were set down, and continuing into the second.

One claim on which most these schools of thought, Vedāntic and Tāntric, agree is that truth, ultimately, is beyond what can be captured in finite words and concepts. 'That from which words recoil, together with the mind, unable to attain it, that is the bliss of Brahman.'[44]

In this chapter, we have traced the development of Indian philosophy from the end of what is often termed the 'classical period' – the centuries from the decline of the Maurya Empire to that of the Guptas – and into the medieval period of India, marked by the decline of Buddhism and the rise of the theistic systems of Vedānta and Tantra.

In our next chapter, we shall conclude our exploration of Indian philosophy by examining how Indian philosophical traditions have continued to develop and evolve in the modern period: a period in which it may truly be said that Indian thought has 'gone global'.[45]

Notes

1 Portions of this chapter have appeared previously, in considerably different form, in the *Journal of Vaiṣṇava Studies* and *Prabuddha Bharata*. They are included with permission.

2 Recall from our earlier discussion that the authority of smṛti texts is derivative from or dependent upon the śruti texts, which are the highest textual authority in at least most Hindu traditions. The *Bhagavad Gītā* is cited accordingly in premodern commentarial literature.

3 *Brahma Sūtra* 2.2.33 See *Brahma Sūtras According to Śrī Śaṅkara*, trans. Swami Vireshwarananda (Mayavati: Advaita Ashrama, 2001), pp. 200–1. This is according to the versification of the text found in the commentary of Śaṅkara. The commentary of Rāmānuja gives this verse as 2.2.31. See *Brahma Sūtras According to Śrī Rāmānuja*, trans. Swami Vireshwarananda (Mayavati: Advaita Ashrama, 1998), p. 264.

4 *Bhagavad Gītā* 13:4, translation mine.

5 *Bhagavad Gītā* 2:19, George Thompson, trans., *The Bhagavad Gita: A New Translation* (New York: North Point Press, 2008), p. 10.

6 *Bhagavad Gītā* 13:1.

7 See Jeffery D. Long, 'War and Nonviolence in the *Bhagavad Gītā*: Correcting Common Misconceptions' (*Prabuddha Bharata*, October 2009).

8 *Bhagavad Gītā* 2:12–13, based on Thompson, trans., p. 9.

9 *Bhagavad Gītā*, 2:42–4 (p. 12).

10 *Bhagavad Gītā*, 2:45 (pp. 12–13).

11 *Bhagavad Gītā*, 2:46 (p. 13).

12 *Bhagavad Gītā*, 2:47–8 (p. 13).

13 *Bhagavad Gītā*, 3:4–5 (p. 16).

14 *Bhagavad Gītā*, 3:9 (p. 17).

15 *Bhagavad Gītā*, 4:28 (p. 24).

16 *Bhagavad Gītā*, 12:2–7 (pp. 60–1).

17 *Bhagavad Gītā*, 4:8.

18 *Bhagavad Gītā*, 4:11.

19 'It is almost universally accepted that the GK [the *Gauḍapādīya Kārikā*, another name for the *Māṇḍūkyopaniṣad Kārikā*] has been influenced, at least in terms of [its] argumentation, by the philosophy of Nāgārjuna.' (Richard King, *Early Advaita Vedānta and Buddhism: The Mahāyāna Context of the Gauḍapādīya Kārikā* (Albany: State University of New York Press, 1995), p. 89.

20 This, of course, is not a view that a Buddhist would accept. 'Nāgārjuna does not uphold *ajātivāda* – the absolutistic doctrine of non-origination since the true import of *śūnyatā* is said to be a denial of all views including the absolutistic view that

all things exist in some unoriginated form [the Sarvāstivāda view that Nāgārjuna rejects]." (King, *Early Advaita Vedānta and Buddhism*, p. 128).

21 *Bhagavad Gītā* 2:71–2 (p. 15).
22 *Bhagavad Gītā* 5:24–6 (pp. 28–9).
23 *Aitareya Upaniṣad* 3.3.
24 *Māṇḍūkya Upaniṣad* 1.2.
25 *Chāndogya Upaniṣad* 6:8.7.
26 *Bṛhadāraṇyaka Upaniṣad* 1:4.10.
27 *Chāndogya Upaniṣad* 3:14.1.
28 See, for example, Anantanand Rambachan, *The Advaita Worldview: God, World, and Humanity* (Albany: SUNY Press, 2006).
29 Swami Tyagananda, *Knowing the Knower: A Jñāna Yoga Manual* (Gol Park, Kolkata: Ramakrishna Mission Institute of Culture, 2017), pp. 25–6.
30 Śaṅkara's commentary on *Bhagavad Gītā* 18.66: *Srimad Bhagavad Gītā Bhāṣya of Sri Sankaracharya*, trans. Dr. A. G. Krishna Warrier (Calcutta: Sri Ramakrishna Math, 1983).
31 Alasdair Macintyre, *Whose Justice? Which Rationality?* (Notre Dame: University of Notre Dame Press, 1989), pp. 361–9.
32 Paul J. Griffiths, *Religious Reading: The Place of Reading in the Practice of Religion* (New York: Oxford University Press, 1999), p. 183.
33 *Bhagavad Gītā*, 4:33 (p. 24).
34 *Bhagavad Gītā* 12:2 (p. 60).
35 Kencho Tenzin, 'Shankara: A Hindu Revivalist or a Crypto-Buddhist?' (Thesis: Georgia State University, 2006). doi: https://doi.org/10.57709/1062066.
36 Michelle Voss Roberts, *Body Parts: A Theological Anthropology* (Minneapolis: Fortress Press, 2017), p. 57.
37 Jeffery D. Long, *A Vision for Hinduism: Beyond Hindu Nationalism* (London: IB Tauris, 2007), p. 85.
38 Swami Tapasyananda, *Bhakti Schools of Vedānta* (Chennai: Sri Ramakrishna Math, 1990), p. 49.
39 Deepak Sarma, *An Introduction to Madhva Vedānta* (Farnham: Ashgate, 2003), pp. 70–1.
40 Christopher Chapple, *Key Reconciling Yogas: Haribhadra's Collection of Views on Yoga* (Albany: State University of New York Press, 2003), pp. 75–85.
41 Swami Nikhilananda, trans., *The Gospel of Sri Ramakrishna* (New York: Ramakrishna-Vivekananda Center, 1942), p. 216.
42 Jaini, *The Jaina Path of Purification*, p. 89.
43 Surendranath Dasgupta, *A History of Indian Philosophy* (Delhi: Motilal Banarsidass, 1991), p. 4.
44 *Taittirīya Upaniṣad* 2.4; cited in Keith Ward, *Religion and Creation* (Oxford: Clarendon Press, 1996), p. 88.
45 Jonardon Ganeri, 'Why Philosophy Must Go Global: A Manifesto', *Confluence: An Online Journal of World Philosophies* 4 (June 2016): 134–86.

The modern period

Indian philosophy goes global

Introduction

The second millennium of the Common Era saw several major shifts in Indian religion and philosophy. As we have already seen, the various systems of Vedānta and Tantra, emerging in the prior millennium, continued to develop extensively during this period. Many of the developments of this period particularly in Vedānta, were fuelled by the popular bhakti movements that emerged in various parts of India, and from within various theistic traditions: Vaiṣṇava, Śaiva and Śākta. The coming of Islam, too, marked a major shift as new modes of religiosity and philosophy entered the Indian conversation. By the middle of the second millennium, widespread mutual syncretism was occurring between adherents of Hindu bhakti traditions and of the mystically oriented Sufi tradition of Islam, leading to a great deal of religious ferment and creativity. The Sant movement, represented by such figures such as the mystical poet Kabīr (1440–1518), in whose work the lines between Hinduism and Islam are blurred, and the Sikh tradition of Guru Nānak (1469–1539), who taught, 'There is no Hindu, there is no Muslim', are just two examples of this trend towards integration and synthesis.

In terms of philosophy, in a formal sense, developments on the popular level manifested in the rise of a strong theistic orientation in Indian thought. It was not only the average person who was drawn to a path of bhakti, of faith and devotion. As we have seen, prominent intellectuals like Rāmānuja, Madhva and Caitanya held bhakti to be absolutely central to the relationship between God and humanity.

This era also saw the rise of the Navya Nyāya: the 'New' or 'Neo' Nyāya school of thought. Active from roughly the thirteenth to the eighteenth centuries, Navya Nyāya is essentially a far more rigorous and detailed variation of the earlier Nyāya system of epistemology and logic. Gupta characterizes it as follows:

The most important difference between the old Nyāya and the Neo-Nyāya is as follows: The Neo-Nyāya discussed the same relational facts as the Nyāya did, however, in order to express their contents more adequately, they developed a new terminology and style. What the Naiyāyikas expressed in a simple language, the

Neo-Nyāya expanded into much more sophisticated expressions . . . If the old Nyāya would say that the book is on the table, the neo Nyāya would express the same fact by stating that the book is 'being qualified by the qualifier bookness,' and state the relation of being on the table as the relation of conjunction, and also determine the table as qualified by 'tableness.'[1]

Gupta's characterization here would almost appear to be a caricature. The point, however, of this more detailed, sophisticated and complex mode of philosophical presentation was to express truth with the greatest exactitude possible. Navya Nyāya, like its older ancestor, exerted an enormous influence upon Indian philosophy, as it came to define the standard of logical rigour by which one would need to argue in order to establish one's position. This system was thus studied not only by its own adherents, but by adherents of other systems as well, such as the renowned Jain philosopher Yaśovijaya (1624–88).

The coming of the British and the emergence of Indian modernity

European Christianity and modern science arrived in India through colonization, along with modern philosophy: the thought of Descartes, Hume, Kant and Hegel, and later, the evolutionary thought of Charles Darwin and the 'social Darwinism' of Herbert Spencer. Starting with the Portuguese and continuing with the Dutch and French, and finally culminating with the British, European powers began arriving in India, initially to trade, but ultimately, to control and dominate politically, economically and culturally. European education was introduced with the twin goals of, on the one hand, 'civilising' Indians, making them more like Europeans both religiously and culturally, and on the other, of enabling Europeans to control India through a class of civil servants who had imbibed Western values. In one of the ironies of history, it was from among this Western-educated class of Indians that many leaders of the movement for Indian political independence emerged: an independence finally won on 15 August 1947. It was also from this class, informed by two ancient and sophisticated traditions, European and Indian, that modern Indian philosophy emerged at the beginning of the nineteenth century.

Several general points need to be noted about the influence of European thought on Indian philosophy and culture before proceeding to an exploration of major modern Indian thinkers. First, regarding Christianity, it should be noted that *European* Christianity, specifically, first arrives with Portuguese missionaries in the late fifteenth century. Christianity, though, had been present in India for over a thousand years before the arrival of the first missionary. The Nasrani (Nazarenes), or St. Thomas Christians, as they are also known, and who are traditionally affiliated to the Syrian Orthodox Church, had existed in Kerala for centuries. It was not Christianity as such, but colonial European Christianity that disrupted Indian culture.

Second, regarding modern science, there is a widespread misconception that the British were able to conquer India because of superior technology. This is not, however, the case. In fact, India was, in many respects, more technologically advanced than Europe at the time of the arrival of the first Europeans in India.[2] India was not, however, a united political unit at this point. The Mughal Empire was in decline by the eighteenth century, when the British were beginning their colonization activities in earnest. The gradual incorporation of most of the subcontinent into the British Empire was a process involving at least as much political manoeuvring as direct military confrontation. India was not formally brought under the rule of the British crown until 1858. Prior to this time, British holdings in India were under the control of the British East India Company.

Finally, it should be noted that as with the coming of Islam, many Indian philosophers did not concern themselves with the cultural ideals or philosophies of the dominant political power. Although gradually eclipsed by educational institutions based on a European model, the traditional systems of learning continued to exist in monastic institutions and other kinds of traditional school. These traditional institutions continue to exist in India today, and Indian philosophy continues to be produced in Sanskrit, in which arguments are made utilizing the norms of traditional, system-based Indian philosophy.

What is most noteworthy about the modern period of the history of Indian philosophy is the emergence of new modes of thought, often presented in English, that draw upon earlier Indian models and strike out in new directions, inspired by interactions with Western philosophy, both Christian and sceptical.

Modern Vedānta: Roots in the Brahmo Samāj

The story of the 'new Vedānta' begins in Bengal with Ram Mohan Roy (1772–1833). Roy, a reformer of Hinduism, saw validity in some Islamic and Christian criticisms of Hindu traditions, like their criticisms of Hindu use of images in worship, pejoratively dubbed 'idolatry', and of caste prejudice and patriarchy in Hindu society. Unlike other thinkers, however, who either adopted Islam or Christianity or, more often, became sceptical about all religions, Roy responded to these criticisms by seeking to recover what he believed to be the original and pure teaching of Hinduism: the teaching of the *Upaniṣads*, which he interpreted as an ethical monotheism. Roy contrasted the Upaniṣadic philosophy with both Christianity and popular Hinduism, both of which he found to be morally and rationally wanting. Roy's reforms sparked what has come to be known as the 'Bengal Renaissance', and inspired a host of other reformers from across the Indian subcontinent. A churchlike organization in which songs were sung and sermons given based on the *Upaniṣads*, the Brahmo Samāj or 'Community of Brahman' was established to perpetuate Roy's rationalistic understanding of Hinduism.

The Brahmo Samāj, as an organization, never attracted a massive popular following. Its rejection of the popular practice of mūrti puja (worship using images), which is a central dimension of much Hindu practice to the present, was likely a factor in its failure to become a mass movement.

However, many of the most prominent Hindu thinkers of the nineteenth century were inspired by or in some way affiliated to this organization. The first leader of this organization after Roy, Devendranath Tagore (1817–1905), was known not only for his work with the Brahmo Samāj, but probably even more so for his illustrious son, Rabindranath (1861–1941), a renowned artist, musician, philosopher and essayist.

Keshub Chunder Sen (1838–84), who was probably the most controversial member of this organization, parted company with Brahmo Samāj orthodoxy on several issues. Sen taught a 'new dispensation' that would involve a unification of Hinduism and Christianity. Under the influence of the Bengali sage, Sri Ramakrishna, Sen's views on the use of images softened. Sen was an early mentor to and influence on Narendranath Datta, who would later become a prominent disciple of Ramakrishna. Known to the world as Swami Vivekananda (1863–1902), Datta became the most renowned and influential Vedāntic thinker of the modern era.

The Vedānta of Swami Vivekananda

The Vedānta of Swami Vivekananda develops from the thought of the Hindu reformers who preceded him. It is rooted in the classical Vedānta of the earlier ācāryas (especially Śaṅkara), but it also has distinct features of its own, including an emphasis on direct experience (*anubhāva*) as the ultimate authority in spiritual matters, in contrast with the more traditional emphasis on Vedic texts as the śabda pramāṇa, as well as an emphasis on universalism, as opposed to exclusivism.

Apart from the Brahmo Samāj, an important early influence which would continue to shape his thought in many ways throughout his lifetime, certainly the strongest influence on Vivekananda was the aforementioned sage, Sri Ramakrishna Paramahamsa (1836–86).

It is probably not an exaggeration to say that Sri Ramakrishna is one of the most remarkable figures of not only Indian, but of world religious history. Barely literate, Ramakrishna was not a philosopher in the sense of having specialized training in the study and elucidation of Sanskrit texts. He was born into a poor Brahmin family in the Bengal village of Kamarpukur. When he was nineteen years old, he and his elder brother were hired as priests at a temple of the Goddess Kālī in Dakshineshwar, on the outskirts of Calcutta. Before this time, Ramakrishna was known locally for his ecstatic trances, or *samādhis*, in which he would lose consciousness of the outer world and become immersed in a state of divine bliss. Both during and after his lifetime, sceptics expressed the view that he might have suffered from a neurological disorder.

Ramakrishna came out of these experiences, though, believing he had become absorbed in God-consciousness, and he appeared to have a deep knowledge of many of topics discussed in the Hindu scriptures, even without having studied them. The belief of the community of devotees that developed around him was that this knowledge came from direct experiences of the realities the scriptures describe. His experiences were often induced by devotional activity, like the singing of songs on sacred themes.

The Kālī temple at which he served was on a popular pilgrimage route, and holy persons from diverse traditions frequently stopped there and engaged him in discussion of spiritual topics. Some believed him to be an avatāra, a divine incarnation.

Ramakrishna, according to accounts of his life, performed *sādhana*, or spiritual practice, following a variety of traditions. His aim was to realize God in as many ways as possible. He thus followed various Hindu traditions – Śākta, Śaiva and Vaiṣṇava – as well as Christianity and Islam, until he entered a state of samādhi through their respective practices. According to the beliefs of the community that developed on the basis of his life and teachings, he achieved God-realization in all of them, thus establishing an experiential basis for religious pluralism.[3]

The young Narendranath Datta was an adherent of the Brahmo Samāj; but he also had quite a sceptical mind, having absorbed the thinking of many modern European philosophers over the course of his education. He was encouraged by one of his teachers, a Scottish theologian named William Hastie (1842–1903), to seek out Ramakrishna, whom Hastie had heard was a 'man of God'. Datta dutifully visited Ramakrishna at Dakshineshwar. Initially thinking Ramakrishna to be insane, Datta nevertheless found himself mysteriously drawn to this holy man, who seemed more a product of ancient India than of the modern world in which he found himself immersed. A number of young men of Calcutta, finding themselves caught between traditional Hinduism and the modern world of their education, felt similarly drawn to Ramakrishna. After his death from throat cancer in 1886, they became renouncers and formed a new group of Hindu monks called the Ramakrishna Order. Their leader, Datta, took the monastic name Swami Vivekananda.

Vivekananda wandered the length and breadth of India for several years, learning from a variety of teachers and also, himself, teaching those who were interested in hearing what he had to say. In 1893, at the encouragement of the Rāja of Ramnad, in southern India, he agreed to be a delegate to the first Parliament of the World's Religions, held in Chicago, and to carry the message of Vedānta to the Western world.

Swami Vivekananda's first address to the Parliament of the World's Religions, presented on 11 September 1893. In this address, Vivekananda identifies Vedānta with an ideal of 'universal acceptance'. Citing the *Śiva Mahimna Stotra* (a popular Śaiva hymn) and the *Bhagavad Gītā*, Vivekananda identifies all spiritual paths as being aimed at the same ultimate goal.[4] This focus on religious pluralism is in keeping with his claim that his teaching is his 'own interpretation of our ancient books, in the light which my Master shed upon them'. Ramakrishna's religiously plural sādhanas provide the context in which Vivekananda interprets the Hindu textual tradition.

This pluralistic thread, which becomes a dominant attribute of modern Vedānta, has a long history in Indian thought, being traceable to the teaching of the *Ṛg Veda* that, 'Though reality is One, inspired poets speak of it in many ways'. As we have seen, philosophers in India have not always treated one another's views with 'universal acceptance'. They frequently offer sharp criticisms of one another's views. But Vivekananda is not simply misreading the tradition he has inherited. He is pointing, rather, to a trait of Indian philosophy which we would be remiss not to note. This is the tendency of Indian philosophical systems towards what Indologist Paul Hacker has termed *inclusivism*.[5] This is the idea that the teachings of one's opponents, even if it is not representative of the full truth, as found in one's own view, are nevertheless not wholly mistaken. Rather than a simplistic division of philosophies into 'true' (one's own) and 'false' (everyone else's), Indian philosophers often conceive of a hierarchy of truth, in which other schools of thought are 'rungs' on the 'ladder' leading to the truth: the *siddhānta*, or end perfection of truth.

We have seen this on a number of occasions: the Jain doctrine of the complexity of reality (anekāntavāda), the Mahāyāna teaching of the Buddha's skilful means (upāya kauśalya) and the teaching of the *Bhagavad Gītā* that while Kṛṣṇa is the Supreme Lord, He accepts all who approach Him in any form, and through diverse paths, like the yoga of knowledge and the yoga of devotion. Vivekananda clarifies this in a later lecture, where he says:

> System after system arises, each one embodying a great idea, and ideals must be added to ideals. And this is the march of humanity. Man never progresses from error to truth, but from truth to truth, from lesser truth to higher truth – but it is never from error to truth.[6]

Contemporary Western philosophers of religion make a sharp distinction between religious pluralism – the view that all, or most, religions are relatively equal in their capacity to express truth and lead to some kind of salvation – and inclusivism of the more hierarchical variety that one finds expressed in most forms of Indian philosophy (and in many other traditions as well, such as in the official teaching of the Roman Catholic Church regarding truth and salvation in religions outside itself, and in the Islamic teaching that Christians and Jews are 'People of the Book', possessed of an incomplete, but nevertheless valid revelation from God). And, of course, both pluralism and inclusivism are distinct from *exclusivism*, which teaches that there is only one true religion and path to the ultimate good. In some of his teachings, like when he speaks of universal acceptance, Vivekananda seems to be a pluralist, whereas in other places, such as when he speaks of levels of truth, or in another lecture where he teaches that the *Vedas* are the texts which best embody the highest truth, he seems to be more of an inclusivist. Ramakrishna, on the other hand, is a thoroughgoing pluralist, as is Mohandas Gandhi. Modern Indian philosophy gravitates towards universalism, either in a pluralist or inclusivist form, or a stance somewhere between the two.

This universalism was pioneered most dramatically by Ramakrishna, though both Roy and Sen. drew upon Christianity and professed admiration for Jesus Christ. Roy and Sen, in turn, were drawing upon thinkers like Kabīr and Guru Nānak, who sought a rapprochement between Hinduism and Islam.

What Ramakrishna adds to the picture is the multi-religious spiritual practices by which he is believed to have achieved God-realization, thus placing universalism on an empirical footing. Vivekananda and other teachers of modern Vedānta subsequently present Vedānta not simply as a Hindu system of philosophy, but as the spiritual science underlying all religions. In the words of one of its most renowned modern exponents, Sarvepalli Radhakrishnan, Vedānta is 'not a religion, but religion itself in its most universal and deepest significance'.[7]

Closely related to the universalism of modern Vedānta is its emphasis on direct experience as a pramāṇa – and indeed, the most authoritative pramāṇa. Experience – anubhāva – here refers not only to sensory experience, but also to yogic experience of the kind cultivated in the sādhanas of Ramakrishna. One who places faith in the testimony of a seer like Ramakrishna (or the seers of the *Vedas*) has only second-hand knowledge of the realities they have experienced. The ultimate goal is to have this experience for oneself by following the teachings of those who have achieved it. This is also the basic model of the Śramaṇa traditions – Jainism and Buddhism: that one follows the teachings of those who have attained enlightenment so one may attain it oneself.

Advaita Vedānta scholar Anantanand Rambachan has pointed out that modern Vedānta's emphasis on experience is a departure from classical Advaita Vedānta as expounded by Śaṅkara.[8] For Śaṅkara, the *Vedas* are the śabda pramāṇa. As a pramāṇa, they need no additional validation outside themselves; for a pramāṇa precisely *is* a source of validation. This way of seeing the *Vedas* is in accordance with the Mīmāṃsā understanding of the *Vedas*, which traditional Vedānta shares.

We have seen, though, that this is not the only way to look at Vedic authority among those traditions which take the *Vedas* to be authoritative. The Nyāya tradition bases Vedic authority on the *Vedas'* being the word of an authoritative person: Īśvara. One could say that for modern Vedānta, the *Vedas* are authoritative because they are the word of seers who perceived the truth directly. This is in line with the modern understanding of Vedānta as akin to a spiritual science.

One trusts – one could say one 'has faith' – in what scientists say on the assumption that they have performed the experiments needed to establish the views they are propounding. Prior to attaining realization for oneself, one similarly trusts the Vedas. The ideal, though, of modern Vedānta is to attain this realization oneself. This is why the focus in modern Vedānta has moved from the study of Vedic texts to the cultivation of experience through practices such as meditation.

This distinction between modern and traditional Vedānta, though, can be overstated. It is not that textual study is wholly absent from modern Vedānta. Indeed, some of the best translations of Vedāntic sources in the modern period have been those produced by the Ramakrishna Order. Nor was meditation absent from ancient or classical Vedānta. Like Sāṃkhya, Advaita Vedānta teaches that knowledge – jñāna – constitutes the state of liberation. As in Sāṃkhya, though, this is not simply a matter of cognition, or else anyone who hears or reads and understands the words of the *Vedas* will instantly attain liberation. Traditional Advaita Vedānta teaches a three-step process of realization. One first hears the words of the *Vedas* (śravaṇa, or 'hearing'). One then reflects upon their meaning (manana, or 'thinking'). Then one makes this meaning an object of meditative contemplation (nididhyāsana), leading to direct realization. There is thus substantive continuity between traditional and modern Vedānta. The emphasis has only shifted from the study of the texts based on the experience (and which, properly contemplated, can lead to the experience) to the experience itself as the ultimate foundation of authority. Again, this is in keeping with the shift to a scientific mode of thinking emphasizing direct perception over accepting the authority of the word of others in anything other than a provisional fashion.

A focus on social action: Swami Vivekananda and Mahātma Gandhi on Karma Yoga

Another shift in focus in modern Indian thought is toward service to alleviate concrete human suffering. This shift, much like the shift from scriptural authority to the authority of direct experience, is not without precedent in the premodern period, and does not represent a complete rupture with the past. But it is a shift in emphasis, particularly in regard to the purpose of monastic life.

Traditionally, members of monastic orders – Hindu, Buddhist and Jain – have focused most of their activity upon study and meditation, refraining from ritual activity and worldly work. At most, ascetics would engage in teaching. Their focus, otherwise, was on personal striving for liberation, in which they would be supported by their householder disciples.

Swami Vivekananda, however, made service a central mandate of the Ramakrishna Order. Vivekananda's monks engaged in concrete work for the alleviation of human suffering: poverty relief, education and so on. The Ramakrishna Mission's work in this regard has been its major focus since its inception, with the Ramakrishna Order running hospitals, schools and orphanages across India.

According to Swami Vivekananda's interpretation of the *Bhagavad Gītā*, this focus upon concrete service is in line with the ideal of the karma yoga, in which one does good deeds, serving the suffering beings in the world, not out of desire for good karma – for a renouncer is aimed not at a better rebirth, but at liberation – but simply out of a selfless desire to serve. Such selfless service is a path to liberation. It purifies the mind of egotism, preparing it for the transforming knowledge that constitutes liberation.

While monks engaging in 'worldly' service was initially seen by many as scandalous, in the course of the last century, it has become a standard element of the work of monks from a variety of Hindu traditions. Much of this service had been carried out, traditionally, by rulers and wealthy householders. A good deal of it was unnecessary in the premodern period, when India was highly affluent. However, the poverty that came with colonization and the destruction of much of the indigenous industry by which Indians had earned their livelihood, made such service necessary. It has been alleged that this focus on service in Hindu traditions has been a result of the influence of Christian missionaries. The rationale for such activities, however, can be seen to derive from Indian philosophical sources. What has been modelled on Christian missionary work is the system of *organisation* that Hindu relief efforts have adopted, enabling them to deliver services efficiently on a large scale.

Much Hindu engagement with human suffering has been apolitical. Even during the period of British rule, the monks of the Ramakrishna Order did not take up political activism in the name of Indian independence. Indeed, one of the close Western disciples of Swami Vivekananda, Sister Nivedita (born Margaret E. Noble, 1867–1911) parted company with the Order over this issue, as she wished to pursue activism for the political independence of India.

The figure best known for taking up Swami Vivekananda's call for service and translating it into a political program is Mohandas K. Gandhi (1869–1948), better known as 'great soul', or *Mahātma*, Gandhi – a title bestowed upon him by his admirers among the people of India.

For Gandhi, political liberation and spiritual liberation were two sides of the same coin. In Gandhi's view, *Hind Swarāj*, or 'Indian Self-rule', meant not only political independence from the British Empire, though it certainly implied this. It meant the spiritual transformation of all India and the re-establishment of Indian civilization on a spiritual basis. While his blend of religion and politics was controversial for some, it would prove inspirational for figures around the world involved in similar struggles for peace, justice and human dignity. Martin Luther King, Jr., especially, comes to mind as a civil rights leader who followed Gandhi's model in many ways.

Gandhi is best known for insisting on non-violent methods for bringing about political and social change. If political activism is a kind of sādhana, or spiritual practice – a karma yoga – then it can only be pursued through ethical means. For Gandhi, this implied a commitment to *ahiṃsā* and *satya*: non-violence and truth. Via Gandhi, although he was a devout Vaiṣṇava Hindu, a substantial element of Jain thought on non-violence came to be emphasized in India in the modern era.[9]

Gandhi was, in the mould of Ramakrishna, a religious pluralist. He was committed to a vision of India as a place where all religions would be welcome. Believing, as he did, that all religions are paths to the same ultimate realization, he did not see religious diversity as a source of conflict, but as something to be celebrated.[10]

Gandhi ultimately sacrificed his life for his commitment to inter-religious harmony. He was deeply opposed to the partition of India into the predominantly Hindu (but officially secular) state of India and the Islamic state of Pakistan (which was itself later partitioned into Pakistan and Bangladesh). The partition occurred nevertheless, resulting in countless deaths as many Hindus in Pakistan and many Muslims in India fled their respective homes. Members of both communities engaged in angry reprisals against one another for losses of homes and loved ones. Gandhi fasted, nearly to the death, to bring peace between the two groups. But his attempts at rapprochement with the Muslim community were seen by some Hindus as a betrayal, which led to his assassination on the 30 January 1948 by Nathuram Godse, an adherent of the Hindu nationalist movement who believed Gandhi had not done enough to prevent the partition and that he had appeased Muslims interests against those of the Hindus. Hindu nationalism remains a prominent political movement which seeks to transform India from a secular state to a Hindu state, or *rāṣṭra*. It is an internally diverse movement with both moderate and extreme sub-variations, including the one represented by Godse.[11]

The integral Yoga of Sri Aurobindo

Another figure inspired by Swami Vivekananda, but taking this inspiration in a different direction from that of Gandhi, was Aurobindo Ghose (1872–1950), better known as Sri Aurobindo. Aurobindo, like Gandhi, was from the class of Indians who received a British education, absorbing many of the values and ideals of Western philosophy. He spent much of his childhood and youth in England, studying at

Cambridge University with the intent of joining the British Indian civil service. Like Gandhi, he became radicalized after leaving England on seeing the disparity between European ideals of justice and the realities of life in a British colony, in which the indigenous population was subjugated and subject to numerous indignities. He got involved in the independence movement and was jailed for writing articles critical of British rule.

During his time in prison, Aurobindo dedicated himself to spiritual practice and had several visionary experiences. After being freed from prison, he moved to the small French Indian colony of Pondicherry and continued his spiritual practice and writing. He produced several major philosophical works over the course of his life, including the monumental *The Life Divine*.

The Life Divine is probably the definitive presentation of Aurobindo's philosophical vision. Extending to well over a thousand pages, it encompasses both Western and Indian thought. One of the distinctive aspects of Aurobindo's thought is its incorporation of both Western and Indian sensibilities into a synthesis.

Aurobindo, building upon Vivekananda's teaching, perceives the West as having cultivated mastery of the material world, through its science and technology. From the perspective of most Western thought, life and consciousness have evolved from matter. Even in Christianity, humans are first made, and then life infused into them. From an Indian perspective, though, consciousness has always existed. From the point of view of traditions such as Vedānta and Yogācāra Buddhism, consciousness is prior to matter, which is an appearance or manifestation of consciousness:

> We speak of the evolution of Life in Matter, the evolution of Mind in Matter; but evolution is a word which merely states the phenomenon without explaining it. For there seems to be no reason why Life should evolve out of material elements or Mind out of living form, unless we accept the Vedantic solution that Life is already involved in Matter and Mind in Life because in essence Matter is a form of veiled Life, Life a form of veiled Consciousness.[12]

Darwinian concepts regarding evolution have engaged the imaginations of modern Indian philosophers to a great extent, bearing some resemblance, as they do, to evolutionary concepts found in Sāṃkhya and Vedānta.[13] *Pariṇāmavāda*, or the 'doctrine of evolution' found in Indian philosophical systems does not refer specifically to biological evolution, and certainly not to the random process termed 'natural selection', though this idea is not too far from Lokāyata concepts of consciousness being a result of fortuitous combinations of material elements.

The traditional Indian concept of evolution refers to the transformation of the original conscious principle: its gradual manifestation through various subtle levels of existence, which culminates in awareness arising in, and appearing to evolve from, a material form. To differentiate this Indian concept of consciousness, or spirit, gradually manifesting in matter, from the idea of the evolution of consciousness *from* matter, Swami Vivekananda coins the term *involution*.[14] It is consciousness which is *involved* in matter. When Sri Aurobindo says, 'Life is already *involved* in Matter and Mind in Life' (emphasis mine), he is referring to this concept.

Sri Aurobindo refers to his system of thought and contemplative practice as *Integral Yoga* because he seeks to *integrate* Western and Indian concepts of evolution and involution. The same process seen from the standpoint of Vedānta as the involution of consciousness *into* matter is seen from the standpoint of Western thought as the evolution of consciousness *from* matter. Both are true and lend insight into the process as it occurs. According to Aurobindo, history is the unfolding and manifestation of progressively higher levels of consciousness into the material world. He saw his own life and personal transformation as a major step in this process.

Going global: Vedānta and science and the transmission of Indian philosophy to the West

We have already seen that a major feature of modern Vedānta has been its engagement with Western thought, and modern science in particular, which is today no longer 'Western', but global, with scientists of all nations and cultures contributing to such fields as physics, chemistry and biology.

Vedānta, especially Advaita Vedānta, is seen by many modern Indian thinkers as capable of integrating concepts from traditional Indian culture – specifically, from the complex of ideas and practices known collectively as *Hinduism* – with modern science, and even as explaining scientific developments from a philosophical standpoint. We have seen how Sri Aurobindo, drawing on Vivekananda, develops the concept of involution as a complement to the biological process of evolution.

S. S. Suryanarayana Sastri (1893–1942) and A. C. Mukerji (1888–1968), on the other hand, both use Advaita Vedānta to critique concepts of modern science. Both argue that the materialism adopted by many scientists fails to explain certain phenomena adequately, whereas the Advaita idea of the ontological priority of consciousness addresses these issues.[15]

Scholar Nalini Bhushan summarizes the work of modern Indian philosophers in bringing together Indian and Western thought as follows:

> Professor K.C. Bhattacharyya (University of Calcutta) had an interest in experimental psychology, as well as German phenomenology, and used these ideas to develop a more richly textured notion of the empirical embodied self of daily experience . . . Swami Vivekananda re-imagined the metaphysical and mystical concept of *māyā* and the world of appearances to which it gave rise in robust scientific and empirical terms . . . Ram Mohan Roy . . . re-imagined Hinduism . . . Roy (and the Brahmo Samaj) creatively appropriated certain Christian ideas in order to render more plausible Indian philosophical ideas of transcendence. And finally, both Sri Aurobindo . . . and Rabindranath Tagore . . . subtly shifted the focus of the significance of Indian philosophy from the core idea of the world as *māyā* to the core idea of the world as a manifestation (*līlā*) of God's divine aesthetic play. Thus, the perfected life for them was not in a world other than this one, but rather in seeing this very mundane world as divine.[16]

In 'seeing this very mundane world as divine', Aurobindo and Tagore are of course echoing the ancient teaching of Nāgārjuna that saṃsāra and nirvāṇa are one: that Indian thought is not about being 'otherworldly', about fleeing from the material world to a realm of transcendence, but about radically *transforming* how this world is perceived. This idea is also at the core of the Advaita Vedānta concept of *jīvanmukti*: becoming liberated while in this lifetime, not in some future realm. This transformation does involve transcendence in a number of important senses: seeing *through* the details of the material world to the spiritual reality towards which they point, or which they can be said to manifest. One could say that India's encounter with the West has refocused its attention on the ways in which the material world – the world of here and now with which Western thought is concerned – serves as the all-important staging ground in which the spiritual life occurs. From attending to the concrete sufferings of living beings through karma yoga, or to the details of how consciousness manifests in biological organisms as revealed in modern science, Indian philosophy has been infused with a Western sensibility of focus on the material present without losing sight of the vision of the highest good that has traditionally motivated it.

In addition to 'going global' in the sense of engaging deeply with non-Indian thought, it is also the case that Indian philosophy has 'gone global' in another sense. Indian ideas have become available world wide through the processes of Indian emigration to countries around the world and diffusion through books and, increasingly today, the internet.[17]

Even before the arrival of Vivekananda on the stage at the Chicago World Parliament of Religions in 1893, generations of American and European enthusiasts, like the Transcendentalists and the Theosophists, had been devotedly studying and disseminating Hindu and Buddhist thought through their works.

Of course, both the Westerners who have adopted facets of Indian thought and the Indians who have sought to propagate it have done so for their own purposes and ends. And each of these persons has also been about promoting a particular mode of Indian thought, and not Indian thought in its totality, since, as we have seen in this book, Indian thought is extremely diverse. Often, some facets of Indian thought have been given strong emphasis, with others being downplayed or even derided. Those with an enthusiasm for Buddhism, for example, have at times cast Hindu thought as medieval and backward, connected with the domination of a priesthood, while enthusiasts for Vedānta have presented their preferred system as the be-all and end-all of Indian philosophy, able to incorporate the essential elements of Buddhism, Christianity and modern science into their all-encompassing, all-inclusive world view. Romantics have found the tools in Indian philosophy to critique the cold, mechanistic thinking of the modern world, while analytic philosophers have looked to Indian thought to supplement their logical investigations.

In the words of an anonymous reviewer of an early draft of this book, the richness of Indian philosophy is such that those of us who encounter and study it will be ill-served simply to look for what we want to see: for confirmation of our own beliefs or prejudices. 'We should instead expect Indian philosophy to challenge and surprise us, sometimes in delightful ways, sometimes in ways that perplex or infuriate us.

Conclusion

This book has been written with the conviction that understanding is possible across vast distances of time, space and cultural difference, even when one is looking into some of the most profound questions that have fascinated humanity from the distant past to the present. It has also been written from the further conviction that Indian philosophy, in particular, has much to offer the contemporary world. It is not merely a relic of the past, but a living tradition, full of insight that has yet to be appreciated fully by the wider world. It is sobering to know that vast numbers of Indian texts exist in libraries across the subcontinent which have yet to be translated into a modern language (Indian or otherwise). Should this translation work ever occur, it is possible that not only this book, but all of the books that have been written about Indian philosophy in the last couple of centuries, will be rendered obsolete.

It is my sincere hope that this introduction, presented partly as a conversation and partly as a chronological record through history of the schools of thought making up this tradition, has given some sense of the depth and richness of this field of study. In conveying the basics of a tradition that is at least 4,000 years old, there is much detail that could not be covered. I apologize to any reader whose favourite thinker or school of thought was not covered here or was covered inadequately.

If you have read to this point, you have just begun to scratch the surface of all that there is to know about to learn from the thinkers of India. I hope that this is only the beginning of your journey into Indian philosophy. Should you continue to pursue this field of inquiry, many great intellectual adventures await you!

Notes

1 Gupta, *An Introduction to Indian Philosophy*, pp. 171–2.
2 Rockets, to name just one example, were first introduced to the British through their conflicts with the ruler Tipu Sultan, of Mysore, who deployed this technology against them. See A. Bodown Van Riper, *Rockets and Missiles: The Life Story of a Technology* (Baltimore: Johns Hopkins University Press, 2007).
3 Nikhilananda, *The Gospel of Sri Ramakrishna*, p. 60.
4 Ibid., vol. 1, pp. 4–5.
5 Wilhelm Halbfass, *Philology and Confrontation: Paul Hacker on Traditional and Modern Vedanta* (Albany: State University of New York Press, 1995).
6 Ibid., vol. 2, p. 365.
7 Sarvepalli Radhakrishnan, *The Hindu View of Life* (New York: Macmillan, 1973), p. 18.
8 Anantanand Rambachan, *The Limits of Scripture: Vivekananda's Reinterpretation of the Vedas* (Honolulu: University of Hawaii Press, 1994).
9 See Uma Majmudar, *Gandhi and Rajchandra: The Making of the Mahatma* (Lanham: Lexington Books, 2020).
10 Cited in Glyn Richards, *A Sourcebook of Modern Hinduism* (Surrey: Curzon Press, 1985), pp. 156, 157.
11 For two radically different interpretations of Hindu nationalism, see Christophe Jaffrelot, *Modi's India: Hindu Nationalism and the Rise of Ethnic Democracy*

(Princeton: Princeton University Press, 2021) and Aravindan Neelakandan, *Hindutva: Origin, Evolution, and Future* (Noida: Kali, 2022).

12 Sri Aurobindo, *The Life Divine* (Pondicherry: Sri Aurobindo Ashram, 1973), p. 3.

13 Many Indian thinkers in the modern period have had a fascination with science. See Yiftach Fehige, ed., *Science and Religion: East and West* (London: Routledge, 2016).

14 Swami Vivekananda, *Complete Works*, vol. 1, p. 369.

15 Nalini Bhushan, 'Ancient Indian Philosophy Meets Modern Western Science: Discussions of Causality and Consciousness in the Colonial Academy', in *Science and Religion: East and West*, ed. Yiftach Fehige (London: Routledge, 2016), pp. 123–39.

16 Ibid., 136.

17 See Long, *Hinduism in America*.

Bibliography

Adluri, Vishwa and Joydeep Bagchee, *The Nay Science: A History of German Indology*. New York: Oxford University Press, 2014.

Allen, Michael. 'Inquiry as Spiritual Practice: The Role of Philosophy in Late Advaita Vedānta'. *Proceedings of the XXIII World Congress of Philosophy* 16 (2018): pp. 15–19.

Arnold, Dan. *Buddhists, Brahmins, and Belief: Epistemology in South Asian Philosophy of Religion*. New York: Columbia University Press, 2008.

Babb, Lawrence. *Absent Lord: Ascetics and Kings in a Jain Ritual Culture*. Berkeley: University of California Press, 1996.

Balcerowicz, Piotr. *Early Asceticism in Jainism: Ājivikism and Jainism*. London: Routledge, 2016.

Batchelor, Stephen. *Buddhism without Beliefs: A Contemporary Guide to Awakening*. New York: Riverhead Books, 1998.

Beckwith, Christopher I. *Greek Buddha: Pyrrho's Encounter with Early Buddhism in Central Asia*. Princeton: Princeton University Press, 2015.

Bhaskar, Bhagchandra Jain. *Jainism in Buddhist Literature*. Nagpur: Alok Prakashan, 1972.

Bodhasarananda, Swami. *Stories from the Bhagavatam*. Mayavati: Advaita Ashrama, 2014.

Brekke, Torkel. *Makers of Modern Indian Religion in the Nineteenth Century*. Oxford: Oxford University Press, 2002.

Brereton, Joel. '"Tat tvam asi" in Context'. *Zeitschrift der Deutschen Morganländischen Gesellschaft* 36, no. 1 (1986): pp. 98–109.

Bronkhorts, Johannes. 'The Riddle of the Jainas and Ājīvikas in Early Buddhist Literature'. *Journal of Indian Philosophy* 28 (2000): pp. 511–29.

Bronkhorst, Johannes. *Greater Magadha: Studies in the Cultures of Early India*. Leiden: Brill, 2007.

Bronkhorst, Johannes. *How the Brahmins Won: From Alexander to the Guptas*. Leiden: Brill, 2016.

Bryant, Edwin Bryant. *The Quest for the Origins of Vedic Culture: The Indo-Aryan Migration Debate*. Oxford: Oxford University Press, 2004.

Bryant, Edwin, trans. *The Yoga Sūtras of Patañjali: A New Edition, Translation, and Commentary*. New York: North Point Press, 2009.

Buddhaghosa (Bhikkhu Ñāṇamoli, trans.), *The Path of Purification: Visuddhimagga*, 5th ed. Kandy: Buddhist Publication Society, 1991.

Chapple, Christopher. *Key Reconciling Yogas: Haribhadra's Collection of Views on Yoga*. Albany: State University of New York Press, 2003.

Chattopadhyay, Debiprasad. *Lokāyata: A Study in Ancient Indian Materialism*. New Delhi: People's Publishing House, 1968.

Clements, Richa Pauranik. 'Being a Witness: Cross-Examining the Role of Notion of Self in Śaṅkara's *Upadeśasāhasrī*, Īśvarakṛṣṇa's *Sāṃkhyakārikā*, and Patañjali's *Yogasūtra*'. In *Theory and Practice of Yoga: Essays in Honour of Gerald James Larson*, edited by Knut A. Jacobsen, pp. 75–97. Leiden: Brill, 2005.

Collins, Steven. *Selfless Persons: Imagery and Thought in Theravāda Buddhism*. Cambridge: Cambridge University Press, 1982.

Cort, John, ed. *Open Boundaries: Jain Communities and Cultures in Indian History.* Albany: State University of New York Press, 1998.

Cort, John. 'Intellectual *Ahiṃsā* Revisited: Jain Tolerance and Intolerance of the Other'. *Philosophy East and West* 50, no. 3 (July 2000): pp. 324–47.

Cort, John. *Jains in the World: Religious Values and Ideology in India.* Oxford: Oxford University Press, 2001.

Dasgupta, Surendranath. *A History of Indian Philosophy.* Delhi: Motilal Banarsidass, 1991.

Dasti, Matthew and Stephen Phillips, trans. *The Nyāya-sūtra: Selections with Early Commentaries.* Indianapolis: Hackett Publishing Company, 2017.

Donaldson, Brianne, ed. *Beyond the Bifurcation of Nature: A Common World for Animals and the Environment.* Cambridge: Cambridge Scholars Publishing, 2014.

Doniger, Wendy and Brian K. Smith, trans. *The Laws of Manu.* New York: Penguin, 1991, p. lv.

Drew, Rose. *Buddhist and Christian? An Exploration of Dual Belonging.* London: Routledge, 2013.

Dundas, Paul. *The Jains*, 2nd ed. London: Routledge, 2002.

Eyre, Ronald. *The Long Search, Volume 3: Footprint of the Buddha.* Ambrose Video, 1977.

Farmer, Steve, Richard Sproat, and Michael Witzel, 'The Collapse of the Indus-Script Thesis: The Myth of a Literate Harappan Civilization'. *The Electronic Journal of Vedic Studies (EJVS)* 11–12 (2004): pp. 19–57.

Fehige, Yiftach, ed. *Science and Religion: East and West.* London: Routledge, 2016.

Flueckiger, Joyce Burkhalter. *Everyday Hinduism.* Chichester: Wiley Blackwell, 2015.

Freschi, Elisa and Alessandro Graheli. 'Bhāṭṭamīmāṃsā and Nyāya on Veda and Tradition'. In *Boundaries, Dynamics, and Constructions of Traditions in South Asia, Volume III: How to Produce, Construct and Legitimate a Tradition*, edited by Federico Squarcini, pp. 287–324. Cambridge: Cambridge University Press, 2012.

Ganeri, Jonardon. 'Why Philosophy Must Go Global: A Manifesto'. *Confluence: An Online Journal of World Philosophies* 4 (June 2016): pp. 134–86.

Garfield, Jay, trans. *The Fundamental Wisdom of the Middle Way.* New York: Oxford University Press, 1995.

Ghose, Aurobindo. *The Life Divine.* Pondicherry: Lotus Press, 1973.

Ghose, Aurobindo. *The Secret of the Veda.* New Delhi: Lotus Press, 1995.

Gier, Nicholas F. *Spiritual Titanism: Indian, Chinese, and Western Perspectives.* Albany: State University of New York Press, 2000.

Gold, Jonathan C. 'Yogācāra Strategies against Realism: Appearances (*ākṛti*) and Metaphors (*upacāra*)'. *Religion Compass* 1 (2006). doi:10.1111/j.1749-8171.2006.00014x.

Gombrich, Richard. *What the Buddha Thought.* London: Equinox Publishing, 2009.

Goodman, Charles. *Consequences of Compassion: An Interpretation and Defense of Buddhist Ethics*, Paperback Reprint. Oxford: Oxford University Press, 2014.

Griffin, David Ray. *Parapsychology and Spirituality: A Postmodern Exploration.* Albany: State University of New York Press, 1997.

Griffiths, Paul J. *On Being Mindless: Buddhist Meditation and the Mind-Body Problem.* Chicago: Open Court, 1991.

Griffiths, Paul J. *On Being Buddha.* Albany: State University of New York Press, 1994.

Griffiths, Paul J. *Religious Reading: The Place of Reading in the Practice of Religion.* New York: Oxford University Press, 1999.

Gross, Rita Gross. *Buddhism After Patriarchy: A Feminist History, Analysis, and Reconstruction.* Albany: State University of New York Press, 1993.

Gross, Rita Gross. 'Buddha Dharma'. In *Dharma: The Hindu, Jain, Buddhist, and Sikh Traditions of India*, edited by Veena R. Howard, pp. 144–208. London: IB Tauris, 2017.

Gupta, Bina. *An Introduction to Indian Philosophy: Perspectives on Reality, Knowledge, and Freedom*. London: Routledge, 2011.

Hadot, Pierre. *Philosophy as a Way of Life*. Oxford: Blackwell Publishing, 1995.

Halbfass, Wilhelm. *On Being and What There Is: Classical Vaiśeṣika and the History of Indian Ontology*. Albany: State University of New York Press, 1992.

Halbfass, Wilhelm. *Philology and Confrontation: Paul Hacker on Traditional and Modern Vedanta*. Albany: State University of New York Press, 1995.

Hall, David L. and Roger T. Ames. *Thinking Through Confucius*. Albany: State University of New York Press, 1987.

Hamilton, Sue. *Indian Philosophy: A Very Short Introduction*. New York: Oxford University Press, 2001.

Hanh, Thich Nhat. *Interbeing: Fourteen Guidelines for Engaged Buddhism*. Berkeley: Parallax, 1987.

Harrison, George Harrison. *All Things Must Pass*. London: Apple Records, 1970.

Hartshorne, Charles. *The Divine Relativity: A Social Conception of God*. New Haven: Yale University Press, 1982.

Herberman, Charles G., Edward A. Pace, Condé B. Pallen, Thomas J. Shahan, and John J. Wynne, eds. *The Catholic Encyclopedia*, vol. I. New York: Robert Appleton Co., 1907.

.Howard, Veena R. Howard. 'Toward an Understanding of Dharma: The Questions of Identity, Hybridity, Fluidity, and Plurality'. In *Dharma: The Hindu, Jain, Buddhist, and Sikh Traditions of India*, edited by Veena R. Howard, pp. 1–37. London: IB Tauris, 2017.

Ishigami, Zenno ed. *Disciples of the Buddha*. Tokyo: Kōsei Publishing Company, 1990.

Jaffrelot, Christophe. *Modi's India: Hindu Nationalism and the Rise of Ethnic Democracy*. Princeton: Princeton University Press, 2021.

Jain, Pankaj. *Dharma and Ecology of Hindu Communities: Sustenance and Sustainability*. New York: Routledge, 2016.

Jaini, Padmanabh S. *The Jaina Path of Purification*. Berkeley: University of California Press, 1979.

Jamison, Stephanie W. and Joel P. Brereton, trans. *The Rigveda: The Earliest Religious Poetry of India*, vol. I. Oxford: Oxford University Press, 2014.

Jenkins, Stephen L. 'Buddhism and Nonviolence'. In *Nonviolence in the World's Religions: A Concise Introduction*, edited by Jeffery D. Long and Michael G. Long, pp. 39–50. London: Routledge, 2021.

Kamenetz, Rodger. *The Jew in the Lotus: A Poet's Rediscovery of Jewish Identity in India*. New York: HarperOne, 2007.

King, Richard. *Early Advaita Vedānta and Buddhism: The Mahāyāna Context of the Gauḍapādīya Kārikā*. Albany: State University of New York Press, 1995.

Knitter, Paul F. *Without Buddha I Could Not Be a Christian*. London: Oneworld Publications, 2013.

Krishna Warrier, A.G., trans. *Srimad Bhagavad Gītā Bhāṣya of Sri Sankaracharya*. Calcutta: Sri Ramakrishna Math, 1983.

Lamotte, Etienne, trans. *Śuraṃgamasamādhisūtra*. Delhi: Motilal Banarsidass, 2003.

Larson, Gerald James. *Classical Sāṃkhya: An Interpretation of its History and Meaning*. New Delhi: Motilal Banarsidass, 2011.

Long, Jeffery D. *A Vision for Hinduism: Beyond Hindu Nationalism*. London: IB Tauris, 2007.

Long, Jeffery D. *Jainism: An Introduction*. London: Bloomsbury, 2009.

Long, Jeffery D. 'War and Nonviolence in the *Bhagavad Gītā*: Correcting Common Misconceptions'. *Prabuddha Bharata*, October 2009.

Long, Jeffery D. *Historical Dictionary of Hinduism*, 2nd ed. Lanham: Rowman and Littlefield, 2020a.

Long, Jeffery D. *Hinduism in America: A Convergence of Worlds*. London: Bloomsbury, 2020b.

Long, Jeffery D. 'From a Certain Point of View: Jain Theism and Atheism'. *Sophia* 60, no. 3 (2021): pp. 623–38.

Macintyre, Alasdair. *Whose Justice? Which Rationality?*. Notre Dame: University of Notre Dame Press, 1989.

Madaio, James. 'Rethinking Neo-Vedānta: Swami Vivekananda and the Selective Historiography of Advaita Vedānta'. *Religions* 8, no. 101 (2017): 3.

Majmudar, Uma. *Gandhi and Rajchandra: The Making of the Mahatma*. Lanham: Lexington Books, 2020.

Mandair, Arvind Pal-Singh. *Sikh Philosophy: Exploring Gurmat Concepts in a Decolonizing World*. London: Bloomsbury, 2022.

Mark, Joshua J. 'The Dates of the Buddha'. *World History Encyclopedia*. https://www .worldhistory.org/article/493/the-dates-of-the-buddha/ (accessed 18 June 2023).

Matilal, Bimal Krishna. *Anekāntavāda: The Central Philosophy of Jainism*. Allahabad: L.D. Institute of Indology, 1981.

Matilal, Bimal Krishna. *Logic, Language, and Reality*. New Delhi: Motilal Banarsidass, 2008.

McClish, Mark. *The History of the Arthaśāstra: Sovereignty and Sacred Law in Ancient India*. Cambridge: Cambridge University Press, 2019.

Mills, Ethan. *Three Pillars of Skepticism in Classical India: Nagarjuna, Jayarasi, and Sri Harsa*. Lanham: Lexington Books, 2018.

Mus, Paul. *Barabudur*. Hanoi: Imprimerie d'Extreme Orient, 1935.

Neelakandan, Aravindan. *Hindutva: Origin, Evolution, and Future*. Noida: Kali, 2022.

Nicholson, Andrew. *Unifying Hinduism: Philosophy and Identity in Indian Intellectual History*. New York: Columbia University Press, 2013.

Nikhilananda, Swami, trans. *The Gospel of Sri Ramakrishna*. New York: Ramakrishna-Vivekananda Center, 1942.

O'Brien-Kop, Karen. *Rethinking Classical Yoga and Buddhism*, Paperback ed. London: Bloomsbury, 2023.

Olivelle, Patrick, trans. *Upaniṣads*. Oxford: Oxford University Press, 1996.

Olivelle, Patrick. *The Early Upaniṣads: Annotated Text and Translation*. Oxford: Oxford University Press, 1998.

Ollett, Andrew. *Language of the Snakes: Prakrit, Sanskrit, and the Language Order of Premodern India*. Berkeley: University of California Press, 2017.

Pahlajrai, Prem Pahlajrai. 'Doxographies–Why six *darśanas*? Which six?'. https://www .scribd.com/document/249196183/Doxographies-Why-Six-Dar%C5%9Banas-Which -Six# (accessed 18 June 2023).

Panikkar, Raimundo, trans. *The Vedic Experience: Mantramañjarī–An Anthology of the Vedas for Modern Man and Contemporary Celebration*. Delhi: Motilal Banarsidass, 1977.

Parikh, Vastupal. *Jainism and the New Spirituality*. Lahore: Peace Publications, 2002.

Parpola, Asko. *The Roots of Hinduism: The Early Aryans and the Indus Civilization*. New York: Oxford University Press, 2015.

Parpola, Asko and Simo Parpola, 'On the Relationship of the Sumerian Toponym Meluhha and Sanskrit Mleccha'. *Studia Orientalia* 46 (2015): pp. 205–38.

Patil, Parimal. *Against a Hindu God: Buddhist Philosophy of Religion in India*. New York: Columbia University Press, 2009.

Perrett, Roy W., ed. *Indian Philosophy: A Collection of Readings, Volume Four, Philosophy of Religion*. New York: Routledge, 2001.

Prasad, Rajendra. *A Conceptual-Analytic Study of Classical Indian Philosophy*. Delhi: Concept Publishing Company, 2008.

Radhakrishnan, Sarvepalli. *The Hindu View of Life*. New York: Macmillan, 1973.

Radhakrishnan, Sarvepalli and Charles Moore, *A Sourcebook in Indian Philosophy*. Princeton: Princeton University Press, 1967.

Rahula, Walpola. *What the Buddha Taught*. New York: Grove Press, 1974.

Rambachan, Anantanand. *The Limits of Scripture: Vivekananda's Reinterpretation of the Vedas*. Honolulu: University of Hawaii Press, 1994.

Rambachan, Anantanand. *The Advaita Worldview: God, World, and Humanity*. Albany: SUNY Press, 2006.

Ranganathananda, Swami. *Bhagavan Buddha and Our Heritage*. Mayawati: Advaita Ashrama, 2001.

Reps, Paul and Nyogen Senzaki. *Zen Flesh, Zen Bones: A Collection of Zen and Pre-Zen Writings*. Tokyo: Tuttle Publishing, 1985.

Richards, Glyn. *Sourcebook of Modern Hinduism*. Surrey: Curzon Press, 1985.

Roebuck, Valerie, trans. *The Upaniṣads*. New York: Penguin, 2004.

Ruzsa, Ferenc. 'The Fertile Clash: The Rise of Philosophy in India'. In *Indian Languages and Texts Through the Ages: Essays of Hungarian Indologists in Honour of Prof. Csaba Töttössy*, edited by Csaba Dezso, pp. 63–85. Delhi: Manohar, 2007.

Sagan, Carl. *Cosmos*. New York: Random House, 1980.

Sanderson, Alexis. 'Tolerance, Exclusivity, Inclusivity, and Persecution in Indian Religion During the Early Medieaval Period'. In *In Honoris Causa: Essays in Honour of Aveek Sarkar*, edited by John Makinson, p. 159. Northwood, Middlesex: Allen Lane. See also Nicholas F. Gier, *The Origins of Religious Violence: An Asian Perspective*. Lanham: Lexington Books, 2014.

Santayana, George. *The Letters of George Santayana, Book Eight, 1948–1952*. Cambridge, MA: The MIT Press, 2008.

Sarma, Deepak. *An Introduction to Madhva Vedānta*. Farnham: Ashgate, 2003.

Sarma, Deepak. *Classical Indian Philosophy: A Reader*. New York: Columbia University Press, 2011.

Seymour, Laura. *An Analysis of Roland Barthes's* The Death of the Author. London: Macat International, 2018.

Sipe, Jnana Sipe, 'Reflections on Mara'. *Urban Dharma*. http://www.urbandharma.org/udharma8/mara.html (accessed 30 August 2022).

Staal, Frits. *Discovering the Vedas: Origins, Mantras, Rituals, Insights*. New York: Penguin, 2009.

Strong, John. *The Experience of Buddhism: Sources and Interpretations*, 3rd ed. Belmont: Thomson Wadsworth, 2008.

Tapasyananda, Swami. *Bhakti Schools of Vedānta*. Chennai: Sri Ramakrishna Math, 1990.

Tarnas, Richard Tarnas. *The Passion of the Western Mind: Understanding the Ideas That Have Shaped Our World View*. New York: Ballantine, 1991.

Tenzin, Kencho. 'Shankara: A Hindu Revivalist or a Crypto-Buddhist?'. Thesis: Georgia State University, 2006. https://doi.org/10.57709/1062066.

Trainor, Kevin Trainor, ed. *Buddhism: The Illustrated Guide*. Oxford: Oxford University Press, 2004.

Tull, Hermann. *The Vedic Origins of Karma*. Albany: State University of New York Press, 1989.

Tulsi, Ācārya Tulsi, *Transmutation of Personality through Preksha Meditation*. Ladnun, Rajasthan: Jain Vishva Bharati, 1994.

Tyagananda, Swami. *Knowing the Knower: A Jñāna Yoga Manual*. Gol Park, Kolkata: Ramakrishna Mission Institute of Culture, 2017.

Van Riper, A. Bodown. *Rockets and Missiles: The Life Story of a Technology*. Baltimore: Johns Hopkins University Press, 2007.

Vireshwarananda, Swami, trans. *Brahma Sūtras According to Śrī Rāmānuja*. Mayavati: Advaita Ashrama, 1998.

Vireshwarananda, Swami, trans. *Brahma Sūtras According to Śrī Śaṅkara*. Mayavati: Advaita Ashrama, 2001.

Vivekananda, Swami. *Complete Works*. Mayawati: Advaita Ashrama, 1979.

Voss Roberts, Michelle. *Body Parts: A Theological Anthropology*. Minneapolis: Fortress Press, 2017.

Ward, Keith. *Religion and Creation*. Oxford: Clarendon Press, 1996.

Warren, Herbert. *Jainism in Western Garb as a Solution to Life's Problems*. New Delhi: Crest Publishing House, 1993.

White, David Gordon. *Sinister Yogis*. Chicago: University of Chicago Press, 2011.

Whitehead, Alfred North. *Adventures of Ideas*. New York: The Free Press, 1967.

Whitehead, Alfred North. *Process and Reality*, Corrected ed. New York: The Free Press, 1978.

Williams, Paul. *Mahāyāna Buddhism*. London: Routledge, 1989.

Wright, Robert. *Why Buddhism is True: The Science and Philosophy of Meditation and Enlightenment*. New York: Simon and Schuster, 2018.

Zysk, Kenneth. *Asceticism and Healing in Ancient India*. Oxford: Oxford University Press, 1991.

Index